Duquesne Studies

LANGUAGE AND LITERATURE SERIES

VOLUME TWENTY–ONE

General Editor:
Albert C. Labriola

Advisory Editor:
Foster Provost

Editorial Board:
Judith H. Anderson
Donald Cheney
Ann Baynes Coiro
Mary T. Crane
Patrick Cullen
A. C. Hamilton
Margaret P. Hannay
A. Kent Hieatt
William B. Hunter
Michael Lieb
Thomas P. Roche, Jr.
Mary Beth Rose
John M. Steadman
Humphrey Tonkin
Susanne Woods

"Through a Glass Darkly"

"Through a Glass Darkly"

Milton's Reinvention of the Mythological Tradition

John Mulryan

DUQUESNE UNIVERSITY PRESS
Pittsburgh, Pennsylvania

Copyright © 1996 by Duquesne University Press
All Rights Reserved

No part of this book may be used or reproduced,
in any manner whatsoever, without written permission,
except in the case of short quotations
for use in critical articles and reviews.

Published in the United States of America by

DUQUESNE UNIVERSITY PRESS
600 Forbes Avenue
Pittsburgh, Pennsylvania 15282–0101

Library of Congress Cataloging-in-Publication Data

Mulryan, John, 1939–
    "Through a glass darkly": Milton's reinvention of the
mythological tradition / by John Mulryan.
      p. cm. — (Duquesne Studies. Language & literature series;
v. 21)
    Includes bibliographical references and index.
    ISBN 0-8207-0267-6 (alk. paper)
    1. Milton, John, 1608–1674—Knowledge—Mythology.
2. Classicism—England—History—17th century. 3. English
poetry—Classical influences. 4. Mythology, Classical, in
literature. I. Title. II. Series: Duquesne studies. Language &
literature series ; v. 21.
PR3592.M96M85 1996
821'.4—dc20   96-9980
                                                                              CIP

In loving memory of Michael,
my dear brother

Contents

	Acknowledgments	xi
	Abbreviations	xiii
	Introduction	1
ONE	Milton and the Classics	14
TWO	Milton and the Church Fathers	54
THREE	Milton, Martianus Capella, Bernard of Sylvester, and Alan of Lille	67
FOUR	Milton and the *Trattato d'amore*	89
FIVE	Milton and the Emblematic Tradition	114
SIX	Milton and the Egyptological Tradition	160
SEVEN	Milton and the Renaissance Dictionaries	172
EIGHT	Milton and the Mythographers	197
NINE	Milton, Vincenzo Cartari and Natale Conti	229
TEN	Conclusions	287
	Notes	291
	Bibliography	315
	Index	339

Acknowledgments

Most of this book was written in summers with the support of fellowships from the American Philosophical Society, the Bibliographical Society of America, the Folger Library, the Henry E. Huntington Library, the Newberry Library, the John Carter Brown Library, St. Bonaventure University, and an NEH travel grant. A very welcome Andrew W. Mellon Fellowship grant made it possible for me to examine a microfilm of the unique manuscript of the medieval mythographers, preserved at the Vatican Film Library of Saint Louis University. I have also been extended every courtesy that a scholar could wish for by the staff at the Folger, Huntington, Newberry, Princeton, University of Illinois (Champaign-Urbana), and Yale University libraries.

I wish to thank the Newberry library for permission to reprint figure 13, and the Henry E. Huntington library for permission to reprint figures one through 12, and 14.

Numerous friends and colleagues offered valuable advice and counsel in the completion of this book. The following merit special mention: Steven Brown, Richard Cooper, Davide del Bello, Dan and Elizabeth Donno, Edward K. Eckert, Dan Inman, Peter Medine, Frederick Nash, Claude Rawson, Winfried Schleiner, John Shawcross, John Steadman, Stanley Stewart, Jeffrey White, Robert J. Wickenheiser and Paul Wood, as well as the departed spirits of

Don Cameron Allen, Marian Harman and Gordon W. O'Brien. Several pleasant summers of writing were spent in the idyllic setting of the beautiful Pasadena home of Jerry and Kit Johnston. My wife Sandra and our six children provided me with the protection from other responsibilities that made such writing vacations possible.

Finally, I wish to offer my thanks to St. Bonaventure University for a subvention to defray the costs of publication, to Albert Labriola and Susan Wadsworth-Booth for shepherding the book through the various stages of publication, to Michael Lieb for a careful reading of the manuscript, and to the anonymous reader for the press, whose demands for a more coherent presentation of the argument resulted in, I hope, a better book.

Abbreviations

Aen	*Aeneid*
Il	*Iliad*
Od	*Odyssey*
PL	*Paradise Lost*
PR	*Paradise Regained*
SA	*Samson Agonistes*
Verg	*Vergil*
YP	*Yale Prose*

INTRODUCTION

It is a bewitching paradox that our most Christian poet chose to communicate his vision of reality in the language of ancient Greek and Roman mythology. Writing after a period of intense bibliographical activity, when Renaissance printer-publishers like Aldus Manutius and the Estienne family[1] were discovering and disseminating ancient texts, and after having experienced a first-rate classical education,[2] Milton, as no poet before him, had mastered the texts of classical mythology in their original languages and would seldom write a line that did not betray their influence.

E. M. W. Tillyard in his seminal essay, "Milton and the Classics," observes that as the classics fell out of fashion at the end of the nineteenth century,[3] Milton also fell out of fashion. Milton, Tillyard explains, used both the classics and the Bible not for their own sake but rather to focus on contemporary issues that were important to him, like human culpability, the thirst for fame and the inexorability of fate. Tillyard dwells on verbal echoes and plots derived from the classics, but he does not discuss mythology *per se*.[4]

The first systematic study of Milton's use of classical mythology was C. V. Osgood's *The Classical Mythology of Milton's English Poems*. Unfortunately, Osgood limits himself almost exclusively to the classical texts themselves and takes little notice of the uses and abuses of classical myth in editions, translations and commentaries in the Middle Ages and the Renaissance. Osgood's study can be supplemented by the heavily annotated edition of Milton by Merritt Y. Hughes, who does take some account of postclassical sources of mythology. More recent studies of Milton and classical mythology tend to focus on Milton's debt to individual writers like Vergil and Ovid (see especially Du Rocher) or his relation to a single facet of the mythological tradition, like the Renaissance dictionaries[5] or the emblem books (Anand). Don Cameron Allen's useful study of arcane Renaissance lore, *Mysteriously Meant*, owes its title to Milton[6] and covers much of the tradition to which Milton was exposed and from which he profited. Allen's masterful surveys of the Homeric, Ovidian, and Vergilian traditions in the Renaissance have laid the groundwork for all future studies of the classical tradition in this period. Douglas Bush's earlier *Mythology and the Renaissance Tradition in English Poetry* skims the surface of the subject, while Charles Martindale puts Milton's classical learning in the perspective of his many learned contemporaries. Francis C. Blessington concentrates on Milton's dialogue with Homer and Vergil, and touches only briefly on his use of classical mythology. Jonathan Collett sees Milton's use of mythology in the early poems as decorative and superficial, and traces what he feels is an ultimate rejection of mythology in the later poems—a linear pattern that does not, I feel, mirror Milton's actual practice. William M. Porter's *Reading the Classics and "Paradise Lost"* focuses on Milton's allusions to the classics, but Porter's real purpose is to defend the classics against what he is pleased to call Milton's "insolence" (82).

Mythopoeic Milton:
A Contextual Approach

My own approach to this enterprise is to make the reader aware of the mythological milieu in which Milton flourished, and to show how the details of particular myths and their varying interpretations shaped his poetry and prose. While this study will not focus exclusively on which editions or which sources of classical mythology Milton read or had read to him, it should be emphasized that there was no shortage of books and articles on classical mythology in England during Milton's lifetime, and what he could not find there he could find in Italy, during his Italian tour (1638–39).[7] To state the obvious, Milton was a voracious reader, fluent in all the major European and ancient languages; he frequented the booksellers from a very early age, and attended St. Paul's school, which was well stocked with books on classical mythology. As D. L. Clark observes, "When Milton was a boy in school all his texts for the elegantist authors were overloaded with critical and explanatory apparatus" (11), including prose versions of the verse originals. Then as now, his teachers would select and impose interpretations on the classical texts based on their own readings, including texts obviously not familiar to the students. There has never been a period in English literature, before or since, when classical mythology was of such crucial importance to writers, or yielded such rich results as in the seventeenth century. Standing on the shoulders of Fletcher, Allen, Bush, Seznec (*Survival*), John Steadman,[8] Edgar Wind (*Pagan Mysteries*) and Erwin Panofsky (*Studies in Iconology*), I shall attempt to focus on Milton's use of this rich tradition and avoid retelling the oft-told tale of Milton's education and the cultural explosion of mythological sources in Renaissance England.

When examining texts of similar genres or subjects, I try to evaluate the same groups of myths, but at times an individual source may contain more significant commentary on one myth than on another, rendering it impossible to be entirely consistent in this matter. Different traditions yield different results and bear different fruits. However, I do attempt to connect one myth to another through a system of cross references, thus reminding the reader of the interconnections and continuity that prevail from one tradition to another.

This book focuses on traditions established on the European continent, and the reader might well be justified in questioning the assumption that Milton would choose a continental (or even an ancient classical) source in preference to one written in his own native tongue. However, while the twentieth century speaker of English can expect most scholarship to be available in English or to be eventually translated into English, a different linguistic hierarchy prevailed in seventeenth century England. While "imperial English" subdues all other tongues in the twentieth century, in the seventeenth century the most authoritative scholarship was composed in Latin, while English writings on myth were often derivative of continental classical scholarship, and much less subtle in both scope and execution than the sources they obviously emulated. Many English sources of myth are simply abridgments or epitomes of continental sources—what might be termed "knock-offs." In Milton's hierarchy of sources on classical myth, it seems clear that the texts of the ancient Greek and Latin classics come first, the continental commentaries and editions second, and the more fragmented English (native) negotiations with classical myth a distant third.

Despite my best attempts to keep my argument within manageable and rational limits, I am sure that some readers will interpret this study as an attack on Milton's originality. There will always be those who bristle with indignation at even the hint of a suggestion that Milton might borrow a passage directly from a source without winnowing it through the complex threshing machine of his creative imagination, or that Milton would consult *any* type of classical commentary in addition to the original ancient text. For such scholars, the measure of Milton's achievement is the extent to which he has distanced himself from his sources. The effect is simultaneously to transform Milton into a romantic poet and to disassociate him from the learned tradition that nourished his genius.

Again, by foregrounding this material, I have necessarily brought into question some recent feminist readings of Milton's poetry, particularly of *Paradise Lost* and the issue of Adam and Eve's sexuality. While recent critics like Diane McColley[9] have downplayed the physicality and passion of Adam and Eve, I endorse the opposing view of Le Comte (*Milton and Sex*) and Jean Hagstrum. Milton approaches crudity in describing intercourse after the fall, and sixteenth and seventeenth century versions of the myths of Venus and Cupid parallel this (almost) animalistic view of the sex act. Dissenting voices, on this and other controversial readings of Milton's *oeuvre*, will be cited at the appropriate points of the argument.

Beginning with the most immediate and concluding with the most remote sources of mythology that were available to Milton, I want to comment on their accuracy, depth, accessibility and approach. Since the number of texts within any given category is immense, I shall restrict myself to a few representative examples. Unfortunately, repetition of passages from Milton's prose and poetry that apply to more than one mythological tradition is inevitable.

My goals are as follows. I want to demonstrate the incredible richness of the mythological tradition that was available to Milton, and to highlight sources that have either been ignored or depreciated in Milton scholarship. I want to gain some insight into Milton's own view of classical myth, especially as it relates to the problem of reconciling pagan learning and Christian thought. Finally, I want to show how Milton enriched his poetry through his use of classical mythology, and how his particular historical moment—the prerationalistic seventeenth century—was enthusiastically open to and profoundly supportive of such creative mythologizing.[10]

My study begins with that shopworn subject, "Milton and the Classics" (chapter one), referring both to printed Renaissance editions of the classics in their original languages and to contemporary English, French and Italian translations. My point here is that Milton never read his authors "straight"; Renaissance editions of Vergil, Ovid and Homer are filled with learned annotations, introductions and appendices.[11] Thus a page from a folio edition of Vergil might contain three lines of text, and the rest would consist of annotation. The *scholia* of Homer, Vergil and Ovid are very extensive, and offer a cumulative commentary on the great triad that has never been equalled. It would be virtually impossible for Milton to bypass such commentary completely, and as a student of the classics he would be expected to be familiar with it. The earliest of these commentaries focused on etymology and philology, but as more and more allegorical interpretations of individual lines and references to other treatments of the same myth were added, the editions swelled in size and grew ever more ubiquitous.

Next in importance would be translations of the classics, translations that are themselves interpretations, and also contain commentaries and annotations. Sandys's Ovid, for example, is full of commentary on the myths and would certainly have been known to Milton, and this is examined in chapter two. Milton would also have been aware of French and Italian translations of the classics, especially of Ovid, and they are treated here as well. Although Milton would have no need of translations in the sense of grasping the meaning of the text, he might well have wished to compare the translator's rendering of a line with his own, the translator's commentary on a particular line or listing of parallel sources drawn from other classical authors.

Somewhere between translation and commentary is the allegorized Ovid, that great body of Christianized paraphrase from the *aetatis Ovidiana* of the late twelfth and early thirteenth centuries. This rich medieval legacy of mythological commentary has received some attention by scholars, but, like most matters relating to the Middle Ages, has been downplayed by Milton scholars.¹² Although not adhering to strict chronology, chapter two, "Milton and the Church Fathers," offers a comprehensive analysis of attitudes toward and approaches to theories of mythology found in the Latin fathers. These treatments (and sometimes *mis*treatments) of classical mythology raise the question of Milton's uneasy synthesis of biblical and classical mythology—like Milton, the church fathers are sometimes uncomfortable with the mythic strain in the Bible, and are careful not to tar themselves with the same brush they apply so liberally to the classical authors. Since, for Milton, the church fathers were second in authority only to the Bible, his intimate knowledge of their texts is a given.¹³

Before taking a final leave of the Middle Ages, in chapter three, "Milton and Martianus Capella, Bernard Sylvester, and Alan of Lille," I examine Milton's putative relationship with some of the most important mythological texts in medieval literature. This close analysis of *The Marriage of Mercury and Philology*, the *Cosmography* and *The Complaint of Nature* leads naturally into my study of the great Renaissance texts of love in chapter four, "Milton and the *Trattato D'Amore*." Giordano Bruno expounds Renaissance love theory from an occult perspective in his *Vision of Love* and *The Expulsion of the Triumphant Beast*, while Leone Ebreo's *Dialogues of Love* and Marsilio Ficino's commentary on Plato's *Symposium* situate the myths of Venus and Cupid within a literary context immensely more sophisticated than any earlier approach to these myths.

Next in importance is the visual tradition, the treatment of classical myth in plaster and in paint as well as in book illustration and emblem books. Since much of this has already been covered by Roland M. Frye, chapter five, "Milton and the Emblematic Tradition," is limited to emblems, *imprese* and similar combinations of word and pictures. The emblem, a form effectively invented by Andrea Alciato, combines written comment with picture. The emblems are written in all the major European languages and are abundant to the point of superfluousness in the Renaissance, as Mario Praz and others have informed us. Frye has covered the first part of this tradition, but in his study the emblem books are dealt with spottily and unsystematically at best.[14] The visual tradition is complicated by Milton's blindness, but his visual memory was so acute (as *Paradise Lost* amply demonstrates) that it cannot be discounted.[15] Related to the emblem tradition is the work of Egyptologists like Athenaeus Kircher and Pietro Valeriano, who produced extensive commentary on myth based on their wrongheaded notions of the Egyptian hieroglyphs (chapter six, "Milton and the Egyptological Tradition"). The storied wisdom of Egypt and its link to ancient occult wisdom, as well as Moses's access to its traditions and their possible influence on the Bible, were hotly debated questions in both the Middle Ages and the Renaissance.

Chapter seven, "Milton and the Renaissance Dictionaries," deals with the Renaissance dictionaries and reference books, loosely referred to as the lexicographical tradition. In these sometimes superficial, sometimes extensive definitions are provided for the pagan gods as well as real and fancied etymologies of their names. Also treated here are the learned commentaries on classical texts that do not deal with a single author—the main example of this is the *Lectionum Antiquarum* (*Ancient Readings*) of Ludovicus Rhodiginus Caelius, a huge encyclopedia of commentary on selected passages from ancient Greek and Roman authors.

Chapter eight, "Milton and the Mythographers," traces the broad tradition of mythography from the ancient period to the Renaissance. Here myths are summarized, apposite texts are quoted, and complex systems of interpretation are applied to the classical myths. The tradition began with Hesiod, matured in the Middle Ages with Fulgentius and Boccaccio, and reached full flower in L. G. Giraldi, Vincenzo Cartari and Natale Conti. Brief treatment is also accorded to the English mythographers, including Daniel,

Bacon, Ross, King and Batman. Because of their ubiquity, popularity and massive, systematic interpretations of classical mythology, a separate chapter examines Conti and Cartari: chapter nine, "Milton, Vincenzo Cartari and Natale Conti." A final assessment of all these traditions and authors is attempted in chapter ten, "Conclusions."

To demonstrate the importance of this material, constant reference is made to Milton's poetry and all of the relevant prose. I have decided to omit any separate study of Milton's response to other poets' engagements with classical myth, like Chaucer and Spenser in England, or Tasso and Ariosto in Italy. There are many detailed studies of Milton's relationship to these towering figures; moreover, these poets were also subject to the mythological traditions treated here, and it would be unprofitable, I feel, to attempt to disentangle the various accretions from, say, Ovid and Martianus Capella in Chaucer, and then to isolate a Chaucerian as opposed to a Capellan influence in Milton. My categories are not watertight, but they do enable me to trace the development of the mythological tradition in Europe and to add an important chapter to an unfinished book on Milton's intellectual milieu.[16]

OTHER VOICES

While my methods of approaching Milton's text are primarily historical in the traditional sense, they are not without value for practitioners of structuralism, deconstruction, feminism, new historicism, multiculturalism and other postmodernist approaches to literature. Myth is itself a kind of language that Milton, in a sense, "deconstructs." He *decodes* the mythological tradition, only to *encode* it in another way. Certainly Milton's interest in the logos extends beyond the Bible to the logos of myth as well.[17] Milton's struggle with the logos recalls Martianus's Philology vomiting up books and papers that bear numerous and often contrary significances (chap. 3, pp. 72–73)—

a disgorgement that recalls, in turn, the Son's contemptuous repudiation of Satan's book learning in *Paradise Regained*. In a similar vein, the Egyptologist John Spencer illustrates his faith in the logos by relating Jewish laws to the Egyptian, Syrian, Phoenician, Greek and Roman languages (chap. 6, p. 163). And while Milton seeks to control the logos of the Old and New Testaments in *Paradise Lost*, Leone Ebreo's Philo (in his *Dialoghi D'Amore* my chap. 5, pp. 96 ff.) seeks to seduce Sophia by controlling the texts of both Plato and the Old Testament.

Milton's tongue-wagging snake (chap. 8, p. 201; *PL* 9.527, 529–30) suggests an almost Derridean distrust of rhetoric, epitomized in the myth of Mercury, the original messenger god. The speechmaking Mercury takes another form in the Gallic Hercules, whose imbonding tongue bears irrefutable testimony to the power of the logos; the logocentrism of a hero whose words literally bind men in chains is obvious (chap. 5, pp. 135–38). Alain's *The Gods* cautions us that a belief in the power of speech as a substitute for true labor is the first illusion of the child, while Milton's resistance to Satan's and Belial's "eloquence" rescues him from the charge of logocentrism. In fact, Herman Rapaport claims that ". . . Milton's conception of devout discourse, of true speaking, is radically opposed to the Greco-Roman ideology of the text as logos, of the word as an incarnation of the truth" (209).

In generic studies, both M. M. Bakhtin and his commentators have failed to notice how Milton's use of classical myth and classical sources anticipates many of the features that the great Russian critic associated exclusively with the novel and earlier comic forms that anticipated it. For example, "the theme of the hero's inadequacy to his fate or his situation" may be "one of the basic internal themes of the novel" (Bakhtin, 37), but it is also an exact description of the plight of Milton's Adam after the Fall. Again, Bakhtin's concept of *polyglossia*, of one language speaking to another and thereby enriching both (61 passim), is evident in Milton's appropriation not only of the Greek and Hebrew languages of the Bible, but also the entire Greco-Roman tradition of pagan thought. Apropos of my chapter six, "Milton and the Egyptological Tradition," Bakhtin lists a hieroglyph as one of the visible forms language can take to become meaningful for us (258). Certainly the persuasive power of the god Mercury (see my chaps. 5–9), as realized in Milton's Satan, also relates to Bakhtin's claim that the writer is ". . . polemically invading the reader's belief and evaluative system" (283). Finally, Milton's network of Greek, Latin and Hebrew quotations, as well as his appropriation of the literary forms of Homer and Vergil, relate to Bakthin's discussion of "the forms of direct, half-hidden and completely hidden quoting . . .," (68) as well as his observation that in the Middle Ages, "certain types of texts were constructed like mosaics out of the texts of others" (69).

Feminist interpretations of myth might well be enriched by tracing the evolution of the figure of Venus as it is renegotiated through the classical tradition and as it shapes Milton's vision of Eve. Conti's genderless god (chap. 9, p. 236) might serve as a feminist model, as would Cartari's remark that wisdom is born of woman (ch. 9, p. 240, on Athena-Minerva). Certainly Jacques Lacan's view of context and allusion can be related to the packaged summaries of myth contained in the dictionaries and the emblem books, the summaries of the tradition in the epigrams that precede the emblems, and the strain of occultism that moves through the Egyptological tradition. Lacan's theory of one's mirror image as the beginning of narcissism (1–7) can be profitably used to look at George Sandys's interpretation of the Narcissus myth as an unhealthy fascination with the physical beauty of the body (my chap. 1, pp. 38–39)—a fascination centered, Donald F. Bouchard insists, in Adam's identification of Eve with his own image (88).[18] Signified and signifier come together in a new way in the emblem tradition, and the marginalized writer-author (long-since dead, according to the structuralist Roland Barthes)[19] is deconstructed in the textual tradition by the marginal annotations of the scholia that enclose the texts of Homer, Vergil and Ovid. And according to Harold Bloom, Milton adds his own deconstructive twist to the classical canon through his "allusive triumph over tradition," a contextualizing of Homer, Vergil, and Ovid that makes them seem as if they were Milton's followers rather than his precursors (142).

Alan of Lille's comparison of himself with "the writer's silent page" (my chap. 4, p. 85) also evokes claims of the death of the author, and Milton's own medley of authoritative voices in *Paradise Lost* submerges the author almost as successfully as Shakespeare's characters eclipse the personality of their creator. Alan of Lille's grammatical approach to gender (chap. 3, p. 82) reminds one of the linguistic games of Derrida and the sexual function of Milton's language, focused on by Catherine Belsey (46–67), as well as Joseph Wittreich's claim that both the Bible and Milton have been deconstructed by the misogynistic readings of Milton's critics.[20]

The church fathers (chap. 2) attempt to "deconstruct" the classical texts, and they are in turn deconstructed by Milton, who writes his own text over their heavy rhetoric of resistance to the classical authors. Lactantius's remarks on the emptiness of pagan philosophy (85–86) anticipate the "inverifiability" thesis of desconstructionists like Derrida, and are clearly related to Christ's rejection of pagan philosophy in *Paradise Regained*. In an intriguing way, Lactantius anticipates Richard Rorty's claim that philosophy does not really mirror reality or present a coherent, Cartesian model of the universe—for Rorty, it is just another part of the "conversation" (389–94; Kolenda, 95). Rorty (4) sees philosophy as the modernist's substitute for religion (the very issue Milton wrestles with in *Paradise Regained* 4), and follows Lactantius in wondering aloud if we can do without philosophy (as "a field of professional inquiry") altogether (391).

William Kerrigan's Freudian view of Milton can certainly be clarified by confronting the mixed nature of mythological commentary in the Renaissance, and avoiding a simplistic identification of the classical version of the Oedipus myth and Milton's alleged Oedipal impulses. Kerrigan's musings on femininity and creativity in *Paradise Lost* (185 ff.) are obviously relevant to the birth of Athena from the head of Jupiter, an event that receives careful scrutiny in both the emblem books and the mythographers. Freudians who posit a sexual rivalry between God the Father and Satan (his son) for Eve (his daughter) might also find grist for their incest mill in Conti's chapter on Ixion (book 6, chapter 16), where Ixion attempts to seduce Jupiter's wife, Juno, and ends up embracing an empty cloud. Finally, Cartari's merging of rhetoric and erotic desire (my chap. nine, p. 273) might be taken as a definition of Lacanian psychiatry; in fact, Cartari's interplay of iconic and verbal images suggests the polysemous nature of his discourse, the interplay of signifiers that Milton deconstructs in his reinvention of the mythological tradition, which is the abiding concern of my own discourse.

ONE

Milton and the Classics

It is interesting to note that the first designated category of mythological exegesis, the classical texts themselves, looks forward to the last, the Renaissance mythographers.

HOMER

The Johannes Spondanus commentary on Homer, which accompanies the Greek-Latin edition published at Basel in 1583, repeatedly cites the Renaissance mythographer Natale Conti (1520?–1582?; see chaps. 8–9) as an interpretive authority on Homer's mythological milieu. For example, Spondanus cites book and chapter (6.21) of the *Mythologiae* to explain the bloody generation of the Giants, and he includes a cross reference to Natale Conti's translation of Athenaeus (2o1ᵛ ff.).[1] For Spondanus, the myth of Circe signals Satan's presence in the world (2M3). Milton's own Comus is the offspring of Circe and Bacchus, and, like Circe, Eve has the power to turn a man (Adam) into a beast. Spondanus anticipates Milton's ontological problem by arguing that the gods (for Milton the angels) were depicted in human shape to make them more believable to his audience (2R1ᵛ). The oxymoronic stereotype of a woman as both passive and dangerous (pre- and post lapsarian Eve?) is explored in Spondanus's sketches of Penelope's compliance and submissiveness toward Odysseus (2Z2ᵛ), and the almost virile force of the woman slayer Diana (2R1ᵛ). Thus Spondanus's commentary might have been helpful to Milton in shaping his anthropomorphic angels, or in addressing both the dangerous and the "feminine" sides of Eve. But I must admit to having singled out some of the more interesting interpretations; much of the commentary is simply a prose summary of the action in the *Iliad* and the *Odyssey*.

Ioachim Cameriarus's Greek-Latin edition of Homer's *Iliad* (Strasbourg, 1583) includes a long preface extolling the teachings of Homer, but his editing never rises above the conventional assignment of place names and etymological analysis of Homer's Greek. Zachary Bogan's (1625–1659) *Comparatio Homer: Cum Scriptoribus Sacris* (Oxford, 1658) attempts to place Homer in a Christian context by setting up parallel passages from Homer's Greek and the Hebrew of Scripture. He translates most of the Hebrew into Latin, and occasionally translates a tag line from Homer or the Bible into English. Bogan also published a supplement to Francis Rouss's *Archaelologiae* (1658) on matters relating to Eros, Anteros, aphrodisiacs, sacrifices, burial customs, and female behavior in general, including some remarks on the common isolation of menstruating women in the Jewish and the Greek traditions. Several other Renaissance editions of Homer have interesting cross references to Vergil, which Milton could have used in comparing the two great epic writers.

Lodovico Dolce's Italian translation of the *Odyssey* in *ottava rima*, his "L'Vlisse" (1573), contains "argomenti et allegorie" for each canto, for both history and fable. He presents a straightforward Christian interpretation of the poem with one table identifying each book of the *Odyssey* with a different idea or opinion relating to Christianity, including Divine Providence, Divine Goodness, Wisdom, Poverty, Divine Justice. Each "canto" (book) contains both a summary and a prose allegorical interpretation. Calypso in canto one, for example, represents the boldness and lustfulness of a woman (1), the defunct heroes of canto 11 the fact that death is common to us all (91). Ulysses' men are turned into swine (10.82) because men who give themselves up to prostitutes become nothing better than brute animals, mostly pigs, who are lustful and unclean, perhaps "To roul with pleasure in a sensual stie," as Milton puts it in *A Mask* (hereafter referred to as *Comus*) (77). Ulysses (12.100), who had himself tied to the mast so that he could hear the song of the Sirens, represents the diligence of a man who has taken up an honorable quest, and who is himself so honorable that no number of obstacles can dissuade him from his high moral purpose. Ulysses' weak men, their ears stuffed with wax to prevent them from hearing the Siren songs, are clearly emblematic of Milton's "fugitive and cloister'd vertue" in *Areopagitica*, while Ulysses meets his adversary, "not without dust and heat" (*YP* 2.515). Dolce's misogynistic interpretation of Penelope as irresolute (19.163) and untrustworthy (15.127) is balanced by his praise for her courtesy (17.145) and heartfelt affection for her spouse (19.163).

Dolce also published a combined translation of the *Iliad* and the *Aeneid* in *ottava rima*, his *L'Achille* (1572); it consists of 52 cantos, with a separate allegorical interpretation for each canto (see fig. 1). In canto ten we learn, when Venus saves Paris from death, that the recipient of a favor is much more grateful when the favor is tendered at an opportune moment and on an occasion [*occasione*] of extreme necessity. As a follow-up to this interpretation, in canto 19 the vacillating fortunes of the Greeks in the Trojan war reveal the instability of Fortune, who seldom takes a firm position on anything.[2] In reference to Milton's

Figure 1. Ludovico Dolce, *L'Achille*. Venice, 1572.

angels, the goddess (in canto 28) who helps Achilles ford a dangerous river, reminds us that men are often assisted by those demons or angels who protect them through divine help, when human assistance is inadequate to the situation. On the other hand (canto 31), Fortune also conducts Aeneas into the kingdom of the Harpies, displaying how powerful her malignity can be when she sets out to persecute a man. And in canto 34, when Venus has Cupid take on the appearance of Aeneas's son Ascanius in order to inspire Dido with love, it is recognized, Dolce insists, that cupidity and carnal desire enter our spirits through the agency of these earthly resemblances. Both Eve and the devil alter their appearances ("But to *Adam* in what sort / Shall I appear?" [*PL* 9.816–17]) and Raphael warns Adam of the dangers of unduly focusing on Eve's "outside" (*PL* 8.568). Where Raphael sees only externals, Adam would agree with Dolce that in the outward form invisible beauty shines forth, and strikes up the flame and fire of love in us. And Dido (in canto 34), by telling her sister about her love, shows that it is impossible to keep that fire hidden in our souls, a fire that manifests itself in a thousand ways, above and beyond anything we might say; here one might recall Eve's appearance after she eats the apple ("in her Cheek distemper flushing glowd," *PL* 9.887), or the violent sexual intercourse of Adam and Eve after the fall.

Milton actually owned a copy of one of the earliest of the Homeric allegories, the *Allegoriae in Homeri fabulas* ("Allegories in Homer's Myths")[3] by Heraclides of Pontus [fl. 4th c. B.C.] (Basel 1544).[4] Heraclides, in responding to the complaints of the Platonists about the immorality and shallowness of Homer, assumes an allegorical interpretation of the text (as the title indicates), and proceeds to apply euhemeristic (after Euhemerus, ca. 400 B.C., who claimed that all the gods were originally men),[5] astrological and moral (battle of the vices and virtues—the battle for supremacy between the followers of Zeus and his enemies) interpretations to morally suspect episodes of both the *Iliad* and the *Odyssey*.

In this chaotic blending of physical, historical and moral interpretations of Homer, Heraclides claims that Homer could not possibly have taken an offensive or sacrilegious attitude toward the gods; otherwise people could not both esteem the poet and worship the gods through complex rituals enacted in extravagantly built temples (1.1). He also takes refuge in the argument that many people really don't understand Homer's codes—either the allegorical language (as he defines it, saying one thing and meaning something entirely different) or the occult wisdom concealed beneath. While most of his interpretations of classical myths are mundane and jejune in the extreme, he does make an interesting distinction between the two messengers of Zeus, Iris and Hermes. Iris speaks the god's message, but Hermes (as we shall see in later commentaries) both delivers and explains the divine communication (28.3). The tongue is sacrificed to Hermes, since it is the one part of the body that makes language possible (72.19). We shall also have occasion to discuss Hercules the learned (himself a derivative of Hermes) as well as Hercules the powerful, particularly as the distinction applies to Milton's Samson in *Samson Agonistes*. Heraclides also explores the complexities of Hercules; in fact, he is one of the first commentators to speak of Hercules as both a man and a sage (33.1). Heraclides looks beneath the erotic surface of the Homeric epics to discover moral directives and virtuous heroes. It only appears that Homer is condoning the abduction of Helen which sparked the Trojan war; in fact he is ridiculing the foolishness of amorous passion (28.4). Ulysses, that wild womanizer and reckless adventurer, is in reality the instrument by which Homer shapes all the virtues. In fact, the entire corpus of Homer is a continual song of wisdom that conveys the truth about the gods through allegories (60.1).

While Heraclides' attempt to clear Homer of moral blame was commendable, one assumes that a reader of Milton's moral and linguistic sophistication would not be swayed by such interpretations. Heraclides' allegories do, however, defend literature as a positive moral force and indicate, however bizarrely, that the text of Homer could be adapted for purposes its author probably never intended.

A later but even more famous allegory of Homer was *Porphyry: The Cave of the Nymphs in the Odyssey*, a gloss on *Odyssey* 13.102–12. Porphyry [fl. 350 A.D.] examines Homer's claim that the cave had one entrance for gods and another for human beings, which he later interprets to mean that separate entrances were provided for good and bad men: "One is proper to the gods and to good men, while the other is proper to mortals and to baser natures" (p. 31, sec. 31). Segments of the work were extant as early as the eleventh century, but the rationale of Porphyry's symbolism is much closer to Renaissance than medieval critical theory:

> For the ancients did not consecrate sanctuaries without mystical signification, and Homer does not describe them haphazardly. The more one attempts to show that Homer's cave is not a piece of fiction of his own but was dedicated to the gods before his time, the more this place proves to be full of ancient wisdom; and for this reason it will deserve to be investigated and require to have the symbolism of the sacred objects in it explained. (p. 7, sec. 4)

Clearly, "... the poet, in this instance, is speaking allegorically and, for a mysterious purpose" (p. 5, sec. 4). Porphyry cites earlier Homeric commentators (e.g. Artemidorous the Ephesian [fl. 104–101 B.C.]), and relates the passage to a broader philosophy of Nature, which has, like the cave, both an exit and an entrance (birth and death?). Indeed, because of their primordial nature, "in the most remote periods of antiquity, ... caves and grottoes were consecrated to gods before temples were even thought of ..." (p. 21, sec. 20). It is also a sacred space where neophytes are initiated into the mysteries: "... the Persians call the place a cave where they introduce an initiate to the mysteries, revealing to him the path by which souls descend and go back again" (p. 9, sec. 6). And "since nature arose out of diversity, the ancients everywhere made that which has a twofold entrance her symbol" (p. 29, sec. 29).

For Milton the cave can be a symbol of barbaric primitivism (the caves, woods and desert of *Comus*), a place of refuge (*Prolusions* 1, 7), a thing of beauty (*PL* 9.118) or the dwelling place of evil ("Hell ... sigh'd / From all her Caves" [*PL* 2.788–89]). The olive tree that fronts the cave is the tree of Athena, goddess of wisdom, and a general symbol of divine wisdom (p. 31, sec. 32). For Athena emerged from the head of Zeus, just as the tree is at the head of the cave (p. 33, sec. 34). In this cave one follows the example of Ulysses and rids oneself of all one's possessions, and then takes advice from Athena, "seated with her at the foot of the olive tree ..." purging "the treacherous passions of one's soul" (p. 33, sec. 34), rejecting them "vehemently at one time, charming and beguiling them at another ....." till one can finally "exterminate" them all (p. 35, sec. 35).

Milton's Satan tempts the Son with Athena's own city, Athens, the "Olive grove of *Academe*," a place of "retirement" and "studious musing" (*PR* 4 244, 245, 249), while the human race, bereft of all of its possessions, is regenerated after the flood by the appearance of an olive branch, a "pacific signe" (*PL* 11.860).[6]

Porphyry ends by insisting on the validity of an occult interpretation of Homer, and the presence of substantial wisdom beneath the guise of a superficial fiction:

> When the wisdom of antiquity, all the intelligence of Homer, and his perfection in every virtue are taken into account, one should not reject the possibility that in the form of a fairy-tale the poet was intimating images of higher things. For it would not have been possible for Homer to fashion the whole subject plausibly, if he had not modeled his creation on certain truths. (p. 35, sec. 36)

Milton would probably have a different notion about what those "certain truths" might be, but he would certainly read the text of Homer with this same kind of attention to symbolic detail and occult meaning.

Vergil

While Homer was hardly neglected by the commentators, the erudition expended on the Vergilian corpus was nothing short of stupendous. As Don Cameron Allen remarks, "the early editions of Virgil's *Opera* are the most profusely annotated classical texts the world has ever seen" (*Mysteriously Meant* 140–41).

We begin with the Nuremberg 1492 edition, which boasts commentaries from Servius and Aelius Donatus (both fl. 4th c. A.D.), Domizio Calderini (1447–1478), and Cristoforo Landino (1424–1504). The first two focus almost exclusively on etymological commentary, and Calderini contributes little beyond a literal interpretation of the text. Only Landino makes any meaningful contribution to an interpretation of Vergil's work. For Landino the Sirens (v. 862 ff., fol. 187b) are both excessively voluptuous and representative of prostitutes. Since they are notorious for making virile men effeminate, Ulysses has himself tied to the mast so that he will not succumb to their charms. Adam, too, succumbs to the charms of Eve, "fondly overcome with Femal charm" (*PL* 9.999) while Milton's Samson, like the Greek Hercules and the Hebrew Samson before him, becomes effeminized, "Effeminately vanquish't" (*SA* 562) by Dalila. It would have been much wiser for him if he had followed the example of Ulysses' men, and had stuffed his ears with wax. Only after the fact can he reply to Dalila: "So much of Adders wisdom I have learn't / To fence my ear against thy sorceries" (*SA* 936–37). The other Sirens, the "Sphear-born, harmonious sisters" (cf. "At A Solemn Musick," 2) are also discussed: the Sirens, according to Landino, control the motion of the "sphaerarum coelestium." Landino, commenting on *Aen* 4.510 (fol. 167), connects Chaos with Demogorgon, the supposed parent god of generation discussed by Boccaccio and others, and co-terminus with the three fates[7] (see Milton, *PL* 2.965). Minerva (*Aen* 2.31; fol. 114b) is discussed at length by Landino, including her motherless birth from the head of Jupiter, the accounts of the many different parents attributed to her (no doubt from Cicero's *On the Nature of the Gods*), her symbolism as goddess of both war and peace, her perpetual virginity, and her creativity as "inventrix" of many crafts.

The Lyon 1529 edition of Vergil has a long section on the Muses and a careful description of the Sirens. It includes annotations from no less than ten commentators, a full set of (often lurid) illustrations, and a careful etymological and grammatical analysis of Vergil's texts, including the minor poems. There is some physical description of the gods, but little in the way of moral or ethical commentary. The Paris 1532 edition also describes the Sirens in detail (p. 394, commenting on *Aen* 5.864) but has little to say about the Muses or other pagan deities. The appendix by Pierio Valeriano (see chapter six) deals more with textual problems than myths. The Venice 1562 edition of Vergil cites many commentators, and includes a separate section of miscellaneous readings of the text by the great philologist and encyclopedist Ludovicus Caelius Rhodiginus (discussed in chapter seven).

The Antwerp 1575 edition, edited by no less a scholar than Julius Caesar Scaliger (1484–1558), has a rather succinct definition of Chaos that Milton may well have admired

> [Et chaos.] Elementorum confusio. Inuocat utem rerum primordia, quae in elementorum fuerant confusione. (p. 298)
> (And chaos. The disorder of the elements. It calls forth the origins of things, which were within the disorder of the elements. . . .)

Compare Milton's "ever-threatening storms" and "loud misrule" of Chaos (*PL* 3.425, 7.271). The edition goes into a great deal of detail in the annotations about the underworld rivers, and also supplements Vergil with physical descriptions of the gods, no doubt based on Pausanias and other sources of "paper archaeology."[8] As one would expect, the most detailed and most fruitful commentaries involve the sixth book, on Aeneas's descent into the underworld.

The Geneva 1599 edition of Vergil is the most complete of all the Renaissance editions, and incorporates dozens of sources, including the Renaissance mythographers Giglio Gregorio Giraldi and Natale Conti (to be discussed in chaps. 8–9), Augustine and Lactantius (see chap. 2). As usual, the sixth book is the one that receives the most detailed comment, but it may also stand as an example of the kind of commentary Giovanni Pontano (1426–1503) showers on the rest of Vergil's works. A lengthy synopsis details every event in the narrative, and there are several comments at the foot of the page just on the synopsis, including one from Ludovicus Caelius Rhodiginus (see chap. 7). Servius comments on Vergil's extensive borrowing from Egyptian theologians and philosophers, and Caelius relates the same material to man's knowledge of his soul and his moral makeup (2.1359–60). Fabius Paulinus (1361–62) describes Vergil as a kind of *uomo universale*, who has put all fields of scholarly knowledge into a single book. The actual entries on mythology, however, are not very enlightening or helpful. They are too text-bound to provide a comprehensive view of myth, and are piecemeal at best.

The Italian edition of Vergil, the *L'Opere* of Giovanni Fabrini, Malatesta da Rimene, and Filippo Venuti da Cortona (Venice 1609), is more of a school text than a scholarly edition of Vergil. Each section of the poem is followed by one to three explanatory units in Italian: a close paraphrase of the text with alternative word choices in brackets, the allegorical and moral senses of the passage (in some instances replaced by a physical or purely rhetorical interpretation), and an explanation of the words, fables, histories and points of grammar. In some cases the glosses (which include paraphrases of commentaries by Servius and Landino) spill over into several double-columned quarto pages.

Some of the interpretations belabor the obvious. For example, in the sixth book of the *Aeneid* (ll. 9–10), when Aeneas enters the temple of Apollo, his purpose is to contemplate divine things: "... perche come dicono i Theologi, Initium sapientiae est timor Domini" (fol. 141ᵛa [*Ps* 111.10]); (For as the theologians say, fear of the Lord is the beginning of Wisdom).

The threefold divinity of the lunar goddess is represented by Hecate in the heavens, Diana in the woods and Proserpina in the underworld (*Aen* 4.510–11; fol. 112a), the exact distinction Conti makes in his chapter on Proserpina (3.16.253).[9] The young Aeneas represents man in the first stages of his youth (*Aen* 1.1, fol. 2ᵛa). The Muse is invoked to convey Aeneas's (or the narrator's) amazement at the inscrutable will of the gods (*Aen* 9.77, fol. 246ᵛa) as well as to explain why Juno seeks so viciously to harm Aeneas (*Aen* 1.8, fol. 2ᵛa).

A fanciful etymology reveals that the Sirens really represent the (nautical) ties of lust (*Aen* 5.864, fol. 139a), but the editors are also aware that Plato has assigned a Siren to each sphere:

> Sò bene che Platone pone che ogni sfera celeste habbia una Sirena, nel libro della Republica, & Macrobio medisamente. (fol. 139b) (I am well aware that Plato claims that each celestial sphere has a Siren—in the book of the *Republic*, and Macrobius has a similar account.)

Modern scholars cite Plato's *Republic* as Milton's source for the account of the Sirens in "At a solemn Musick" ("Blest pair of *Sirens*....," l. 1). And where Milton associates sadness with the underworld river Acheron, and weeping and grief with the underworld river Cocytus ("Sad *Acheron* of sorrow, black and deep; / *Cocytus*, nam'd of lamentation loud / Heard on the ruful stream...," *PL* 2.578–80), the commentators link these traits to deliberate acts of sin on the part of the damned souls:

> Et perche la volontà entra nel peccato per la deliberatione, che ella ha fatto di peccare, per questo i poueri pongono in questo fiume la barca, & il barcharuolo: la barca, che significa la volontà, & il barcharuolo il libero arbitrio della volontà. Ma doppò questo transito, cioè doppò il peccato commesso, ne seguita la mestitia, che è portata a l'animo dalla Stige, & al fine al pianto causato dal Cocito. (fol. 160a)

> (And because the will consciously embarks upon sin, and has committed sin, the poor souls place the boat and also the boatman in the river. The boat signifies the will, and the boatman the free exercise of the will. But after that voyage, that is after the sin has been committed, the sadness of it follows, that is brought to the soul from the Styx, and finally to the weeping brought on by the Cocytus.)

Moving from the editions of Vergil to pure commentary, a popular commentator (reputed to be Bernard Sylvester, noted luminary of twelfth century France),[10] interprets the *Aeneid* as an allegory of the various ages of humanity, from birth to death. Unlike many of the other Vergilian commentators, who tend to comment only on the historical or linguistic aspects of the text, "Bernard" revels in the ambiguity of pagan symbolism and judges the capacities of Aeneas on the basis of the interpretations to which his mother, Venus, is subjected:

> The lawful Venus is the harmony of the world, that is, the even proportion of worldly things, which some call Astraea, and others call natural justice. This subsists in the elements, in the stars, in the seasons, in living beings. The shameless Venus, however, the goddess of lust, is carnal concupiscence which is the mother of all fornications. . . . Hence, one must pay attention to the dire aspects of poetic fictions and the multiple interpretations of all allegorical matters if in fact the truth cannot be established by a single interpretation. (11)

Thus both the piety and the passions of Aeneas can be explained through Venus's motherhood—his just veneration of his father, his passionate affair with Dido—just as

Adam duly worships his father, God, at the moment of his birth, while almost dissolving into passion at his first sight of Eve: "... here passion first I felt, / Commotion strange, in all enjoyments else / Superiour and unmov'd, here onely weak / Against the charm of Beauties powerful glance" (*PL* 8.530–33).

The aftermath of the Fall, where confusion reigns and the man has acted at the behest of the woman, can be paralleled by Aeneas's first entry into Carthage, which sounds almost like postlapsarian Eden: "In this city he finds a woman [Dido] ruling and the Carthaginians enslaved, because in this world such is the confusion that desire rules and virtues are oppressed" (13).[11] For "Bernard" the Muse Urania represents understanding,[12] which is what Milton seeks when he invokes her in the proem to book seven of *Paradise Lost*:

> Descend from Heav'n *Urania*, by that name
> If rightly thou art call'd, whose Voice divine
> Following, above th'*Olympian* Hill I soar,
> Above the flight of *Pegasean* wing.
>
> (1–4)

Just as Milton compares himself to Perseus on the horse Pegasus, making his way above the pagan horseman to the heavens themselves, so immediately after the account of Urania "Bernard" presents the myth of Daedalus, soaring on high in an ecstacy of contemplation: "Daedalus travelled the aerial paths with feathers (*pennis*) and came to Apollo's temple—that is, by reason and intellect he contemplated the sublime and inwardly moved himself to philosophical study.... the exercise of reason and intellect" (39). "Bernard" also provides allegorical interpretations of the three Fates and of Orpheus, who represents Wisdom and Eloquence: "Orpheus has a harp, that is, rhetorical speech in which diverse colors as if diverse strings resound" (53). Orpheus and the Fates, as we shall see in chapter nine, converge in Milton's *Lycidas*. Finally, the Son's choice in *Paradise Regained* (for or against Satan's wishes) and Samson's in *Samson Agonistes* (submit to the Philistines or defend God's law) resemble both Hercules' choice and the Pythagorean Y,[13] the letter shaped like a tree (both discussed below), which Sylvester refers to: "Pythagoras called humanity a tree which is divided into two branches, that is, into virtue and into vice" (58).

John Boys's (1614?–1661) English translation and commentary on the sixth book of the *Aeneid*, *Aeneas His Descent into Hell* (London, 1661), announces itself on the title page as a comprehensive, learned and wise treatment of Vergil's text: "*. . . Together with an ample and learned comment upon the same, wherein all passages* Critical, Mythological, Philosophical, *and* Historical, *are fully and clearly explained.*" He cites both Sandys (discussed below) and Ludovicus Caelius Rhodiginus (see chapter seven) as well as the "Mythologists," currently termed mythographers (see chaps. 8–9). Boys—speaking, he feels, for Vergil—says hell represents the frustration of the spirit, which cannot overcome the crushing amoral weight of the body, so that "few can raise themselves to the contemplation of divine verities, and dive into the more abstracted knowledge of heavenly things, unless by extraordinary temperaments of mind, which are granted to none but some few" (55). Pluto as god of the earth and the spirit that invades all aspects of the earth, merits an entire bull as a sacrifice; Boys's source for this tidbit of information is Natale Conti's *Mythologiae*, which is cited as a general authority on mythology, as he is for Johannes Spondanus (see above). Apparently Boys's "abstracted knowledge of heavenly things" is derived almost exclusively from continental sources.

While Richard Stanyhurst's English translation of the *Aeneid* (Leiden, 1582, Smith, 1.135–47) is not terribly distinguished, the simple fact of its existence indicates that the Vergilian tradition was very strong in England. He still speaks of Virgil the magician (a medieval rather than a Renaissance Vergil),[14] but he also sees (with Boys) the *Aeneid* as a book of hidden knowledge: "What deepe and rare poynctes of hydden secrets *Virgil* hath sealde vp in his twelve bookes of *AEneis*, may easelye appeere.... (136).[15] Like Boccaccio and many other Renaissance allegorists, Stanyhurst uses the bark-rind analogy to stress that different readers of Vergil react and get more or less from the text according to their different capacities: "thee outward ryne of a supposed historie . . . thee shallow reader may bee delighted wyth a smooth tale, and thee diuing searcher may be aduantaged by sowning a pretiouse treatise" (136).

Ovid

The s*cholia* for editions of Ovid are almost as extensive as those we find in the editions of Vergil, and the mythological references are of course much denser.[16] The editions usually contain a life of Ovid and many crossreferences to his other works, as well as to Plato and other ancient philosophers. As one would expect, there is a great deal about the physical description of the gods. The notes constantly supply other information about the pagan gods from other pagan authors to supplement the graceful accounts of Ovid. Like the mythographers, these include a great deal of detail about parentage, especially when it is in dispute.

The 1493 edition of the *Metamorphoses*, one of the earliest printed editions of Ovid, contains the commentary of Raphael Regius (d. 1520). Most of his annotations are simply explanations of what is being said in the text, glosses of individual words (the usual incorrect derivation of *Aphrodite* as "from the foam") and extended crossreferences, both to other classical authors and to other texts of Ovid. Among the more interesting allegorical commentaries on Ovid is an essay in the Basel 1549 edition (commenting on the *Metamorphoses*, book 4) on the nature of love—how it starts with sight and hearing, then moves on to touching and kissing, and finally culminates in sexual intercourse (fol. 85a). Here we might think of the "seduction" of Eve by Adam. The Lyon 1518 edition of

Ovid contains the important annotations by Pierre Bersuire (d. 1362). The title page identifies Ovid as both a poet and a theologian, and boasts a tropological interpretation of the myths, harking back to a medieval allegorical mode of scriptural exegesis. The erudition and eloquence of the entries is also proclaimed. This sounds suspiciously like the moralized Ovid, our next topic of discussion. The story of Daphne is a monument to the glory of virgins, the fall of the reckless Phaethon a warning to sons. Satan also falls, less than majestically, and as a son of God (a point he makes about himself in *Paradise Regained*) he too should heed the lesson of Bersuire. In some cases the commentary on just two or three lines goes on for four or more pages. On the Giants, he has crossreferences to Moses and sacred history and to the *Antiquities* of Josephus (37–95? A.D.), all precisely geared to his text. Here we might recall that when Satan and his followers entered the hall of Pandemonium in book two of *Paradise Lost*, they had to reduce themselves to pygmy size, but they are otherwise depicted as giants, and enemies of Zeus or "God," just as they are in the *Metamorphoses*. But the point to be made is that the Bersuire annotations provide Milton with the opportunity to introduce a pagan myth into a Christian context—a bit of secular history to mingle with the sacred (fol. 12b).

Bersuire also has a "sensus historicus," where he gives the myth a euhemeristic[17] twist, perhaps to trivialize it, or to place it in a subordinate position to Christian myth—Milton's own habitual disposition. His comment on Cupid in Ovid is traditional—the conventional reference to Eros and Anteros (Love and the Love that returns love),[18] as well as the citation from Plato's *Cratylus*. Much of the commentary is supplemented by material appropriated from other classical sources, particularly from Cicero's *On the Nature of the Gods*, one of Natale Conti's favorite sources and one of the most comprehensive treatments of ancient Roman attitudes toward the pagan gods. Sisyphus is a symbol for inappropriate ambition (fol. 64) and the folly of fighting against the gods, the very essence of Milton's Satan. For the commentators, Orpheus is the poet (fol. 141) torn to pieces for spurning women; the women who tore him apart represent the animallike urges that make war with the spirit, the mindless forces of nature like the raging sea that took the poet-priest Edward King ("Lycidas") to his watery grave.

The early French translation of the *Metamorphoses* by Jean de Tournes, *Le Metamorphose D'Ovide Figuree* (Lyon, 1583) paraphrases rather than translates large portions of the text and also leaves substantial portions out, and it offers little in the way of commentary. In contrast, the *Le Metamorphoses D'Ovide Traduites en Prose Francoise* ... by N. Renoüard (Paris 1651), tries to plumb "le secret des Fables" (5), concentrating on scientific or "natural" and ethical meanings. Thus Mars represents heat and Venus moisture, while the behavior of the pagan gods in heaven is an abominable disgrace ("Thir Gods ridiculous, and themselves past shame," *PR* 4.342):

> Un docte Chrestien combattant l'aveuglement des ancients Idolatres, avoit raison de leur reprocher, qu'ils faisoient du Ciel un Theatre d'impieté & d'impudicité, sur lequel ils ne representoient qu'habominables exemples de tous vices practique par leurs Dieux; afin que par ce moyen ils fissent plus facilement glisser le Peuple grossier au precipice de leurs erreurs. (51–52)

> (A learned Christian warring against the blindness of the ancient idolatrers, was right to rebuke them, saying that they had made heaven into a theater of impiety and shamelessness, in which they displayed heinous examples of all the vices practiced by their gods, making it easier for the common people to take a fall from the precipice of their sins.)

The Italian translation of the *Metamorphoses* by Giusseppe Andrea dell'Anguillara with the notes of Giuseppe Morologgi (Venice 1584) is one of the most heavily annotated and perversely interpreted of the Ovid translations (see fig. 2). Both historical and allegorical meanings are attached to the text, but the allegorical are the most bizarre. For Morologgi, Orpheus represents the power and force of eloquence, which can move the trees and forests and attract the love of Eurydice. The power of his eloquence keeps her on the path of natural desire and away from Aristaeus, who wants to restrain her natural affections and put her on the path to a more cerebral, neoplatonic love (book 10, 2B2^v). This is a complete reversal of Ovid's account of the lustful adulterer Aristaeus pursuing the chaste wife Eurydice. For Milton, the song (or eloquence) of Orpheus "Drew Iron tears down *Pluto's* cheek, / And made Hell grant what Love did seek" (*Il Penseroso* 107–08). Eve, however, draws herself into the underworld of death by attending to the eloquence of the Devil and fleeing the (arguably) nobler desires of Adam.[19] Where Eurydice steps on a snake in her flight from Aristaeus, Eve of course encounters a true reptile when she leaves the faithful side that gave her being, that shaded and protected her from harm (*PL* 9.265–66). Similarly (2B2) Pygmalion flees the natural, authentic love of man for woman and seeks his own selfish pleasure in the love of an unworthy object like a painting, a sculpture, or a medal ("... si danno ad amare alcune cose di poco frutto, solamente per proprio loro piacere, come pitture, sculture, medaglie..."). In a way, Milton's Adam turns Eve into a work of art, a goddess to be worshiped instead of a woman to be loved, or as Eve puts it, "a liveless Rib" (*PL* 9.1154).

The moral English had already met the challenge of Ovid's supposed obscenity in William Webbe's *A Discourse of English Poetrie* (London, 1586) (Smith 1.206–302): "*Ovid*, in his most wanton Bookes of loue and the remedies thereof, hath very many pithie and wise sentences, which a heedefull Reader may marke and chose out from the other stuffe" (254). This strategy of finding occult truths in the midst of apparent obscenities was part of the interpretive tradition of Ovid on the continent as well as in England.

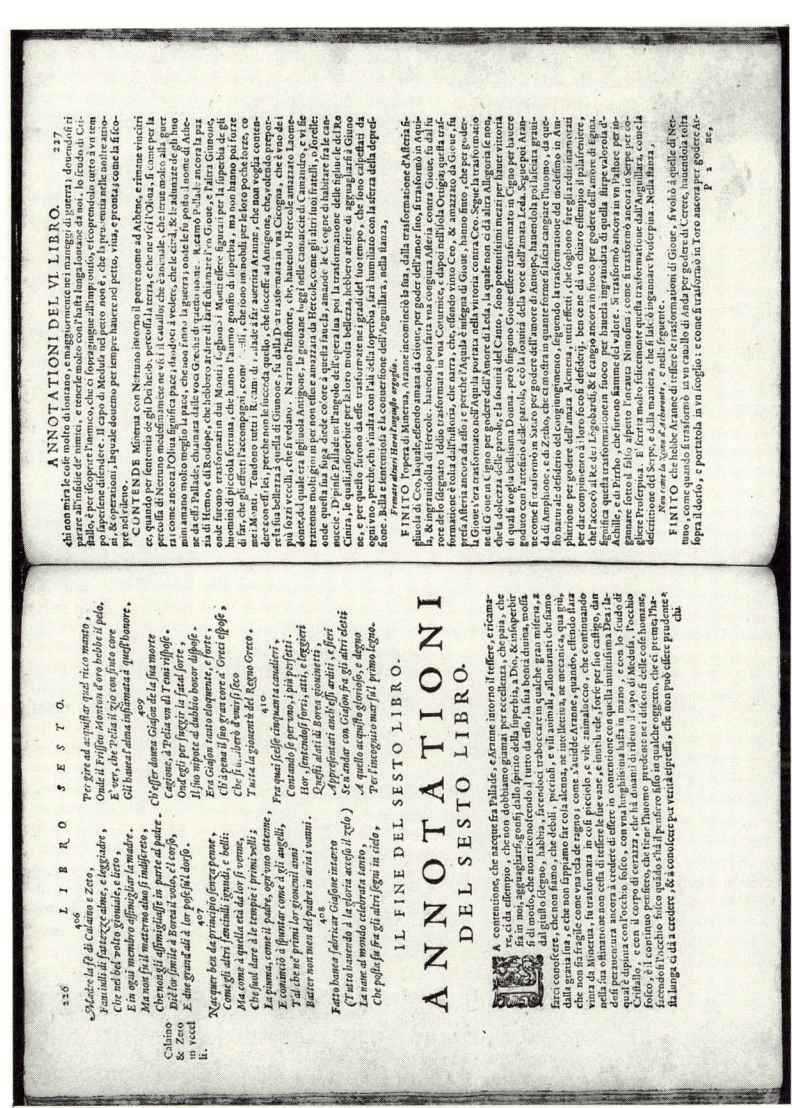

Figure 2. Ovid, *Le Metamorfosi*. Translated into Italian by Gio Andrea dell'Anguillara. Venice, 1584.

In the first great English translation of Ovid, that by Arthur Golding, there is no marginal commentary, but there is a lengthy verse preface that is not without interest, and which shows that Golding himself was familiar with the earlier Latin commentators. Milton's own notion of the inherent dignity of humanity under the rule of reason shines forth in these lines from Golding:

> And finally hee [Ovid] dooth procede in shewing that not all
> That beare the name of men (how strong, feerce, stout, bold, hardy, tall,
> How wyse, fayre, rych, or hyghly borne, how much renownd by fame,
> So ere they bee, although on earth of Goddes they beare the name)
> Are for too be accounted men: but such as under awe
> Of reasons rule continually doo live in vertues law:
> And that the rest doo differ nought from beasts, but rather bee
> Much woorse than beasts, bicause they doo abace theyr owne degree.
>
> ("The Epistle," 55–62)

Compare Milton's hymn to married love in *Paradise Lost*, where he praises Adam and Eve for the spirituality of their love, and associates raw passion with beasts rather than with human beings:

> Hail Wedded Love, mysterious Law, true sourse
> Of human ofspring, sole proprietie,
> In Paradise of all things common else.
> By thee adulterous lust was driv'n from men
> Among the bestial herds to raunge, by thee
> Founded in Reason, Loyal, Just, and Pure
>
> (4.750–55)

Adam and Eve "doo abace theyr owne degree" in many ways, from their sexual lust to their degrading abasement of themselves before the tree of the knowledge of good and evil. Golding (p. 2) adopts the interpretation of Daphne as an emblem of virginity which we have already seen in the commentaries on the Latin editions; similarly Phaethon's fabled fall (cf. Lucifer being thrust out of Heaven in *Paradise Lost* 1) comes from those very same sources. Just as Adam gives in to Eve, "Against his better knowledge," but "fondly overcome with Femal charm" (*PL* 9.998, 999), so the fables of Hermaphroditus and Narcissus, Mars and Venus, and Salmacis, show us ". . . that voluptuous life breedes sin: which linking all toogither / Make men too bee effeminate, unweeldy, weke and lither" ("The Epistle," 115–16).

At the end of this long epistle, Golding brashly (and incorrectly) claims to have interpreted all of the fables in Ovid's great work, but "Not adding over curiously the meening of them all" ("The Epistle," 300). He is proud of his achievement, but is quick to add that Holy Scripture is superior to any type of pagan learning:

> If any man will say theis things may better lernèd bee
> Out of divine philosophie or scripture, I agree
> That nothing may in worthinesse with holy writ compare.
> Howbeeit so farre foorth as things no whit impeachment are
> Too vertue and too godlynesse but furtherers of the same,
> I trust we may them saufly use without desert or blame.
> And yet there are (and those not of the rude and vulgar sort.
> But such as have of godlynesse and lerning good report)
> That thinke the Poets tooke their first occasion of theis things
> From holy writ as from the well from whence all wisdome
>   springs.
>
> ("The Epistle," 332–41)

Milton seems to echo both the first and the second point of this passage in *Paradise Regained*. In responding to the temptation to learning, Milton's savior proclaims the self-sufficiency a knowledge of Scripture conveys: ". . . he who receives / Light from above, from the fountain of light / No other doctrine needs, though granted true;" (4.288–90); and then goes on to denigrate the classical knowledge Milton himself held in such great esteem. But the Savior completes his harangue against classical learning with Golding's second point—"That rather *Greece* from us [the Hebrews] these Arts deriv'd; . . ." (338).[20] It is a classic formulation, and Milton could have got it from any one of a dozen places, including St. Augustine. But such a dichotomy was clearly part of the mythological tradition, which is the focus of our study. Golding goes on to declare that the account of creation in Ovid was taken from Moses:[21]

> What man is he but would suppose the author of this booke
> The first foundation of his woorke from Moyses wryghtings tooke?
> Not only in effect he dooth with Genesis agree,
> But also in the order of creation, save that hee
> Makes no distinction of the dayes.
>
> (342–46)

He also makes the parallel between Deucalion's and Noah's flood, a parallel obviously developed in the seventh and eighth "creation" books of *Paradise Lost*.

While Golding limits himself to an explanatory and interpretive verse preface, George Sandys is the only Renaissance commentator writing in English who has produced a full-scale interpretation of the *Metamorphoses* (1632)— not only a meticulous series of explanatory notes, but a commentary on each book as well. To be sure, Sandys draws heavily on all of the learned lore that had accumulated around Ovid's work, but as the most erudite English commentator on the poem, he could hardly be ignored by Milton.[22] He even begins with a life of Ovid, in imitation of the continental editions of the *Metamorphoses*. As with Golding, the annotations on the first book point directly to Scripture as the source of Ovid's account of the creation. He goes into great detail on the nature of Chaos, which he believes, with Milton, is a substance and not a condition, hence "that deformed *Chaos*. . . ." (57). The human being is, according to Sandys, made in the image of God, not only in the soul, but also "in the symetry and beauty of his body" (57). The beauty of Adam's body is emphasized by both the narrator of *Paradise Regained* and Adam himself. Both Adam and Eve are made in the image of God:

> ... for in thir looks Divine
> The image of thir glorious Maker shon, ...
> His fair large Front and Eye sublime declar'd
> Absolute rule; and Hyacinthin Locks
> Round from his parted forelock manly hung
> Clustring, but not beneath his shoulders broad
> (4.291–92, 300–03)

The "symetry" of Adam's body is declared by Adam himself, when he examines and admires his glorious body: "My self I then perus'd, and Limb by Limb / Survey'd, and sometimes went, and sometimes ran / With supple joints, as lively vigor led" (8.267–69).

Like the continental commentators, Sandys takes Phaethon to stand for the sin of pride, and his profile of that hapless fool bears a close resemblance to the character of Satan in *Paradise Lost*: "This fable to the life presents a rash and ambitious Prince, inflamed with desire of glory and dominion: who in that too powerfull, attempts what so ever is above his power; and gives no limits to his ruining ambition" (106). These words form a brilliant epitome of the character and actions of Milton's Satan, so evocative of Milton that it is almost a redundant impertinence to support it with lines from Milton's text. But let these suffice:

> his Pride
> Had cast him out from Heav'n, with all his Host
> Of Rebel Angels, by whose aid aspiring
> To set himself in Glory above his Peers, ...
> But what will not Ambition and Revenge
> Descend to? who aspires must down as low
> As high he soard, obnoxious first or last
> To basest things. Revenge, at first though sweet,
> Bitter ere long back on itself recoils
> (1.36–39, 9.168–72)

As Sandys observes, Ovid compares Phaethon to "a falling star" (106), the very words Milton uses to describe the fall of Mulciber, the architect of hell, the Vulcan of the *Metamorphoses*:

> from Morn
> To Noon he fell, from Noon to dewy Eve,
> A Summer's day; and with the setting Sun
> Dropt from the Zenith like a falling Star,
> On *Lemnos*, th'*AEgaean* Ile....
> (1.742–46)

An obvious parallel between Milton and Ovid is the Narcissus myth—first because of the famous scene in which Eve falls in love with her own reflection:

> As I bent down to look, just opposite,
> A Shape within the watry gleam appeerd
> Bending to look on me, I started back,
> It started back, but pleas'd I soon returnd,
> Pleas'd it returnd as soon with answering looks
> Of sympathy and love; there I had fixt
> Mine eyes till now, and pin'd with vain desire,
> Had not a voice thus warnd me, What thou seest,
> What there thou seest fair Creature is thy self
> (*PL* 4.460–68)

And second, because Sandys interprets the tale as an immortal soul reduced to a mortal body by the extravagance of self-love:

> *Narcissus*, a youth; that is, the soule of a rash and ignorant man; beholds not his owne face, nor considers of his proper essence or virtue, but pursues his shadow in the fountaine, and strives to imbrace it; that is, admireth bodily beauty, fraile and like the fluent water; which is no other then the shadow of the soule: for the mind doth not truly affect the body, but its owne similitude in a bodily forme. Such *Narcissus*, who ignorantly affecting one thing, pursues another; nor can ever satisfie his longings. Therefore he resolves into teares and perisheth: that is, the soule so alienated from it

selfe, and doting on that body, is tortured with miserable perturbations; and dyes, as it were, infected with that poyson: so that now it rather appeareth a mortall body then an immortall soule. (160)[23]

Thus Sandys connects the mortality of the body with the sin of pride, and Adam, overcome with the love of Eve—that is the love of himself—condemns himself (and us) to mortality.

Milton also draws on classical mythology when he creates his unholy parody of the Trinity through the incestuous relationships of Satan, Sin and Death. Conceiving Sin from his own imagination (to be compared with the myth of Athena springing from the head of Zeus in later chapters, esp. five and nine), Satan lies with her and produces Death, who in turn rapes his mother Eve. Thus Sin is the mother to her brother Death, and sister to her own son. Another analogue in classical mythology is the story of Myrrha, who fell in love with her own father Cinyras. Sandys's translation highlights the incestuous relationships implicit in this union in Myrrha's soliloquy: "Thy father's whore! a rivall to thy mother! / Thy owne sonnes sister! mother to thy brother!" (10.348–50). Sandys takes this unholy passion to be a manifestation of the sickness of melancholic love: ". . . being too strong an affection of the soule, allied, and like unto Melancholy; which continually agitates the mind, and inflames it with the conceaved beauty & graces of the beloved; let in by the eye, and inthroned in the heart of the lover. This ardor increaseth dayly, incensed by desire, and fomented by hope, until it attaine to fruition" (486). As we shall note later, Adam is too enamored of "the conceaved beauty & graces of the beloved," and his love is both incestuous and narcissistic, since Eve is a product of his own body. He is the mother, father and brother of Eve—and she is in turn his daughter and sister. And just as Myrrha seeks death as an escape from her dilemma, so Adam's love for his other self drives him (and later ourselves) to death.

The treatment of the church fathers is reserved for our next chapter, but one of the most significant patristic interpretations of the fallen angels (also concerning unnatural sexual relations) is quoted and then glossed by Sandys. In commenting on the myth of Chione (book eleven), who is supposed to have been impregnated by two gods (Mercury and Apollo) on two successive nights, Sandys compares the pagan gods to the fallen angels and cites Lactantius as his authority:

> But can we believe that Divells, for these Gods were no better, can carnally lust and ingender with mortals?.... That such there were, was almost the generall opinion of the ancient; not only of the *Pagans*; but of some of the Fathers: among whom *Lactantius*; *The Angells whom God had appointed to guard mankinde, being commanded to beware of loosing their coelestiall dignity by earthly pollution; not withstanding were allured by their daily conversation with women, to knowe them carnally: For which they were kept out of heaven and throwne downe to earth; whom the Divell entertained for his agents. But those whom they begot, being neither absolute Angels nor men, but mixed of either, were not cast into Hell, as their parents, nor yet assumed into heaven. Thus became their two sorts of Divels, the one coelestiall and the other terrestriall.* (527)

Milton may be alluding to Lactantius's account (as filtered through Sandys) in his preface to the roll call of the rebel angels, for he remarks that those demons took different names and shapes when they came to earth to corrupt humankind:

> Godlike shapes and forms
> Excelling human, Princely Dignities,
> And Powers that earst in Heaven sat on Thrones;
> Though of thir Names in heav'nly Records now
> Be no memorial blotted out and raz'd
> By thir Rebellion, from the Books of Life.
> Nor had they yet among the Sons of *Eve*
> Got them new Names, till wandring ore the Earth,

> Through Gods high sufferance for the tryal of man,
> By falsities and lyes the greatest part
> Of mankind they corrupted to forsake
> God thir Creator, and th'invisible
> Glory of him that made them, to transform
> Oft to the image of a Brute, adorn'd
> With gay Religions full of Pomp and Gold,
> And Devils to adore for Deities:
> They were known to men by various Names,
> And various Idols through the Heathen World.
>
> (PL 1.358-75)

And while Milton does not go as far as Lactantius in making women so corrupt that they actually corrupt the devils themselves,[24] he does link Adam's passion for Eve with (as we shall discuss later) his disordered intellect.

In writing *Paradise Lost*, Milton is attempting to fuse a Christian theology with a pagan aesthetic, and while most commentators on classical mythology were careful not to overstate the parallels between Christian Scripture and pagan poem,[25] Sandys does so constantly, and thus forms a contemporary English precedent for Milton's great synthesis. For example, while Milton (apparently) describes the birth of Eve in terms of the hermaphrodite,[26] Sandys makes the relationship explicit: "But nothing is here spoken of the creation of Woman. *Aristophanes* tells a fable in *Plato* how Man at the first was made double, after cut in two, and distinguished by their sexes, an obscure notion of *Eves* being taken out of the side of *Adam*" (58).

As Adam learns in the final two books of *Paradise Lost*, he has subjected his entire posterity to horrible disease and death, while the reader learns in the second book that Satan's sin has created devouring Death (more commonly known in the Renaissance as devouring Time).[27] Death is a force unleashed on earth by Adam's sin, whereby humankind becomes, as we learn from mother Sin, the pièce de resistance of Death's diet:

> Thou therefore on these Herbs, and Fruits, and Flowrs
> Feed first, on each Beast next, and Fish, and Fowl,

> No homely morsels, and whatever thing
> The Sithe of Time mows down, devour unspar'd,
> Till I in Man residing through the Race,
> His thoughts, his looks, words, actions all infect,
> And season him thy last and sweetest prey.
>
> (*PL* 10.603–09)

Thus in a way Adam "devours" his own children and can be regarded as a cannibal like Saturn and a child murderer like Moloch. Again, Sandys makes these parallels explicit in his commentary on the first book of Ovid's *Metamorphoses*:

> *Saturne* is fained to be the sonne of *Coelus*, or Heaven, and *Cybel*, which is the Earth: so *Adam* had God to his Father and the Earth, whereof he was made, to his Mother. *Saturne* was the first that invented tillage, the first that ever raigned; and so was *Adam*: *Saturne* was throwne out of Heaven, and *Adam* out of Paradice: *Saturne* is said to devoure his owne children, and *Adam* over-threw his whole posterity, (perhaps the occasion of their sacrifizing their children to *Saturne* or *Moloch*; for both were the same, as is apparent by their Idols and Ceremonies) *Saturne* hid himselfe from *Jove*, and *Adam* from the presence of *Jehovah*. *Saturne* being an Hebrew word which signifies to lie hid. (59)

Sandys expands on the Saturn-Moloch comparison in his commentary on Ovid's sixth book:

> The feasting of their Gods with the blood of their owne children was a wretched custome, introduced by the subtilty of the divell, and derived, as *Vives* conjectures, from the immolation of *Isaack*: used not only by the Heathen but the *Jewes*; who offered their sonnes and daughters unto *Molock*, which bloody sacrifice was convaied by the spirit of Darknesse unto the salvages of *Florida*; in the same manner as *Diodorus* describes them to be offered unto *Saturne*. (297)

Moloch is the fiercest of Milton's evil angels and as cannibalistic as Saturn:

> First *Moloch*, horrid King besmear'd with blood
> Of human sacrifice, and parents tears,
> Though for the noyse of Drums and Timbrels loud
> Thir childrens cries unheard, that past through fire
> To his grim Idol.
>
> (*PL* 1.392–96)[28]

Milton's account of the bad angels being overwhelmed by mountains in the war in heaven ("When coming towards them so dread they saw / The bottom of the Mountains upward turn'd, / Till on those cursed Engins triple-row / They saw them whelm'd, and all thir confidence / Under the weight of Mountains buried deep" [*PL* 6.648–52]) obviously derives from Ovid's account of the Giants, but he could also have taken the hint of the parallel from Sandys' commentary: "*Pherecides* the *Syrian* writes how the Divels were throwne out of heaven by *Jupiter* (this fall of the Gyants perhaps an allusion to that of the Angells) the chiefe called *Ophioneus*, which signifies Serpentine: having after made use of that creature to poyson *Eve* with a false ambition" (61).

The myth of Phaethon, to which we shall return in later chapters (especially five) obviously relates to Milton's Satan, for like Satan, Phaethon was ambitious to ascend too high and then was cast down. Riding the horses of his father Helios (the Sun), he failed to control them and went down in flames. Just as Satan and the other angels fall "with ruine and hideous combustion," so Phaethon scorches the earth through his folly: "And in those daies there fell such abundance of fire from heaven (which *Ficinus* [see chap. four] conjectures to be the same that is mentioned by *Moses*) as destroyed many of the Easterne regions: whereupon it was fained that his misguidance had set the whole world on a conflagration" (106). The language of Milton seems almost to have been lifted from Sandys's commentary. Satan himself castigates himself for his ambition, while Sandys focuses on ambition as the core meaning of the fable: "This fable to the life presents a rash and ambitious Prince, inflamed with desire of glory and dominion: who in that too powerfull, attempts what so ever is above his power; and gives no limits to his ruining ambition" (106). Like Satan, Phaethon is "altogether unfit for government" (107), afflicted by pride, and where Satan is "insatiate to pursue / Vain Warr with Heav'n" (2.8–9), Phaethon is overcome by "insatiate ambition":

> Pride diminishing love, and facility authority: or to attempt what is above their power, or to fall beneath it, the middle way being only safe; which not observed by our lusty *Phaeton* accelerates his ruine. This also may allude unto those, who straying from their proper spheares, their kingdomes; set the World on fire with the flame of warre, which seemes too little for their insatiate ambition. (107)

On a smaller point, Milton's muse Urania is for Sandys "one of the *Muses* so named of heaven, as the intelligence of celestiall things" (233n.).

Although Sandys's effort was the most erudite of the translations of Ovid into English, there were other more modest efforts that also testify to the tenacity of the Ovidian tradition in England. For example, in John Jones's translation of *Ovid's Invective Against Ibis* (2nd ed. London, 1667), Jones takes the same occult approach to the myths that we have noticed in Stanyhurst and Sandys: "And without all question, as before Letters the Ancients expressed their conceptions in Hieroglyphics, so did their Poets their Divinity under Fables and Parables" (n.p.). In addition to his own interpretations of Ovid, Jones also cites the readings of Sandys himself, as well as the founder of the emblem book, Andrea Alciato (see chap. 5).

Commentaries on Ovid were not, of course, limited to marginal annotations bound up with the Latin or translated text of the poetry. Independent allegorizations of Ovid had been a thriving industry since the last quarter of the eighth century,[29] and it would clearly have been impossible for Milton to remain unaware of them. Lactantius (or Luctatius) Placidus (fl. bet. 400 and 500 A.D.) provided summaries of Ovid's text in his *Narrationes*, and the twelfth century editions by Raphael Regius and Jacobus Micyllus supplied learned lexical commentary, but no substantial interpretation of the meaning and significance of Ovid's text. One of the earliest texts that comments extensively on Ovid's poetry is the thirteenth century exegesis in verse by John of Garland.[30] This very brief poem intersperses Garland's own commentary with references to the prose allegorization of Ovid by Arnolph of Orleans (fl. ca. 980–1,000 A.D.). He provides a euhemeristic interpretation of some of Ovid's figures and does not neglect the moral sense, but he does evince a genuine enthusiasm for the "scientific" or "natural" explanation, particularly of the creation of the universe. Most of his interpretations are fairly standard: Midas's love for gold obviously represents greed (425), the dismemberment of Orpheus by the Bacchae is the punishment for misogyny (422), Circe's transformation of Scylla into a site for shipwrecks indicates that prostitutes are a constant source of destruction (477–78). In contrast, the fifteenth century epitome of selected stories from Ovid (*Fabularum Ovidii Abbreviato*, Padua, 1474), attributed to Lactantius Placidus, does little more than provide a prose summary, perhaps as a substitute for reading the tales themselves.

Since, as the editor C. de Boer has emphasized, the *Ovide Moralisé* influenced many French authors in the fifteenth and sixteenth centuries, and it is a direct outgrowth of the Ovidian allegorical tradition, it constitutes a crucial link in what constituted the mythological tradition for Milton. The work was itself influenced by the Ovidian commentator Pierre Bersuire (see above). There are 19 manuscripts of the work, one of which is now in the British Library (#10324), originally part of the Heber collection, so there is at least a chance that Milton may have perused an original copy.[31] The gloss on the myth of Cupid and Venus, or Love and Beauty, is typical of the type of allegorizing found in the *Ovide Moralisé*. Venus is first of all a planetary god, and Friday is her special day. The daughter of Caelum, she has a benign nature, but she also represents the notorious nature of love, for she is the "mistress" and "dame" of love. Luxury, wicked excess, iniquity and other evils flow from her. The more sinful something is the more it pleases her, and she delights in her own wrongdoing [meschieé] (1.738). These are the kinds of glosses that would appear apart from the text in Bersuire; here they become part of the poem. One might relate this passage to Milton's attack on sexual dalliance in the fourth book of *Paradise Lost*, and the lascivious women of Michael's prophecy in book 11:

> ... the bought smile
> of Harlots, loveless, joyless, unindeard,
> Casual fruition, nor in Court Amours,
> Mixt Dance, or wanton Mask, or Midnight Ball,
> Or Serenate, which the starv'd Lover sings
> To his proud fair, best quitted with disdain.
> (4.765–70)

> For that fair femal Troop thou sawst, that seemd
> Of Goddesses, so blithe, so smooth, so gay,
> Yet empty of all good wherein consists
> Woman's domestic honor and chief praise;
> Bred only and completed to the taste
> Of lustful appetence, to sing, to dance,
> To dress, and troul the Tongue, and roul the Eye.
> (11.614–20)

It is interesting that in both Milton's *Paradise Lost* and the *Ovide Moralisé*, love represented in female form (i.e., Venus for the French and the harlots for the English writer) is negative, but represented as the male, Cupid, it is positive. In the *Ovide Moralisé*, a wise Cupid shows us the right path to good love and leads us to God, whom we reach through love:

> L'amour Dieu, por home secourre,
> Dou dars de bone amour ploia
> Sapience, et l'envoia
> Au monde en humaine figure,

> Pour soi joindre a nostre nature.
> Cupido, cil qui nous avoie
> Et nous monstre la droite voie
> De bone amour, a mon avis,
> C'est Dieus, li rois de paradis,
> Qui en amours nous endouctrine,
> Se nous tenons bien sa doctrine.
> Bien nous moustre signe d'amer,
> Quant ciel et terre, monde et mer
> Et toutes les riens qu'il y a
> Pour nostre avancement cria.
>
> (1.3292–306)

(The god of love, in order to shake man up, bends the dart of good love toward him. And he dispatches wisdom to the world in mortal shape, in order to join himself to our nature. Cupid is the one who leads us and points us in the right direction of good love, it seems to me. It is God, the king of Paradise, who instructs us in our love affairs if we hold fast to his teaching. Even if he does display signs of bitterness toward us, heaven and earth, the world and the sea, and everything else that exists really shout encouragement for our success.)

Again, the fourth book:

> Here Love his golden shafts imploies, here lights
> His constant Lamp, and waves his purple wings,
> Reigns here and revels
>
> (763–65)

Taking up the myth of Phaethon (2.645–730), the author of the *Ovide Moralisé* again invokes the euhemeristic theory that all the gods were originally human beings, but that Phaethon was a particularly astute intellectual who studied the motions of the planets. He became overcome with pride and was thus destroyed by Jupiter and is a lesson to us all not to overstep our bounds: "Que nulz ne se doit orgueillir / De trop grant emprise acueillir" (2.691–92.) (For no one should become swelled up with pride because he has reached too great a height). Again, the analogy with the pride of Satan is obvious.

Unlike other commentators, the author of the *Ovide Moralisé* christianizes the myth of another proud man, Narcissus, by connecting his self-love with the fall of the rebel angels from hell. Their presumption and pride sent them to hell:

> Par lor fole presumption,
> Dont il perdent le cors et l'ame.
> Orgeulz desconfit home et fame.
> Par orgueil cheïrent jadis
> Li fol angle de Paradis.
>
> (3.1872–876)

(By their foolish presumption, they lost heart and soul, through the defect of pride mankind was lost, as well as his former place of residence, the left corner of Paradise.)

Like Adam and Eve, too much love of themselves causes "Homes et femes" to die:

> Homes et femes enhaï,
> Et trop s'ama, si le traï
> Li mireoirs de la fontaine,
> Ou sa biautez faintive et vaine
> Mira tant que la mort en vint.
>
> (3.1881–885)

(Men and women in hate, and surfeited with self-love, if they are attracted to the mirrors of the fountain, or its weak, vain beauty, become so enraptured by wonder that they are vanquished by death.)

The allegory of Venus, Mars and Vulcan is very similar to what we have covered in the other Ovidian commentaries. Venus represents luxury as opposed to the ardor of Vulcan, while Mars the destroyer is the adulterer and the bringer of death. The sin of Adam and Eve also brought death to both. Illicit sex can only bring death and destruction: "Grief mort et grief destruction / Vienent par fornication." (4.1640–641) (Ruination and death are the sad fruits of fornication.) Neither wisdom nor power can prevail against love: "Contre amours ne puet force avoir / Riches ne sages ne poissans. (4.1691–692) (Against love affairs neither riches, nor wisdom, nor power have any force.)

The story of the judgment of Paris, in which the apple of Discord is presented to Aphrodite (Venus), the goddess of love, rather than to Athena the goddess of wisdom (and power as well, according to the author of the *Ovide Moralisé*), and Hera (Juno) the goddess of marriage or wealth or virtue, affords an ironic parallel to the "gift" of the fruit[32] to Eve, who is perhaps selected on the basis of the same criterion as Venus: physical beauty. But while Venus bribes the judge Paris in the Greek tale, in the biblical account and in Milton, in the *Ovide Moralisé* it is the devil who bribes Eve with the qualities possessed by Athena and Juno: wealth, status and power:

> Juno, deesse de richesce,
> Pallas de force et de sagesce,
> Venus, la deesse d'amours,
> Qui les cuers embrase en amours.
> (11.1501–504)

(Juno, goddess of riches, Pallas, goddess of power and wisdom, Venus goddess of love affairs, the one who entangles our hearts in the things of love.)

And Satan's paean to the forbidden tree invites Eve to share in the snake's supposed advance in wealth, status and power:

> O Sacred, Wise, and Wisdom-giving Plant,
> Mother of Science, now I feel thy Power
> Within me cleere, not onely to discern
> Things in thir Causes, but to trace the wayes
> Of highest Agents, deemd however wise.
> Queen of this Universe, . . .
> . . . . you shall be as Gods,
> Knowing both Good and Evil as they know.
> (9.679–84; 708–09)

To conclude this discussion of adaptations of Ovid, we move to a second moralized Ovid, the so-called *Ovide*

Moralisé En Prose, published in the fifteenth century.[33] This is an adaptation and loose paraphrase of the *Ovide Moralisé*, which also implements later sources, like Boccaccio's *Genealogy of the Gods*. It exists in only one manuscript in the Vatican library (Reg. 1686).[34] In the initial book, the anonymous author posits a direct relationship between Saturn's involuntary exile from his own Paradise and the casting out of Adam from Paradise: "*Comment Adam fut mis hors de paradis terrestre*" (1.20.50) (How Adam was cast out of an earthly Paradise.) In the description of the fall of Phaethon, the author refers specifically to "la dite combustion" (2.9.84) (the burning referred to) given off by the falling Phaethon and to the length of his fall ["abismes parfondes" (2.8.84) (bottomless abyss)], circumstances unforgettably related to Satan by Milton in his *Paradise Lost*: "Him the Almighty Power / Hurld headlong flaming from th'Ethereal Skie / With hideous ruin and combustion down/ To bottomless perdition..." (1.44–47).

The *Ovide Moralisé En Prose* follows the same interpretation as the *Ovide Moralisé*, blaming Phaethon for his pride and for aiming too high in life, but adding a detail directly parallel with Satan:

> A grant honte aussi et à grant meschief tresbucha jadis Lucifer de paradis par son orgueil, car il se vouloit aparier à Dieu son createur, mais il en fut de par Dieu tresbuchié es abysmes infernaulx comme le plus mauldit de toutes les creatures qui oncques furent. (2.10.85)

> (Lucifer was covered with shame for his great crime which originated in his pride, a crime that caused him, in times past, to be cast out of Paradise. For he wanted to be on an equal basis with God his creator; instead God snared him in the bottomless pit as one of the most accursed creatures who ever existed.)

He also interprets Phaethon as Antichrist (2.15.88).

For the author of the *Ovide Moralisé En Prose*, following many of the commentators (including Pierre Bersuire),

Echo represents one's good name, and Juno the world. As a whole, the tale symbolizes the danger of losing one's good name, and emphasizes the rudeness and incivility of Narcissus in spurning the love of Echo, (3.11, 12.123–24), a lesson all too well absorbed by Milton's uxorious Adam. Although it is not rendered explicitly, the myth of Hermaphroditus and Salmacis (4.10, 11.144–146), which figures prominently in the *Ovide Moralisé En Prose*, can be related to *Paradise Lost* in that Eve, through her strategy of keeping the still sinless Adam from falling out of love with her, drags him to death through the eating of the fruit, just as the author warns men against dangerous women like Salmacis. She represents the type of woman who is dangerous to all men, no matter how courageous they might be:

> Et de telle femme est la frequentacion tant perilleuse et dommaigeuse à homme qui la hante que à peine en peut aucun eschapper depuis qu'il en est lié, tant soit il saiges ou vaillant. (4.11.146)
>
> (Spending any amount of time with such a woman is so dangerous and so injurious to the man who sees her regularly, that, once he is ensnared, he has no more chance of escaping his punishment than a brave or a wise man would.)

And she will eventually lead them to shame and error ("à honte et à confusion"). While Salmacis unites her female form with the male form of Hermaphroditus, Eve's dominance over Adam reunites her female form with Adam's male form, thus producing the hermaphrodite—in effect rejoining what God had put asunder![35] Thus commentators have often accused Adam of effeminate slackness, because the superior power of Eve in drawing him to sin feminizes him and forces him to partake in her being. This myth, joined with the myth of the Judgment of Paris, combines the notion of sexual identification with the complexities of moral choice. In fact in an earlier work, the *Tetrachordon*, Milton, while not overtly rejecting the hermaphrodite myth, gave his readers to understand that the image of God is consistently male and not female; therefore any concept of the hermaphrodite blurs God's image in the male:

> It might be doubted why he saieth, *In the image of God created he him*, not them, as well as *male and female* them; especially since that Image might be common to them both, but *male and female* could not, however the Jewes fable, and please themselvs with the accidentall concurrence of *Plato's* wit, as if man at first had bin created *Hermaphrodite*: but then it must have bin male and female created he him. So had the Image of God bin equally common to them both, it had no doubt bin said, In the image of God created he them. (YP 2.589)[36]

On the same theme, the great Hercules, after so many labors, succumbs to the blandishments of Yole and so forgets himself that he exchanges clothes with her and becomes her slave; he is also destroyed by his wife Deyanira after the dying Centaur Nessus gives Deyanira a poisoned cloak to avenge his death at Hercules's hands (9.2.239–41). Adam is a type of both Samson and Hercules in Milton's *Paradise Lost*, two men shorn of their strength by a woman's "wiles." After the Fall, Adam and Eve rut like beasts[37] and the "fallen" Adam then "rises" to a new "low" of lost power and strength: "So rose the *Danite* strong / *Herculean Samson* from the Harlot-lap / Of *Philistean Dalilah*, and wak'd / Shorn of his strength . . ." (*PL* 9.1059–62).[38] The Hercules of the *Ovide Moralisé en Prose* becomes a pawn between two women, the enslaving Yole and the shrewish Deyanira. He ravishes the one and is destroyed by the other. Deyanira takes the poisoned cloak from the centaur Nessus, who has falsely claimed that it will insure her husband's love for her. It drives him mad, he kills all of their children, and then immolates himself on the pyre. It might not be too fanciful to suggest a parallel with Adam and Eve. Eve "gives" Adam of the fruit to eat, and as a result he tastes death, and with him all his progeny. In effect he has taken his and his ancestors' death sentence from the gift of his wife, just as Hercules did with Deyanira (9.2.239–41).[39]

In short, the interpretations of both the *Ovide Moralisé* and the *Ovide Moralisé en Prose* offer a merging of text and commentary, with a reinforcement of the commentaries imbedded in contemporary Renaissance editions of Ovid. A few more Christian parallels to the Ovidian text are contained in the *Ovide Moralisé,* and some of these are presented in greater detail in the *Ovide Moralisé en Prose.* The *Ovide Moralisé en Prose*, while it fails to comment on large sections of the *Ovide Moralisé*, does work in numerous references to the other works of Ovid, as well as other works of French and ancient Roman literature.[40] Both works attest to the persistent tradition of allegorical commentary of Ovid, and their "christianization" of the text indicates that precedent existed for mingling theological ideas with pagan in medieval and late Renaissance literature.

Milton, of course, would have been familiar with the texts of Homer, Vergil and Ovid in their original languages, and in French, Italian or English translations, as well as the various commentaries appended to all of these texts. Clearly, however, the Ovidian complex offered the richest possible vein of mythological commentary to the Christian poet in search of mythological parallels to Christian ideas. Indeed, this was a mythological tradition of cultural synthesis that Milton would be hard put to ignore.

Two

Milton and the Church Fathers

The church fathers provide an interesting perspective on the mythological tradition. While they formally denounced the various classical myths and their explicators, they also developed recondite and often farfetched readings of sacred Scripture. Yet at the same time they denied that classical myth could be similarly interpreted, particularly since methods of scriptural interpretation were arguably derived from the various readings of other ancient texts. More ironically still, in setting up the classical texts and myths for attack, they themselves became repositories of such materials.[1]

St. Jerome

The ambivalent attitude of the church fathers toward pagan thought is best expressed in the famous dream of St. Jerome (345–420). After suffering from a near-fatal illness,

Jerome reports[2] that he had a dream in which he was called before God's judgment seat:

> I was asked to state my condition and replied that I was a Christian. But He who presided said: "Thou Liest; thou art a Ciceronian, not a Christian".... At last the bystanders fell at the knees of Him who presided, and prayed Him to pardon my youth and give me opportunity to repent of my error, on the understanding that the extreme of torture should be inflicted on me if ever I read again the works of Gentile authors. In the stress of that dread hour I should have been willing to make even larger promises, and taking oath I called upon His name: "O Lord, if ever again I possess worldly books or read them, I have denied thee".... And I acknowledge that henceforth I read the books of God with a greater zeal than I had ever given before to the books of men.[3]

Of course Jerome did not fulfill his oath to the letter, but his remarks pinpoint the tension suffered by Christian thinkers who wanted to hold on to the beauties of the classical culture in which they were educated.[4] As we shall see, Lactantius and Marcus Minutius Felix Octavius tried to resolve the dilemma by claiming that some pagans actually knew the truths of Christianity, but were afraid to embrace or publicize them, lest they be exposed to violent retribution.

St. Augustine

St. Augustine's (345–430) *City of God*[5] is a full-scale diatribe against the pagan deities, embodying three contradictory views of their nature: 1) the pagan gods are figments of our imaginations, 2) they are the reincarnations of the fallen devils from hell and 3) they are of human origin (Euhemerus). He presents all three theories in the tenth chapter of the second book:

> As for the defence that is offered, namely, that what is said of the gods is not true but false and imaginary, that is even

more outrageous if you are concerned for religious devotion [1]. If, however, you imagine the possibility of malice on the part of the demons, what device to deceive could be shrewder or more clever?.... These malign spirits, however, whom they hold to be gods, choose to be charged with crimes that they did not commit, so long as they can enmesh men's minds with such beliefs as with nets and drag them along with themselves to a predestined punishment [2]. This is the case whether the crimes were actually committed by men—by men who are held to be gods to the joy of those whose joy it is to see men go astray [3], and for whom the demons substitute themselves as objects of worship by a thousand harmful and deceitful tricks—or whether, though no such crimes were really committed by any men, the utterly deceitful spirits gladly welcome such inventions about divinities to the end that sufficient authority may seem to have been transferred to earth from heaven itself for the perpetration of such crimes and villainies. (1.175)

Minucius Felix Octavius (fl. 200) seems to be anticipating Augustine when he characterizes the pagan gods as reincarnations of the fallen devils from hell:

There exist deceitful and wandering spirits who have lost their heavenly vigor from having been dragged down by earthly stains and lusts. These spirits, then, burdened with and steeped in vice, have forfeited the original simplicity of their nature; now damned themselves, they seek to bring others to damnation as a consolation for their own ruin; ... cast out by God, they seek, by introducing wicked cults, to win others away from Him. (ch. 26, p. 378)

And St. Justin Martyr (ca. 100–ca. 165):

Seized with fear and unaware that these were evil demons, they called them gods and greeted each by the name which each demon had bestowed upon himself.... those who pass down the myths fabricated by the poets give no proof of their truth to the youths who learn them, yet we can now show that these myths were first related through the instigation of evil demons to deceive and seduce all men.[6]

In the first book of *Paradise Lost* the narrator refers to the pagan gods as "numberless" (344), echoing Augustine's charge that the very number of the pagan gods indicated their inferiority and imperfection:

> So many were the gods who thus protected Rome, and who can count them: native gods and foreign-born, gods celestial and terrestrial, infernal and marine, fountain gods and river gods, and, as Varro says, gods certain and uncertain, and in every class of gods, as in every kind of animal, the male and the female? Surely, Rome founded as she was under the protection of so many gods, should not have been assailed and afflicted by such great and terrible calamities, of which I shall mention only a few out of many. (3.12.1.303)[7]

And again in the eighth chapter of the fourth book: "But how is it possible in one passage of this book to record all the names of the gods and goddesses that they were scarcely able to find room for in the huge volumes in which they divided up the services of the deities among the departments, assigning each to his own?" (2.31). And again in Tertullian (ca. 160–ca. 230): "And now, shall I quickly run through the list of deities, one by one, numerous and important as they are, the new and the old, barbarian and Greek, Roman and foreign, captive and adopted, private and public, male and female, belonging to the country, the city, the sailor, the soldier?"[8]

The narrator of *Paradise Lost* claims that the fallen angels lost their original names—were struck from the family Bible so to speak—and then took on new names to deceive and subdue humankind:

> . . . Godlike shapes and forms
> Excelling human, Princely Dignities,
> And Powers that earst in Heaven sat on Thrones;
> Though of thir Names in heav'nly Records now
> Be no memorial blotted out and raz'd
> By thir Rebellion, from the Books of Life.
> Nor had they yet among the sons of *Eve*

> Got them new Names, till wandring ore the Earth,
> Through Gods high sufferance for the tryal of man,
> By falsities and lyes the greatest part
> Of Mankind they corrupted to forsake
> God thir Creator,. . . .
> And Devils to adore for Deities:
> Then were they known to men by various Names,
> And various Idols through the Heathen World.
>
> (*PL* 1.358–69, 373–75)

Augustine also attacks the worshipers of the pagan gods, paralleling the Son's line in *Paradise Regained*: "Thir Gods ridiculous, and themselves past shame" (4.342). And, in exhorting the Romans to turn to Christianity, he says: "Do not pursue false and fallacious gods. Abandon them, rather, and despise them, break away into true liberty. They are not gods, they are malignant spirits, for whom your eternal happiness is their punishment" (2.29.1.261).

Recalling Milton's description of the wandering fallen angels ("... disguis'd in brutish forms / Rather then human ... *PL* 1.481–82) to us, Augustine speaks of the Egyptian gods who resembled dog-headed apes: "What am I to say of the Cynocephali, whose dogs' heads and actual barking are evidence that they are rather beasts than men?" (16.8, 5.43). On this same shape-shifting theme, the myth of the hermaphrodite constitutes the creature that Adam was before God severed a rib to separate him from his female self. Augustine also refers to this myth:

> Although androgyni, whom men also call hermaphrodites, are very rare, yet it is difficult to find periods when they do not occur. In them the marks of both sexes appear together in such a way that it is uncertain from which they should properly receive their name. However, our established manner of speaking has given them the gender of the better sex, calling them masculine. (16.8, 5.47)

But Adam disagrees, and even describes Eve as if she herself were a hermaphrodite:

> The Rib he formd and fashiond with his hands;
> Under his forming hands a Creature grew,
> Manlike, but different sex, so lovely fair,
> That what seemd fair in all the World, seemd now
> Mean, or in her summ'd up, ...
>
> (*PL* 8.469–73)⁹

On the famous debate between Athens and Jerusalem, Augustine has an intriguing apposite passage. Where Milton's Christ singles out the Greeks and the Romans for abuse, Augustine concentrates on the Egyptians:

> Therefore let no nation with any false pride boast of the antiquity of its wisdom as surpassing that of our patriarchs and prophets, in whom divine wisdom was found; since not even Egypt, who is wont falsely and foolishly to boast of the antiquity of her learning, is found to antedate with any wisdom of her own, whatever its quality, the wisdom of our patriarchs. Nor in fact will any one dare to say that they were most skilled in scientific lore before they knew letters, that is, before Isis had come and taught letters in their country. Furthermore, what was that memorable learning of theirs, which is called wisdom, unless it was chiefly astronomy and such other like sciences as commonly serve to exercise men's talents rather than to enlighten men's hearts with true wisdom?
>
> For as far as philosophy is concerned, which professes to teach men the way to happiness, studies of that kind won a place in those lands somewhere near the era of Mercury, whom they called Trismegistus, long before the wise men and philosophers of Greece, to be sure, but yet after Abraham and Isaac and Jacob and Joseph, and indeed after Moses himself. For research shows that it was at the time of Moses' birth that Atlas lived, that great astronomer, brother of Prometheus and maternal grandfather of the elder Mercury [recall "thrice-great Hermes" in *Il Penseroso*], whose grandson was the aforesaid Mercury Trismegistus. (18.40.6.15)

TERTULLIAN AND LACTANTIUS

The very terms of the controversy were introduced by Tertullian (155–222) with his famous taunt: "What indeed has Athens to do with Jerusalem? What concord is there between the Academy and the Church? what between heretics and Christians?.... With our faith, we desire no further belief."[10]

Milton's debt to Lactantius (ca. 260–ca. 318) has already been studied by Kathleen Ellen Hartwell (*Lactantius and Milton*) but not specifically from the point of view of mythological tradition. Since Lactantius wrote for the educated pagans, whom he wanted to convert to the new religion while also enriching Christianity with their vigorous intellectualism, he is very sparing in his quotations from Christian sources. A convert from paganism himself, he attempts to reach the pagans on their own terms and in their own language.

Lactantius's scornful dismissal of the pagan gods as false and unworthy of worship in the first book of his *Divine Institutes* may be seen as yet another gloss on Milton's line "Thir Gods ridiculous, and themselves past shame" (*PR* 4.342). Lactantius seems to use the same pattern we find in *Paradise Regained*, where Milton excoriates the pagans not only for their literature but also for their philosophy. Where Augustine refers to Hebrew thought as "true wisdom," Satan in *Paradise Regained* urges pagan wisdom as the road to glory: "Be famous then / By wisdom..." (4.221–22), while the Son refers to the same learning as "Thin sown with aught of prophet or delight" (4.345). Lactantius, however, defines philosophy as the *search* for wisdom, and contends that *all* philosophy is empty of wisdom and that it is the wrong place to search! After refuting the pagan religion as false in the first two books of *Divine Institutes* (including the blasphemous transformation of images into gods—1.22.90),[11] he goes on in the third book to show

how empty and false philosophy is also, that when all error has been removed, the truth may shine forth revealed.... If, then, philosophy seeks wisdom, and is not itself wisdom, for it is necessary that it be other than what it seeks and other than what is sought, neither is the seeking itself right, because it is not possible to find anything. Therefore, I would concede that the philosophers are not even students of wisdom, because wisdom is not arrived at by that study. For if the chance of coming upon truth were subject to this study, if this study were the path to wisdom, as it were, then it would be found at some time.... Those who philosophize, therefore, do not pursue or study wisdom, but think that they study it, because that which they seek they do not know where or what it may be. (3.2.166–67)

He then cites the philosophers against themselves, particularly Zeno, the Stoics and Socrates: "If, then, it is not possible for anything to be known, as Socrates thought, and if speculation is not fitting either, as Zeno held, then all philosophy is taken away" (3.4.170). Thus Lactantius takes the position that for the believing Christian, philosophy is unnecessary; in addition, it does not do what it claims to do.

In *Paradise Regained*, the Son takes exactly the same view and, like Lactantius, attacks certain philosophers as part of the tradition:

> he who receives
> Light from above, from the fountain of light,
> No other doctrine needs, though granted true;
> But these are false, or little else but dreams,
> Conjectures, fancies, built on nothing firm.
> The first and wisest of them all profess'd
> To know this only, that he nothing knew;
> The next to fabling fell and smooth conceits,
> A third sort doubted all things, though plain sence;
> . . . .
> Alas what can they teach, and not mislead;
> Ignorant of themselves, of God much more,
> And how the world began, and how man fell
> . . . .

> Who therefore seeks in these
> True wisdom, finds her not, or by delusion
> Far worse, her false resemblance only meets,
> An empty cloud.
>
> (4.288–96, 309–11, 318–21)

Or as Lactantius puts it, "If, then, the individual sects are convicted of foolishness by the judgment of many sects, all are, therefore, found to be vain and empty; thus philosophy itself consumes and exhausts itself" (3.4.171).[12] And the pagan philosophers, according to Lactantius, have condemned themselves out of their own mouths: "And does anyone bear ill-will to us because we deny that the philosophers are wise, when they themselves confess that they do not know anything and that they are not wise?" (3.28.238).

There are a number of places in *Paradise Lost* and *Paradise Regained* where Milton seems to be echoing the concerns, if not the language, of the *Divine Institutes*. For example, when Adam discusses his own creation, he immediately rises to his feet, examines the created world and finds it good, and then seeks to worship the great maker who created him. He is thus *homo erectus*, the only animal who stands on two feet, and the one who looks upward for his maker:

> Strait toward Heav'n my wondring eyes I turnd,
> And gaz'd a while the ample Skie, till rais'd
> By quick instinctive motion up I sprung,
> As thitherward endevoring, and upright
> Stood on my feet....
> ... how came I thus, how here?
> Not of my self; by some great Maker then,
> In goodness and in power praeeminent;
> Tell me, how may I know him, how adore
>
> (*PL* 8.257–61, 277–80)

Citing Ovid rather than the Scriptures as his source (*Met* 1.84–86), Lactantius makes these same points, uniting pagan concepts of human dignity with a Christian emphasis on our instinctive love for God:

> For this reason, surely, the Greeks called him *anthropon* because he looks upward. Thus, they renounce themselves and rob themselves of the name of man who do not look above but below, unless, perhaps, they think that the very quality of upright stature has been given to man without cause. Certainly, God has willed us to look to heaven, and not uselessly. (2.1.97)

Again, Lactantius condemns those who follow the fallen angels in their new guise as pagan divinities, a point that Milton makes in the first book of *Paradise Lost*: "... known to men by various Names, / And various Idols through the Heathen World" (374–75); and Lactantius as follows: "... those destroyers of souls ... destroy themselves by serving the most depraved demons whom God has condemned to eternal punishments ..." (5.19.376).

Finally, two emblems of choice, the Pythagorean Y and the Choice of Hercules,[13] are alluded to by Milton in describing the temptations of the Son in *Paradise Regained* and Samson in *Samson Agonistes*. Both refer to the road not taken, the path not chosen, and will be discussed in more detail in the chapters concerning the emblematic tradition (five) and Natale Conti-Vincenzo Cartari (nine). Lactantius mentions the first emblem without attributing it to Pythagoras: "For they say that the course of human life is like the letter Y because each man, when he has touched the threshold of his first youth and has come into that place, "where the way separates itself into two parts," [*Aen* 6.540], may cling waveringly and not know toward which direction he should rather incline" (6.3.397). Lactantius does not explicitly define the second emblem, which includes two women, one beautiful and one plain, inviting us to take opposite directions—the beautiful one, the smooth road to perdition; the ugly one, the rocky path of virtue—another Y-shaped pattern. In Lactantius the paths remain, but the women have been removed. For Lactantius these become the roads to heaven and hell, respectively: "We, however, do better and we speak more truly who say that those two ways are of heaven and of the lower regions, because immortality has been determined for the just, punishment for the unjust" (6.3.397). In short, both Lactantius and Milton address their learned audiences in the language of classical humanism purged of unbelief.

Marcus Minucius Felix Octavius

Perhaps no commentator among the church fathers offers a better gloss of the line "Thir gods ridiculous, and themselves past shame" (*PR* 4.342) than Marcus Minucius Felix Octavius:

> Moreover, do not the very forms and appearances of your gods expose them to ridicule and contempt?—Vulcan, a lame and crippled god; Apollo still beardless after all the years; Aesculapius, with a bushy beard, although he is the son of the ever-youthful Apollo,[14]. . . . These fables and absurdities we learn from our unenlightened parents. What is worse, we improve them with great care by our own studies and subjects of instruction, especially in the works of the poets who have done the greatest possible harm to the truth because of the high esteem in which they are held. (chaps. 23, 24, pp. 369, 370)

St. Justin Martyr

Finally, St. Justin Martyr launches a full-scale attack on pagan learning and theology in his *Exhortation to the Greeks* and *Discourse to the Greeks*. In the *Exhortation*, pagan learning is vigorously attacked, while at the same time Justin claims that Plato and other pagan philosophers had a foreknowledge of Christianity and the Holy Spirit. The ideas of the gods found in the Greek poets are dismissed as "silly." And while it may be true of the poets "that poetic license permits them to fabricate myths and, under the guise of mythology, to attribute many false things to the gods," the theology of the learned men and philosophers of Greece "is much more ridiculous than that of your poets" (chaps. 2, 3, pp. 74, 77). Justin also follows the traditional Christian view that Hebrew lore reached the Greeks and the Romans indirectly through Egypt. He claims that Plato learned about the teachings of Moses when he was visiting Egypt, and that he feared to reveal these truths, lest he be condemned to death like Socrates (chap. 20). He also credits Homer with prescient Hebrew wisdom derived from Egypt (chap. 28).

Justin continues this attack in his *Discourse to the Greeks*. Athena, the model for Milton's Sin; Bacchus, the father of Milton's Comus as well as the role model for Charles and his dissolute court; the women who follow Bacchus and whose murder of Orpheus is lamented in Milton's *Lycidas* and *Paradise Lost*—all are dismissed in a single contemptuous sentence: "What majesty is depicted by the scene of a woman clothed in armor, or of a man in female attire, decorated with cymbals and garlands, and followed by a frenzied mob of female devotees?" (chap. 2, p. 433).

Thus Milton could learn much about the mythological tradition from St. Augustine and the church fathers. The three theories of the pagan gods—that they are false, that they are demons, and that they are only men—are expounded by Augustine and given detailed treatment by many of the church fathers. The demon theory is at the very core of Milton's treatment of the fallen angels in *Paradise Lost*. The second great influence is detectable in *Paradise Regained*. The two-pronged attack on pagan learning by Justin Martyr and Lactantius—first on the poets and then on the philosophers—is mirrored almost exactly in the poem. Lactantius denies that pagan philosophy yields any truth at all, while Justin claims that pagan thinkers like Plato and pagan poets like Homer had to suppress their knowledge of Christianity because their culture was unwilling to accept its truth. The words of the Son in *Paradise Regained*, when he rejects Athens for Jerusalem, have a chauvinistic ring to them that can be traced directly to the church fathers, especially St. Augustine and St. Jerome.

As we have seen, the ambivalent attitude of these writers establishes a tradition where one can pick and choose—to emphasize the terrifying and repugnant reality of the pagan gods, or to dismiss them as figments of the pagan imagination.

THREE

Milton, Martianus Capella, Bernard of Sylvester and Alan of Lille

The four works to be discussed here (two by Alan of Lille) have a single theme: the intimate fusion of creation and learning in a hostile universe, a theme that Milton made his own in *Paradise Lost*. One might say they deal with the poetry of creation, or the intellectual basis for human perfection. They are all, in one way or another, explications of Plato's *Timaeus*, the philosopher's "creation book," roughly corresponding to the seventh book of *Paradise Lost*. These poems seriously address the problems of personal responsibility, the relation of Nature to humankind, and the problems of spiritual and physical survival in a postlapsarian, hostile world—the world Adam faces after the visitation by the archangel Michael.

MARTIANUS MINEUS FELIX CAPELLA

Martianus Mineus Felix Capella's (fl. A.D. 480) *The Marriage of Mercury and Philology*[1] is usually associated with the Middle Ages rather than the Renaissance, but there were nine printed editions of this fascinatingly elusive and allusive work in the sixteenth and seventeenth centuries. Milton would at least have been aware of its existence, even if he made no direct use of it. Again, like the works of Giordano Bruno (see chap. 4), it is a discussion of myth in a literary form and hence shapes part of the mythological tradition that Milton inherited. Moreover, Martianus (like Augustine) had access to works of Varro that have since been lost and that also form part of this tradition.

Without having recourse to the text of Martianus, Milton's interest in the figure of Mercury (and to a lesser extent Philology) is worth pursuing. Milton's "thrice great *Hermes*" (l. 88) of *Il Penseroso* refers to the mythical nephew of Hermes or Mercury, Hermes Trismegistus, but this is only one of the many places where Mercury might work his magic in Milton's poetry. Pan, the son of Mercury, the god of universality and pastoral poetry, is also an iconographic symbol for the devil. At the same time, Pan is identified by some Christian commentators with Christ, based on the (mistaken) etymology of *Panas* (Pan) as "all," and the myth that the death of Pan, recorded in Plutarch, evoked, according to Christian commentators, the birth of the Savior and the ushering in of a new age (see below, on the *Nativity Ode*). Mercury is the messenger god, traveling like Milton's Raphael between earth and heaven to communicate God's will to Adam and Eve. But he is also the conveyor of the dead to the underworld, and is like Satan in his attempt to destroy humankind, or like Michael, passing an implicit death sentence on the original pair by banishing them from the garden. Mercury is derived from the Greek Hermes and is the god of occult wisdom, the hermetic art. In iconography, he is one half of the *Hermathena* (to be discussed as an emblematic form in chapter five), the combination of learning (Hermes) and wisdom (Athena). He is also the masculine principle of learning and wisdom that accompanies the feminine principle of love in the Hermaphrodite. He is the trickster god, the shrewd bargainer, the slightly disreputable point man for Zeus, who attempts to cover up Zeus's affair with Io and do Zeus's dirty work.[2] He also communicates the irreverent ways of mortals to Zeus in Lucian's scornful dialogues of the underworld, and he is connected to the aging or "Gallic" Hercules, who exchanges wisdom and learning for physical strength in his old age, pulling men along by golden chains attached to his tongue.[3] He is also an alchemical god of formidable proportions, and Mercury's water is an essential ingredient in the process of turning base metals into gold. His winged sandals, the *talaria*, speed him along on his journeys between the sublunar world and the afterworld, for Mercury accompanies men on their journeys across the underworld rivers of the pagan afterlife (Juno performs that office for women).

Mercury is a strangely asexual god, except where he functions as a type of Pandarus, arranging or facilitating Zeus's various amours. In Botticelli's *Primavera*, for example, Mercury stares into space in neoplatonic fashion, ignoring the various emblems of love and lust that surround him.[4] As the *clericus* or scholar who prefers wisdom to sensual pleasure, he would have no sympathy with Eve's passion or Adam's uxoriousness. The caduceus or *virga*, wrongly associated by Martianus with the art of medicine (the actual province of the god Aesculapius), represents peacemaking or treatymaking power; and the snakes that couple in mutual amity at the crest of the staff the peace that ambassadors hoped to achieve before returning to their respective countries. It is also the golden bough, the *virga* or staff that Vergil carries to guide Dante through the afterworld. After attempting to steal the cattle of Apollo, not to mention the thunder of Zeus (the ancients, as Norman O. Brown points out in his *Hermes the Thief*, made no real distinction between a good bargain and theft),[5] Mercury exchanges his lyre, the instrument of poetry, for Apollo's staff. In effect, he exchanges control of poetry for control of time, death and the totality of social relationships.

In short, the god Mercury invites comparison with many characters and ideas in Milton's poetry, but he particularly embodies the characteristics associated with the devil: deceit, speed, wisdom, learning, occult knowledge, wealth (see the temptation to wealth in *Paradise Regained*), misogyny, poetry, ambiguous gender, a pandering disposition and the learned impotence of the *clericus* who flees the joys of heterosexual love (note Satan's leer of envy in book 4 of *Paradise Lost*: ". . . aside the Devil turnd / For envie, yet with jealous leer maligne / Ey'd them askance, . . ." [502–04]. He is a rather suspect god, wise without charm or courtliness, acquisitive but not discriminating, powerful more for what he knows rather than for what he is, despised and feared by both gods and men, as callous and efficient as an assassin, as dreamlike and unworldly as the most irrelevant poet.

In the *Marriage*, Mercury sees the happy union of all deities in marriage and he too decides to marry. He loves Wisdom or Philology, and he seeks out the great oracle Apollo to advise him on his courtship:

> Then, as usual, he gave his caduceus to Virtue, so that she could penetrate the secret parts of the world with him, and with equal swiftness could break into the more remote quarters of heaven. He himself bound on his feet the golden sandals and they made a thorough search for Apollo. (1.9.8)

As we can see from this passage, Mercury or learning must be accompanied by virtue if he is to find wisdom. As the messenger god, he wears the winged sandals (the *talaria*) and his occultism is suggested by his access to "the secret parts of the world" and "the more remote quarters of heaven."

Jupiter calls a council of the gods to discuss whether Mercury should be permitted to marry. In introducing the subject of the Council, Jupiter defines the powers and offices of his son Mercury:

> For he is my trust, my speech, my beneficence, and my true genius, the loyal messenger and spokesman of my mind, the sacred Nous. He alone can give the number of the gods, he alone can know the glittering stars, the dimension of the heavens and their depth; he knows the number of the ebb tides, how great are the flood tides the ocean sweeps along its shores; he knows the bond that joins the contrary elements, and I, the father, enforce those bonds through him—perhaps Duty alone will reckon what rewards this obedience will pay. (1.92.31)

The gods assent unanimously to the marriage, and Philology then prepares herself. After an attempt to dress for the wedding, her mother Phronesis (Wisdom) intervenes and outfits her in a white dress and robe, and places a crown on her head. Her feet are shod in papyrus leaves, by the learned pages inspired by her. Here Martianus touches on the visual tradition, particularly the discipline of iconography. She is then addressed by each of the Muses in turn. Of particular interest is Urania, the Muse of Astronomy, whom Milton invokes in his creation book (*Paradise Lost* 7). Since Philology is to be wedded to Mercury or Learning, she will, according to Martianus's Urania, learn all the hidden secrets of the universe:

> With trust in the divine will and without disputing, behold the assemblies of the stars and the sacred vaults of the heavens; you formerly studied what cause whirled the interdependent spheres, now as their leader you shall assign causes to their sweeping motions. You should perceive what is the fabric that connects their circuits, what bond encompasses them, and what huge spheres are enclosed within a curving orbit; you will see what drives on and what delays courses of the planets, which rays of the sun inflame the moon or diminish its light, what substance kindles the stars in heaven, and how great are the bodies which heaven spins around, what is the providence of the gods, and what its mode of operation. Ascend into the

temples of heaven, maiden, deserving of such a marriage; your father-in-law Jupiter asks you to rise to the lofty stars. (1.118.41)

Like Philology, Milton has, with the aid of Urania, ascended to the Heavens. At the beginning of the seventh book of *Paradise Lost*, he asks Urania to return him to earth. Like Mercury, Urania is linked with Wisdom, and like Philology, she is associated with "th'Almighty Father," or in pagan terms, Jupiter:

> Descend from Heav'n *Urania*, by that name
> If rightly thou art call'd, whose Voice divine
> Following, above th'*Olympian* Hill I soar,
> Above the flight of *Pegasean* wing.
> The meaning, not the Name I call: for thou
> Nor of the Muses nine, nor on the top
> Of old *Olympus* dwell'st, but Heav'nlie born,
> Before the Hills appeerd, or Fountain flow'd,
> Thou with Eternal Wisdom didst converse,
> Wisdom thy Sister, and with her didst play
> In presence of th'Almightie Father, pleas'd
> With thy Celestial Song. Up led by thee
> Into the Heav'n of Heav'ns I have presum'd,
> An Earthlie Guest, and drawn Empyreal Air,
> Thy tempring; with like safetie guided down
> Return me to my Native Element
>
> (1–16)

In an odd form of "publish or perish," Philology relieves her swollen innards by vomiting up a great store of books and papers, including the occult wisdom of Egypt:

> Then that nausea and labored vomit turned into a stream of writings of all kinds. One could see what books and what great volumes and the works of how many languages flowed from the mouth of the maiden.... There were some written with a sacred ink, whose letters were thought to be representations of living creatures; when Immortality saw the writings of these books, she ordered them to be inscribed on certain imposing rocks and placed inside a cave within the sanctuaries of the Egyptians, and she called

these stones *stelae* and ordained that they should contain the genealogies of the gods. (2.136–37.47)

Recall the Egyptian-Greek-Hebrew controversy (to be reviewed in chap. 6) and Milton's insistence on the supremacy and priority of Hebrew in *Paradise Regained* ("That rather *Greece* from us these Arts deriv'd" 4.338).

The arrival of the various liberal arts is pretty routine until astronomy is introduced. Then Bacchus's sidekick, Silenus, belches loudly and triggers a spate of ribaldry by Venus, Cupid and the maidservants that attend Bacchus (8.804 ff.; 314 ff.). Satire reproves them, and the narrator jests with her. The material on astronomy is what one would find in an elementary textbook, and to some extent it parallels Milton's own description of the universe in *Paradise Lost*, but it contains nothing that he could not find in a dozen other sources. The book concludes rather cleverly with a description of Harmony, the last of Philology's bridesmaids.

What are we to make of this strange work of the fifth century? While most of the material on the seven liberal arts would be useless or old hat to Milton, there are certain mythic themes in "The Betrothal" and "The Marriage" books that are repeated in *Paradise Lost*. As we have seen, the ascent of the poet to heaven to sing of its glory and activities parallels the ascent of Philology to heaven and to godlike status as wife of Mercury. Mercury as messenger god parallels the messenger angels Michael and Raphael. Milton's favorite muse, Urania, promises to provide Philology with the secrets of the universe, as she does to Milton when he celebrates the glories of heaven and the beauties of the created universe. Finally, the notion of an apotheosis, an ascent to heaven, is stated for Philology and implied for each person, who will have, according to Milton's Michael, "A Paradise within thee, happier farr" (12.587). The spatial metaphors of Milton represent the fruits of a long tradition that can be said to have begun with Martianus, whose confusing, chaotic text

74   *"Through a Glass Darkly"*

forms one of the more bizarre examples of the mythological tradition.

BERNARD OF SYLVESTER

As Winthrop Wetherbee observes, the fusion of *sapientia* and *eloquentia* in Bernard of Silvester's *Cosmographia* marks (in that work) the point at which literature and philosophy meet in the *Cosmographia*.[6] And while this approach in Bernard is derived from the Chartrian method of commenting on the *auctores*,[7] for Milton it moves from two more inclusive sets of *auctores*, the Bible and the church fathers on the one side, and the classical Greek and Latin texts on the other. Milton is confident that he can express the hidden ways of God "if answerable style [he] can obtain" (*PL* 9.20) from his celestial Muse, Urania. For Milton there is a merging of wisdom and eloquence in the poem itself, which is an eloquent exposition of the wisdom of the universe.

Milton's view of Chaos as intractable matter from which only God could achieve creation, and as the evil substance through which Satan must travel to reach earth, is certainly reflected and anticipated in Bernard.[8] Bernard's Nature complains that Chaos (Hyle or Silva) is "intractable, a formless chaos, a hostile coalescence, the motley appearance of being, a mass discordant with itself" (67). Nature even denies that Chaos was created by God: "Because she is lacking in all these Silva may scarcely lay claim to her true title as the work of God; rather she appears a giddy contrivance of blind fortune, bereft of the protection of any higher power" (68). Milton, in turn, introduces us to the real horrors of Chaos in the second book of *Paradise Lost*, after Sin opens the gates of hell to allow Satan to proceed to earth and to tempt Eve. This is the place

> ... without bound,
> Without dimension, where length, breadth, and highth,
> And time and place are lost; where eldest Night

And *Chaos*, Ancestors of Nature, hold
Eternal *Anarchie*, amidst the noise
Of endless Warrs, and by confusion stand.

(892–97)

In this mad kingdom, Disorder rather than Order rules, for Chaos and Chance determine the outcome of events:

... *Chaos* Umpire sits,
And by decision more imbroils the fray
By which he Reigns; next him high Arbiter
Chance governs all....

(2.907–10)

As does "Blind Fortune" in Milton's version of Chaos.

Bernard (speaking through Noys or Reason) is just as negative about Chaos (Hyle) as Milton is: "Now Hyle exists in an ambiguous state, suspended between good and evil, but because her evil tendency preponderates, she is more readily inclined to acquiesce in its impulses" (69). She is definitely an ambivalent substance: "Hyle was Nature's most ancient manifestation, the inexhaustible womb of generation, the primary basis of formal existence, the matter of all bodies, the foundation of substance" (70). However, even though she forms new beings and reassimilates those who have died, she provides no real identities for the creatures, and assigns their shapes at random (70). She also has a component of evil that threatens the physical and spiritual integrity of creatures formed from her: "Yet to the very extent that her nature proved fertile and prolific in conceiving and giving birth to all creatures in common, it was equally impartial with respect to evil" (71). She has within her "a certain malign tendency" (71): "When she had so nearly refined away that coarseness which is the property of Silva [Hyle], Noys, reflecting inwardly upon eternal ideas, fashioned the species of created life in close and intimate resemblance to these" (72).

Thus evil is implicit in Chaos, and the breakdown in nature after the Fall, which Milton documents in the eleventh and twelfth books of *Paradise Lost*, can be linked to the release of this destructive force. After Adam and Eve pray to be forgiven for their disobedience, they witness an eclipse and the flesh-eating eagle and lion pursuing their prey. Adam recognizes the import of these ominous signs and counsels his spouse: "O *Eve,* some furder charge awaits us nigh, / Which Heav'n by these mute signs in Nature shews / Forerunners of his purpose, or to warn" (*PL* 11.193–95). After Michael introduces Adam to the thousand and one forms of death, Adam asks if there is a better, less painful way, only to be confronted by another irony that emanates from a flawed creation. For a healthy way of life only leads to a painful and degrading old age, as Adam learns:

> There is, said *Michael,* if thou well observe
> The rule of not too much,....
> This is old age; but then thou must outlive
> Thy youth, thy strength, thy beauty, which will change
> To witherd weak and gray; thy Senses then
> Obtuse, all taste of pleasure must forgoe
> (11.530–31, 538–41)

While Milton deals mainly with natural sites in *Paradise Lost* (in the vision of Eden) and historical sites in *Paradise Regained* (the kingdoms of the world, the Parthenon), Bernard deals with both in his "garden," which is neither the garden of Paradise nor the particular inspiration of any religious source. Instead "The Pierian grove of the Academy, surpassing in its charm, destined to harbor the high-sounding Sophists and Plato himself, comes into bloom. The Nine Sisters have abandoned the vault of the firmament, so great is the splendor of the Pierian grove" (83). Here both poets and rhetoricians (i.e. Sophists) are mentioned, and the "Grove of *Academe*" (*PR* 4.244), but also the notion of *sapientia* and *eloquentia*—the poets have both, the sophists only *eloquentia,* which gives literature the edge in manifesting the secrets of the universe. Milton's Satan attributes "resistless eloquence" (*PR* 4.268) to the Greek orators and wisdom to "sage Philosophy" (272).

In response, the Son attacks pagan eloquence by reducing Plato's grand manner to "fabling" and "smooth conceits" (295), and Greek poetry to ". . . swelling Epithetes thick laid / As varnish on a Harlots cheek . . ." (343–44). As for wisdom, ". . . Who therefore seeks in these / True wisdom, finds her not, or by delusion / Far worse, her false resemblance only meets, / An empty cloud . . ." (318–21).

The *Cosmographia*, Bernard's account of the creation of the perfect man, Nature's final attempt to surpass all of her other flawed works, posits a mysterious universe where the power of evil as well as of good is locked in the womb of Chaos, Hyle or Silva: "For there was infused in her seedbed from of old the taint of a certain malign tendency which would not readily abandon the basis of its existence" (71). Even the fully formed planets pose a threat to the creation of the perfect man, particularly Saturn, who embodies Time and Death, the twin evils of postlapsarian existence:

> Far below this level resided the Usiarch of Saturn, an old man everywhere condemned, savagely inclined to harsh and bloody acts of unfeeling and detestable malice. Whenever his most fertile wife had borne him sons, he had them cut off at the first budding of life, devouring them newly born. Ceaselessly on guard against childbirth, he neither paused for deliberation nor succumbed to pity, whereby he might sometimes have been sparing because of the sex or comeliness of the child. Nature was horrified by the old man's cruelty, and lest she should profane her divine gaze with so foul a sight, turned away her face in virginal alarm. One evil passion obsessed the old man, and he indulged in one form of savagery: he was still vigorous, and with a strength not yet impaired, and whenever there was no one whom he might devour, he would mow down with a blow of his sickle whatever was beautiful, whatever was flourishing. . . . By the spectacle he presented he prefigured the hostility with which he was to menace the race of men to come by the poisonous and deadly propensities of his planet. . . . Chronos [Saturn] was the son of eternity and the father of time. (99–100)

Milton's Death "snuff'd" "with delight" "the smell / Of mortal change on Earth . . ." (*PL* 10.272–73) in anticipation of the feast his mother Sin would be preparing for him from the carcasses of fallen man and nature. Here Milton (unlike Bernard) appears to distinguish between Death and Time, the first being a product of the second, but the devouring, scythe-wielding Saturn is clearly the basis for his concept of Death and the process of corruption that inevitably accompanies it:

> To whom th'incestuous Mother thus repli'd.
> Thou therefore on these Herbs, and Fruits, and Flowrs
> Feed first, on each Beast next, and Fish, and Fowl,
> No homely morsels, and whatever thing
> The Sithe of Time mows down, devour unspar'd,
> Till I in Man residing through the Race,
> His thoughts, his looks, words, actions all infect,
> And season him thy last and sweetest prey.
>
> (10.602–09)

Bernard goes beyond a mere description of the fabulous garden; he also treats it as the future site of the great learning of Greece, a passage that is clearly relevant to the temptation to learning in *Paradise Regained*: "The grove of the Academy, surpassing in its charm, destined to harbor the high-sounding Sophists and Plato himself, comes into bloom" (83). And in Milton:

> Where on th' *AEgean* shore a City stands
> Built nobly, pure the air, and light the soil,
> *Athens*, the eye of *Greece*, Mother of Arts
> And Eloquence. . . .
>
> (*PR* 4.238–41)

The "high-sounding Sophists" of Bernard have several applications to the "eloquent" Milton, including the temptation to learning the Son endures in *Paradise Regained*, and the fallacious temptation of Eve in the ninth book of *Paradise Lost*.

Bernard also makes a substantive distinction between the heavens and humankind: whereas the planets are immortal, human beings are subject to mortality because of their intrinsic weakness: "So now the hapless race of men, whose existence is not sustained by a perfect fusion of the elements, lives in constant fear of falling subject to external accidents" (73). Bernard suggests, in fact, that since human beings have more imperfect bodies than the planets, they also experience greater suffering. The upwardly mobile stance of Milton's Adam as he becomes *homo erectus* at the very moment of birth, is also anticipated by Bernard: "... man alone, his stature bearing witness to the majesty of his mind, will lift up his noble head toward the stars, that he may employ the laws of the spheres and their unalterable courses as a pattern for his own course of life" (113).

Bernard posits several groups of angels (who, in their hermetic character as messengers, may be regarded as an aspect of the mythological tradition), the largest under the command of Michael, and Milton may well have borrowed some of his angelic lore from Bernard. Bernard's most important reference to angels involves their influence in dreams: "Often they insinuate themselves invisibly into minds at rest, or concerned with their own thoughts, through the power of suggestion" (108). This passage explains, with admirable concision, how Satan employs a dream to "insinuate" himself into the mind of Eve:

> Assaying by his Devilish art to reach
> The Organs of her Fancie, and with them forge
> Illusions as he list, Phantasms and Dreams,
> Or if, inspiring venom, he might taint
> Th'animal Spirits that from pure blood arise
> Like gentle breaths from Rivers pure, thence raise
> At least distemperd, discontented thoughts,
> Vain hopes, vain aimes, inordinate desires
> Blown up with high conceits ingendring pride.
> (*PL* 4.801–09)

Thus Bernard touches on a number of mythologically based ideas that receive further amplification in Milton:

Chaos, Creation, Time, Wisdom, Eloquence, the Angelic intelligences and the inherent dignity of the human person.

ALAN OF LILLE

Alan of Lille, the twelfth century poet and philosopher who came to be known as "Doctor Universalis," wrote two poetical satires in Latin that bear marked thematic and stylistic resemblances to Milton's *Paradise Lost*: the *Plaint of Nature* (a Menippean Satire) and the *Anticlaudianus*.[9] In the *Plaint* Alan explores two themes that also occupied Milton: the corruption of the natural world through the sin of humankind, and the proper relationships between the sexes. In the *Anticlaudianus* there are three motifs (or image clusters) that reappear in *Paradise Lost*: the garden, the infernal council and the celestial voyage. All of these themes or motifs, in both Alan and Milton, are accessed through myth. Alan's works have as their common concern the search for moral perfection in an imperfect world populated by flawed human beings; the Christian stories of the Fall and human redemption effected through Christ are implicit in Alan's works, although there are no explicit references to either account. While the Christian narratives are externalized in Milton, their mythic underpinnings can be profitably explicated through comparison with both the *Plaint of Nature* and the *Anticlaudianus*.

Aside from a brief note by the classicist J. E. Sandys comparing Milton's invocation to light in *Paradise Lost* to the similar passage in the *Anticlaudianus*,[10] there appear to be no comparative studies of these two great epic poets. Yet both poets take the entire cosmos for their subject, with particular emphasis on heaven, hell and the pre- and post-lapsarian earth; and both aim for a sublimity of style and a seriousness of tone (albeit one in Latin and the other in English) that have almost come to be defined as Miltonic.

Alan was a distinguished product of twelfth century French humanism, as it emanated from the school of

Chartres.¹¹ Milton, in turn, is the last great Renaissance humanist, the most distinguished graduate of the English school system (fundamentally Latin in its orientation) that developed beneath the shaping hands of Grocyn and Lincare in the fifteenth century.¹² They were both learned, epic, moral, linguistically ornate poets engaged in justifying the ways of God to men (and women).

Milton could certainly have read Alan of Lille firsthand, for there was an edition of his works published by Carl de Vish in 1654,¹³ but even if he did not, there are certainly grounds for comparison. And, while it may be finally impossible to link Milton's work with the work of Alan, it can be seen as at least an indirect source. For Milton, as Edward Sichi persuasively notes, surely knew Jean de Meun's account of Nature in the *Romance of the Rose*,¹⁴ and that same attitude of a personified Nature, who feels cheated and corrupted by Adam's sin, proceeds in a direct line from Alan to Jean de Meun to Milton.¹⁵

The theme of the corruption of the natural world, a corruption brought on by human weakness, is stated with lucidity and force by Nature herself in the *Plaint*:

> Man, however, who has all but drained the entire treasury of my riches, tries to denature the natural things of nature and arms a lawless and solecistic Venus to fight against me.... I regret that for the most part I have honoured man's nature with so many graces and privileges, seeing that he disgraces his graces by abuse of propriety, that he disfigures the fair figure of Venus by ugliness, that he discolours the colour of beauty by the meretricious dye of desire, that he deflowers the flower of pulchritude by having it bloom into vice. (131, 134–35)

Once Eve has eaten of the apple from the fruit of the forbidden tree, "Earth felt the wound, and Nature from her seat / Sighing through all her Works gave signs of woe, / That all was lost..." (*PL* 9.782–84). For Alan, humankind "deflowers the flower of pulchritude by having it bloom into vice." Milton's Eve is, in the words of Adam, "Defac't, deflowrd" (901). Alan's sinful human "discoulours the color of beauty by the meretricious dye of desire," while the narrator of *Paradise Lost* observes of Eve that "in her Cheek distemper flushing glowd" (887). This sinful person of Alan's "disfigures the fair figure of Venus by ugliness," while both Adam and Eve disfigure the act of Venus with passion's heat. Adam is "inflamed" by her newfound beauty, and Eve "on fire" to return it:

> For never did thy Beautie since the day
> I saw thee first and wedded thee, adorn'd
> With all perfections, so *enflame* my sense
> With ardor to enjoy thee, fairer now
> Then ever, bounty of this vertuous Tree.
>   So said he, and forbore not glance or toy
> Of amorous intent, well understood
> Of *Eve*, whose Eye darted contagious *Fire*.
>   (1029–36; my emphasis on "enflame" and "Fire")

Alan's discussion of the natural union of man and woman is expressed through the extended metaphor of language—the coupling of male and female is analogous to the coupling of subject and predicate, male and female are related to the masculine and feminine genders of nouns; and the (respectively) aggressive and receptive roles of man and woman in the sexual act are identified with the active and passive moods of the verb. (67–70) Such linguistic wit might be dismissed as gratuitous cleverness on Alan's part, but for Milton the generative power of the Word in the Bible mirrors the poet's creative power over language. He is, in fact, an interpreter of the Word, commenting directly on the book of Genesis but also alluding to The Song of Songs, recreating prelapsarian sexuality from the prophetic utterances of the Old Testament. Milton also attacks stereotypical views of sexuality in grammatical terms in the sixth *Prolusion*, where he criticizes his auditors for confusing secondary sexual characteristics with the true integrity of gender. After comparing himself to the man-woman Tiresias (for disturbing two coupling snakes;

Ovid, *Met* 3.322 ff.) and the woman-man Caenis (a change she requested from the gods, after being raped; Ovid, *Met* 12.189 ff.), Milton attacks crudity and immorality as standards of manhood:

> But why do I seem to them too little of a man? Have they no regard for [the ancient grammarian] Priscian? Do these bungling grammarians attribute to the feminine gender what is proper to the masculine, like this? It is, I suppose, because I have never brought myself to toss off great bumpers like a prize-fighter, or because my hand has never grown horny with driving the plough, or because I was never a farm hand at seven or laid myself down full length in the midday sun; or last perhaps because I never showed my virility the way these brothellers do. But I wish they could leave playing the ass as readily as I the woman. (YP 1.283–84)

If we refer to the "Hail wedded Love" speech of Milton's narrator in *Paradise Lost* (4.750 ff.), true marriage is contrasted with "adulterous lust" (753), while in *The Plaint*, Nature is betrayed by her lieutenant Venus, who engages in adulterous love with Antigenius, producing *Jocus* or *Sport*, Frivolity (163–65). This demon god represents the kind of selfish, superficial unions that the narrator mocks in the same speech:

> ... the bought smile
> Of Harlots, loveless, joyless, unindeard,
> Casual fruition, nor in Court Amours
> Mixt Dance, or wanton Mask, or Midnight Ball,
> Or Serenate, which the starv'd Lover sings
> To his proud fair, best quitted with disdain.
>
> (765–70)

The question of forbidden knowledge or knowledge rightly ordered is also addressed by the narrator. He states that the disposition of knowledge from God to ourselves is organized by the angelic choirs:

> Man, however, like a foreigner, living on the outskirts of the universe, does not refuse to show obedience to the hosts

of angels. In this state, then, God gives commands, the angels carry them out, man obeys. God creates man by his command, the angels by their operation carry out the work of creation, man by obedience re-creates himself. . . . Our chain of reason extends too far when it dares to lift our discourse to the ineffable secrets of the godhead, although our mind grows faint in sighs for a knowledge of this matter. (120–21)

Milton's Adam also yearns to know "the ineffable secrets of the godhead," but Raphael is careful to keep his revelations within the "chain of reason":

> . . . such Commission from above
> I have receav'd, to answer thy desire
> Of knowledge within bounds; beyond abstain
> To ask, nor let thine own inventions hope
> Things not reveal'd, which th'invisible King,
> Onely Omniscient, hath supprest in Night,
> To none communicable in Earth or Heaven:
> Although is left besides to search and know.
> But Knowledge is as food, and needs no less
> His Temperance over Appeite, to know
> In measure what the mind may well contain,
> Oppresses else with Surfet and soon turns
> Wisdom to Folly, as Nourishment to Wind.
>
> (7.118–130)

In the fifth book of Alan of Lille's *Anticlaudian*, to mark the ascent from heaven to earth of Phronesis (Prudence), and to celebrate the shift from poetry to prophecy, Alan sets aside his Apollinian Muse and invokes the heavenly Muse, whom he seems to identify with God the Father. He himself becomes the unwitting scribe, almost like Philology in Martianus vomiting out the books and papers of her Wisdom:

> The earthly Apollo will yield to the heavenly Muse; the Muse will give place to Jupiter [often taken as an ancient substitute for God the Father]; the language of earth will yield to and wait on the language of heaven and Earth will give place to Olympus. I will be the pen in this poem, not

the scribe or author. I will be a sounding brass, the writer's silent page, the singer's pipe, the sculptor's chisel, the orator's muse, the thorn bearing a rose, the reed bringing a potion of new honey, the night with its light from another source, the earthen vase flowing with nectar. Father on high, eternal God, ... direct first on me a ray of divine light; send your rain upon me to bedew still further my mind with heavenly nectar, cleanse me of blemishes of mind, wipe out and dispel the darkness, grant me the clear calm splendour of your light. (146–47)

Milton, in the seventh book of *Paradise Lost*, does exactly the opposite: in order to relate the story of creation, Urania must *descend* from heaven rather than *ascend* to earth as a prelude to Raphael's description of the creation: "Descend from Heav'n *Urania*, by that name / If rightly thou art call'd.... / For thou art Heav'nlie, shee an empty dream" (1–2; 39). However, just as Milton begs the Muse to allow him to see clearly the artifacts of Creation as explained by Raphael, so the exhausted Alan, speaking in his own voice, looks to heaven for assistance in describing the strange things that he sees. Where Alan shifts from poet to prophet in the *Anticlaudianus*, Milton "must change / Those notes to Tragic" in the pivotal ninth book of *Paradise Lost* (5–6), and switch to the prophetic mode in the apocalyptic vision of the eleventh and twelfth books.[16]

Alan's description of the journey itself, however, is more germane to Satan's ill-fated expedition than the easy peregrinations of angels and God in *Paradise Lost*. The journey of Phronesis through the threatening realms of the various galaxies resembles Satan's perilous voyage through Chaos. Phronesis is "in a feverish turmoil since she sees that the approaches are difficult, a fall ever imminent" (139). Similarly, Satan hesitates for a moment before passing from hell through the vast abyss of Chaos: "Into this wild Abyss the warie fiend / Stood on the brink of Hell and look'd a while, / Pondering his Voyage; for no narrow frith / He had to cross....." (*PL* 2.917–20).

Again, Milton, like Alan (who in turn follows Martianus's example), follows the convention of reducing the author's role to that of a stenographer, or amanuensis, who takes dictation from the Muse. Thus in the ninth book of *Paradise Lost*, he speaks "Of my Celestial Patroness, who deignes / Her nightly visitation unimplor'd, / And dictates to me slumbring, or inspires / Easie my unpremeditated Verse:" (21–24). It might, however, be more accurate to say that both authors are comparing themselves with the authors of the Bible, writing under the inspiration of the Holy Spirit, and endued with the gift of prophecy.

Where both Adam and Samson are "fondly overcome with Femal charm" (*PL* 9.999) and bow before the will of love and the wills of their wives, the perfect man of Alan's poem kills Venus herself, who dies recalling her mastery over two other great men whom she feminized:

> Now my arms lie idle, my arms through which Achilles, counterfeiting a girl in his degenerate clothes, was once overcome and yielded. The descendant of Alceus [Hercules], degenerate in arms, exchanges his staff for a distaff, his arrows for a day's supply of wool, his quivers for a spindle and basely unsexed himself completely in womanish action. (211)

And while the conflation of Fortune and Occasion is most often seen as a Renaissance phenomenon (see Milton's *Comus*, 743, "If you let slip time . . ."),[17] it is already present in Alan. For "the front of her [Fortune's] head is covered with a rich growth of hair, the back bemoans its baldness" (190). And, just as the Renaissance Fortune is often depicted with the Cornucopia or Horn of Plenty, so "one hand gives a gift, the other takes it away; one increases the gift, the other diminishes it; one offers it, the other withdraws it" (190), just as Comus offers both life and death with the poisoned cup.

Both Milton and Alan (in the *Anticlaudianus*) address the question of the right ordering of knowledge: what type of knowledge is necessary to succeed in the world and what relations exist among the various forms of knowledge. After Adam "dares to lift [his] discourse to the ineffable secrets of the godhead" (*PL* 8.121) by making some dangerous comments about the superfluity and potential wastefulness of nature, the angel Raphael rebukes him strongly and reminds him of the (God-given) limitations of his knowledge:

> Sollicit not thy thoughts with matters hid,
> Leave them to God above, him serve and fear;
> Of other Creatures, as him pleases best,
> Wherever plac't, let him dispose: joy thou
> In what he gives to thee, this Paradise
> And thy fair *Eve*; Heav'n is for thee too high
> To know what passes there; be lowlie wise:
> Think onely what concerns thee and thy being;
> Dream not of other Worlds, what Creatures there
> Live, in what state, condition or degree,
> Contented that thus farr hath been reveal'd
> Not of Earth onely but of highest Heav'n.
>
> (*PL* 8.167–78)

Since Alan's new man is being created for the postlapsarian world, and is supposed to be as near perfection as possible, he needs learning as well as natural goodness to survive. Thus this new and "perfect" man is formed by Reason, with the assistance of the seven liberal arts. The council of the seven liberal arts and the debate about creating the perfect man resemble the devilish councils of Satan and his cohorts in both *Paradise Lost* and *Paradise Regained*. In the former, the devils plot the demise of prelapsarian "man," Adam and Eve; in the latter, the destruction of the Son, the perfect postlapsarian man ("till one greater Man / Restore us" (*PL* 1.4–5). Since the Son is living in the postlapsarian world, he needs knowledge to refute the devil, and he provides it in abundance: "To whom our Saviour *sagely* thus repli'd" (*PR* 4.285; emphasis mine).

Finally, just as Milton's new man, the Son of God, must confront and refute the fraudulent rhetoric of Satan, "the perswasive Rhetoric / That sleek't his tongue...," the rhetoric he used to accomplish "his fraud" (*PR* 4.4–5, 3), so Alan's New Man, emerging victorious from the battle of the Virtues and Vices, must face Fraud herself, who "propitiates him with sweet words and cloaks her artifices with the ornaments of Rhetoric" (214). Again, when the devil tempts Eve in *Paradise Lost*, "his words replete with guile / Into her heart too easie entrance won" (9.733–34). And while Adam is overcome by Venus in the shape of Eve, "The New Man, however, in Parthian fashion, shoots an arrow at Venus while he is retreating and it does not miss its mark. It first strikes and causes a wound and thus finally brings about her death; nor can Desire urge any opposing argument when Venus is thus thwarted" (210). Like the Son and unlike Adam, Alan's new man will not be "fondly overcome with Femal charm" (*PL* 9.999). Nor will his reason be subject to his passions, the condition of postlapsarian man outlined by Milton's archangel Michael: "And upstart Passions catch the Government / From Reason, and to servitude reduce / Man till then free..." (*PL* 12.88–90). In fact the *Anticlaudianus* concludes with a battle royal between the Virtues and the Vices, with the perfect man leading the Virtues to victory.[18]

In reviewing this collage of medieval epic poetry, one common subject emerges: the relation between the nature of human beings and the nature of the physical universe they inhabit, a relationship that can only be negotiated by the creative, learned, "perfect" man. Thus all human beings must cultivate both wisdom and eloquence to cope with their environment (Mercury, Philology, Urania), must recognize its chaotic nature (Mars, Saturn, Fortune), must come to terms with their own sexuality (Venus), must acknowledge superior beings and control the inferior (God, the Angels, the animals of Genesis), and must attempt to recapture their former glorious prelapsarian state (Nature, the Garden). In short, there are ample grounds for comparison between Milton and any of these philosopher-poets who wrote during an age he affected to despise.

Four

Milton and the Trattato d'amore

The *trattato d'amore* ("treatise about love"), which embraced not only the mythological figures of Venus and Cupid, but also the idea of love as a philosophical concept, expounds a philosophy of love that would have been familiar to Milton and that can be profitably related to the love existing between his Adam and Eve. My remarks will be restricted to four of the most influential and comprehensive treatises: Marsilio Ficino's (1433–1499) *Commentary on the Symposium*,[1] Leone Ebreo's (1437–1508) *Dialoghi D'Amore*,[2] and Giordano Bruno's (1548–1600) *Eroici Furori*[3] and *Lo Spaccio*.[4]

Marsilio Ficino

As Ficino's English translator Sears Jayne argues, the thesis of Ficino's treatise is the "defense of human love," which Diane McColley and John Shawcross have argued is one of the central themes of *Paradise Lost*.⁵ Jayne further explains that the *De amore* was meant to have an esoteric meaning, inaccessible to the ordinary reader. This tradition was common to both the Egyptologists (cf. chap. 6) and the mythographers (cf. chaps. 8 and 9): "Because the *De amore* was written as a Platonic work and because it was written for the Medici, any renaissance reader would have expected it to follow the Platonic mode of nondiscursive form but also to conceal some more esoteric meaning than was apparent on the surface" (18). Or as Ficino himself says: "For it was the custom of the ancient theologians to conceal their holy and pure mysteries in the shadows of metaphors, lest they be defiled by the prophane and impure" (4.2.72).⁶

Like the zany Egyptologist Athanasius Kircher (see chap. 6) and consistent with Milton's account, Ficino sees Chaos as preceding Love: "Who, therefore, will doubt that Love immediately follows Chaos, and precedes the World and all the gods who are assigned to the parts of the World, since the appetite of the Mind precedes its receiving of the Forms, and it is in the already formed Mind that the gods and the World are born?" (1.3.39). Love is defined as "the desire for beauty" (1.4.40), which is certainly consistent with Adam's compelling desire to enjoy Eve's beauty—so compelling in fact, that he gives up his own life and all of ours to retain it!

> O fairest of Creation, last and best
> Of all Gods Works, Creature in whom excell'd
> Whatever can to sight or thought be formd,
> Holy, divine, good, amiable, or sweet!
> . . . .
> And mee with thee hath ruind, for with thee
> Certain my resolution is to Die;
> How can I live without thee, how forgoe
> Thy sweet Converse and Love so dearly joyn'd,
> To live again in these wild Woods forlorn?
> (*PL* 9.896–99, 906–10)

Or as Ficino says: "For men are not ensnared by love from the fact that they are brave, but very often, from the fact that they are wounded by love, they become very bold, and fearlessly undergo any dangers, for the sake of the beloved" (5.8.97). Even before the temptation, Adam admits that he is "... onely weak / Against the charm of Beauties powerful glance" (8.532–33). Adam is made in the image and likeness of God, Eve in the image and likeness of Adam. Yet, God's splendor also shines through Eve, and leaves Adam, paradoxically, trapped by his love of the divine. Or as Ficino puts it, "... even brave and wise men, I say, have been accustomed to suffer in the presence of the beloved, however inferior.... But that splendor of divinity, shining in the beautiful like a statue of God, compels lovers to marvel, to be afraid, and to worship" (2.6.52)

When Adam admits to God that he has eaten the fruit of the forbidden tree, he attempts to excuse his act by stressing the divine element in Eve:

> This Woman whom thou mad'st to be my help,
> And gav'st me as thy perfet gift, so good,
> So fit, so acceptable, so Divine,
> That from her hand I could suspect no ill,
> And what she did, whatever in it self,
> Her doing seem'd to justifie the deed
>
> (*PL* 10.137–42)

And God in turn accuses Adam of worshiping Eve, in the words of Ficino, "however inferior":

> Was shee thy God, that her thou didst obey
> Before his voice, or was shee made thy guide,
> Superior, or but equal, that to her
> Thou did'st resign thy Manhood, and the Place
> Wherein God set thee above her made of thee,
> And for thee, whose perfection far excell'd
> Hers in all real dignitie....
>
> (145–51)

Beginning with the second speech of his seventh chapter,[7] Ficino expresses his views of love directly through classical myth, viz. the myths of Cupid and Venus (53 ff.). Of the two Venuses that are derived from Plato, the second, earthly Venus transfers the divinity of the first Venus to the world, but with the attendant danger of exalting the passions at the expense of the spirit. For if anyone "prefers the form of the body to the beauty of the soul, he certainly abuses the dignity of love.... He who properly uses love certainly praises the form of the body, but through that contemplates the higher beauty of the Soul, the Mind, and God, and admires and loves that more strongly" (7.2.54). In rebuking Adam for his fascination with Eve, Raphael invokes the first Venus, the Venus *caelistis*,[8] and expounds a philosophy of love that is perfectly consistent with the remarks of Ficino:

> In loving thou dost well, in passion not,
> Wherein true Love consists not; love refines
> The thoughts, and heart enlarges, hath his seat
> In Reason, and is judicious, is the scale
> By which to heav'nly Love thou maist ascend,
> Not sunk in carnal pleasure, for which cause
> Among the Beasts no Mate for thee was found.
> (8.588–94)

Given the outcome of the temptation in Eden, it is perhaps ironic to invoke the words of Ficino: "And whoever loves, dies" (2.8.55).

Ficino's section on the hermaphrodite[9] is especially pertinent to Milton. Ficino stresses the interdependency of each half of the hermaphrodite, its desire to be reunited with its other half:

> But each human half seeks its own half. And so whenever his own half meets someone, of whichever sex he may be desirous, he is most violently aroused, clings to it with burning love, and does not even for a moment permit being separated from it. And so the desire and longing for the whole to be restored receives the name of love. (4.1.72)

Milton's Adam, as we have seen, divides himself from himself by insisting that God provide him with a companion like himself. The crisis occurs in Milton's *Paradise Lost* when Eve, already divided from Adam, seeks further division by suggesting that they divide their labors. Adam, echoing Ficino's claim that the lover seeks reunion with the beloved, balks at this additional division: ". . . leave not the faithful side / That gave thee being, still shades thee and protects" (*PL* 9.265–66). And, as already noted, Adam, after Eve eats the apple, tells her that he cannot live without her, cannot part from his own flesh: ". . . no no, I feel / The Link of Nature draw me: Flesh of Flesh, / Bone of my Bone thou art, and from thy State / Mine never shall be parted, bliss or woe" (*PL* 9.913–16).

For both Ficino and Milton, the newborn soul turns instinctively toward heaven and its Maker and is illuminated by His divine rays. Ficino says:

> Further, immediately after the soul is born from God, it turns toward Him as its parent by a certain natural instinct, just as a fire created on earth by the power of higher things is immediately directed toward the higher things by an impulse of nature. Having turned toward Him, the soul is illuminated by His rays. (4.4.75)

Adam's eyes rove heavenward from the first moment of birth: "Strait toward Heav'n my wondring Eyes I turnd, / And gaz'd a while the ample Skie, till rais'd / By quick instinctive motion up I sprung, / As thitherward endevoring, . . ." (*PL* 8.257–60).[10]

Adam's choice of Eve's love over obedience to God can be regarded as a form of self-sufficiency (as well as an overdependence on the body) that ignores the human being's contingency and dependence on God:

> Only God, to whom nothing is lacking, above whom there is nothing, remains content with Himself, sufficient to Himself. Therefore the soul made itself equal to God when it wished to be content with itself alone, as if it could be sufficient to itself no less than God. (4.4.76)

And, in arguing with God for a mate, Adam admits his own contingency and contrasts it with God's self-sufficiency:

> Thou in thyself art perfet, and in thee
> Is no deficience found; not so is Man,
> But in degree, the cause of his desire
> By conversation with his like to help,
> Or solace his defects.
>
> *(PL* 8.415–19)

So although Adam recalls that both he and Eve are dependent on God (9.943), he sacrifices disunion with God for union with Eve: "Our State cannot be severd, we are one, / One Flesh; to loose thee were to loose myself" (9.958–59). Adam, who had heard Raphael's account of the angel's rebellion, might well have recalled Satan's blatant claim for self-sufficiency for both himself and the other rebel angels: "We know no time when we were not just as now; / Know none before us, self-begot, self-rais'd / By our own quick'ning power, ..." *(PL* 5.859–61).

Ficino emphasizes that our desire for sexual intercourse distorts our view of beauty and leads us away from it: "But our soul, created in a condition such that it is surrounded by an earthly body, inclines to the function of procreating. Weighed down by this inclination, it neglects the treasure hidden in its own heart" (5.4.90). Beauty, that quality whose pursuit defines love,

> is a certain lively and spiritual grace infused by the shining ray of God, first in the Angel, and thence in the souls of men, the shapes of bodies, and sounds; a grace which through reason, sight, and hearing moves and delights our souls; in delighting, carries them away, and in carrying them away, inflames them with burning love. (5.6.95)

Adam, in defending himself against Raphael's charge that his passion for Eve has distorted his judgment, claims that it is this very "lively and spiritual grace" that motivates his love for Eve, and not his desire for sexual intercourse with her:

> Neither her out side formd so fair, nor aught
> In procreation common to all kinds
> (Though higher of the genial Bed by far,
> And with mysterious reverence I deem)
> So much delights me as those graceful acts,
> Those thousand decencies that daily flow
> From all her words and actions mixt with Love
> And sweet compliance, which declare unfeign'd
> Union of Mind, or in us both one Soul;
> Harmonie to behold in wedded pair
> More grateful then harmonious sound to th' ear.
> (8.596–606)

In the very last speech of Ficino's work, the narrator remarks that "by the divine madness he [the lover] is raised above the nature of man and passes into a god" (7.13.168). It is interesting that, caught in their own self-love, both Adam and Eve aspire to be gods and to lose their dependency on God Himself. This applies to Satan as well, and all three fall under the rubric of, in Ficino, vulgar love or madness. Hence, Satan feels that he is "self-begot" and tries to displace God by becoming God himself. Eve believes the devil when he says "ye shall be as Gods, / Knowing both Good and Evil as they know" (*PL* 9.708–09, *Gen* 3.5). And, just before he succumbs to the fatal temptation, Adam muses fallaciously that, since the Serpent has moved to humanlike state after eating the fruit, he and Eve would move to the next state, the state, presumably, of gods:

> [Fruit] Profan'd first by the Serpent, by him first
> Made common and unhallowd ere our taste;
> Nor yet on him found deadly, he yet lives,
> Lives, as thou saidst, and gains to live as Man
> Higher degree of Life, inducement strong
> To us, as likely tasting to attain
> Proportional ascent, which cannot be
> But to be Gods, or Angels Demi-gods.
> (*PL* 9.930–37)

Thus Ficino appropriates the myths of Love and the Hermaphrodite from the thought of Plato to defend the sanctity and worth of human love, an adaptation of the mythological tradition that Milton also employed with great profit in *Paradise Lost*.

LEONE EBREO

Leone Ebreo's *Dialoghi d'Amore* or *The Philosophy of Love* (1501–02) was a very popular example of the *trattato d'amore*. It was translated from Italian into French, Spanish, Latin and Hebrew, and the original text went through five editions in the Renaissance. Since it is often cited in Robert Burton's *Anatomy of Melancholy*, Milton would at least have known it indirectly, although he may very well have read it in the original Italian or in any of the extant translations. It influenced Castiglione's *The Courtier*, and was influenced by both Boccaccio's *Genealogiae Deorum* and Ficino's *De Amore*. It is therefore a pivotal work in the application of love theory to literature in the Renaissance.

The participants in the dialogue, Philo and Sophia ("Love of Wisdom"), mix flirtation with true philosophy and provide a heterosexual model for the love of Adam and Eve, both in its essence and expression. The first dialogue, on love and desire, bears on Adam's desire for a companion. Philo's definitions of love and desire can be used to gloss the difficulties Adam experiences by desiring a companion to share his joy in Paradise: "However for my present purpose it is enough to define desire as an affect of the will aimed at the coming to be or coming to be ours of a thing we judge good and have not; and to define love, as an affect of the will to enjoy through union the thing judged good" (dial. 1.12). Adam lacks a companion; he wants God to create or bring one into being for him, and he wants to *possess* it. Paradoxically, if he desires "to enjoy through union the thing judged good," he really wants to reunite with himself and therefore be without a companion once more. Desire suggests a lack, but once one is united with the object of desire, the loved one, the threat of losing the beloved darkens the relationship and destroys the love one experienced in the first place. Hence Adam's "How can I live without thee" plaint in book 9 of *Paradise Lost* (908), as well as Eve's refusal to be possessed as an object: "Was I t'have never parted from thy side? / As good have grown there still a liveless Rib" (*PL* 9.1153–54). Sophia, for her part, is willing to allow for an "excess" of love and desire in pursuing the good: "So that in respect of the Good: virtue consists in overflowing love thereof and vice in lack of such love..." (l. 24). Satan's embittered wish, "Evil be thou my Good" (*PL* 4.110) clearly expresses a hatred for the good, while Adam's joyous response to Christ's sacrifice and boundless love for men, "O goodness infinite, goodness immense!" (12.469), is the epitome of "excess" love and desire.

In discoursing of the mutual love among the elements, Philo refers, citing Pythagoras, to the harmony they exude, the so-called music of the spheres:

> He assigned to each sphere and planet its own peculiar sound and tone, and set forth the harmony composed by all. According to him we do not hear or perceive this heavenly music because of the remoteness of Heaven from us, or else our habituation to it.... (2.107–08)

For Milton we do not hear "... the heav'nly tune, which none can hear / Of human mould with gross unpurged ear" (*Arcades* 72–73) because we have sinned and jarred the harmony of the universe:

> That we on Earth with undiscording voice
> May rightly answer that melodious noise
> As once we did, till disproportion'd sin
> Jarr'd against natures chime, and with harsh din
> Broke the fair musick that all creatures made
> To thir great Lord....
> ("At A solemn Musick," 17–22)

Since Ebreo does refer to Moses and the Old Testament (unlike Ficino, who restricts himself to a totally pagan context), the idea of heaven's remoteness could be related to the Fall as discussed in Genesis.

Where Milton veers between regarding the gods as the fallen devils from hell or simply ridiculous figments of one's imagination, Ebreo sees the pagan deities as susceptible to allegorical interpretation, including the euhemeristic tradition that they were all originally men:[11]

> Not one but many meanings, called "senses," were woven by the ancient poets into their poems. First of all they set down in the literal sense, as a kind of outer husk, the history of certain people and of their noteworthy and memorable deeds. Within this same fiction, like an inner rind nearer to the kernel, they included the moral sense, useful for the active life of men, which justified the acts of virtue and condemned the vices. Moreover the same words concealed some true knowledge of facts, natural or heavenly, astronomic or theological, and sometimes two or even three scientific senses are contained in the tale, like the seeds of a fruit within its rind. And these inmost senses are called "allegorical." (2.110–11)

This rather standard version of the allegorical interpretation of the myths reappears in the mythographers and will be noticed in the Egyptological tradition (chapter six). Since Ebreo is outside the Christian tradition, he cannot find glimmerings of Christian truth in the pagan myths, as other commentators do.[12] He does share Milton's antipathy for revealing the "exalted secrets" of the ancients to the vulgar, "for too much divulgation of true and deep knowledge involves communicating it to those who are unfit for it...." (2.112).

Ebreo signals his probable debt to Boccaccio's *Genealogiae* with his reference to the Demogorgon as the "dread god," (2.117), for Demogorgon is the parent god of Boccaccio's genealogical tree.[13] Milton also mentions Demogorgon, although he is more likely to have picked up the reference directly from Boccaccio, including his "dreadful nature": "... and by them stood / *Orcus* and *Ades*, and the dreaded name / Of *Demogorgon* ..." (*PL* 2.963–65). Ebreo also touches on the euhemeristic theory, suggesting (through Philo) that only men of superior intellect or soul were worthy of being named as gods (2.120). His detailed analyses of the pagan gods (including Pan as Universal Nature) are probably derived from the *Genealogiae* and in a few instances directly from Ovid. Unlike the church fathers, he treats the adulterous liaisons of the pagan gods without irony or condemnation and accompanies this, like the *Ovide Moralisé*, with a flatfooted allegorical interpretation. The whole encyclopedia of genealogies is precipitated by Sophia's request: "Now I desire to know of the birth, marriages, adulteries and love affairs of the other heavenly gods and the allegorical sense thereof" (2.132). She later congratulates Philo for reconciling the accounts of Jupiter's adulterous amours with Moses's [sic] account of creation in the Bible (2.145). He repeats the account of the heavenly and earthly Venuses, but also names the Cyprian Venus as the founder of prostitution (the meretricious Venus).[14] His account of the hermaphrodite emphasizes the union of intellect and the passions, and can be related to the carnal union of Adam and Eve after the Fall:

> And they say truly that these are born of a conjunction of Mercury and Venus, the reason being that these two planets do not combine well and naturally together, because Mercury is wholly intellectual and Venus wholly material, so that, when their two natures mingle, they produce a counterfeit and unnatural lust. (2.159)

Ebreo also alludes to the golden-leaden arrow account from Boccaccio's *Genealogiae* (ultimately from Ovid), the leaden for bad and the gold for good love:

> S. So you would have it that Cupid has wounded you with a golden, me with a leaden, dart.

> P. I would not have it, but I see that it is, so: for your love I desire more than gold, but mine weighs on you like lead. (2.193)

In the Epithalamium imbedded in the fourth book of *Paradise Lost* ("Hail Wedded Love"), Milton connects this image with the quality of married love: "Here Love his golden shafts imploies . . ." (4.763).¹⁵

Ebreo (through Philo) joins Plato (and Ficino) in "defining love as the desire of the beautiful . . ." (3.257). As the narrator of *Paradise Lost* makes clear, Adam's desire for the beautiful went wrong when he exaggerated the presence of the divine in Eve, to the point where he practiced obedience to her instead of to God Himself. Following Plato and perhaps Ficino, Ebreo also has Philo attribute divinity to the beloved, and even to substitute the worship properly extended to God for one of his creatures, woman:

> I am showing you that it is the beloved who is divine and not the lover: for the beloved is actually beautiful like the Godhead, and the lover who desires the beloved is only potentially beautiful; and although he is made godlike by his desire, he does not partake of the divinity of the beloved. (3.273)

In his many definitions of love, Ebreo centers on Cupid as the "voluptuous and wanton love and the lust of the body" (3.339) and denies that there is a heavenly Cupid to balance the heavenly Venus. However, he does posit a virtuous Cupid as the son of the heavenly Venus:

> . . . as there are two Venuses, so there must also be two Loves; and the first Venus, the great, being heavenly and divine, her son is virtuous love, whereas the second Venus, being lower and wanton in her pleasures, her son is evil love. In this way love is twin, and there are two Loves, the virtuous and the base. (3.342)

When Ebreo switches to a discussion of the Old Testament account of creation in Genesis, he immediately focuses on the question of division in creation. The text is contradictory, he notes, because Adam is first supposed to be created male and female in one person, and then woman—or the female half of the human being—is supposed to have been created from a rib of Adam. He relates the account to the story of the androgyne in Plato's *Symposium*, and God's trial of Adam before he presents him with the "gift" of Eve:

> And God made trial of man by bringing all the beasts of the field and the birds before him to see if he would be content with any of the female species as his mate. And Adam named each of the animals after its own kind, but none was found meet to be his trusted companion. Therefore God caused a sleep to fall upon him, and took one of his sides, the word in Hebrew being equivalent to rib.... (3.349)

Milton's God also describes this trial period, but in much richer detail, perhaps concluding with an ironic emphasis on how much Adam wanted this "gift":

> Thus farr to try thee, *Adam*, I was pleas'd,
> And find thee knowing not of Beasts alone,
> Which thou hast rightly nam'd, but of thy self,
> Expressing well the spirit within thee free,
> My Image, not imparted to the Brute,
> Whose fellowship therefore unmeet for thee
> Good reason was thou freely shouldst dislike,
> And be so minded still; I, ere thou spak'st,
> Knew it not good for Man to be alone,
> And no such companie as then thou saw'st
> Intended thee, for trial only brought,
> To see how thou coulds't judge of fit and meet:
> What next I bring shall please thee, be assur'd,
> Thy likeness, thy fit help, thy other self,
> Thy wish exactly to thy hearts desire.
>
> (*PL* 8.437–51)

Philo emphasizes that the division in Plato is a punishment and weakens humankind; in the Hebrew account, however, it is supposed to be a positive change. And while Christian commentators were often anxious to show that the pagans really had some glimmerings of Christianity concealed beneath the mask of fables, Ebreo stops with the Jewish tradition, and has Sophia make the connection between Plato and Moses: "It is indeed pleasing to learn that Plato drank of the waters of the sacred fount" (3.350); however, as Philo later informs Sophia, Plato also "learnt from the ancient fathers in Egypt..." (3.419) and thus, unlike Aristotle, runs the gamut of classical, Egyptian and Hebrew teachings.

Philo's elaboration of the principle of division in man and woman relates directly to Milton's exemplification of its perils in the ninth book of *Paradise Lost*:

> When man was first created as male and female in one person, as I have told you, there was no possibility of sin, because the serpent was unable to deceive the woman when she was joined to man, as he did when she was separated from him, and his cunning and wisdom did not avail to deceive both united as one. But when they were cut in twain by the hand of God... there followed the possibility of sin, because the serpent was able to deceive the woman separated from man, [and to tempt her][16] to eat of the forbidden tree of the knowledge of good and evil. And the woman also made the man to eat with her, and so the punishment for the sin fell upon them both. (3.351)

The separation of male and female implies weakness since Adam (intellect) is divided from Eve (the passions)[17] and he can no longer control her/them:

> P. Every man or woman has a masculine part which is perfect and active, to wit the intellect, and a feminine part which is imperfect and passive, to wit the body and matter.... In the beginning, therefore, these two parts, masculine and feminine, were joined in absolute union in the perfect man whom God had made, so that the sentient and feminine body was the obedient servant of the masculine intellect and reason. (3.354-55)

Thus according to Philo (Ebreo), the division not only enabled the devil to tempt Eve by herself, but also left her free to tempt her other self, Adam. This is worked out in precisely the same way in the pivotal ninth book of *Paradise Lost*. Eve, in insisting to Adam that she should be free to leave his side and work on her own, assumes that the devil will not seek out the weaker side of man: "... not much expect / A Foe so proud will first the weaker seek, / So bent, the more shall shame him his repulse" (382–84). She is, of course, wrong: "He sought them both, but wish'd his hap might find / *Eve* separate, he wish'd, but not with hope / Of what so seldom chanc'd, when to his wish, / Beyond his hope, *Eve* separate he spies" (421–24). And after Eve has taken the fatal bite of the fruit, and is infected by evil, she wants to become "the better half" of the androgyne by withholding her recently acquired knowledge from Adam: "... so to add what wants / In Femal Sex, the more to draw his Love, / And render me more equal, and perhaps, / A thing not undesirable, somtime / Superior..." (821–25). But she changes her mind and, as Ebreo notes, being separate she can tempt him to "share" her fate: "... Confirm'd then I resolve, / *Adam* shall share with me in bliss or woe:/ So dear I love him, that with him all deaths / I could endure, without him live no life" (830–33).

Ebreo, through Philo, also makes a rather interesting point about the dangers of intellectual activity that is completely cut off from sensual experience, and how this might be construed to argue for some sort of independence in Eve: "... the sensual and feminine part should not be so subservient to the intellect that it will offer no resistance, but should draw it somewhat to bodily things for the benefit of both the individual and the race" (3.356). What happened before the Fall, according to Philo, was that desire "overstepped the dividing line between intellect and matter..." (3.357).

Just as Adam was trapped by the divine in Eve (*PL* 10.3), and the lover reacts to the divine in the beloved (Ficino, *De Amore* 1.3.39), so Philo is held captive to the divine wisdom (sophia) *in* Sophia:

> P. I spoke truly when I told you that the highest beauty is divine wisdom. And this is so mirrored in the form and grace of your person and in the angelic loveliness of your soul, though not as yet fully fledged, that your image is made divine in my mind and as such it is esteemed and adored. (3.464)

In sum, these two treatises combine a number of facets of the mythological tradition while focusing on the nature of love. Both deal with the occult tradition and forbidden knowledge, although Ebreo places it within the context of the allegorical tradition. Where Ficino moves from the idea of Chaos to creation, Ebreo emphasizes the internal harmony of the universe that results in the music of the spheres. Both give equal emphasis to the idea of the divine in the beloved. Both deal with the myth of the hermaphrodite, but Ebreo gives much more attention to the concept of separation and division, and how it enhances and even provides the opportunity for sin. Both deal with the ancient Greek-Latin-Hebrew-Egyptian controversy, but only Ebreo connects them with "our rabbi Moses" (p. 183) and sees Plato as actually borrowing from Moses' account of the creation (he believes Moses to be the author of Genesis). Ebreo actually draws on the medieval mythographers as well as Ovid, and his love treatise has embedded within it multiple accounts of the pagan gods. Where Ficino stresses the impulse of the sinners to attain independence from God, Ebreo takes the principle of division as an invitation to sin and the breakdown of the holistic concept of the human being. These two treatises focus on the myths of love, so crucial to *Paradise Lost*, but they also situate those myths within a theological and philosophical context that vastly enriches their range of meaning and evocative power.

Giordano Bruno

Another author whose work serves as a kind of spin-off from classical literature is the philosopher and martyr to truth, Giordano Bruno.[18] Bruno wrote two works with a strong mythical base, the *Eroici Furori* and the *Lo Spaccio*. Both are written in the form of Platonic dialogues and demonstrate a high degree of literary art, and both are also related to the emblem tradition, to be discussed in chapter five. Since Bruno also spent a great deal of time in England, and dedicated both the *Eroici Furori* and the *Lo Spaccio* to Sir Philip Sidney, it is more likely that Milton knew of his work than that of other Italian masters (the *Eroici Furori* was actually first published in London, and Milton's own competence in the Italian language is, of course, beyond question). The theme we have been stressing since the Ovidian commentaries—the association of impure, bodily love with women (Venus) and pure love with men (Cupid)[19]—reappears in the very first sentence of the dedication in the *Eroici Furori*: "Most illustrious knight [Sidney], it is indeed a base, ugly and contaminated wit that is constantly occupied and curiously obsessed with the beauty of a female body!" (59). He continues, giving us what is almost a perfect picture of the woebegone Adam hankering after Eve: "What spectacle, oh good God, more vile and ignoble can be presented to a mind of clear sensibilities than a rational man afflicted, tormented, gloomy, melancholic, . . ." (59).

It is interesting that Bruno talks of love in terms of Paradise—here we may think of the physical Paradise of Adam and Eve, as well as "a Paradise within thee, happier farr" (*PL* 12.587). According to Bruno, the beloved is the Paradise he seeks, because the sight ennobles him: "Love therefore shows him paradise because it makes him know, understand and accomplish the highest things, or because it gives grandeur at least in appearance to the things loved" (1.94).[20] Quoting himself, Bruno says "*Fate snatches paradise away* he says, for often fate does not concede to the deceived lover all love has shown him, inasmuch as what he sees and longs for is distant and opposed to him" (1.94). In a way, fate, chance, or circumstance snatched Paradise away from Adam when Eve succumbed to the devil. Paradoxically, Adam lost Paradise (the physical paradise of Eden) to retain what he regarded as the true Paradise (Eve).

Bruno's gloss on "the contrariety represented by the tree of the knowledge of good and evil" would also interest Milton: "From this we see that ignorance is the mother of felicity and sensuous happiness; and this same happiness is the garden of paradise of the animals. . . ." (2.98). Bruno thus joins the myth of Cupid afflicting the lover with sorrow and pain, with the loss of Paradise in the Judeo-Christian tradition, just as Milton does in his marriage song in *Paradise Lost* (4.750 ff.).

Recall that Adam, when faced with a sinful Eve, tells her that it is his certain resolution to die for her. Recognizing her as the thing that she is, his love does not falter. Obviously, then, Adam has failed to take full account of the nature of love, and rather than make a heroic gesture on Eve's behalf, he has permitted himself the luxury of leaving his love unexamined. This demented spirit is captured beautifully and definitively in this passage from *The Heroic Frenzies*: ". . . sometimes, although we discover a vicious spirit, we remain none the less enflamed and ensnared by it; for although the reason recognizes the evil and baseness of such love, it does not have the virtue of throwing off the disordered appetite" (3.112). Virtue, appetite—these terms are the very essence of *Paradise Lost*. The aftermath of the Fall, when Adam seizes Eve's hand and leads her "nothing loath" (9.1039) to their bower for a near-rape, is perfectly captured in the following passage, which could be seen as a gloss on the mutuality of their sin, and the mutuality of their lustful pleasure: "This [yielding to passion] occurs when both souls are vicious and as though spotted by the same ink, so that, because of their likeness love is aroused, enkindled and confirmed" (3.113).

While the *Heroic Frenzies* does not afford any obvious parallels to Milton's poetry and prose, it still provides an interesting literary model for creative mythologizing. In effect, there is a system within a system whereby emblematic lines of poetry are quoted, then evaluated and interpreted symbolically. In addition, there is an extended gloss on the myth of Actaeon who, like the lover, is devoured by his own thoughts. One thinks of the destruction of Orpheus in Milton, done in by the beauty of his own songs.[21]

Bruno's second mythological work, *Lo Spaccio de la bestia trionfante* (translated as *The Expulsion of the Triumphant Beast*), is in the form of a dialogue with three principal speakers: Mercury, Sophia and Solino. Sophia or wisdom is the intermediary who imparts the learning of Mercury to Solino, the man in search of wisdom. We have a similar situation in *Paradise Lost*, in which Raphael and Michael impart the wisdom of God to man. The topic of discussion is Jupiter, a god who has been weakened by endless debauchery and is burnt out and used up. Jupiter leads a council in heaven, just as God the Father does in Milton's heaven, and Satan in Milton's hell—all three being modeled on the divine counsels led by Zeus in Homer (and mocked in Lucian, the more probable model for Bruno's acerbic wit[22]) and Jupiter in Vergil. Like Adam and Eve, Bruno's gods are subject to the ravages of time, and Bruno's Jupiter is clearly aging. But as weak as he is, this Jupiter still asserts his authority over lesser deities, for when he convenes the gods in council, he deliberately excludes the half-beast, half-human gods of Egypt:

> The great father of the celestial realm, sighing from time to time as he spoke, now having terminated his discussion with Venus, decided to change the proposal calling for dancing into one convening the grand council of the gods of the round table, consisting, that is to say, of all those gods who are not false, but are genuine, and who have a head for counselling; but excluding the ram-headed, the oxen-horned, the goat-bearded, the donkey-eared, the dog-toothed, the pig-eyed, the monkey-nosed, the goat-browed, the chicken-stomached, the horse-bellied, the mule-footed, and the scorpion-tailed. (1.2.103)

Similarly, in his ritual recital of the names of the pagan gods presented as the reincarnations of the devils from hell,

Milton, as we have seen,[23] singles out the Egyptian gods for particular contempt:

> After these appear'd
> A crew who under Names of old Renown,
> *Osiris, Isis, Orus* and thir Train
> With monstrous shapes and sorceries abus'd
> Fanatic *Egypt* and her Priests, to seek
> Thir wandring Gods disguis'd in brutish forms
> Rather then human.
>
> (1.476–82)

But the impulses are clearly different. Bruno the heretic wants to reverse the status of mortals and gods—the gods are humanly weak, men and women godlike in their aspirations. In fact, according to Sophia's euhemeristic view, all of the gods were originally mortal beings: "Likewise, you must understand that all the other gods [in addition to Venus] have been known as men" (3.2.237). Milton uses the Greek and Roman contempt for the Egyptian deities as a method of elevating Christian mythology (the angels) at the expense of pagan mythology (the polytheistic system of Greece and Rome), while Bruno (through his mouthpiece Sophia) seems almost nostalgic for the sweet mysteries of Egyptology:

> Oh Egypt! oh Egypt! Of your religions there will remain only the fables, still incredible to future generations, to whom there will be nothing else that may narrate your pious deeds save the letters sculptured on stones, which will narrate, not to gods and men (because the latter will be dead and deity will have transmigrated into heaven), but to Scythians and Indians, or other people of a similarly savage nature. (3.2.241)

Bruno's Jupiter confesses the debauchery of the gods and leads a call for reform:

> Come now, come now, oh gods! Let there be expelled from the heaven these ghosts, statues, figures, images, portraits, recitations, and histories of our avarice, lusts, thefts, disdains,

spites, and shames. May there pass, may there pass this black and gloomy night of our errors; for the enticing dawn of the new day of Justice invites us. And let us prepare ourselves, in such a manner, for the sun that is about to rise, so that it will not disclose how impure we are. We must cleanse and make ourselves beautiful; it will be necessary that not only we but also our rooms and our roofs be spotless and clean. We must purify ourselves internally and externally. (1.2.115)

Milton, staunch anti-Catholic that he was, would also welcome this identification of religious iconography with idolatry.

The Son (who comes in for some extremely vicious satire in *Lo Spaccio*) of Milton's *Paradise Regained*, in a chauvinistic diatribe against both the worshipped and the worshippers, not only ridicules the pagan gods for their barbaric morals, but also claims that Greek literature is a pale derivative of Hebrew:

> All our Law and Story strew'd
> With Hymns, our Psalms with artful terms inscrib'd,
> Our Hebrew Songs and Harps in *Babylon*,
> That pleas'd so well our Victors ear, declare
> That rather *Greece* from us these Arts deriv'd;
> Ill imitated, while they loudest sing
> The vices of thir Deities, and thir own
> In Fable, Hymn, or Song, so personating
> Thir Gods ridiculous, and themselves past shame.
> (4.334–42)[24]

But for Bruno's Jupiter, "Fanatic *Egypt* and her Priests" (*PL* 1.480) rather than the landless Jews are the true source of Greek culture, including Greek mythology:

> But let him [Aquarius] not infer that the sufficiency of Chaldaean magic has come out of, and is derived from, the Jewish Cabala; because the Jews have been proved to be the excrement of Egypt, and there is no one who could have imagined with any verisimilitude that the Egyptians have taken some worthy or unworthy principle from them.

> Therefore, we Greeks recognize Egypt, the great monarchy of letters and nobility, as parent of our fables, metaphors, and doctrines, and we do not so recognize that generation that never had a span of land which naturally or by virtue of civilized justice was theirs. Whence we can with sufficiency conclude that they have neither naturally nor because of the long enduring violence of fortune ever been part of the world. (3.2.251)

The basic Renaissance position, echoed by Natale Conti (see below, chaps. 8 and 9) and others, was that the occult wisdom of the *Cabala* descended from the Hebrews to the Greeks, from the Greeks to the Romans, and from the Romans to the rest of the world.[25] Milton was obviously very much aware of this tradition, and felt the need to emphasize Hebrew cultural superiority through the mouth of the Son, who lays claim to all knowledge, both sacred and secular.

One of the gods who petitions for a seat in Bruno's reformed Pantheon is Fortune, who equates happiness with wealth and material goods. Both Bruno and Milton critique the naive equation of personal worth with external symbols of success: Bruno by having Fortune point out that, by drawing lots for success, the thinner population of the good have no chance against the army of the bad; and Milton (through the Son's contemptuous rejection of Satan's "gifts") by suggesting that wealth without character is meaningless:

> Why this? Why? Prudence comes and drops only two or three names into the urn. Sophia comes and puts only four or five names into it. Truth comes and leaves only one name in it and would leave less if it were possible. And then, out of the hundreds of thousands of lots which are poured into the urn, you expect that my sorting hand should chance upon one of these eight or nine, rather than the eight or nine hundred thousand others. (*Lo Spaccio* 2.2.174)

> Get Riches first, get Wealth, and Treasure heap,
> Not difficult, if thou hearken to me,

Riches are mine, Fortune is in my hand;
They whom I favour thrive in wealth amain,
While Virtue, Valor, Wisdom sit in want.
To whom thus Jesus patiently reply'd;
Yet Wealth without these three is impotent,
To gain dominion or to keep it gain'd.
Witness those antient Empires of the Earth,
In highth of all thir flowing wealth dissolv'd:
But men endu'd with these have oft attain'd
In lowest poverty to highest deeds.
(*PR* 2.427–38)

However, whereas in Bruno Sophia (Wisdom) loses the debate to Fortune and Jupiter acknowledges that Fortune really possesses *all* of the seats in the Pantheon, the Son in *Paradise Regained* treats Fortune and Fate as false sources of wisdom:

              to themselves
All glory arrogate, to God give none,
Rather accuse him under usual names,
Fortune and Fate, as one regardless quite
Of mortal things. Who therefore seeks in these
True wisdom, finds her not, or by delusion
Far worse, her false resemblance only meets
An empty cloud.
(4.314–21)

Both Bruno and Milton distinguish between Fortune and Occasion or Opportunity,[26] as do most of the emblem books (see chap. 5). Bruno's Fortune uses Occasion to create "opportunities" to exercise her power, while Milton's Satan uses Occasion to create a sense of urgency and pressure to do his bidding: "You, Occasion, walk ahead, precede my footsteps, open thousands and thousands of paths to me. Go irresolutely, unrecognized, and hidden, because I do not want my coming to be too easily foreseen" (2.3.179). "If Kingdom move thee not, let move thee Zeal, / And Duty; Zeal and Duty are not slow; / But on Occasions forelock watchful wait" (*PR* 3.171–73).

Ultimately, because she exercises capricious control over *all* centers of power, whether divine or human, Fortune is denied her own seat in Jupiter's pantheon. Her own ironic defense of herself is to pervert the place of integrity and moral worth in human destiny. The goddess Virtue, she claims, determines the fate of individuals by either extending or withholding (in the manner of Fortune herself) moral strength: "'And Fortune, who gives him the being of a prince and the being of an affluent man, is not the cause of this evil, but rather the cause is the goddess Virtue, who does not give him, nor did give him virtuous being'" (2.2.176). Similarly—but without Fortune's ironic intent—the chorus in Milton's *Samson Agonistes*, while punning extravagantly on the ascent and descent of Fortune's wheel, associates true character with the virtuous exercise of one's abilities, rather than pedigree and possessions:

> To lowest pitch of abject fortune thou art fall'n.
> For him I reckon not in high estate
> Whom long descent of birth
> Or the sphear of fortune raises;
> But thee whose strength, while vertue was her mate,
> Might have subdu'd the Earth,
> Universally crown'd with highest praises.
>   (*SA* 169–75)

Virtue once again triumphs over Fortune.

In both of these powerfully persuasive works, Bruno sets up the evolution of moral positions through dialogue and impassioned discourse, the interplay of Love and Desire in *The Heroic Frenzies*, the evaluation of personal merit in *The Expulsion of the Triumphant Beast*; tensions between antithetical positions are resolved through the aesthetic structure of the works. Personalities are assigned to the various individuals that populate both works, and the historical data of classical myth is drawn upon to illuminate the actions and ideas of the participants in the dialogues. It is clear, I hope, that this summary of Bruno's methods could easily be substituted for Milton's own approach to myth. But what essentially makes these three great philosophers such interesting precursors to Milton is the literary structures they employ to convey their concepts of love, beauty, and (in Bruno's case) power to audiences every bit as erudite as Milton's seventeenth century English readers, and just as receptive to the seductive pleasures of classical myth.

FIVE

Milton and the Emblematic Tradition

Roland Mushat Frye's great study, *Milton and the Visual Arts: Iconographic Tradition in the Epic Poems*,[1] makes a convincing argument that Milton would have seen and enjoyed much continental art in his travels through Italy. But once we leave the visual arts and move on to so-called "paper archaeology"[2] (here restricted to the emblem books) of visual representations with printed explanations, the scholarship is sparse and is haunted by monolingualism.[3] That is, almost all the studies of Milton and the emblem books focus on the English emblem books, sorry imitations of the much superior emblem books on the continent. And why Milton would consult, say, George Wither[4] or Francis Quarles[5] rather than Andrea Alciato (1492–1550, the founder of the emblem genre)[6] has never been convincingly argued by the proponents of an "English" rather than a "continental" Milton.[7]

An emblem, if one uses Alciato as a model, consists of a motto, a poem and an explanation that expands on both the motto and the poem. They were one of the more ubiquitous forms of popular literature. Mario Praz's book length bibliography of the genre[8] attests to the staggering number of editions of Alciato, as well as the many French, Dutch, Spanish, Italian, English and German emblem writers, all stemming from Alciato but continually borrowing from each other as well. The whole is too difficult to encompass, so I shall restrict myself to emblematic versions of myths that are exemplified in Milton's work, and how those emblems support or expand on other mythological traditions. As already noted, there was a constant crisscrossing of mythological traditions in the Renaissance. Thus the mythographer Cartari (discussed in chaps. 8 and 9) cites Alciato several times and builds on his emblems, as well as the *Discours* of Guillaume du Choul (fl. 16c., see below), while the Renaissance dictionaries (see chap. 7) appropriate both the mythographers and the emblem books, not to mention the editions and translations of ancient Greek and Latin authors. And the final (Latin) edition of Alciato (Padua 1621) contains comments from *all* of the above-named sources. In effect, the emblems in this edition become mere jumping off places for the copious notes that dominate the text.

Emblems of Fortune, Occasion, Opportunity

The images of Occasion (Opportunity) and Fortune are often confused and misunderstood. For example, in Gayle Edward Wilson's article, "Emblems in *Paradise Regained*," he cites Satan's appeal to Occasion (Opportunity) from *Paradise Regained*: "If Kingdom move thee not, let move thee Zeal, / And Duty; Zeal and Duty are not slow; / But on Occasions forelock watchful wait" (3.171–73). The emblem that Williams reproduces is by Geoffrey Whitney (1548?–1601) and clearly imitates many continental emblems of both Fortune and Occasion. A nude woman standing on Fortune's wheel in the midst of a turbulent sea and looking blindly into space would immediately be taken as Fortune, save for the forelock of Occasion. The razor denotes her sharpness and ability to cut down anyone or anything that gets in her way. And although Whitney glosses the figure as Occasion in his own poem, the epigraph from Horace's letters names the figure Fortune. (As we shall see in chapter nine, the Renaissance mythographer Vincenzo Cartari connects Occasion with the Greek idea of *kairos* or the *appropriate time* to do something, without the sense of urgency the devil applies to the situation).

Since God controls all times and opportunities anyway, any undue haste in grasping the good times could be seen as a lack of faith.[9] Were Milton looking for an emblem to express this idea, he might well have preferred the Alciato original, "In Occasionem" [On Opportunity].[10] Or he might have been intrigued by the more complex emblem of Jean Jacques Boissard (1528–1602), where a knight actually attempts to grasp the forelock of Occasio while *Metanoeia* (Regret) whips her from behind (no. 54) (fig. 3).[11] This emblem conveys much more graphically and immediately the sense of urgency that the devil attempts to communicate to Milton's Christ. The brief Latin description is followed by a more lengthy verse analysis in French. A great many men have been lost, we are told, for having neglected the opportune, appropriate moment, and thus their lives have been full of trials. In fact, throughout history all of humanity has been afflicted by troubles and pains because of Occasion. Even though she is bald, she does have a forelock ("le crin frontal") we can grasp when she suddenly comes on the scene. But if we fail, something worse awaits us: Penitence (*Metanoea* in the Latin verse), who will make us repent anew for having allowed Opportunity to escape us.

This emblem was so familiar in the Renaissance that it could be discussed without actually providing the illustration. Robert Greene's poem on Fortune (1587), for example, is really a combination of emblem and explanation:

Milton and the Emblematic Tradition   117

Figure 3. Jean Jacques Boissard. #34: "A Tergo Calva Est."
           Emblemata. Metz, 1584.

>   The fickle seat whereon proud Fortune sits,
>   the restles globe whereon the furie stands,
>   Bewraies her fond and farre inconstant fits,
>   the fruitfull horne she handleth in her hands,
>   Bids all beware to feare her flattering smiles,
>   that giueth most when most she meaneth guiles.
>   The wheele that turning neuer taketh rest,
>   the top whereof fond worldlings count their blisse,
>   Within a minute makes a blacke exchaunge;
>   and then the vild and lowest better is:
>   Which embleme tels vs the inconstant state,
>   of such as trust to Fortune or to Fate.[12]

Sir Antonye Cope (d. 1551), in his *The Historie of Two The Moste Noble Capitaines of the Worlde, Anniball, and Scipio . . .* (London 1544), gives an emblematic description of Occasion, similar to Greene's of Fortune. What is important about Cope's description is its very early date (1544), just 13 years after the first emblem book, and its casual appearance in his dedication to King Henry VIII, as if the image were common knowledge. Cope begins by noting that Time both devours and manifests the truth of all things, and then moves into his rather sharply drawn portrait of Occasion:

> Wherefore *VERITIE* is called the doughter of tyme. She hath also a sister called *OCCASION*, whom the saied sage poetes (vnder whose woordes, as vnder a vaile are hidden many depe misteries) wyllynge to descriue, dooe feigne to haue wynges on hir fete, to declare therby her swift passying awaie. And also they feigne hir to haue all hir heare growing and hanging long downe on the forpart of hir hedde, the hynder part being smothe bare and balde: signifiyng therby, that as she cometh towarde a man, he may take sure holde of hir, by hir longe heares. But in case he mysse to take than his holde, suffryng hir to passe by hym: than is there no holde to be taken of hir behynde, but that she runneth awaie without recouerie. There is also iuigned vnto hir a compaignion called *REPENTANCE*, whiche is nothyng so lyght of foote as is the other, whom Occasion after hir escape from a man, leaueth behynde hir, to kepe hym compaignie. Whereby is ment, that if occasion be not taken, whan she offereth hir selfe to any manne: the partie that refuseth hir offre, shall after not ceasse, duryng his lyfe, to forthynke his folie, in suffryng hir departure. (a2ᵛ)[13]

An emblem that connects the idea of Occasion with the Greek *kairos* is the "Occasionem Qvi Sapis Ne Amiseris" (#71) (fig. 4) in the *Bonon. Symbolicarvm* (Bologna, 1574) of Achilles Bocchi (1488–1562) (T4ᵛ, 3.152–53).[14] Here the term "Occasion" is in the title; a woman, Occasion, with forelock, is tied to the wheel of Fortune, and the word *kairon* appears in the support beneath the wheel. The caption, "Occasionem Qvi Sapis Ne Amiseris" ("Occasion is gone before you know it"), refers to the turning of Fortune's wheel and the disappearance of the forelock, and all our hopes along with it. The accompanying poem warns us that she may fly away at any moment, and if we are too slow, she will be gone: "Momento praeteruolat haud vnquam reditura. / Occiput en calua est. lentus es? illa abijt" ("She flies away in an instant, not likely to return. Notice that the back part of the head is bald. Are you slow? That woman is gone").

There are other references to Occasion in Milton, almost all unfailingly negative. For example, when the second brother in *Comus* wants to emphasize the danger to their sister's chastity, he invokes the goddess Opportunity:

> You may as well spred out the unsun'd heaps
> Of misers treasure by an outlaws den,
> And tell me it is safe, as bid me hope
> Danger will wink on opportunity,
> And let a single helpless maiden pass
> Uninjur'd in this wild surrounding wast.
>
> (398–403)

And Comus to the Lady: "If you let slip time, like a neglected rose / It withers on the stalk with languish'd head" (743–44). Or Satan to his vengeful followers in *Paradise Lost*: "Let us not slip th' occasion. . . ." (1.178); and to himself as he prepares to tempt Eve: ". . . Then let me not pass / Occasion which now smiles, . . ." (9.479–80). And in a terribly ironic play on words, Manoa points out to Samson that while Samson claimed to have a calling from God to "Find some occasion to infest" their common enemies, those same enemies "Found soon occasion thereby [through the wiles of Dalila] to make thee / Thir Captive, and thir triumph . . ." (*SA* 423, 425–26). Thus Dalila grasped the occasion to revenge her people in the shape of Samson's forelock and shaved him bald before and behind! Samson's own hair became the forelock of opportunity, his

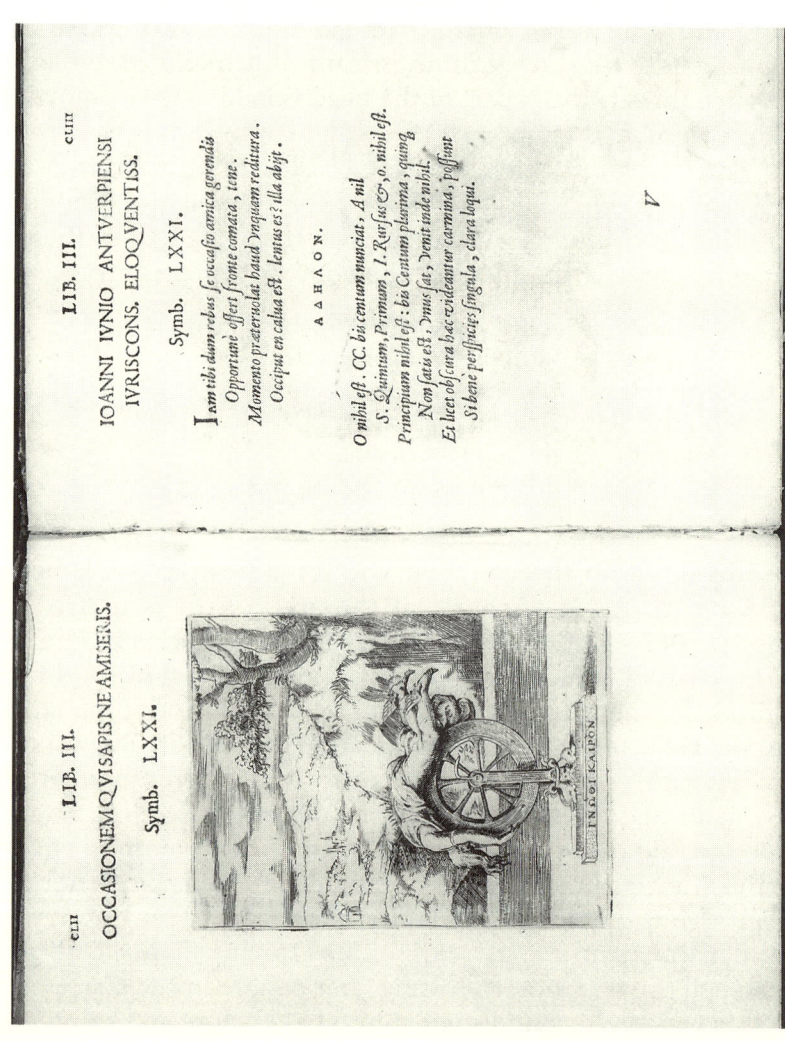

Figure 4. Achilles Bocchi, *Bonon. Symbolicarvm*. Bologna, 1574.

own person the victim of opportunists. More ironically still, Dalila "seized" the *kairos* or opportune moment to act the part of the grim reaper and harvest Samson's hair, thus bringing on his death and her own: ". . . so treacherously / Had shorn the fatal harvest of thy head" (1023–024).[15] Occasion draws Samson to Dalila, she seizes the Occasion to enslave him, and he in turn seizes the Occasion of the "occasion" of the celebration for Dagon. As the messenger who reports Samson's triumphal demise declares, "Occasions drew me early to this City" (1596). Finally, Manoa urges the newly honored and freed Israel to "Find courage to lay hold on this occasion" (1716) to honor Samson and his father's house (1717). Occasion builds on occasion until God seizes the moment, both exonerating and honoring his champion, Samson.

Thus Milton turns the tradition of Occasion or Opportunity on its head: the devil tries to make Christ move with haste before the "due time," while the second brother warns the first that the really vigilant ones looking for an opportunity are the evil ones, those who live in time rather than eternity. Both Satan's search for an opportunity for revenge and the clever vigilance of the Philistines (especially Dalila) support this belief. Of course what one is supposed to find through Opportunity is Fortune, wealth, whatever one most desires. Fortune herself, as Milton was well aware, was mocked even in Roman times by Juvenal (see chap. 9) and was denounced by the church fathers (see chap. 2) as a goddess invented to excuse immoral behavior and to argue against God's influence in the world.

Since Occasion or Opportunity is often related to matters of love and sexuality, the emblem of the goddess in Octavio Van Veen's (1560?–1629?) *Amorvm Emblemata*, in which Love is grasping the forelock of an apparently willing Occasion (175) (fig. 5), can be related to the attempted seduction of the Lady in *Comus*, or indeed the devil's successful seduction of Eve. A more detailed image of Occasion is available in Giles Corrozet's (1510–1568) *Hectamographie* (Paris, 1543, M2^v–M3), where her instability and slipperiness are explained in a long poem (M3) that accompanies the emblem. Both the sail and the wheel push her back and forth, while her hair blowing in the wind poses yet another challenge—you can grasp her locks in only one place, because she is bald behind. Those who don't grasp her with a firm hand and take what she has to offer will be doomed to suffer regret (the *Metanoeia* of Boissard). But Corrozet also has an image of Fortune (F7ᵛ–F8), displaying the broken mast and with one foot on a revolving, unstable ball and the other on a dolphin. This symbolizes danger, instability and her subjection to the various winds of change (F8). A Fortune with amputated feet balancing her footless left leg on a ball symbolizes the profoundly unstable nature of Fortune in Adrian Junius's (1511–1575) emblem, "Fortunae instabilitas" (no. 26)[16] and again in Laurens Van Haecht Goidtsenhoven's (fl. 1600) *Mikrokosmos Parvvs Mvndvs* ("Fortvnae Natvrae," no. 21) (fig. 6).[17] The Chorus in *Samson Agonistes* seems to be evoking both Fortune and Occasion when they commiserate with Samson for allowing Dalila to lead him astray: "What Pilot so expert but needs must wreck / Embarqu'd with such a Stears-mate at the Helm?" (1044–045).[18]

Fortune as opposed to Occasion is depicted alongside Mercury (Emblem no. 99) in Alciato's *Emblemata*. Mercury bears the caduceus while Fortune is seated on a globe and holds a ship's rudder in her right hand and a cornucopia (horn of plenty) in her left. Her unfocused gaze indicates that she gives her favors according to whim. She is fully clothed and does not have a forelock, the trademark of Occasion. In Henry Peacham's (1546–1634) *Minerva Britannia*, there is an emblem (p. 25) that combines the characteristics of Fortune and Mercury. Peacham's Felicity carries a caduceus on her right arm and a cornucopia on her left. Happiness, it would seem, consists in the right combination of wisdom and worldly goods.

Guillaume du Choul, in his *Discours De La Religion Des Anciens Romains Illustré*, has four images of Fortune, again with the ship's rudder in the figure's right hand and

Figure 5. Octavio Van Veen, Amorvm Emblemata. Antwerp, 1608.

the cornucopia in the left, denoting "instabilité & inconstance" (B4ᵛ). "L'imaige de fortune fut encores paincte aueugle: pource que souuentesfois elle donne les biens à ceux, qui ne l'ont pas merité" (C1ᵛ) (Fortune was also depicted as blind, because she often bestows good things on people who haven't done anything to deserve them.) Satan, as the very model of instability and inconstancy, has his own cornucopia, full of wealth and riches, which he carries in his hand, and which he rewards to whomever he favors:

> Get Riches first, get Wealth, and Treasure heap,
> Not difficult, if thou hearken to me,
> Riches are mine, Fortune is in my hand;

124   "Through a Glass Darkly"

Figure 6. Laurens Van Haecht Goidtsenhoven, "Fortuna Natura," #21. *Mikrokosmos: Parvvs Mvndvs*. Amsterdam, 1610[?].

> They whom I favour thrive in wealth amain,
> While Virtue, Valour, Wisdom sit in want.
>
> (*PR* 2.427–31)

It is interesting that almost all the references to Fortune in Milton's poetry[19] are concentrated in *Paradise Regained* and *Samson Agonistes*, where Satan masquerades as a "giftgiver" to the reluctant Son, and God's own hero wallows in *mis*fortune. The Satan of *Paradise Regained* even "offers" the Son the kingdoms of the world ("The Kingdoms of the world to thee I give," *PR* 4.163) on the condition that he worship him, a condition the Son rejects with abrupt contempt: ("I never lik'd thy talk, thy offers less," *PR* 4.171). As we have seen, the Son also accuses the devil of pretending that God the Father really is Fortune: ". . . to themselves / All glory arrogate, to God give none, / Rather accuse him under usual names, / Fortune and Fate. . . ." (*PR* 4.314–17).[20] In *Samson Agonistes* the Chorus refers to the medieval concept of Fortune and her false wheel:

> Strongest of mortal men,
> To lowest pitch of abject fortune thou art fall'n.
> For him I reckon not in high estate
> Whom long descent of birth
> Or the sphear of fortune raises
>
> (168–72)

In Claude Paradin's (d. 1573) *Devises Heroïqves* (Lyon, 1557; first ed. 1551) we see the Wheel of Fortune with two cornucopiae meeting at the crest; on the lower half of the wheel, however, are spikes or arrows sticking out of each one of the spokes. The caption speaks of the difficulty and pain that accompanies the quest: "Pour paruenir à quelque felicité & bonne fortune, le chemin est dificile & mal aisé . . ." (L1, p. 161) (In order to arrive at some kind of happiness and good fortune, the route is difficult and painful.) In short, the many emblems of Fortune and Occasion made it possible for Milton to distinguish the two. As we have already noted, the iconography of Fortune was readily available in Greene's poem, "The fickle seat whereon proud Fortune sits," and as we shall have "occasion" to notice, the most detailed analysis of Fortune appears in the mythographers Cartari and Conti.

EMBLEMS OF THE FALL

In the dramatic conclusion to *Paradise Regained*, ". . . Satan smitten with amazement fell" (4.562) from the very pinnacle from which he had threatened to cast down the Son. Drawing on Spenser[21] or one of the emblem books, Milton compares Satan's fall to that of Antaeus:

> As when Earths Son *Antaeus* (to compare
> Small things with greatest) in *Irassa* strove
> With *Joves Alcides*, and oft foil'd still rose,
> Receiving from his mother Earth new strength,
> Fresh from his fall, and fiercer grapple joyn'd,
> Throttl'd at length in th'Air, expir'd and fell;
> So after many a foil the Tempter proud,
> Renewing fresh assaults, amidst his pride
> Fell whence he stood to see his Victor fall.
>
> (PR 4.563–71)

Most of the details of Milton's account are caught in Jean Mercier's (d. 1570) emblem of Antaeus (no. 45) (fig. 7), which appeared in his *Emblemata*. The motto, "Erige Te Qvisqvis Vanos Sectaris Honores" (You raise up whoever seeks vain honors), captures the futility of Satan's quest to gain glory at the expense of others. This image of Antaeus being lifted up to be destroyed can also be applied to Satan's *second* fall as Antaeus in *Paradise Regained*. The concluding lines in the poem accompanying the Mercier emblem pick up, in an odd way, the separation of Antaeus from the earth: "Flectere qui mentem cupiet, quam saeva libido / Vexat; ab humanis temperet illecebris" (Whoever wants to improve his mind will be vexed by savage lust; he should resist human desires.)

Goidtsenhoven, in his *Microcosmus: Parvus Mundus*, explicitly compares the pagan myth of Jupiter casting Cupid out of heaven and the similar fall of Satan ("De Cvpidine Et Iove," no. 3, B1ᵛ). Jupiter brandishes his thunderbolt and Cupid's confiscated arrows in his left hand and the wings he has torn from Cupid in his right; the gods and goddesses (plus Jupiter's eagle) look down in dismay as the boy is hurled headlong to earth. Cupid, as the poem tells us, caused dissension among the gods until Jupiter despoiled him of his wings and his quiverfull of arrows and then cast him down to earth, just as Lucifer was cast out of heaven, for the heavenly city can tolerate nothing that is unclean (B2).

Satan's spectacular fall from heaven in the first book of *Paradise Lost* is clearly meant to evoke the image (as we have seen) of Phaethon falling from the chariot of the Sun (his father) because he lacks the skill to drive it. In Alciato's *Emblemata* this is, appropriately, an emblem of *temerarios* or rashness (in people), just as Satan is rash for attempting to appropriate the reins of power from *his* Father, God (no. 56). Satan also flies too close to the Son of God, and in attempting to displace him, he follows the flaming path of Phaethon:

> ... Him the Almighty Power
> Hurld headlong flaming from th'Ethereal Skie
> With hideous ruin and combustion down
> To bottomless perdition, there to dwell
> In Adamantine Chains and penal Fire,
> Who durst defie th'Omnipotent to Arms.
>
> (PL 1.44–49)

The explanation of the motto could well refer to Satan's self-destruction and the ruin he almost brought upon all humankind:

> You see that Phaeton, the driver of his father's chariot, dared to guide the fire-spewing horses of the Sun. After he sprinkled the earth with the greatest fires, the wretch slipped out of the car that he had mounted so rashly. Thus many kings, whom youthful ambition drives on, are carried to the stars on the wheels of Fortune. After great disasters to the human race and to themselves, they finally pay the penalty for all their crimes. (56)

It is interesting that Alciato conflates the myths of Fortune and Phaethon to describe the nature of rashness. By defying God, Satan sets himself on the wheel of Fortune and

Figure 7.   Jean Mercier, *Emblemata*. Bourges, 1592.

exposes himself to his richly deserved Fate, certainly outdoing the ambitious kings Alciato refers to, in bringing the greatest of disasters upon all humankind.

One might also relate the fall of Satan to the downfall of an "impostor," predicting victory over God, just as the fall of Icarus is related to the false predictions of the astrologer by Alciato (no. 104):

> Icarus, you who were snatched through the upper air, until the molten wax sent you headlong to the sea, now the same wax and burning fire are reviving you, so that you might teach us sure lessons by your example. Let the astrologer be wary of predicting anything; for the imposter will fall headlong, while he is flying beyond the stars.[22]

Another image of the "fall" of Satan can be found in Giles Corrozet's *Hecatomgraphie*, "Discorde haye de Dieu" (E6ᵛ) (fig. 8) (Discord, the hammer of God), where, à propos of Satan, the comment emphasizes the continual presence of war and Discord on the Earth, after her "descent" from Heaven:

> Lors que discorde eust esté expulsée
> Des cieulx luysantz par le dieu Iupiter
> Et qu'il la feit en bas precipiter,
> La guerre fut en terre commencée. (E6ᵛ)
>
> (At the same time as Discord was being cast out of the sacred heavens by Jupiter, and was falling down from on high, war had started on earth.)

The illustration shows God (Jupiter or God the Father) flanked by two of his subordinates watching as Discord is hurled headlong from heaven, presumably by the upraised left hand of the Omnipotent.

EMBLEMS OF HERCULES

Emblems of Hercules (in addition to the ones describing the famous Antaeus episode) touch on the characters and actions of the three protagonists of Milton's three most famous poems: Adam in *Paradise Lost*, the Son in *Paradise Regained*, and Samson in *Samson Agonistes*. The most obvious emblem knitting all three together is the so-called choice of Hercules, where in a dream he is accosted by two women.[23] The one (*Voluptas*), half-clothed, is ready to lead him through "the primrose way to the everlasting bonfire," while the other (*Virtus*) sees him through the rocky road to virtue. The emblem is reproduced in Goidtsenhoven's *Mikrokosmos: Parvvs Mundus* ("Hercules Elegit Virtvtis Callem" [Hercules chooses the hardness of Virtue]), complete with a cautionary quotation from Matthew, 7.13: "Spatiosa via est quae ducit ad perditionem, & arcta via est quae ducit ad vitam" (fig. 9) (Wide is the path that leads to ruin, narrow the path that leads to life). The fully clothed Lady is Virtue; the other is Venus the Temptress (blanda), also Venus the false (fallax), who recalls the two Venuses appropriated from Plato by Ficino and Ebreo (see chap. 4).

The first of our three protagonists, Adam, obviously made the wrong choice, and Eve takes on the characteristics of both Venus the false and Venus the temptress:

> So saying, she embrac'd him, and for joy
> Tenderly wept, much won that he his Love
> Had so enobl'd, as of choice t'incurr
> Divine displeasure for her sake, or Death.
> In recompense (for such compliance bad
> Such recompense best merits) from the bough
> She gave him of that fair enticing Fruit
> With liberal hand: he scrupl'd not to eat
> Against his better knowledge, not deceav'd,
> But fondly overcome with Femal charm.
>
> (*PL* 9.990–99)

Adam has indeed "ennobled" his love for Eve by placing her above God, and his "choice" yields nothing but the bitter "recompense" of death. By allowing Eve to leave the garden and depend "On what [she] . . . hast of vertue . . ."

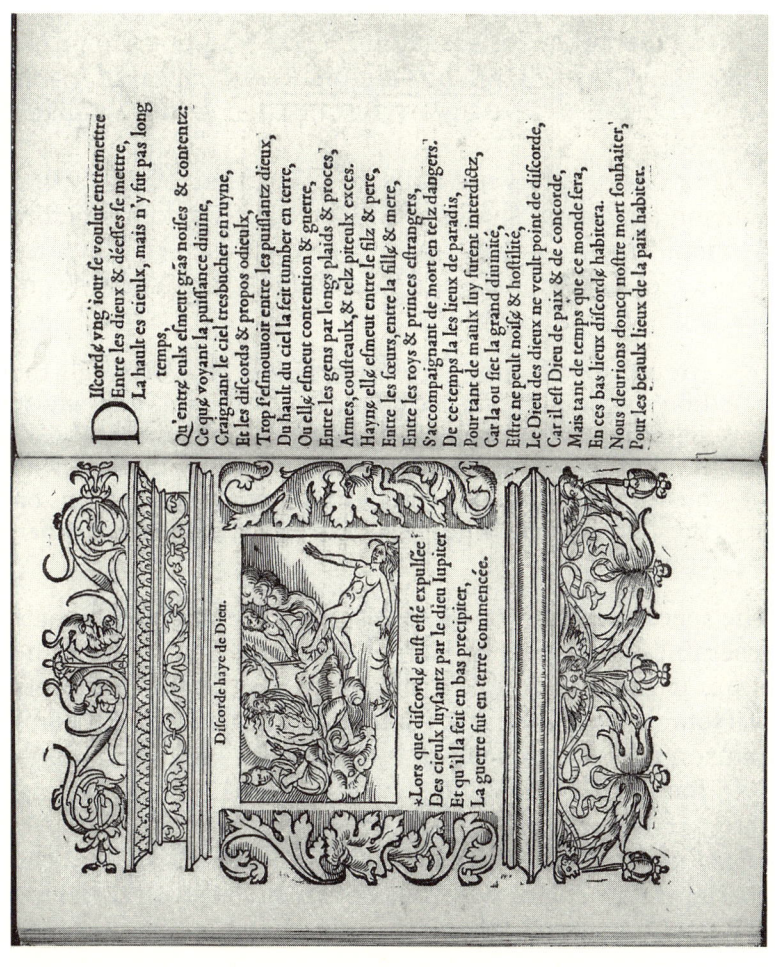

Figure 8. Giles Corrozet, *Hecatomgraphie*. Paris, 1543.

(*PL* 9.374), Adam has already dismissed *Virtus* and made *Voluptas* welcome.

Satan, of course, offers the Son several comfortable paths to glory, wealth, ease and power, but he stands firm against them all, and even evokes Satan's grudging admiration for the path he has "chosen": "Hard are the ways of truth, and rough to walk" (*PR* 1.478). Samson attends to the blandishments of another Venus "blanda," Dalila. He even calls her a "Traytress" (725) and "sorceress" (819), although he takes full responsibility for his choice: "She was not the prime cause, but I my self, / Who vanquisht with a peal of words (O weakness!) / Gave up my fort of silence to a Woman" (234–36).

This faulty choosing calls to mind that other failing Samson (or Adam) shares with Hercules: weakness before women.[24] I refer to the emblem of the enslaved Hercules at the feet of Omphale, a figure soundly mocked by Seneca in his *Hercules Furens*:

> Are we to call him brave from whose shoulders fell the lion's skin and club, made present for a girl, and whose side shone resplendent, decked out in Tyrian robes? Call him brave, whose bristling locks dripped with nard, who busied those famous hands with unmanly strummings on the tambourine, whose warlike brow a barbaric turban crowned? (465–71)

The speech of Lycus on Heracles' enslavement by Omphale resembles the taunt of Harapha to Samson; at the same time, it exposes some of the more disgraceful accounts of Heracles, particularly his effeminacy, which Milton's Samson relates to his defeat by Dalila: ". . . foul effeminacy held me yok't / Her Bond-slave; . . . / What boots it at one gate to make defense, / And at another to let in the foe / Effeminatly vanquish't? . . ." (410–11, 560–62).[25] And the postlapsarian Adam who awakens from sleep after having debilitating sexual intercourse with Eve is also "effeminately vanquish't," in the manner of both Samson and Hercules: ". . . So rose the *Danite* strong / *Herculean*

Figure 9. Lauren Van Haecht Goidtsenhoven, "Hercvles Elegit Virtvtis Callem," #23. Amsterdam, 1610[?].

Samson from the Harlot-lap / Of *Philistean Dalilah*, and wak'd / Shorn of his strength . . ." (*PL* 9.1059–062). But the Son is proof against such effeminacy. A woman, as Satan reminds the dissolute Belial, ". . . beguil'd the heart / Of wisest *Solomon*, and made him build, / And made him bow to the Gods of his Wives" (*PR* 2.169–71), just as Dalila attempted to do with Samson. But the Son, like other worthy men, is proof against such assaults: "How many have with a smile made small account / Of beauty and her lures, easily scorn'd / All her assaults, on worthier things intent?" (*PR* 2.193–95).

Another emblem of Hercules that may help to explain the cerebral orientation of Milton's Samson, and which is not found in other treatments of his legend, is the Gallic Hercules. This emblem, found in Alciato (no. 181) and many other emblem writers,[26] depicts Hercules as drawing two men (later expanded to a crowd) in chains emanating from his mouth. He is an aged, bald figure, but the power of rhetoric and wisdom, usually associated with Mercury, has compensated for his lack of physical strength. He bears a bow in his left hand and a club in his right, symbols of his 12 labors. He is also a symbol of eloquence, which may explain the fluid speeches of Milton's Samson, as these have no precedent either in the biblical account of Samson or in the more traditional accounts of Hercules.[27] The caption in the Alciato emblem emphasizes the triumph of eloquence over strength, the power of language to move human hearts:

> Is this then the figure of Hercules? This is not appropriate because he is old and his temples are grey because of old age. Why, then, is his tongue pierced by light chains, by which he easily draws men to him, their ears being pierced? Is it not because the French say that Hercules, excelling in speech, not in strength, gave laws to the nations? Arms yield to the toga, and he whose strength is in eloquence draws even the hardest hearts to his wishes. (181)

Where Lucian, who is the source of the account in the emblem books, mocks this Gallic Hercules (*Heracles* 1.63.65), the emblem writers take it quite seriously. For example, Jean Baudoin (1590?–1650), in his *Recveil D'Emblemes Divers* (1638), appends a nine-page essay on the emblem, which begins with a close paraphrase of Lucian's remarks on the figure (again, one mythological source collapsing into another). Baudoin first speculates that the Gauls created this image of Hercules (or Mercury) to make fun of the Greeks and to depreciate their claim that Hercules was divine. On second thought, however, he finds a deeper meaning there:

Au contraire, transportés d'vne allegresse incroyable, ils loüent le Dieu qui les conduit, & marchent si viste, en le suiuant, qu'à voir leurs chaines si lâches, il semble qu'ils ayent enuie de le deuancer, & qu'il leur fâcheroit fort de n'estre plus captifs: tant s'en faut qu'à la façon des personnes lassées, ils ayent de la peine à mettre vn pied deuant l'autre. (1.536)

(On the contrary, transfixed by an unbelievable joy, they praise the god who leads them, and they march along so openly as they follow him, and their chains are so loose, that they seem to want to get ahead of each other, and that it annoyed them that they weren't even more subjugated: so much so that, very much like people who have been worn out, they can scarcely put one foot in front of the other.)

Conflating the myths of Hercules and Mercury (done with more finesse, as we shall see later, in Cartari), Baudoin concludes that the courage of the physical Heracles is inseparable from wisdom and learning, and all are united by eloquence:

Mais ce fut faussement & sans raison, puis qu'on sçait bien que toutes ces grandes qualitez furent particulieres à l'Hercule Gaulois, homme diuin, à vray dire, & en qui le tiltre d'Eloquent fut inseparable d'auec celuy de Sage, de Vaillant, & de Courageux. (1.540).

(But this was false and unreasonable, for one can easily see that all of these great qualities were particular to the Gallic Hercules, a divine man in fact, and one in whom the title of Eloquent was inseparable from the title of the Wise one, the Brave one, the Courageous one.)

In Goidtsenhoven's emblem (*Microcosmus: Parvus Mundus*, no. 43) (fig. 10), the men attached by chains to Hercules's mouth jump around like so many puppets on strings, backwards and forwards, totally enslaved by his every movement. Here there is a negative interpretation of the emblem, as signified by the biblical quotation from

136 "Through a Glass Darkly"

1 Corinthians 13.1: "Si linguis hominum loquar & angelorum, charitatem autem non habeam: factus sum velut aes sonans: aut cymbalum timiens" [Though I speak with the tongues of men and of angels, and have not charity, I am as brass and tinkling cymbals.] The wordly wisdom rejected here could well refer to Satan

> Squat like a Toad, close at the ear of *Eve*;
> Assaying by his Devilish art to reach
> The Organs of her Fancie, and with them forge
> Illusions as he list, Phantasms and Dreams,
> Or if, inspiring venom, he might taint
> Th'animal Spirits that from pure blood arise
> (*PL* 4.800–05)

The strength of Hercules (as shown in the Son's "ten thousand Thunders," *PL* 6.836), Samson's ability to bring the altar of Dagon down on the heads of the Philistines (1588–889), and Adam's commanding physical form (*PL* 4.300–03) were legendary. In fact Sir Antonye Cope, perhaps combining images of Hercules' physical and intellectual power, envisions King Henry VIII as a new Hercules:

> Furthermore the actes of Hercules be moste sette forthe by poetes, who (as it is thoughte) haue feigned many thinges more than the trueth was: but of your highnes actes, that ar our english Hercules, no man doth or can doubt, they ar so well knowen, euen of your ennemies to theyr peines. (a4ᵛ)

EMBLEMS OF ATHENA

Perhaps one of the most famous images or emblems in Milton's *Paradise Lost* is Sin springing from the head of Satan:

> All on a sudden miserable pain
> Surpris'd thee, dim thine eyes, and dizzie swumm
> In darkness, while thy head flames thick and fast
> Threw forth, till on the left side op'ning wide,
> Likest to thee in shape and count'nance bright,
> Then shining heav'nly fair, a Goddess arm'd

Milton and the Emblematic Tradition 137

Figure 10. Laurens Van Haecht Goidtsenhoven, #25. "Gallorvm Hercvles," *Mikrokosmos: Parvvs Mvndvs*. Amsterdam, 1610[?].

> Out of thy head I sprung: amazement seis'd
> All th'Host of Heav'n; back they recoild affraid
> At first, and call'd me *Sin*, and for a Sign
> Portentous held me....
>
> (2.752–61)

The account is of course based on the myth of Athena springing from the head of Zeus, and the emblem (no. 4, B2ᵛ) in Goidtsenhoven's *Microcosmos: Parvus Mundus* gives it in full detail. One of Vulcan's workmen stands at his forge while Vulcan, splitting Zeus's head open with an axe, allows Athena (Wisdom) to issue forth. It is interesting that Vulcan is termed Mulciber in the poetic narrative explaining the image (B3), for that is his name, as we have seen, in *Paradise Lost*. Athena, the narrative continues, comes not from the flesh, but from the mind, for she represents wisdom: "Sapientia namque / Non ex carne fluit, mens pretiosa parit" [For wisdom is not a product of the flesh, but of man's invaluable mind] (commentary on his fig. 4).

The Lady of *Comus*, who is, according to her oldest brother, "clad in [the] compleat steel" (421) of chastity, and is therefore impervious to the claims of love, presents a demeanor similar to the Pallas Athena described in Giles Corrozet's "Chasteté vaincq Cupido" (*Hecatomgraphie*, C5ᵛ–C6). Here Athena holds her shield bearing the face of the Medusa against the arrow of Cupid. Pallas, the very pure, has vanquished Cupid, the impure, with the shield of chastity:

> Contre Pallas Cupido son dard lance,
> Mais au deuant elle met son escu,
> Et faict si bien qu'elle le rend vaincu,
> Tout desnué d'armes & de puissance.
> Saincte Pallas déesse trespudicque
> L'honneur t'est deu & pris victorieux,
> Tu as vaincu Cupido l'impudicque,
> . . .
> C'est chasteté qui faict crier mercy
> A fol Amour, quand il veult persister:
> . . .
> Sy vous voyez que Venus vous assaille,
> Prenez pour vous l'escu de chasteté,
> Lors ne craindrez son pouuoir vne paille
> Sy vous auez armes d'honnesteté.
>
> (Cupid hurls his arrow against Pallas.
> But she puts her shield in front of her
> And does so well that she vanquishes him.
> Completely stripped of weapons and power.
> Holy Pallas, most shamefast goddess

Honor and the prize of victory are yours,
For you have defeated the shameless Cupid.
. . . .
It is chastity that makes foolish love cry for mercy,
when love wants to persist.
If you see Venus attacking you,
Take up chastity as your shield
Thus you will have no more fear of her power than a straw,
If you are armed with decency.)

Emblems of Sexuality

Eve's attempt to achieve independence from Adam, a manifestation of female power—but also a breach of decorum and a revolt against duly constituted authority—is foreshadowed in Corrozet's emblem "Nature foemine" (L7ᵛ–L8), symbolized by a naked woman pursuing free-flying birds. The whole purport of the emblem is toward protectiveness and control:

> Vne femme quoy qu'elle face
> En reigle ne veult estre mise,
> Elle desire estre en espace,
> Sans estre à personne submise:
> Soit en la rue ou en l'eglise
> Elle est aussi sotte & volaige
> Querant liberté & franchise
> Que le petit oyseau ramaige.

> Les femmes sans toutes blasmer,
> Sont à garder assez fascheuses
> Quand sont subiectes à aymer,
> Et trenchent trop des precieuses,
> Ie le dy pour les vicieuses:
> Les bonnes ie ne veulx taxer
> Qui sont de l'honneur curieuses
> Au faict, au dict, & au penser.

> Les tendres & ieunes pucelles,
> Ce sont petis oyseaux volans,
> Elles ont vne couple d'aelles
> Qui les portent es premiers ans

En deduictz & esbatz plaisans,
L'une est la chair amyant lyesse
Qui vole en la ville & aux champs,
Et l'aultre c'est sotte ieunesse.

[A woman, no matter what she does or says, does not want to be controlled. She wants to be free, without being subordinate to anyone. Either in the street or in Church, she is just as silly and flighty as the warbling prattle of a little bird seeking freedom and liberty.

Without blaming them all, I would say that women are really a nuisance to control when they are in love and affecting to be prima donnas. I am speaking here of the depraved ones. I have no desire to speak ill of good women, who are careful of their honor in thought, word, and deed.[28]

These young and tender maidens are little flying birds. They have a couple of wings that bear them in their early years toward delights and joyous revels. One is the wing of flesh that loves joy and flies to the city and the fields, while the other wing is silly youth.]

Continuing with the theme of unusual births and feminine dominance, Barthelemy Aneau (d. 1565) provides an interesting twist on the myth of the hermaphrodite[29] in *Picta Poesis* (14–15) in his famous emblem "Matrimonii Typvs." This is often cited by Spenser scholars in relation to the stanzas rejected from the third book of *The Faerie Queene*. Here husband and wife come together in love and become part of the branches of a tree. In a way, in *Paradise Lost* Adam and Eve are also brought together by a tree, and by eating the fruit of that forbidden tree they are united in death. This can also be related to another emblem in Achille Bocchi's (1590?–1650) *Bonon Symbolicarum*. Boreas and Pan are rival suitors for Pitym, and rather than make love to either of them, she becomes a tree (1555 ed., 344 no. 150). Since Pan is the archetype of the devil, it may not be too farfetched to say that Satan has turned Eve into a tree, or at least has integrated her into the substance of the tree of the knowledge of good and evil. Eve, in fact, worships the tree after eating the forbidden fruit:

> O Sovran, vertuous, precious of all Trees
> In Paradise, of operation blest
> To Sapience, hitherto obscur'd, infam'd,
> And thy fair Fruit let hang, as to no end
> Created; but henceforth my early care,
> Not without Song, each Morning, and due praise
> Shall tend thee, and the fertil burden ease
> Of thy full branches offer'd free to all;
> Till dieted by thee I grow mature
> In knowledge, as the Gods who all things know;
> Though others envie what they cannot give;
> For had the gift bin theirs, it had not here
> Thus grown....
> ....
>   So saying, from the Tree her step she turnd,
> But first low Reverence don, as to the power
> That dwelt within, whose presence had infus'd
> Into the plant scientical sap, deriv'd
> From Nectar, drink of Gods....
>   (*PL* 9.795–807, 834–38)

Again, in Aneau's *Picta Poesis*, the forcible embrace of Hermaphroditus by the nymph Salmacis ("Fons Salmacidos. Libido Effoeminans," pp. 32–33), and the resultant creature of ambiguous sex, is interpreted as the assault of a prostitute. One could see Eve in this role, as she effeminizes Adam by taking away his will and giving him "of that fair enticing Fruit / With liberal hand...." (*PL* 9.996–97). Aneau labels the emblem "Libido Effoeminans" or "feminizing lust." This love that effeminizes Adam also brings on his death. Thus in another emblem from Goidtsenhoven's *Mikrokosmos: Parvus Mundus*, "De Morte Et Cupidine" (no. 13), Love and Death exchange arrows—the old man loves, the young man dies. The connection between love and death is strengthened by the epigraph from Romans 6.23: "Stipendium peccati mors," (The wages of sin is death.)

The same notions of effeminacy and moral slackness are conveyed in Nicholas Reusner's emblem, "Forma viros neglecta decet" (no. 3.136–37) [It is right for men to be indifferent to physical beauty]. Salmacis enters the water as a man, and emerges as a half man, just as Adam testifies to his link with Eve: "Our State cannot be severd, we are one, / One Flesh; to loose thee were to loose my self" (*PL* 9.958–59).[30] Hermaphroditus is shown resisting the embracements of Salmacis and then becoming the two-headed monstrosity, the hermaphrodite,[31] as he bathes in her stream, recalling Adam's predicament: "fondly overcome with Femal charm" (*PL* 9.999). The captions sound the appropriate moral warnings:

> Salmacidis qui fonte lauat vir, semivir exit:
> Mollescit tactis illicò corpus aquis.
> Quisquis desidiam sectatur, luxuriamque:
> Qui lautè comedit, qui lauat, atque bibit:
> Qui fingit vultus, ornatque subinde capillos
> Ad speculum: captans sic simulacra sui:
> Nec sua cum duris sudoribus ocia miscet:
> Nec, quod agat semper, quodque sequatur, habet:
> Denique qui se stultus amat: sine corde virili
> Semimarem meritò dixeris esse virum.
> Forma viros neglecta decet: cultusque virilis
> Legitimum finem convenienter amat.
>
> (136–37)

(Any man who bathes in the stream of Salmacis comes out as half a man. His body softened after it came in contact with the waters there. Anyone who seeks idleness and extravagance, anyone who luxuriates in bathing or drinking there, is consumed by the stream. The man who falsifies his appearance and then dresses his hair in front of a mirror, instead of just keeping it in place with his own hard sweat, has nothing to keep him continually occupied, except for reaching out for his own reflection. Finally, anyone who loves himself is silly: for you would be right to say that a man without a man's heart is half a man. A carefree appearance is becoming to men. For a man, personal grooming is appropriate only when it is not excessive.)

Another image of the hermaphrodite that emphasizes female power is emblem 38 in Michael Maier's *Atalanta Fvgiens* (fig. 11),[32] where a heavily muscled Aphrodite takes an enervated Mercury in her arms—his caduceus is flung to one side and a displeased (and blind) Cupid flanks Aphrodite. The epigram cautions that we should not spurn the female in ourselves: "Ancipitem sexum ne spernas, nam tibi Regem / Mas idem, mulierque una eademque dabit" (p. 161) [Do not despise the bisexual being. For man as well as woman, who together are one and the same, will give birth to the King for you].[33]

EMBLEMS OF DEATH

In keeping with the image of enervated males, Reusner's emblem, "Vita Mors" (no. 4, p. 206, *Emblemata*) (fig. 12), shows a docile, querulous Adam being pulled toward the forbidden tree, while the sly snake places an apple in Eve's hand with his fangs. The caption highlights the living death we suffer as children of Adam and Eve, and the contrary principles of good and evil so emphasized in *Paradise Lost*:

> Primus Adamus homo sator est cum crimine vitae:
> Mortis iter sator est primus Adamus homo.
> Vita Dei, Sathanae mors est opus: ille bonorum
> Auctor: at hic scelerum primus in orbe fuit.
> Eua parens hominum mortem propagat in omnes:
> Dum veteris culpae nos facit esse reos.
> Mors culpae merces: fruimur quod duplice vita
> Mortales: bonitas est tua magna Deus.
>
> (p. 206, f4ᵛ)

(Adam the first man is the planter with the charge of life. Adam, the first man, is the sower of death. Life is the work of God, death of Satan. God is the creator of good things, but this Satan was the first inhabitant in the world of evil things. Eve the parent of man brings forth death for everyone, because she makes us the defendants against ancient wrong. Death is the price of sin. The devil is the death merchant of sin; we mortals reap the fruits of that sin through our duplicitous way of life. God, your goodness is great.)

Milton's Satan frames the argument in almost the same terms: "... If then his Providence / Out of our evil seek to bring forth good, / Our labour must be to pervert that end, / And out of good still to find means of evil" (*PL* 1.162–65).

We may conclude with a brief but pointed analysis of two classical myths that are treated by both Milton and the emblem writers: the three Fates and Moloch. Milton refers to the three fates in *Arcades*, where the Sirens

> ... sing to those that hold the vital shears,
> And turn the Adamantine spindle round,
> On which the fate of gods and men is wound.
> Such sweet compulsion doth in musick lie,
> To lull the daughters of *Necessity*
> And keep unsteddy Nature to her Law
>
> (65–70)

This very scene is reenacted in Principio Fabrici's *Delle Allusione* (Rome, 1588, p. 319) (fig. 13) with Necessity at the top of the spindle. The motto, "On the sanctity of life," seems deliberately obfuscating, since the Fates ordinarily signal the brevity and instability of life.[34]

In the Dutch emblem book by Johan de Brune (1589–1658) (*Emblemata of Zinne-werck*, Amsterdam, 1624), there is an emblem (no. 49, p. 345) (fig. 14) of Moloch's statue bearing a child in its metal arms; the statue functions as an oven; flames issuing from the body cremate the child's living body as a sacrifice to the god. In Milton's description of Moloch, the horrible human sacrifice of children is stressed:

> First *Moloch*, horrid King besmear'd with blood
> Of human sacrifice, and parents tears,
> Though for the noyse of Drums and Timbrels loud

Milton and the Emblematic Tradition

Figure 11. Michael Maier, "Rebis, vt Hermaphroditus," *Atalanta Fvgiens*. Oppenheim, 1618.

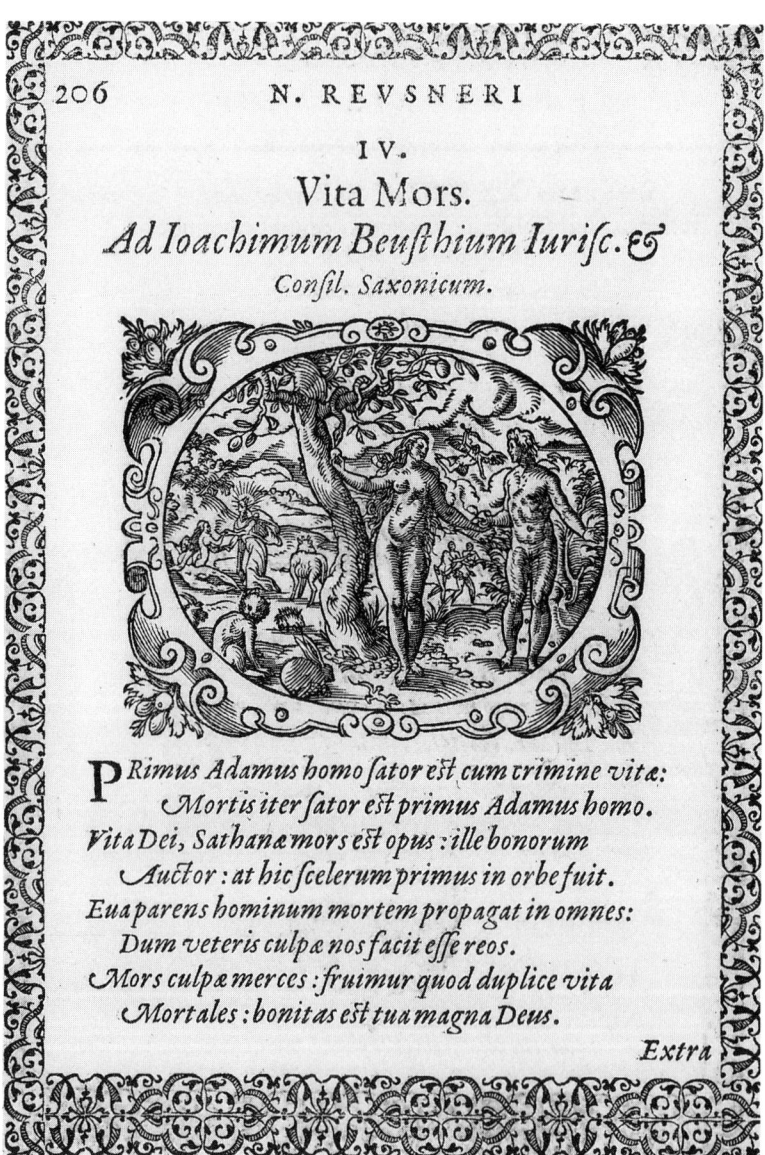

Figure 12. Nicholas Reusner, #4 "Vita Mors," *Emblemata*. Frankfurt, 1581.

> Thir childrens cries unheard, that past through fire
> To his grim Idol. . . .
>
> (*PL* 1.392–96)

Accounts of Moloch as god of human sacrifice also appear in the Renaissance dictionaries and the mythographers, and in the pages of Martin Luther,[35] but the De Brune emblem more powerfully conveys the perfidy of human sacrifice than any merely verbal account.

As this brief survey has indicated, the ubiquity of the emblem books (many examples are found in every country in Europe) indicates that they were very popular and very heavily used. The interconnection of picture and poem, plus the gloss on both, produced repeated images (with explanations) of love, death, ambition, fortune, occasion, gender ambiguity, woman and beauty. They were, of necessity, superficial, but they contain some ideas on love reminiscent of Ficino, make intelligent and important distinctions between Fortune and Occasion, and pick up on some of the spatial metaphors that are so characteristic of *Paradise Lost* (e.g., the "foul descents" of Phaethon, Icarus and Cupid). As I have already stated, their contribution to the mythological tradition was absorbed by both the mythographers and the Renaissance lexicographers. Conversely, late editions of Alciato pick up references to the mythographers Conti and Giraldi.

Milton could then depend on the visual memory of his readers to associate the images of the emblem books with this appropriation of classical myth in his major works. Over a thousand volumes of these emblems rolled off the presses of Europe[36] and into the hands of thousands of readers, Milton doubtless among them.

Figure 13. Principio Fabrici, *Delle Allusione*. Rome, 1588.

EMBLEMATA.
XLIX.

Wacht u, ô menfch, van by-gheloof!
Of anders wert ghy 's duyvels roof.

Zie, waer heen dat de menfch, ô fchrick! niet wert
    ghedreven,
Wanneer, door by-geloof, zijn herte light verstrickt:
Een moer-ftruyck van onheyl en grouwel is zijn leven,
En wat ons God oyt gaf, wert in hem ganfch verftickt.
Natuere wert verzaeckt, want ouders hebben konnen
    Met haere oogen zien, jae wreedelick begeert,
Dat 't geen was uyt haer zelf, eē ander-zelf gewonnen,
    Zou van een gloeyend' beeld tot afschen zijn verteert.

Figure 14. Johan de Brune, #49, *Emblemata of Zinne-Werck*. Amsterdam, 1624.

Six

Milton and the Egyptological Tradition[1]

The Egyptological tradition has several claims on Milton's attention. As an accomplished linguist, Milton would have had more than a passing interest in the search for meaning in the ancient hieroglyphs. As a theologian, he would also have been concerned about the relationship between the hieroglyphs and the tetragrammaton,[2] the sacred name of God. In addition, the hieroglyphic approach to mythology was another attempt to legitimize recondite, even far-fetched interpretations of classical myth, the search for hidden and obscure meanings related to one's own intellectual preoccupations.[3] Milton hints at this view in *Paradise Lost* 3.516: "Each Stair mysteriously was meant," attributing mystical significance to the ascent to heaven's gate, now beyond Satan's reach. Renaissance artists, Erik Iversen maintains, shaped hieroglyphs "with supreme disregard of all traditional and historical facts" (4). These occult symbols were, according to Milton's (early) contemporary Thomas Heywood (1574–1641), the aesthetic embodiments of scientific truths: "So did th'Aegyptians in the Arts best try'd, / In Hierogliphickes all their science hide."[4] And Martianus Capella's Astronomy makes the same mystical claim for Egypt: "Moreover, matters which over the vast span of ages have been reposited in the sanctums of Egyptian priests, I was keeping secret, not wishing to divulge and profane them" (8.812.318).

Emblem Writers as Egyptologists

Andrea Alciato, Henri Estienne

Since hieroglyphs are images of a sort, it is not surprising that they were taken up by Andrea Alciato, author of the first emblem book, or that their animal-like shapes were connected (however loosely) with the twelfth-century bestiary, the *Physiologus*.[5] Henri Estienne, in his *The Art of Making Devices*,[6] also connects these pictograms with the emblems. For Estienne, "the Embleme is properly a sweet and morall Symbole, which consists of picture and words, by which some weighty sentence is declared" (7). Thus an emblem is a subclass of symbol, and all symbols emanate from science or wisdom, the preserve of both the Hebrews and the Egyptians: "There is no doubt, but that after the Hebrewes, the Egyptians were the first that did most precisely addict themselves to all manner of Sciences; nor did they profess any one, which they esteemed more commendable, then that of *Hieroglyphicks*" (1). In fact, we learn from Estienne that Moses was perfectly conversant with all aspects of Egyptian learning.

Francis Quarles

The emblem writer Francis Quarles also conflated emblems and hieroglyphics in his emblem book, *Hieroglyphikes of the life of Man* (London, 1638), and in his book of emblems of the trinity, *Trinitas Emblemes* (London, 1635). In his various prefaces he treats the terms interchangeably.

His *Hieroglyphikes* are "an AEgyptian dish, drest on the English fashion" (A5), but also divine emblems: "Before the knowledge of Letters God was known by *Hieroglyphicks*. And indeed what are the Heavens, the Earth, nay, every Creature, but *Hieroglyphicks* and *Emblemes* of His Glory?"(A3).[7]

"Horapollo"

Editors and commentators on Horus Apollo (or Horapollo), the imagined founder of Egyptology (the MS of "his" *Hieroglyphica* was discovered in the sixteenth century), continue the emblematic approach to the hieroglyphics and occult objects of Egyptian worship. In the Paris 1551 edition of *Hieroglyphica*, the depiction of the three Fates (see also chaps. 5, 7, and 9) recalls Milton's references to these infernal deities in *Lycidas* and *Arcades*. A spindle depicted on a table symbolizes the last extremity of death (219).[8] In *Lycidas*, although the spindle is not mentioned, the fatal sisters certainly use a spindle to "spin out" the threads of lives they may terminate at will. In *Arcades*, Milton refers to the Fates as ". . . those that hold the vital shears, / And turn the Adamantine spindle round, / On which the fate of gods and men is wound" (65–67). In the "Horapollo" emblem, Atropos is the incontrovertible or the inexorable Fate who terminates life, for Milton "the blind *Fury* with th'abhorred shears, / [that comes] And slits the thin-spun life . . ." (*Lycidas* 75–76).

On a related subject, Horapollo attacks the Egyptians for claiming that heaven is of the male gender (23), since the generation of the Sun and Moon and other planets is clearly an act of female gestation. Milton continually refers to heaven in the female gender, as in the reference to the devils' expulsion from heaven: "Disburd'n'd Heav'n rejoic'd, and soon repaird / Her mural breach, returning whence it rowl'd" (*PL* 6.878–79). Attempting to relate the Egyptian hieroglyphs to the Greek and Roman gods, Horapollo also interprets two crows as Mars and Venus, respectively. This provokes a discussion of male-female sexuality and the behaviors appropriate to each (12–13), a cross-cultural essay on sexual difference that emphasizes the essential similarity of male and of female behavior in all civilizations, just as Adam and Eve are Milton's paradigmatic man and woman.

In his *Symbolica AEgyptiorvm Sapientia* (Paris, 1634), Nicholas Caussin (1583–1651) provides both an edition of Horapollo with extensive learned commentary and an interpretive work of his own, the *Polyhistor Symbolicvs*. In the latter he describes the image of Venus among the Corinthians as a seductive symbol of luxury and destruction (2.84, 2G3^v). The apple that she offers with one hand symbolizes the deceptions of luxury—"She gave him of that fair enticing Fruit / With liberal hand . . ." (*PL* 9.996–97)—and the poppy in the other both sleep and death, perhaps the ". . . grosser sleep / Bred of unkindly fumes, . . ." (9.1049–050) that Adam and Eve experience after they satisfy their lust for each other, perhaps the death that awaits them for accepting the "Bad Fruit of Knowledge" (1073). The Venus sculpted by Phidias (ca. 490 B.C.) (2.86, 2G4) stands on the tortoise, the symbol (see Valeriano, below) of domestic responsibility and maidenly fear. Caussin contrasts Phidias's Venus with the one sculpted by Scopas (4th c. B.C.) (2.87, 2G4), the one who is flanked by a goat, a shameless, ugly animal, fit companion for a shameless woman like Venus (or Eve?).

Perrière, Corrozet, Appianus, Baudoin

Guillaume de Perrière (1499–1565), as introduced in the Thomas Combe translation (fl. 1590), also focuses on the connection between the emblem and the hieroglyph: "Wherein if the verse be anie thing obscure, the impreses or pictures make it more liuely, and in a manner actuall" ("To the Reader" unsigned).[9] Giles Corrozet in his *Hectamographie* (see chap. 5) and Petrus Appianus in his *Inscriptiones* (Ingolstadt, 1534), also make the connection, the former in his image of the crocodile (D6ᵛ) and the latter in his magisterial image of Isis (xxxvi). The anonymous *Rime De Gli Occvlti Academici Con Le Loro Imprese Et Discorsi* (Brescia, 1568) (Poems on Obscure Scholarly Subjects, Along With Their Emblems and Commentaries) asserts that the Egyptian priests used figures of natural bodies to express recondite meanings that were inaccessible to the commonality ("Discorso" **1), while Jean Baudoin (1590?–1651) refers to them as "Lettres mystiques" (a5ᵛ). Eventually the term degenerated into a synonym for symbol or image, as it does in Ben Jonson, who connects hieroglyphics with the bogus historical prestige of the Egyptians and the bizarre novelty of interpretation imposed on these pictographs. In his notes to *The Masque of Blacknesse*, for example, Jonson candidly admits the trendiness associated with hieroglyphics. The Tritons in that masque are carrying in one hand "*a mute* Hieroglyphick *expressing their mixed qualities. Which manner of* Symbole [note the conflation] *I rather chose, then* Imprese, *as well for strangeness, as relishing of antiquitie, and more applying to that originall doctrine of sculpture, which the* AEgyptians *are said, first, to have brought from the* AEthiopians."[10]

Cesare Ripa

Cesare Ripa's (fl. 1600) *Iconologia* (Padua, 1630) also bridges the emblematic and Egyptological traditions. He presents both philosophical and technical instructions for the formation of images—to get at the essence of an image, one must understand its philosophical underpinnings as well as master the techniques that reflect its soul. The thoughts embodied in these images come from the Egyptians, and the hieroglyphic figures are in fact the sources of Plato's teachings ("Proemio," [Foreword] 7). His depiction of the goddess "Abondanza" (Abundance), with the cornucopia in her right hand and various grains and vegetables in her left (1.9–10) contrasts with the deceitful cornucopia of Fortuna, the blind goddess who distributes the world's goods without observing the conduct or the morals of the fortunate ones (1.271-72).¹¹ Because of their sin, all abundance is lost to Adam and Eve, and fecundity of earth or womb will be accomplished only with excruciating toil and pain. Eve will experience pain in childbirth ("... Children thou shalt bring / In sorrow forth..." [10.194-95]) while Adam must wrestle with the barren, weed-infested ground:

> Curs'd is the ground for thy sake, thou in sorrow
> Shalt eat thereof all the days of thy Life;
> Thorns also and Thistles it shall bring thee forth
> Unbid, and thou shalt eat th'Herb of the Field,
> In the sweat of thy Face shalt thou eat Bread.
>
> (201-05)

Three female figures in Ripa that relate to fallen Eve are "Pudicitia" (2.597-99) (Modesty), "Vergogna Honesta" (3.165-68) (Honorable Shame), and "Lascivia" (2.434) (Lust). Modesty is a required feminine virtue only after the Fall, as is "honorable shame," while lust is its product. Even in modern Italian, *vergogna* also refers to the "shameful parts" of woman and hence the nakedness and shame Eve (as well as Adam) experience. Adam and Eve "discover" their own nakedness only after they have sinned and joined themselves in a "lascivious" (since it is motivated by lust) embrace, and experience "guiltie" rather than "honorable" shame: "... dewie sleep / Oppress'd them, wearied with thir amorous play" (9.1044-045), and they awaken "... naked left / To guiltie shame..." (1057-058) "... destitute and bare / Of all thir vertue..." (1062-063).

Pierre Dinet

Pierre Dinet's (fl. 17c.) *Cinq livres des hieroglyphiqves* (Five Books of Hieroglyphs) (Paris, 1614), which the author claims is full of the "plus rares secrets de la nature" (the rarest of Nature's secrets) and deems "necessaire à toutes professions," (crucial to all professions) is at once an emblem book and a study of hieroglyphics. Dinet relates the hieroglyphs to the sacred letters that hold the key to the principles and secrets of nature, and he also claims they are the origin of the armories and devices of princes (preface unsigned). Once again, the Egyptian hieroglyphs become a convenient excuse to indulge in farfetched interpretations of classical mythology. The myth of Medusa and her Gorgon sisters, for example, is really a treasury of Greek, Hebrew and Egyptian lore:

> Les Rabins Mecubales, la theologie des Egyptiens, & de la doctrine Platonique, qui a coulé de ces deux fources, les plus anciennes de toutes autres, tirent le faict de ces trois soeurs en vn autre sens: constituans trois sortes d'ames en l'homme, qui les representent. La sensuelle, animale, & vivante, que les Hebrieux appellent *Nephes*, laquelle nous est commune avec les bestes brutes: figuree par la Meduse mortelle, & subiecte comme elles aux passions, & affections de la chair, avec lesquelles ceste ame sensibile. (2T3)

> (The Mercubalean [a very learned group] rabbis, have taken the theology of the Egyptians, and the Platonic teaching, and drawn from these two powers, the oldest powers of all, an interpretation of the existence of these three sisters that has another sense: constituting three kinds of souls in men, which they represent. The sensual, animal, and living, which the Hebrews call *Nephes*. This living soul we have in common with the brute beasts. It is presented figuratively by the mortal Medusa, and is subject, just as she is, to the passions and affections of the flesh, with these types of sensible souls.)

ALCHEMISTS AS EGYPTOLOGISTS

Michael Maier's *Atalanta Fugiens* (see chap. 5) and Nicholas Flamel's (d. 1618) *His Exposition of the Hieroglyphicall Figures* (London, 1624) shift the focus from emblems to alchemy. Both attempt to interpret the hieroglyphs as alchemical symbols that could be used to turn base metals into gold or base men into finer "mettle." Maier's subtitle promises the reader an insight into "De Secretis Naturae Chymica" (the secrets of chemical nature), the nature of elements and fluids. Since, in alchemical terms, all metals take their origin from Mercury, Maier is particularly interested in the metamorphosis that results in the hermaphrodite or androgyne,[12] and Mercury/Hermes as the source of occult knowledge. Flamel, emphasizing a different aspect of the tradition, views the alchemical process as an instrument of salvation that is revealed through the hieroglyphs:

> These *Hieroglyphicke figures* shall serue as two wayes to leade vnto the heauenly life: the first and most open sence, teaching the sacred *Mysteries* of our saluation; (as I will shew heereafter) the other teaching euery man, that hath any small vnderstanding in the *Stone*, the lineary way of the worke; which being perfected by any one, the change of euill into good, takes away from him the roote of all sinne (which is *couetousnesse*) ... (35)

All is done according to "the *Maistery* of *Hermes*" (37) who is also master of the cabala, the occult oral wisdom of the Jews.

Milton's own devils practice a kind of alchemy, digging deep within the veins of hell to mine the "precious bane" (*PL* 1.692) that lies there. And just as Flammel promises that humanity will be purified through alchemizing the four elements, so Milton's Mammon suggests that the "Elements" of the rebel angels will be transformed to promote toleration of the "penal fire" that afflicts them, even as they search for gold:

> ... This Desart soil
> Wants not her hidden lustre, Gemms and Gold;
> Nor want we skill or Art, from whence to raise
> Magnificence; and what can Heav'n shew more?
> Our torments also may in length of time
> Become our Elements, these piercing Fires
> As soft as now severe, our temper chang'd

> Into their temper; which must needs remove
> The sensible of pain...
>
> (*PL* 2.270–78)

In the description of hell, gold is everywhere, but the devils, we are told, were later to teach humankind to mine it on earth; they themselves use it to build Pandemonium, and their transformation of the gold into supports and embellishments for the building is described as an alchemical process. One might say that they were reversing the alchemical process by turning baser metals into an even baser building, a building described in terms of the riches of ancient Babylon and Egyptian Memphis, "Of *Babel*, and the works of *Memphian* Kings" (1.694). Mammon first taught human beings to mine for gold, and hence they "Ransack'd the Center, and with impious hands / Rifl'd the bowels of thir mother Earth/ For Treasures better hid..." (686–88).[13]

One would not expect the elements of water and air in hell, so the devils must make do with earth and fire:

> Nigh on the Plain in many cells prepar'd,
> That underneath had veins of liquid fire
> Sluic'd from the Lake, a second multitude
> With wondrous Art founded the massie Ore,
> Severing each kind, and scum'd the Bullion dross:
> A third as soon had form'd within the ground
> A various mould, and from the boyling cells
> By strange conveyance fill'd each hollow nook,
> As in an Organ from one blast of wind
> To many a row of Pipes the sound-board breaths.
> Anon out of the earth a Fabrick huge
> Rose like an Exhalation, with the sound
> Of Dulcet Symphonies and voices sweet,
> Built like a Temple, where *Pilasters* round
> Were set, and Doric pillars overlaid
> With Golden Architrave; nor did there want
> Cornice or Freeze, with bossy Sculptures grav'n,
> The Roof was fretted Gold....
>
> (700–17)[14]

"Exhalation" describes the process of the building emerging like a vapor or mist from the foul earth of Hell. But it exhales sound as well as form, "of Dulcet Symphonies and voices sweet." It is perhaps no coincidence that Michael Maier sets his emblems to music, with the score appearing on the printed page, just opposite the illustration, so the pleasing sounds that reach the ears will refresh the spirit. Thus each emblem is a total assault on the senses, "videnda, legenda, meditanda, intelligenda, dijudicanda, canenda & audienda" (title page) (to be seen, read, thought about, understood, judged, sung, and heard).

Michael Maier's other book on Egypt, *Arcana Arcanissima Hoc Est Hieroglyphica Aegyptio-Graeca* (The Most Concealed Concealment, which is the Greek-Egyptian Hieroglyph) (London, 1614), subjects all of classical mythology to alchemical analysis. We learn that the beginnings of all science and knowledge came from Egypt, and that at first not even the great historian of the sacred, Moses, understood what they were about (2). The sun and the moon were worshiped as the gods Isis and Osiris (3). He also refers to the temple of Vulcan that was built in Memphis (28; cf. passage from *PL* 1 quoted above). Maier is, however, concerned that his offbeat interpretations of Egyptology and classical mythology cannot be supported by Scripture, so he offers this defense: "Quod etiam si nos in textu bibliorum sacrorum non legamus, tamen credible est haustum ex glossis antiquorum scriptorum" (48) (Although we don't read about these things in the pages of the sacred books, what we draw from the notations of the ancient writers is believable.)

Returning to *Paradise Lost* and the attack on "Fanatic *Egypt* and her Priests" (1.480), Cicero himself (*On the Nature of the Gods* 1.16) spoke of "the insane mythology of Egypt." And in the fourth century "thrice great *Hermes*" (*Il Penseroso* 88), the reputed author of the so-called hermetic writings, attacked Egypt's privileged theological status: "O Egypt, Egypt, of thy religion nothing will remain but an empty tale, which thine own children in time to come will not believe; nothing will be left but graven words, and only the stones will tell of thy piety" (1.343). There is also an ancient tradition of mockery of the animal-headed and semihuman Egyptian gods (some of whom form the basis of the hieroglyphs), extending from Lucian through Juvenal (we have already encountered it in its late classical form in St. Augustine),[15] which Milton echoes in his famous diatribe against the pagan gods (the reincarnated devils from hell) in the first book of *Paradise Lost*:

> ... After these appear'd
> A crew who under Names of old Renown,
> *Osiris, Isis, Orus* and thir Train
> With monstrous shapes and sorceries abus'd
> Fanatic *Egypt* and her Priests, to seek
> Thir wandring Gods disguis'd in brutish forms
> Rather then human.
>
> (476–82)

The anti-Egyptian tradition Milton is drawing upon is rather neatly epitomized by Natale Conti (to move ahead to the mythographers for a moment) in two apposite quotations from ancient sources.[16] The first is from the comic poet Anaxandrides of Rhodes:

> I couldn't have myself allied with you,
> Our ways and customs differing as they do.
> I sacrifice to God, to bulls you kneel,
> Your greatest god's our greatest treat, the eel;
> You don't eat pork; it's quite my favorite meat;
> You worship *your* dog, mine I always beat.[17]

And Juvenal,

> Who knows not, O Bithynian Volusius, what monsters demented Egypt worships? One district adores the crocodile ... but it is an impious outrage to crunch leeks and onions with the teeth. What a holy race to have such divinities springing up in their gardens! (15.1–2, 9–11)

Samuel Purchas

Samuel Purchas (1577?–1626) in *His Pilgrimage* (London, 1614) wryly observes that the Egyptians worship dogs and other beasts and weep at their funerals (6.4.574); in fact, vanity and superstition, Purchas opines, are characteristic of the Egyptians (581). Unlike the more syncretic and comparatist Spencer (see below), Purchas feels that most of the so-called achievements of the Egyptians should really be credited to the Hebrews: "Husbandrie by some is ascribed to them, but falsely, *Adam, Cain, Noah*, and others were in this before them. Astronomie also is not their inuention, but taught them by *Abraham*" (581).

And yet, while Milton refers contemptuously to the Egyptian deities Isis and Osiris in *Paradise Lost*, in *Areopagitica* he compares the dismemberment of the Egyptian deity Osiris to the dismemberment of truth by the ignorant censors of seventeenth century England: ". . . as that story goes of the *AEgyptian Typhon* with his conspirators, how they dealt with the good *Osiris*, took the virgin Truth, hewd her lovely form into a thousand peeces, and scatter'd them to the four winds" (*YP* 2.549).

John Spencer

The seventeenth century divine John Spencer (1630–1693) takes a more positive approach toward Egyptology, attempting to explain and illustrate the supposed connections between Egyptian and Hebrew thought, and thus to reconcile them. In the *De Legibus Hebraeorum Ritualibus Et Earum Rationibus* (On the Laws for Rituals Among the Hebrews and the Reasons for Them) (Cambridge, 1685), Spencer tries to rekindle interest in long-obscure Jewish laws and also to discuss their relationships to Egyptian, Syrian, Phoenician, Greek and Roman rites. This syncretic approach parallels Milton's attempt to assimilate so many diverse materials into a Christian context. And just as

Milton incorporates ancient lore and modern scientific and technological controversy into his great epic (Aristotle, Galileo, seventeenth century military science), Spencer recognizes the need to reconcile ancient and modern sources: "Sat scio, nonnullis nihil arridere, nisi ex Antiquitatis maximè remotae penetralibus eruatur; aliis è contra, nihil salivam movere, nisi novum sit, & quasi recens ab incude prodeat" (A4) [But I know that many cannot be pleased with anything unless it is plucked out from the deepest and most remote parts of antiquity; others have no appetite for anything unless it is new, unless it is right off the press]. He even promises to use a middle style that eschews false elegance ("affectatam elegentiam," A4; cf. *PL* 1.14), in accordance with the dignity of his subject and the needs of his readers (cf. Milton's "answerable style" [*PL* 9.20]. However, Spencer claims that many Hebrew religious rites were derived from the Egyptians (222 ff.), while in *Paradise Regained* the Son ignores Egypt completely and stresses the line of development from the Hebrews to the Greeks:

> ... All our Law and Story strew'd
> With Hymns, our Psalms with artful terms inscrib'd,
> Our Hebrew Songs and Harps in *Babylon*,
> That pleas'd so well our Victors ear, declare
> That rather *Greece* from us Arts these arts deriv'd
> (*PR* 4.334–38)

In another work, his *Dissertatio De Urim & Thummim* (Cambridge, 1669),[18] Spencer alternates between denouncing Egyptian writings as false and markedly inferior to the Hebrew scriptures, and remarking on the similarities between Hebrew and Egyptian religious practices (208–10). Thus Egypt is both comical and fanatical, but still respected as a source of comparison with Hebrew religious practices.

PIERIO VALERIANO

To conclude our discussion of the Egyptological tradition, let us analyze the encyclopedic treatises of Giovanni Pierio Valeriano Bolzani (1477–1558?) and Athanasius Kircher (1602–1680). Perhaps the most detailed and absurd of all the hieroglyphic texts is Valeriano's *Hieroglyphicorvm Collectanea* (1st ed., Basel, 1556; ed. cited Lyon, 1626). In later editions there are constant accretions from other sources; for example, representatives of the philosophical (Ficino), emblematical (Alciato) and mythographical (Cartari, Conti) approaches to myth are cited in the Lyon 1636 edition. All myths, regardless of their origin, are treated as Egyptian.

In the seventh book of *Paradise Lost*, Milton invokes his Muse Urania, a Muse who has carried him "Above the flight of *Pegasean* wing" (4), a reference to the Greek myth of Pegasus, the winged horse of poetic inspiration that was generated from the blood of Medusa after Perseus killed her. For Valeriano, Pegasus, as an Egyptian phenomenon, is Fame, and represents the swiftness and haste of mortals, no doubt in seeking fame (4.6.38). In his chapter on Bacchus (27.3.274), Valeriano stresses the "historical" as well as the mythical Bacchus, the leader of troops into India as well as the wine god. Milton deals with the mythical Bacchus in *Comus*, for Comus is "Of *Bacchus* and of *Circe* born," (522) and, in a way, with the "historical" Bacchus in his characterization of King Charles and his (effeminate) cohorts as "*Bacchus* and his revellers" (*PL* 7.33), for the king is also a (failed) leader and general like the "historical" Bacchus.

Valeriano's symbolic treatments of the tortoise (which we will encounter once more in Cartari's *Imagini*; chap. nine, p. 273) are relevant to Milton's treatment of Eve's womanly obligations in Paradise. For Valeriano (*Virginvm Cvstodia* 28.33.283) the tortoise pressed beneath the foot of a young woman is a symbol of prudence and the protection of virgins, for it symbolizes a woman's care of the house and how it is best for her to be silent.[19] Following the female principle of the Moon, which is overshadowed by the male principle of the Sun, a woman should be conspicuous for her modesty. The public life is for prostitutes, the domestic life for good women. The Egyptians went so far as to prohibit their women the use of shoes, so that they would stay home, just as the turtle always keeps herself within her house.[20]

In the ninth book of *Paradise Lost*, Eve's actions are diametrically opposed to the counsels of Valeriano. Since a woman should be under the protection of the man, just as the Moon is under the protection of the Sun, and should be as silent as the tortoise is mute, Eve is making a tragic mistake when she speaks up with the imperative statement "Let us divide our labours" (214). When Adam seeks to dissuade her from this rash plan, he reflects the domestic emphasis of Valeriano: ". . . for nothing lovelier can be found / In Woman, then to studie household good" (232–33). His final plea echoes the notion that the Sun protects and generates the energy of the Moon: ". . . leave not the faithful side / That gave thee being, still shades thee and protects" (265–66). And just as women in the public sphere are likened to prostitutes, so the talkative Eve continues to chat with the devil outside the domestic sphere, observing neither silence nor modesty. She is not silent, she does not stay within her sphere to take care of the home, she rejects the natural authority of Adam (as shocking as if the Moon had rejected the Sun's light), and she runs about as freely as if she were a prostitute. In fact, if we take the biblical story literally, there is no woman who brought more shame on herself and others, or exhibited less modesty, than Eve.[21]

In Valeriano, the tongue is sacred to Mercury (33.40.340) and, therefore, so is speech.[22] Mercury is also the first one to organize words in a meaningful pattern. In Milton's *Comus*, we have the seductive rhetoric of Comus; in *Paradise Lost* the unlawful speech of Eve, the bad but skillful speaking of Satan, and the hollow rhetoric of Belial; and in *Paradise Regained* the unsuccessful verbal blandishments of Satan. Nor can we forget Dalila in *Samson Agonistes*, to whose sugary rhetoric Samson lends an all too willing ear, learning to protect himself only after it is too late: "So much of Adders wisdom I have learn't / To fence my ear against thy sorceries" (936–37). Valeriano also makes the point that speech is the only skill that differentiates us from the rest of the animals: ". . . quàm sermonem ipsum, quo solus homo ex terrestribus animalibus honestatus est" (33.40.340) (man, the only earthly being graced by speech.) Here one immediately recalls that the devil attributes human speech to the "spirited sly Snake" (*PL* 9.613) and usurps the order of nature. Milton is vitally concerned about the use and misuse of words, as were theologians who debated the proper method of transmitting the Word of God.

Valeriano's sketch of Fortune (39.18.413) represents her, as in Milton, as instability. He also associates her with Occasion, followed again by Milton. Sometimes she is depicted on a wheel, sometimes on a planet. She is associated with the god of love and carries the cornucopia or horn of plenty. These are all standard references and appear in more substantial form in the emblem books, dictionaries and mythographies. The devil alludes to the cornucopia and puts himself into the mask of Fortune in *Paradise Regained*: "Riches are mine, Fortune is in my hand" (2.429). The Savior, following the tradition of the church fathers (and Juvenal), rejects Fortune (or Fate) as a goddess, labeling her as an excuse men devise to cover up their own failings: "All glory arrogate [to themselves], to God give none, / Rather accuse him under usual names, / Fortune and Fate, as one regardless quite / Of mortal things . . ." (*PR* 4.315–18). The devil invokes Occasion when he tempts the Son to sinful action: "If Kingdom move thee not, let move thee Zeal, / And Duty; Zeal and Duty are not slow; / But on Occasions forelock watchful wait" (*PR* 3.171–73). There are also many images devoted to Venus in Valeriano's treatise (including chapters on Venus with the comb, the symbol of female vanity) (41.46.441–42), and the warlike Venus as a symbol of women's "virtus" or strength ("Mvliebris Virtvs," 42.2.443–44), but, as we have seen, most of this material is available in much more accessible form in the emblem books themselves. Valeriano views Pan (44.26.475) as the traditional symbol of universal Nature, which we have already observed in Milton's *Nativity Ode*. His spotted skin represents the stars, and the different parts of his body the totality of the universe.

Book 54 is of particular interest to students of Milton, as it treats the *malum* or apple,[23] representing "the Fruit. . . . [of] all our woe" in *Paradise Lost* (1.1, 3) What Milton called "that fair enticing Fruit" (*PL* 9.996) is equally tempting in Valeriano: "Inter fructiferas arbores malo nulla voluptuosior, pulchrior nulla, nulla delicatior" (54.1.573) [Among the fruitbearing trees there is none more desirable, more beautiful, more delightful than the apple]. His second chapter on the apple ("Amor," 574) focuses on its relationship to love, including its association with Bacchus and the golden apples strewn in Atalanta's path, which allowed her future spouse Hippomenes to defeat her in a foot race and thereby claim her as his bride. Apples are dedicated to Venus because they are sweet. It was the forbidden fruit whose taste resulted in the ruination of all humanity: ". . . mali eius gustum omnium ferè malorum causam mortalibus extitisse" [the taste of that apple caused almost all of the evils that human beings experience.] According to Valeriano's third chapter ("Amoris Progressvs," 574), the apple tree is dedicated to love, and its progress can be measured by it. The apple reddens in the sun just as the lover reddens when his idleness is discovered or he is publicly reprimanded. Venus (8.575) is also depicted with an apple in her hand, perhaps alluding to the figure of Venus in the Judgment of Paris. Valeriano offers many other interpretations, including the apple's connections with Apollo and Hercules, but it is, fundamentally, for him "Veri Amoris Fructvs" (577.14) (Love's true fruit).

Milton explores the paradoxes of this "fallacious fruit" in *Areopagitica*. It is only by experiencing the evil of the fruit that we can determine its good:

> It was from out the rinde of one apple tasted, that the knowledge of good and evill as two twins cleaving together leapt forth into the World. And perhaps this is that doom which *Adam* fell into of knowing good and evill, that is to say of knowing good by evill. (YP 2.514)

Thus for both Milton and Valeriano, the apple is a "fair, enticing fruit" that is intimately associated with love. Both Venus and Eve offer the fruit with liberal hand, for a profusion of apples represents fecundity, even though it is also the cause of all our woe. Although Valeriano does not develop it, we also have the phenomenon of a woman offering a man something poisonous to eat, making Eve a member of the *veneficiae*, the poisonous witches, like Circe and Medea.[24]

ATHANASIUS KIRCHER

Perhaps the most learned (and the most wrongheaded) of the Egyptologists was Athanasius Kircher (1602–1680). He devoted a lifetime to explicating the symbolism he thought he detected in the Egyptian hieroglyphs, and published a formidable number of books that amounted to an elaboration of his own fancies.[25] We may take as typical his interpretation published at Rome in 1666 of the hieroglyphs found on the obelisk. In his first preface to the reader, Kircher speaks frankly and openly of the joy he feels in untying the knots of occult mysteries, and of his conviction that all his work redounds to God's praise:

> Veruntamen cum ita mihi à natura insitum sit, vt nil gloriosius, aut praestantius esse censeam, quàm in huiusmodi literaturae nodis dissoluendis, ingenij, quantum fieri potest, vires experiri, & quid humeri valeant, quid ferre recusent, tentare; vt si occultos adytorum recessus non

omninò penetrare, saltem aliquousque, vel per rimam introspicere concederetur; Si neque hoc, saltem honorificum esse rebar, vel ipsum conatum in Diuinae laudis meritum reponere (**).

(In fact it's really part of my nature to think that there's nothing more glorious or outstanding than dissolving the knotty passages of this literature, and finding out what my shoulders can bear, and what they can't. So that if my powers are unable to penetrate completely into the inner recesses of the temple, at least I can get far enough to peek through the crack. And if not that, at least I used to think it was honorable to count the attempt itself as something worthy of divine praise.)

In his fifth chapter, "Prolusiones ad Interpretationem" (Preludes to Interpretation), he defines a hieroglyph as a sacred object that is sculpted and built in stone to make sure that it lasts, for it was the Egyptian custom to express themselves this way, rather than through speech or words. It was also, he says, a method of concealing profound truths from the ignorant vulgar:

> ... nihil aliud est, quàm symbolum rei sacrae, lapidibus saxisque durissimis contra omnem corruptionis labem incisum; solebant enim Aegyptij componere & formare sua symbola non sermone, aut verborum nominumque constructione, sed ijs notis figurisque, quae integrum quendam de altioribus naturae Diuinitatisque mysterijs sensum inoluerent, ingeniosa industria suos adaptantes sensus, sub obscuro atque allegorico imaginum inuolucro à profanorum ineruditorumque notitia remotissimo solis cognita sapientibus vti. (16–17)

([A hieroglyph is] simply the symbol of a sacred object, carved in stones and very hard rocks, against all possible blight from deterioration. In fact the Egyptians used to compose and to shape their symbols not from speech, or the coinage of names or words, but from these marks and figures, which encompassed a complete meaning from the more lofty mysteries of nature and the godhead, adjusting the meanings themselves with ingenious labor. And beneath the obscure and allegorical covering of the images, they used to withhold the meaning from the understanding of the unlearned and the populace, a meaning which only philosophers knew how to make use of.)

Milton would probably be quite content to place Kircher in the company of "Fanatick *Egypt* and her Priests" (*PL* 1.480), but he would have been in agreement with Kircher about the access of the vulgar to profane learning. In *Samson Agonistes*, after Samson pulls the walls of the Philistines down upon them, the messenger remarks "The vulgar only scap'd who stood without" (1659). His great epic is written for "fit audience..., though few" (*PL* 7.31), and the Son in *Paradise Regained* speaks in riddles and paradoxes as subtle as anything in the hieroglyphs.[26]

Kircher also takes the standard line on the Egyptian-Hebrew controversy: "Post Hebraeos, Aegyptios primos literarum ab Hermete Trismegisto inuentarum vsum tradidisse, in operibus nostris hieroglyphicis ex innumeris authoribus vbertim docuimus" (1.5.18) (The Egyptians were the first peoples after the Hebrews to pass on the use of the letters discovered by Hermes Trismegistus, which we expounded on at length in our hieroglyphic works, citing innumerable authors.) Thus he combines the Egyptological with the Hermetic tradition when he cites Hermes Trismegistus, and both with the patristic when he cites the church father Clement of Alexandria in support of his position (1.6.19).

We need not dwell on the wild and whirling words of Kircher as he proceeds to dissect the meanings of the various letters of the hieroglyphs, but we should pause for a moment to examine his remarks on Chaos[27] and Love, which are directly relevant to Milton's *Paradise Lost*. Kircher cites Orpheus to the effect that Chaos and Love are coterminus: "Hinc Orpheus in Agronauticis [sic] non sine causa: hunc amorem, vt Mundi Genium, & magum antiquissimum laudat. Cum enim Chaos ante Mundum posuerit, ante Saturnum Iouem, & coeteros Deos, Amorem sanè in sinu ipsius Chaos constituit, tanquam Chaoticae euolutionis Animam" (3.3.91) (Orpheus has good reason [in his account of the Argonauts] to praise this love as the Genius of the World and a magician of very great antiquity. Since he says Chaos in fact existed before the world, and before Saturn, Jupiter and the other gods, he puts Love in Chaos's very own lap, as if Love were the essence of the evolution of Chaos.) Clearly, Chaos for Milton is, as it is for Kircher, something palpable, not just a void. Since Heaven has been "dispeopl'd" (*PL* 7.151) by the Fall of the bad angels, God (as we have seen) out of his infinite love creates a new race of men out of Chaos, that "vast profunditie obscure" (7.229). In Milton, Love overrules and controls Chaos; left to itself, Chaos can create nothing but evil. In *Paradise Lost*, Chaos allows Satan to pass through his realm because Satan can promote the confusion he enjoys so much: "If that way be your walk, you have not farr; / So much the neerer danger; go and speed; / Havock and spoil and ruin are my gain" (2.1007–009).

Kircher continues with an account of Egyptian theories of creation, much of which Milton could have obtained from other sources. He does, however, assert the existence of "Daemones" in different parts of the world (3.8.114), anticipating the narrator of *Paradise Lost*'s statement that the fallen angels

> ... among the Sons of *Eve*
> Got them new Names, till wandring ore the Earth,
> Through Gods high sufferance for the tryal of man,
> By falsities and lyes the greatest part
> Of Mankind they corrupted to forsake
> God thir Creator, and th'invisible
> Glory of him that made them, to transform
> Oft to the Image of a Brute, adorn'd
> With gay Religions full of Pomp and Gold,
> And Devils to adore for Deities:
> Then were they known to men by various Names,
> And various Idols through the Heathen World.
> (*PL* 1.364–375)

Kircher's musings are accompanied by attractive plates and learned quotations in Hebrew, Coptic, Greek, and Latin (the Greek always translated into Latin) from earlier commentators and from the Bible itself. Insofar as he engages in a primitive form of iconography, he occupies a modest chapter in the history of the images of the gods, and can be seen as part of the tradition that Milton drew upon in presenting his own images of the gods, saints, monsters and devils.

In sum, the hieroglyphic tradition reinforced a number of themes and approaches we have seen in examining other sources of mythology. Primitive Egyptologists emphasize the hidden, recondite meanings of the material they examine, and often cross linguistic borders to achieve a kind of comparative literature, however primitive. There is some attempt (especially in Valeriano) to be conscious of form and style, and to reduce the complexity of Egyptological sources to some sort of system. A variety of interpretations is presented for the pagan gods, and the old Egypt-Hebrew-Greece-Rome controversy is continually addressed. Finally, some of the Egyptological sources, like Valeriano, continually draw on other mythological sources, including the mythographer Natale Conti and the inventor of the emblem book, Andrea Alciato. The Egyptological tradition formed part of Milton's intellectual milieu, and the fact that it was misconceived did not deter from its potential as a source for Milton's use of classical myth.

SEVEN

Milton and the Renaissance Dictionaries

The passion for collecting every available fact and interpretation of classical mythology, joined with the humanist impulse to incorporate every facet of the classical world into the learned tradition of the Renaissance, produced a spate of formidable reference books: dictionaries, word lists and the beginnings of an encyclopedic tradition.[1] Since these works take a more structured approach toward the cataloging and analysis of classical myth than other sources available to Milton, I shall limit my analysis to several themes articulated in particular myths: Chance (Fortune, Occasion, *Kairos*); Death, Flight and Fall (Moloch, Phaethon, Icarus, Antaeus); Inspiration and Wisdom (Orpheus, the Muses, the Hermathena, Hercules, the Egyptian hieorglphyics); Love (Venus, Cupid, Mars, Diana); and Woman (Uxor, Mulier, the Hermaphrodite, Samson, Hercules, Omphale, Pandora). I have also added a comment on Robert Stephanus's entry on Vulcan, since it is almost totally lifted from Conti's *Mythologiae*, and supports my view that the lexicographers are heavily dependent on the mythographers.

CAELIUS

A truly encyclopedic repository of myth is the massive tome by Lodovicus Caelius (Riccchieri) (1453–1525), *Lectionvm Antiqvarvm* or *Ancient Readings*. While not a dictionary *per se*, it was meant to be used via the massive index rather than the table of contents, and encourages an approach to its contents through the meanings of individual words. The edition published at Cologne in 1620[2] encompasses some 30 books, and the title page announces that it will cover all sorts of abstruse and recondite subjects. There are 77 references to Venus alone, listing many of her cognomens, her relation with Mars, the allegorical meaning, the etymology of her name (Aphrodite, supposedly "from the foam"), her temples and statues, the bald Venus (Venus *Calva*), the bearded Venus (Venus *Barbata*), etc. Venus *Urania* is pertinent to Milton's muse, and the wide-ranging interpretations listed under the allegorical Venus invite applications to Eve, Milton's own incarnation of love and beauty.

Also pertinent to Milton's interpretation of Eve are Caelius's many entries for *uxor* (wife). One item is even referenced in terms of Adam's "sin," uxoriousness: "vxoris amor nimius, turpis," (16.24.883b) (excessive love of one's wife is ugly). Caelius quotes Hieronymus in his *Sententiae* (ca. third century B.C.), indicating that excessive passion for one's wife is really adultery! The wise man loves a woman judiciously, but not to excess. He also cites Seneca on the treatment of one's wife in public. The section merits quotation in full:

> Sextum in Sententiis scripsisse, auctor Hieronymus est, Adulterum esse quisquis in vxorem suam ardentior est

amator. Quippe in vxorem alienam omnis amor turpis est, in suam verò nimius. Sapientis est, vxorem amare, sed iudicio, non affectu. Libidinis pruritus rationis examine reprimendi, nec praecipites ferri in concubitum debemus: foedius nihil, quàm vxorem amare perinde ac adulteram. Venit in mentem historiae, cuius auctor Seneca est, qui à se cognitum quendam testatur, ornatum hominem, qui exiturus in publicum fascia vxoris pectus alligabat, & ne momento quidem praesentia eius carere poterat, potúmque omnino nullum sibi, nisi alterius praegustatum labris, vir & vxor hauriebat, alia item pleraque, nec inepta minus facientes, in quae improuida vis affectus erumpebat. Origo quidem amoris honesta erat, sed nimietas deformitate non carebat. Nil autem referre arbitramur, quàm honesta causa quis insaniat. (16.24.883.b–d)

(The author Hieronymus said that Sextus wrote in his *Sententiae* that an adulterer is anyone who acts too passionately towards his wife. Certainly love for someone else's wife is ugly, but so is too much love for one's own wife. The wisest course is to love one's wife, but judiciously, not emotionally. The itch of lust ought to be repressed by a swarm of reasons, nor should we be rushed heedlessly into sexual intercourse. For there is nothing so loathsome as to love your wife as if she were an adulteress. This reminds me of a story by the author Seneca, who testifies that he once knew someone, a rather distinguished man. This man, before he appeared in public, used to bind up his wife's breasts with a cloth; and she couldn't be out of his sight for a minute. They used to drink water together, and neither one of them had a drink unless it had also passed through the lips of the other one. And they did a lot of other equally foolish things, and ended up accomplishing very little, whenever the unforeseen power of his emotion overcame his good sense. In fact the source of the love was honest, but excess always brings deformity along with it. We feel that this really means only one thing: someone was out of his mind.)

There are numerous parallels to this line of thought in Milton's *Paradise Lost*. Adam's lust for Eve after the Fall suggests the excessive passion that is condemned by Caelius and others. The lack of judiciousness in Adam is epitomized by the narrator's remark "fondly overcome with Femal charm" (*PL* 9.999). In particular, Adam's attraction toward Eve, which triggers Raphael's warning about his uxoriousness, and Adam's response to Eve after she presents him with the apple, argue for an excess of love lacking in prudence:

> ... here passion first I felt,
> Commotion strange, in all enjoyments else
> Superiour and unmov'd, here onely weak
> Against the charm of Beauties powerful glance.
> Or Nature faild in mee, and left some part
> Not proof enough such Object to sustain,
> Or from my side subducting, took perhaps
> More then enough; at least on her bestow'd
> Too much of Ornament, in outward shew
> Elaborate, of inward less exact.
> (8.530–39)

> O fairest of Creation, last and best
> Of all God's Works, ...
> . . . . .
> How can I live without thee, how forgoe
> Thy sweet Converse and Love so dearly joyn'd,
> To live again in these wild Woods forlorn?
> Should God create another *Eve*, and I
> Another Rib afford, yet loss of thee
> Would never from my heart; no no, I feel
> The Link of Nature draw me: Flesh of Flesh,
> Bone of my Bone thou art, and from thy State
> Mine never shall be parted, bliss or woe.
> (9.896–97, 908–16)[3]

And Eve's own rebuke to Adam recalls the possessiveness of the husband in Caelius's anecdote: "Was I t'have never parted from thy side? / As good have grown there still a liveless rib" (*PL* 9.1153–154). These passages also echo the bias of the Ovidian commentators, who (as we have seen) associate sinful love and passion with the female figure of Venus, and higher love with the male figure of Cupid.

The many entries under *mulier* or "woman" provide additional evidence of Caelius's chauvinism and fill in the mythic context of woman from which Milton drew his figure of Eve. According to the proverb, women love or hate—there is no in-between (14.14.758a). Pauline verses are cited to prove that it is good for a man *not* to possess a woman, indeed, not even to touch a woman ("Bonum est vxorem non habere: sed, Bonum est mulierem non tangere"), and that men only marry to legalize their fornication (28.13.1565d). We learn that lust or passion resides in a woman's navel (14.14.756g), that women have testicles inside their bodies (4.10.189c) and are given to prodigious lust (14.8.744a).

To focus on a more precisely mythological topic, Caelius's sections on the Muses emphasize their importance to humane letters and in schools, as an inspiring force. They can be interpreted as the spirits of the physical world (nine planets, nine Muses) (7.1.316.d–f), while some take them to be the children of heaven and earth (20.10.1107b). For Alexander Milesius (?) they represent the song of the celestial harmony—in other words, the Music of the Spheres (1107e), ". . . the heav'nly tune, which none can hear / Of human mould with gross unpurged ear" (*Arcades*, 72–73). Caelius emphasizes the gift of memory the Muses inherit from their mother Mnenosyme (10.16.529f), a gift central to the enterprise of the epic poet. They are also associated with the art of speech (26.6.1441d), essential to one whose song ". . . with no middle flight intends to soar / Above th'*Aonian* Mount, while it pursues / Things unattempted yet in Prose or Rime" (*PL* 1.14–16).

Caelius provides over 40 entries for Hercules, several for Antaeus, Phaethon and Icarus. Fortune is dealt with at length, but Occasio is barely touched upon. A few entries are devoted to the hermaphrodite, but none to the Hermathena. There is no entry for Moloch. Suffice it to say that Caelius has a wealth of information on a number of abstruse topics related to myth, not unworthy of Milton's perusal.

CAMERIARIUS

Another reference work that touches on myth is the *Comentarii Vtriusque Linguae*... (Glosses on Either Language: Basel, 1551) by the Lutheran theologian and German classicist Joachim Cameriarius (1500–1574), whom Milton refers to in his *Life of Ramus* (*YP* 8.406). Basically a treatise on Greek and Roman etymology, it contains occasional remarks on classical myth. For example, the birth of Hermaphroditus is reinterpreted as an astrological phenomenon. At the confluence of the planets, Venus and Mercury, soft men ("molles") and half-men ("semiviros") (13.20) are born, giving rise to the belief that Hermaphroditus is the son of Venus and Mercury. Venus is a celestial goddess (364.15), but she is also connected with the shamefulness of women (385.32) and divination (405.40). Fueling the controversy over antifeminism, Cameriarius (who also has many mulier entries) reports that the effeminate Scythians were called women, not as a sexual designation, but as a term to describe their weakness and to express contempt for them (12.23). There is no entry for the Muses, or any other deity not directly related to the body. Thus Antaeus, Icarus, Phaethon, Moloch and Samson are not represented. The etymology of Omphale is discussed, within the context of Hercules (351.21). In essence, Cameriarius attempts to place a discussion of body parts within an allegorical or symbolic context, taking the root meanings of Greek and Latin words as the key to successful interpretation. While he might not have agreed with the end results, Milton certainly would have approved of the method.

Starnes and Talbert devote an important chapter to Milton and Renaissance dictionaries in their indispensable *Classical Myth and Legend in Renaissance Dictionaries*;[4] unfortunately, they have overstated many of their claims and overlooked evidence of the greater importance of the mythographers. All the same, there is a great deal of material in the dictionaries, and the amount of mythological lore expanded with each new edition, gradually incorporating the emblem books, the mythographies and most of the other contemporary sources of classical mythology. In bulk, the dictionaries offer a comprehensive analysis of classical mythology, but the same information is often repeated from edition to edition; they offer little in the way of interpretation (except in the very late editions), and some very important myths that relate to love, time and death (Venus, Cupid, Saturn, Fortune, Occasion) often receive only perfunctory treatment. As Starnes and Talbert remind us, later editions of the dictionaries do incorporate a good deal of information from both Lillio Gregorio Giraldi and Conti (26, see my chap. 8), but it is just that: information, not interpretation. Like all good reference books, the dictionaries are characterized by brevity, succinctness, comprehensiveness, and accessibility. Unfortunately, the "read and run" kind of entries they usually contain were most useful to the schoolboys who formed their primary readership, or perhaps to the writer whose acquaintance with the classics was somewhat superficial. One cannot envision Milton consulting a dictionary to discover that Atropos was "One of the fatall ladies, which is feigned to breake the threade of life" or that Aphrodite was the "surname of Venus" or that Venus was the "goddesse of loue" (Cooper 1565, Onomasticon, see below). Bishop Cooper and some of the other pious lexicographers tend to suppress accounts of castration (Saturn), homosexuality (Ganymede) and promiscuity (Venus), possibly out of concern for the schoolboys who consulted their ponderous tomes.

Perhaps it would be best, before examining individual entries, to establish the order of the major Renaissance dictionaries and how Milton came into contact with them. It is the nature of reference books to be constantly revised in terms of user needs, to appear in multiple editions, to be only loosely associated with a particular author, and to be used primarily as school texts. One of the earliest Greek dictionaries, which was later translated into Latin, is attributed to one Suidas (ca. A.D. 975). It appeared in numerous editions during the Renaissance, in both Greek and Latin. The tradition of Renaissance Latin dictionaries begins with an Italian lexicographer, Ambrosio Calepino (ca. 1440–1510), whose *Dictionarium* was first published in Reggio in 1502. This, in turn, became the parent source for the multiple editions of dictionaries by the French lexicographers and printers Charles (1504–1564) and Robert (1503–1559) Stephanus (the brothers' given name was Estienne or Éstienne). These dictionaries were adapted in turn by Thomas Eliot,[5] Bishop of Winchester (ca. 1490–1546) (first edition, 1538), and many of these were coedited by Thomas Cooper (1517?–1594). Cooper became sole author after Eliot's death and continued the tradition of drawing heavily on the Stephanus dictionaries, printing his first revision of Eliot in 1538. (One major innovation, which made it much more convenient to search for mythological entries, was the publication of a separate list of proper names in Cooper's edition of 1565). The first edition of Eliot's *Thesaurus linguae latinae* issued from the press in 1548 and quickly became the standard lexicon in England. Finally, Thomas Thomas (1553–1558), who became first printer to Cambridge University, put out the first edition of his *Dictionarium Summa Fide* in 1587, literally dying in the attempt. At least thirteen other posthumous editions followed, the last being printed at Cambridge in 1644.

Charles Hoole, in his famous work, *A New Discovery of the old Art of Teaching Schoole* (London, 1660), lists Charles Stephanus's dictionary as one of the six sources that every school library should contain to assist students in glossing Ovid's *Metamorphoses*.[6] Since copies of the Stephanus dictionary were available in the library at Christ's College, Cambridge, there can be no doubt that Milton had direct access to one or more editions of the work.[7] But with so many editions of these works extant in Milton's time, he could, as the rest of us do, use one or another dictionary depending on whether he was at school, in his study, or conversing with another scholar at his place of work. Throughout the sixteenth century these dictionaries were constantly being enlarged and were picking up more and more material from the Italian mythographers, particularly L. G. Giraldi and Natale Conti, until the entries on the Greek and Roman gods had swelled from simple definitions to essays in their own right (albeit borrowed from other compilers). As if this were not enough, Milton himself, in his declining years, set out to assemble a Renaissance dictionary on the model of Stephanus, which he did not live to complete (Parker 2.887–88).

SUIDAS

The accounts of mythological figures in the *Historica* (a Latin version of the original Greek text, alphabetized according to the Greek), which was attributed to "Suidas" (Basel, 1564),[8] combine physical description with some rudimentary symbolism. Often, however, the entries are rather perfunctory. For Aphrodite, the author discusses only Venus *calva* (the bald), *barbarta* (bearded), and *equestris* (on horseback). Omphale is simply the navel. Moloch, for example, is simply "idolum Moabitarum" or "Idol of the Moabites," and a hermaphrodite is one "qui aut utrumque sexum habet, aut turpiter & facit & patitur" (who either possesses the characteristics of both sexes or else is someone who acts basely and suffers) (listed under Hermes). The entries on Horapollo and the hieroglyphics reflect the Renaissance interest in occult wisdom. "Suidas" also associates Hermes Trismegistus or "Ter maximus" (listed under Hermes) with the "sapiens Aegyptius" or Egyptian wisdom, even going so far as to claim a connection between the "thrice great Hermes" and the doctrine of the triune God: "Ter maximus autem dictus est, quod de Trinitate locutus est, in trinitate unam esse Deitatem asserens" (Moreover, he was also called 'thrice-great,' because the Trinity is so arranged, manifesting that there is one god within the Trinity.) *Tyché* is interpreted as the Greek equivalent of Fortune, a goddess invented by the ancients to cast doubt on Divine Providence by suggesting that events occur either at random or through untraceable causes. The Muses are connected with both learning and theology. Their names are given in the main entry, but there are no individual entries. Antaeus, Icarus and Phaethon are not listed.

Of particular interest is his sketch of Samson, for he emphasizes Samson's bodily strength and his status as a Hebrew judge, but he also claims that Samson went out of his mind after he became involved with Dalila, a situation Milton presents succinctly in the line "O impotence of mind, in body strong!" (*SA* 52). And like Milton's Adam, "Qui quandiu corporis uoluptatibus imperabat, superior erat hostibus" (as long as he [Samson] kept his bodily desires in check, he kept the upper hand over his enemies.) Finally, both Milton and "Suidas" (at least in this Latin edition) describe the sequence of Samson's defeats in a series of parallel structures defined by the past participle. Suidas has Samson being ". . . ab adversarijs captus, uinctus, caecatus, in pistrinum deditus" (seized by his enemies, vanquished, blinded, put to work pounding grain.) And Milton:

> Betray'd, Captiv'd, and both my Eyes put out,
> Made of my Enemies the scorn and gaze;
> To grind in Brazen Fetters. . . .
>
> (*SA* 33–35)

Milton often incorporated such Latinate structures into his poetry, both for mnemonic and dramatic effect.

CALEPINO

Ambrogio Calepino's (1435–1511) *Lexicon*[9] or *Dictionarivm* (first ed., Venice, 1509) provides a fairly detailed account of *some* myths and a generous number of relatively precise citations from ancient Greek and Latin authors. But in some instances the information provided is perfunctory at best. Since the amount and type of information presented varies considerably from edition to edition, I shall first discuss entries from a simple Latin edition, the *Lexicon* of 1526 (the Hague), and then a polyglot edition published at Basel in 1598. This last edition also contains an onomasticon (*Onomasticon Propriorvm Nominvm*) by the great bibliographer and encyclopedist Conrad Gesner (1516–1565). Since this is part of the edition, some of Gesner's supplemental entries will also be discussed.

In the 1526 edition, Calepino repeats the dubious etymology of Aphrodite[10] rising "from the foam" (*spuma*) and therefore equating the foam of the sea with the sperm of Cronos, but he makes no attempt to relate this myth to the libidinous nature of love (as does Conti, see chap. 9) or to connect it with the physical appearance of the goddess (as does Cartari, see chap. 9). Some sites of worship are listed for individual gods, as well as perfunctory physical descriptions. Even in the sixteenth century, it was old news that Diana carried a bow and arrow, and wore laced-up hunting boots (*coturni*) but that is the only description of the chaste goddess that Calepino provides. His entry on Cupid is a subcategory of *Cupidus*, desire, which he defines as avid longing or greed (*avidus*). From this came Cupid, who was taken for a god and presented as the son of Venus by the poets. There is no entry for Moloch or for Samson. When used alone, Fortune means good fortune, otherwise evil (*mala*) fortune. There is a learned entry on the Muses tracing their names from the Greek and relating the myth to the history of music. There is no entry for Antaeus; Icarus's fall is mentioned, and the source in Ovid, but no interpretation is given. For Hercules, the 12 labors are listed, but no more. Both the Hermathena (listed under *Herma*) and the Hermaphrodite are given substantial entries. The mulier seems to stand for a mature woman, and the ideas of softness and effeminacy are derived from the word. Omphale is connected with both the queen of Lydia and the navel, but no profoundly symbolic meaning is attached to it. There is a brief section on Occasio.

In the Basel 1598 edition, Calepino has an extensive entry on Occasio, which details sources (including Cicero). He describes *Occasio* as a word and then as a goddess, taking note of its relationship to the Greek *kairos*. He also quotes a long epigram from Ausonius on Occasion. He has an equally long entry on Fortune. Like many of the other sources we have examined, he emphasizes Fortune's instability and mentions that only the imprudent will pay any attention to her. Fortune is blind and can make others blind, and is also associated with goods and riches. Many sources, both Greek and Latin, are cited. In *The History of Britain*, Milton also distinguishes between the myths of Fortune and Occasion when he cites the example of one Constantine, a common soldier, who became emperor by accident, because he had the same name as the reigning emperor (see chap. 5, n. 19). But Constantine seized the *occasion* and made the most of it, even improving his mind in the process:

> There was among them a common Souldier whose name was *Constantine*, with him on a sudden so taken they are, upon the conceit put in them of a luckiness in hisname, as without other visible merit to create him Emperor. It *fortun'd* [emphasis mine] that the man had not his name for nought; so well he knew to lay hold, and make good use of an unexpected *offer* [*opportunity*, emphasis mine]. He therefore with a wak'n'd spirit, to the extent of his *Fortune* [emphasis mine] dilating his mind, which in his mean condition before lay contracted and shrunk up, orders with good advice his military affairs. (*YP* 5.pt.1.2.124)

The blindness of Fortune and its association with riches is alluded to very effectively in *An Apology for Smectymnuus* [or *An Apology Against A Pamphlet*], where, in arguing against episcopacy, Milton refers to a Bishopric as a false gift of Fortune, congratulates himself on his own circumstances (Divine Providence "hath ever bred me up in plenty"), and points out that he doesn't need "any such kinde of *rich hopes* as this Fortune-teller dreams of" (*YP* 1.929).

Conrad Gesner

Almost all proper names in the Basel 1598 edition are relegated to Conrad Gesner's onomasticon. Gesner provides richer detail and documentation concerning pagan deities than that found in Calepino's own entries in earlier editions, but the entries vary greatly in quality. Gesner's description of Cupid as "caecus, nudus, alatus, arcitenens, volatilis" (a blind, nude, winged, bow-bearing, flying) god is admirably succinct, and the citations from classical sources marvelously comprehensive; Cupid is partly shameful and partly decent—the mixed heritage he received, respectively, from his parents Venus and Jupiter. The various sets of parents of Cupid are listed, along with the classical sources, beginning with Hesiod and concluding with Cicero. More detailed sections on Mercury and Diana are obviously indebted to Cicero's *On the Nature of the Gods* and Ovid's *Metamorphoses* (sometimes acknowledged, sometimes not), but they do not go beyond listing the alternative versions of the myth that Cicero originally supplied, or simply summarizing the descriptive sketches in Ovid.

Many of the other entries are similarly flawed. The entry on Phaethon, for example, refers to his unfortunate fall from the heavens, but offers no interpretation of the event. The sketch of Antaeus is somewhat more helpful. Gesner takes the euhemeristic view of his writings, and, using Eusebius as his source, attributes his fame as a product of his skill in the wrestling school: "Eusebius in Chronicis scribit, Antaeum, palaestricae artis fuisse doctissimum, & quorumcunque certaminum, & ob id se abritrari fictum, quòd fuerit filius Terrae, & quòd viribus restauraretur ab ea" (Eusebius wrote in his chronicles that Antaeus was very skilled in the arts of wrestling, and in all kinds of contests; this gave rise to the story that he was the son of Earth, and that it was she who restored his powers to him). The entry on Icarus is not terribly helpful, and the entry on Hermaphroditus confines itself to the details of the

Salmacis story, adding that all androgynes are called hermaphrodites, as a result of the merging of the two sexes in the stream. There is a separate entry on Androgyni; Gesner's source is Pliny, who places them in Africa and attributes both male and female sexual characteristics to the creatures. There is also a long entry on Hercules, but, once again, it is merely a noncommittal recital of his 12 labors, while the entry on Omphale simply presents contrasting accounts of why the cross-dressed Hercules was enslaved by her. There is no entry on Moloch or Samson, but there are individual entries on the nine Muses, as well as entries on Athena as the goddess of wisdom and the fount of both the liberal and the practical arts. Since Satan thought that Sin was his wisdom, there is a perverse connection between Athena and Satan's odious female offspring, the "fount" of all physical and moral evil. The entry on Aphrodite informs us once again that she comes "from the foam." There is a separate entry on Venus, which lists the genesis of the various Venuses listed in Cicero's *On the Nature of the Gods*, as well as the quip from Terence's *Eunuchus* (1.733): "Sine Cerere & Baccho friget Venus" (Without Ceres and Bacchus Venus is a-chill); see chaps. 5, 8 and 9). In sum, there are a number of detailed entries in Gesner, capsule histories of some of the pagan gods, but they are far from comprehensive.

CHARLES STEPHANUS

The famous Estienne (Stephanus) family was very active in the making of dictionaries, and there were many editions of the lexicons of these scholar-printers.[11] Typical is the edition of the *Dictionarium Historicum, Geographicum, Poeticum* (London, 1686; first edition, 1553) by Charles Stephanus. The entry on Antaeus provides only about a sentence of actual statement by Stephanus on the god, but it also includes a superb list of apposite quotations and citations from Greek and Latin authors. One, for our purposes, is central: "Mythologiam Antaei vide Nat. Com. lib. 7 cap. 1" (For the mythology of Antaeus, see Natale Conti, "Antaeus," Book 7, chapter 1). Again, in the chapter on Fortune, which follows the same citation and quotation procedure as the chapter on Antaeus, he has a citation to both Conti and Pliny: "De Fortunâ prolixe disserit N. Comes Mythol. 4.9. Plin. lib. 2. cap. 7 . . ." (Natale Conti provided an extensive discussion of Fortune in the ninth chapter of his fourth book, and Pliny in the seventh chapter of his second book. . . .) Thus the reader of Stephanus is being directed to authoritative sources for more information on Fortune, the kind of information that simply cannot be provided within the limited confines of a dictionary.

Charles Stephanus's account of Occasio provides the kind of iconographic details one finds in the emblem books, as well as a reference to the classical source of the description:

> à Poetis Dea fingitur rerum gerendarum opportunitati praesidens. Hujus simulacrum ita pingebatur, ut pennatis pedibus volubili rotae insisteret, vertigine quandam velocissimam se in orbem circumagens, priore capitis parte capillosa, posteriore glabra. Quo commento, Occasionis brevitatem & inconstantiam denotare voluerunt, quae, nisi cum primùm se offerat, arripiatur, statim è manibus elabitur, nihilque nobis remanet praeter poenitentiam, quae perpetua Occasionis fingitur esse comes. De effigie ejus Ausonius Epigrammate 12.
>
> (A goddess the poets imagined as presiding over the opportunities for doing things. The image of this one is depicted with winged feet standing on a moving wheel, whirling and circling around as swiftly as possible. The front part of her head has hair; the back part is bald. The ancients made these observations in order to indicate the brevity and inconstancy of Opportunity. For, unless we seize her and and take up her offer immediately, she suddenly slips from our hands, leaving us nothing except torment, which is imagined to be the constant companion of Opportunity. For her image, consult the twelfth epigram of Ausonius.)

On the hermaphrodite, Charles provides a rare interpretation: "Porro Salmacidis nymphae fabula, non tam ad vitium aquae, quam ad inertiam, & otium, quo vires hominum enervantur, referenda est" (Surely the fable of Salmacis should be related less to any fault in the water than to idleness and inactivity, which sap man's vital powers). Or one might recall Milton's famous denunciation of "a fugitive and cloister'd vertue, unexercis'd & unbreath'd," in *Areopagitica* (*YP* 2.515), or the "ignoble ease" and "peaceful sloath" of Belial in *Paradise Lost* (2.227), perhaps even to the Hercules-Samson figure of *Samson Agonistes*, the enervated, feminized bondslave of Dalila. The Hercules entry itself is arranged by cognomens, but Gallicus, the aged but wise Hercules, so central to *Samson Agonistes*, is not one of them. Charles's description of Venus (his source is Cicero's *On the Nature of the Gods*) emphasizes her voluptuous nature and recalls the seductiveness of postlapsarian Eve ("whose Eye darted contagious Fire," *PL* 9.1036) and Dalila: "*Venus*, ab antiquis amorum, gratiarum, pulchritudnis, deliciarum, voluptatumque omnium habita est Dea . . ." (Venus, who is for the ancients the goddess who encompassed all loves, favors, beauty, delights, and desires.) The many men named Hercules are listed by cognomens. There is no entry for mulier or uxor. The Samson entry lists the biblical account, and quotes an account of Samson from Josephus's *Jewish Antiquities* (75–79 A.D.), but does not tie it in with Dalila. Moloch is, as in Milton, the "idolum Ammonitarum, cui filios suos immolabant Israelitae" (the idol of the Ammonites, to whom the children of the Israelites were sacrificed). His entry on the Muses, which focuses on the etymology of their names, draws on Giraldi's *Syntagma de Musis* (Strassburg, 1511) (see chap. 8).

Finally, there is an uncanny similarity in the phrasing of Charles's description of Vulcan and Milton's of Mulciber. Where Milton has his craftsman god "Dropt from the Zenith like a falling Star, / On *Lemnos* th'*AEgaean* Ile . . . . ." (*PL* 1.745–46), Charles recalls that "Fuerunt qui dixerint

Vulcanum..., qui cum deformis natus esset fertur à Jove in insulam maris AEgaei Lemnum praecipitatus" (Some say that Jupiter [Milton's "angry *Jove,*" 741], because Vulcan was born deformed, cast him down to Lemnos the Aegean sea island.) At first one might be tempted to consider Stephanus as Milton's source for the Lemnos account, but closer inspection indicates that this account of Vulcan in a late edition of Stephanus is cribbed directly from Conti.

This is not the place to list the multiple borrowings of the Stephanus lexicon from Conti, but a few passages should suffice to make the point:

> Hunc, vt dictum est, quidam voluerunt subuentaneo conceptu fuisse genitum sine patre, quem tamen Homerus è patre Ioue Iunonéque matre natum esse putauit.... Fuerunt qui dixerint Vulcanum Iouis fuisse filium, qui cùm deformis natus esset, fertur à Ioue in insulam maris AEgaei Lemnum praecipitatus, vt ipse de se ipso testatur apud Homerum in primo libro Iliadis. (Conti, *Mythologiae* 2.6.146)

> (But other commentators, as we also observed earlier, claimed that Vulcan had a miraculous, fatherless birth. As far as Homer was concerned, Jupiter was his father, and his mother was Juno.... Some said that Vulcan was the son of Jupiter, and that when he was born deformed Jupiter supposedly hurled him down from heaven to the Aegean island of Lemnos. The god gives his own account of the matter in the first book of Homer's *Iliad.*)

And Charles Stephanus:

> Hunc quidam voluerunt subventaneo conceptu fuisse genitum sine patre, quem tamen Hom. è patre Jove Junoneque matre natum esse putavit. Fuerunt qui dixerint Vulcanum Jovis fuisse filium, qui cum deformis natus esset fertur à Jove in insulam maris AEgaei Lemnum praecipitatus, ut ipse de seipso testatur apud Homerum Iliad *a* [1].....

> (Some commentators claimed that Vulcan had a miraculous, fatherless birth, while others asserted that he was

Jupiter's son. And after he was born deformed, Jupiter hurled him down from heaven to the Aegean island of Lemnos. The god himself gives his own account of the matter in the first book of Homer's *Iliad*.)

The same lines from Homer are quoted, and Stephanus's entry continues word for word through an extensive quotation from Cicero, and another from Lucian. Then he omits (in whole or in part) some other quotations from classical sources, before picking up the text of Conti once again. Stephanus acknowledges the use of Conti, but does not say that he has quoted him verbatim: "Plura de Vulcano petenda sunt ex N. Comite lib. 2. cap. 6" (Much of the Vulcan material is taken from Conti, book 2, chapter 6). Hercules's disgraceful behavior with Omphale is emphasized by a quote from Tertullian. Thus Stephanus's entries on mythology borrow heavily from the great Italian mythographer; he not only quotes Conti, but also the exact excerpts from the classical authors that Conti supplies for his own readers.

ROBERT STEPHANUS

Robert Stephanus's *Thesavrvs Lingvae Latinae* (Basel, 1578; first ed., 1531) is essentially an anthology of earlier reference works. Among other authors he lists as sources are Caelius Rhodiginus (see above); Nicolai Perotti (1430–1480), author of the *Cornucopiae* (Venice, 1490), an elaborate Latin word-list; Calepino; Erasmus (perhaps the greatest of the fifteenth century philologists); Alciato, founder of the emblem book; "*& alij complures, quorum nomina, brevitatis ergò, omisimus*" (a4) (and many others, whose names, for the sake of brevity, I have left out). His dictionary also focuses on classical Latin, to the virtual exclusion of medieval usage. While his list of sources is fairly extensive, there are no acknowledged direct quotations from any one of them, although he does quote sparingly from the ancient sources. His definition of *fabula*, which emphasizes both its delightfulness and utility, not only in itself, but in the "untying" or explicating of it, encourages the reader to go beyond the surface meaning of the ancient tales. He defines *mythologia* in complementary fashion as the discourse or "reasoning out" (*ratiocinatio*) of the fables. His entries vary considerably in length; the entry on the Muses is quite extensive, and he devotes two folio columns to the origins and epithets of Venus. The entry on the *Hermathena*, the statue that combines learning (Hermes) with wisdom (Athena) includes a quotation from Cicero's letters to Atticus that stresses the commonality of Mercury (Hermes) or learning and the particular importance (for Cicero) of Minerva (Athena) or wisdom. Here one might recall Raphael's words to Adam, in which the angel recommends a proper balance of learning and wisdom:

> But Knowledge is as food, and needs no less
> Her Temperance over Appetite, to know
> In measure what the mind may well contain,
> Oppresses else with Surfet, and soon turns
> Wisdom to Folly, as Nourishment to Wind.
>
> (*PL* 7.126–30)

His account of the hermaphrodite offers no interpretation of the phenomenon, and declares that hermaphrodite and androgen are synonymous terms. Most of the interpretations are very brief, with emphasis on etymologies, usually followed by strings of epithets. Cicero, Vergil and Servius are his primary sources. There seems to be a preference for Latin rather than Greek sources, although Homer is well represented. Where Milton notes that Mulciber "... with this rebellious rout / Fell long before..." (*PL* 1.747–48), and these demons "Got them new Names, till wandring ore the Earth," (365) they tempted humankind, for Henry "Daemones dicuntur à Christianis spiritus in caelo à Deo creati, qui de caelo deiecti, partim in terrae infimo, partim in hoc aere damnati sunt" (Demons according to Christians are spirits created by God in heaven, who were thrown from heaven; some of them were damned to

the lowest part of earth, some to the earth's atmosphere.)
Fortune, we learn, was declared a goddess by the ancients,
but the numerous epithets that are applied to her indicate
that she is blind, cruel, a mistake and sad. The entry on
Occasio informs us that Occasio was a Greek male god
named *Kairos*. His description of the bald, winged deity
with forelock who stands on the perilous foundation of a
ball is obviously taken from the emblem books. His
Urania, like Milton's, is the heavenly Muse, and she is in
heaven because that is where learned men (*uiros eruditos*)
have placed her. There are no entries for Samson or Moloch. There are brief entries on Icarus and Phaethon. The
Hercules entry is the standard account of his 12 labors. The
entries on mulier, uxor, and the Muses are very general,
although he does provide individual entries for the Muses.
There is a brief reference to Omphale as the agent of
Hercules's effeminacy.

Sir Thomas Eliot

Unlike the works of Suidas, Calepino, Gesner and
Charles and Robert Stephanus, the definitions of the Latin
words in Sir Thomas Eliot's *The Dictionary* (London, 1538)
are in English. Unfortunately for the more sophisticated
reader, *The Dictionary* moves on a fairly elementary level
and provides little information about classical mythology
that is not readily available elsewhere. But the entries are
admirably succinct. It is hard to improve on the definition
of allegory (*Allegoria*) as "a figure or inuersion of wordes,
where it is in wordes one, and an other in sentence or
meanynge," unless we were to invoke Milton's own implied definition in *Il Penseroso* (120): "Where more is
meant then meets the ear." Fortuna is simply "fortune,"
and Occasio, "occasyon." The entry for Pallas (Athena) is
extremely curt: "called goddesse of battaile, and also of
wysedome." All we learn of Hercules is that he is "the
sonne of Jupiter & Alcumena," and there is no entry for

either Omphale or Moloch. Venus is "callyd goddesse of loue, sometyme lechery, also carnall appetite, alsoo beautie, by whiche a man is styred to loue." The hermaphrodite and the Hermathena get two lines each. Mulier and its derivations simply list a woman as a female who is not a virgin and the usual stereotypical remarks about effeminacy and tenderness. The Muses are connected with poetry, eloquence and music, and are simply identified as Muses in individual entries. There is a detailed entry on Icarus (although no moral is pointed), no entry on Antaeus, and Phaethon is simply the Sun. There is no entry for Omphale. These missing entries make it clear that a comprehensive treatment of the pagan divinities cannot be obtained without consulting at least several dictionaries. For it is in the nature of reference books (then as now) to add and subtract material at will.

THOMAS COOPER

Thomas Cooper's revision of Eliot's dictionary, *Bibliotheca Eliotae: Eliotis Librarie* (London, 1548), adds new entries and expands others. The extended title of Eliot's "Librarie" concludes with a swipe at both Calepino's lexicographical labors and Eliot's dependence on them: "*. . . This Dictionarie Now Newly imprinted, Anno Domini. M.D.XLV111, is augmented and inriched with aboue. xxxiij. thousande wordes and phrases, very nedefull for the knowlage of the latine tonge: besyde the descriuyng of the true significacions of wordes, whiche were greatly amisse by ouer muche folowyng of Calepine.*" Where Eliot simply identifies Orpheus as "a poete, sonne of Apollo, and Calliopes," the expanded entry on Orpheus in Cooper includes magical powers, his ability to recall the dead to life, and two versions of his own grisly death: "At the last he was slayne with lyghtnynge, or (as some write) torne in peeces by women." Milton adapts the second version of Orpheus's demise to express his contempt for the dissolute nature of Charles's court: "... that wild Rout that tore the *Thracian* Bard / In *Rhodope*,...." (*PL* 7.34–35). Orpheus could, according to Cooper, move stones with his harmony and beasts with his music. Or, as Milton puts it in the sixth Prolusion in a comic reference to his own lack of audience appeal: "... an audience consisting only of rocks and wild beasts and trees ..." (*YP* 1.269). Cooper also informs us that Orpheus, through his musical ability, "... recouered his wyfe Eurydices out of hell," and as we know from *Il Penseroso*, Orpheus "... made Hell grant what Love did seek" (108). Still, for all of his music and his fidelity to his wife Eurydice, he was exposed to shameful death and ignominious treatment of his remains, for "His goary visage down the stream was sent, / Down the swift *Hebrus* to the *Lesbian* shoar" (*Lycidas* 62–63).

Cooper has a separate entry on Hercules Gallicus (*Hercules Gallus*), giving all the details of his appearance and concluding with the interpretation:

> This ymage sygnified eloquence, whiche for the puissaunce thereof, resembled rather Hercules than Mercurie. And his age beetokened, that for the moste parte eloquence is substanciall and vehemente. That Hercules, or rather eloquence draweth men by the eares tyed to his toungue, signifieth the affinitee betweene the toungue and the eare, and theyr gladde and voluntary folowynge, signifieth with what delectacion eloquence draweth men unto hir persuasions and exhortacions.

Where Cooper (in another one of the added entries) recalls Hesiod's indictment of Pandora as the one "that Jupiter sent ... into the world to deceyue mankynde," postlapsarian Eve puts on a false face for Adam (... But to *Adam* in what sort / Shall I appeer?, *PL* 9.816–17) and the Chorus reminds Samson that "... wisest Men / Have err'd, and by bad Women been deceiv'd;" (*SA* 210–11). Ironically, Pandora, which means "hauynge all gyftes," echoes the idea of Eve as "gift" to Adam from God, Dalila as the "prize" or "gift" Samson is entitled to in return for his astonishing deeds of strength and courage. The narrator of *Paradise Lost's prelapsarian* impression of Eve as "More lovely than *Pandora*, whom the Gods / Endowd with all thir gifts...." (4.714–15) can be juxtaposed with Milton's more precise comparison of Pandora and the dubious "gift" (cf. chap. 1, n. 39) of *postlapsarian* Eve in *The Doctrine and Discipline of Divorce*:

> Whenas the doctrine of *Plato* and *Chrysippus* with their followers the *Academics* and the *Stoics*, who knew not what a consummat and most adorned *Pandora* was bestow'd upon *Adam* to be the nurse and guide of his arbitrary happinesse and perseverance, I mean his native innocence and perfection, which might have kept him from being our true *Epimetheus*. . . . [the man who opened Pandora's box] (*YP* 2.293)

Cooper also adds a useful entry on the one ". . . the *Ammonite* / Worshipt in *Rabba* . . ." (*PL* 1.396–97), Moloch, who "was an ydoll of the Ammonites, signifying in hebrue a gouernour or counsailour. . . ." His interpretation of Antaeus is firmly euhemeristic, even down to supplying his birthyear, 1588 B.C. The entry on Salmacis does not go beyond the details of the story of Hermaphroditus's fusion of sexual characteristics. For the most part he presents the reader with highly abbreviated accounts of the pagan divinities, which are not particularly significant.

Thomas Cooper's *Thesavrvs Lingvae Romanae & Britannicae* (London, 1565)—which is, in effect, a revision and expansion of both Eliot's *Dictionary* and Robert Stephanus's *Thesaurus Linguae Latinae*—follows Gesner's example in creating a separate onomasticon, his *Dictionarivm Historicum & Poeticum propria locorum & Personarum vocabula breuiter complectens* (An Historical and Poetical Dictionary, Briefly Covering the Proper Names of Places and Peoples). Occasio[n] appears in both parts of the dictionary. In the onomasticon, the goddess is specifically described, and is obviously modeled on Robert Stephanus's description:

> The goddesse of oportunitie, whose ymage is this deuised of poetes. She standeth on a tumblynge wheele, with wynges on hir feete, tourning hirselfe rounde very swyftly, on hir head hauyng all the heare before, & cleane balde behynde. By which imagination they signifie, that oportunitie is a thing, that soone passeth, and is cleane lost, onlesse it be presently apprehended.

Although helpful on the concept and deity of Occasio[n], he says nothing about its relation to *Kairos*.

Other entries in the onomasticon are neither comprehensive nor particularly illuminating. For Cooper, Hermaphroditus is simply "The sonne of Mercury and Venus," (shortened from the 1548 edition) while Omphale was "A mayden, whiche was queene of Lydia, whom Hercules dyd serue, and she caused him to spinne on a rocke," a repetition of the definition in the 1548 edition. There are no entries on Fortune, Samson or Moloch in the onomasticon, although there is a detailed entry on the word fortune (rather than the goddess) in the body of the dictionary. In the body of the dictionary, a woman (mulier) is "a weake and effeminate person" (he lists Ulpian as his source).

THOMAS THOMAS

Thomas Thomas's *Dictionarivm Lingvae Latinae Et Anglicanae* (London, 1587) was extremely popular, mainly because of the succinctness of its entries. Thus it may be more valuable as a general dictionary of the Latin language than as an epitome of classical myth. More than any other lexicographer, Thomas borrows heavily and profitably from his predecessors, but not without some loss of significant detail. Yet there are exceptions. For example, in the entry on Venus, Thomas ignores the totally inadequate definition supplied by Cooper in the onomasticon to the 1565 edition ("goddesse of loue") and the perfunctory references to her rising from the sea supplied by the Stephanus brothers. He returns to the more provocative definition supplied by

Eliot and repeated in Cooper's 1548 edition (*Bibliotheca Eliotae: Eliotis Librarie*):

> called goddesse of loue, sometyme lechery, also carnall appetite. also beautie, by whiche a man is stered to loue. Eliot, London 1538.

> The goddesse of wanton loue: carnall lust, lechery, also singular beautie, welfauourednes, comlie countenance ... [various classical citations follow]. (Thomas Thomas, Cambridge, 1587)

But the disapproving tone and the erotic emphasis are both muted in subsequent editions:

> *The goddesse of love, beautie, and all sensuall delightes, fained of Poets to be borne of the froth of the sea.* (Thomas Thomas, Cambridge, 1596, fifth edition)

The same definition reappears in the eleventh edition (London, 1619), but in a separate index of names and places. The 1587 edition contains no entries on Hercules, Antaeus, Icarus, Phaethon, Moloch, Samson or Omphale. What entries it does have are considerably shortened from the original dictionaries from which Thomas Thomas borrows. With the exception of Omphale and Samson, all of these names are restored in the dictionary of proper names and places that appears in the eleventh edition (and other editions as well), but in abbreviated form. The entry on Antaeus may be taken as typical: "*A gyant of Italy.*"

Clearly, the dictionaries and reference books of the Renaissance provided the practical-minded poet with a wide variety of material on mythology in remarkably convenient form. Dictionaries differ in originality and depth of insight, and a careful student of myth would consult a variety of lexicons before settling on the most useful one for his purposes. We now turn to the more exclusively mythological and infinitely more detailed treatises of mythology, the mythographies.

Eight

Milton and the Mythographers

A mythography differs from a purely interpretive study of myth in that it is a compilation as well as an interpretation of classical mythology.[1] While Greek allegory and Greek mythography are as old as Greek literature itself, this chapter will focus on the Renaissance mythographers Vincenzo Cartari and Natale Conti, since, for Milton, they clearly provided the most comprehensive and conveniently accessible mythographies. After placing Cartari and Conti within this tradition, individual chapters of their respective mythographies (the *Imagini* and the *Mythologiae*) will be explored in chapter nine.

ANCIENT MYTHOGRAPHIES

Early mythographies include Hesiod's *Theogony* (ca. 750 B.C.),[2] the *Book of Fables* of Hyginus (1st c. B.C.)[3] and the *Library* of Apollodorus (fl. 2nd c. B.C.).[4] Hesiod and

Apollodorus are basically without interpretation, while Hyginus (in the *Fabulae*, Muncker 1–337) differs mainly in the amount of detail and the number of versions he provides for an individual myth. His name is also associated with the *Poeticon Astronomicon*, a work that describes the constellations, summarizes the myths associated with them, and (usually) provides an illustration. For example, Andromeda (Muncker 428–29) is depicted as being chained to two rocks and covered with stars. The commentary enumerates each star, specifies its location, and sets their total number at 20.

The fourth century Greek Palephatus is more interested in assessing and defending the truth value of the myths than in recording their narratives (*De Incredibilibus Historiis*, "On Unbelievable Events of the Past," Gale, *Opuscula* 1–28). His method is simply to point out that the conditions presented by the myth are impossible (e.g. the human and equine body of the Centaur, 3–5) and then to provide a rational (euhemeristic)[5] explanation for the fantastic account. For example, while it is impossible for Pasiphae to make love to a bull (Taurus), it *is* possible that a woman had a love affair with a man named Taurus (6–8). Similarly, Actaeon neglected his domestic responsibilities, whiling away the time by hunting; hence he was devoured as a stag by his own hunting dogs (9–10). Thus Palephatus's text suggests that there was a tradition as early as the fourth century of systematically providing the details of a myth and then attaching an explanation or justification of its details. While the Son in *Paradise Regained* remarks that the gods of the ancients are "ridiculous" (4.342), Palephatus admits that they are ridiculous (or irrational) and then attempts to rationalize the myths attached to the pagan deities (1–2).

Cornutus or Phornutus (b. A.D. 20) associates Mercury (Gale, *De Natura Deorum*, "On the Nature of the Gods," 28–35) with speech, because this is the power that renders the human being separate from and superior to the animals, a distinction and an honor that Satan perverts when he incarnates the snake and provides him with human speech.⁶ But even this speechmaking ability is false and hollow, for Satan metamorphoses the serpent's "gentle dumb expression" ". . . with Serpent Tongue / Organic, or impulse of vocal Air" (*PL* 9.527, 529–30), either by wagging the serpent's tongue or by creating sounds through vibration of the air. This tongue-wagging windbag of a serpent acts as an antitype to the dignity of human speech. He also acts like Mercury the merchant in making a clever and lucrative bargain that borders on deceit: eat the apple, and ". . . ye shall be as Gods, / Knowing both Good and Evil as they know" (*PL* 9.708–09). Like Milton's Satan, Mercury is associated with sophistry and sly speeches.

Sallustius (fl. 3rd c. A.D.), friend to the emperor Julian the Apostate, tries (in his *De Diis & Mundo*, "On the Gods and the World") to rehabilitate pagan mythology by stressing the intellectual quality of the myths (chap. 3, Gale, p. 7)⁷ and their intimate connection with philosophy. The myths are in fact divine, and as Francis Bacon will recite after him (see below), the apparent absurdity of the myths is only a covering for the truth hidden beneath:

> But why have they put in the myths stories of adultery, robbery, father-binding, and all the other absurdity? Is not that perhaps a thing worthy of admiration, done so that by means of the visible absurdity the Soul may immediately feel that the words are veils and believe the truth to be a mystery? (Murray 189)

The inaccessibility of divine truth is almost a leitmotif in Milton's major works. When Satan moves through Chaos, he finds that "Each stair mysteriously was meant, . . ." (*PL* 3.516), while he admits in *Paradise Regained* that it is much more pleasant to admire truth than to seek it and to abide by it: "Hard are the ways of truth, and rough to walk, / Smooth on the tongue discourst, pleasing to th'ear, / And tuneable as Silvan Pipe or Song" (1.478–80). The Chorus in *Samson Agonistes* is puzzled by the truth of womanly desire and compares it with Samson's riddle:

> It is not vertue, wisdom, valour, wit,
> Strength, comliness of shape, or amplest merit
> That womans love can win or long inherit;
> But what it is, hard is to say,
> Harder to hit,
> (Which way soever men refer it)
> Much like thy riddle, *Samson*, in one day
> Or seven, though one should musing sit
>
> (1010–017)

And the Son, after reminiscing about his youthful precocity and gradual understanding of his divine mission, moves, like his own people, "From shadowie Types to Truth, ..." (*PL* 12.303), confident that divine truth will ultimately be revealed to him: "And now by some strong motion I am led / Into this Wilderness, to what intent / I learn not yet, perhaps I need not know; / For what concerns my knowledge God reveals" (*PR* 1.290–93).

Julius Maternus Firmicus (fl. 330 A.D.) writing against the pagans (*De Errore Profanarvm Religionum*, "On the Ignorance of the Unholy Religions," Commelinus 243–311) summarizes and explains a number of classical myths. For example, the sacred mysteries of the Egyptians are based on the "principle" of incest, between Isis and her brother Osiris. Typhon, the husband, kills Osiris and scatters his limbs all over the Nile. Rejected by Isis, he seeks out Anubis, a dog-headed god who took his shape from the torn limbs of the body of Osiris (244–45). As we have seen, the narrator of *Paradise Lost* introduces these same degraded Egyptian gods with undisguised contempt:

> ... After these appear'd
> A crew who under Names of old Renown,
> *Osiris, Isis, Orus* [son of Isis and Osiris] and thir Train
> With monstrous shapes and sorceries abus'd
> Fanatic *Egypt* and her Priests, to seek
> Thir wandring Gods disguis'd in brutish forms
> Rather then human.
>
> (1.476–82)

Following his attack on the gods of the Egyptians, Firmicus extends the same hostile treatment to the gods of the Assyrians, Phrygians, Persians and other ancient peoples. Thus, while Firmicus is a mythographer and was treated as such in the Renaissance—hence his appearance in a collection entitled *Mythologici Latini* (The Latin Mythologists)—his spirit is with the church fathers, who were forced to summarize the myths they wished to excoriate.

Medieval Mythographers

While these earlier mythographies hint at the comprehensiveness and interpretive nature of the genre, the first full-blown mythography that treats the myths in a systematic way and explores their physical and moral meanings is the *Mythologiae* of Fabius Planciades Fulgentius (fl. ca. 439–533 A.D.), which appeared at the end of the fifth century. As Jean Seznec observes,

> The scholar who believed that he had recovered the secret of the lost wisdom of antiquity was in reality merely returning to the hybrid doctrine that the Fathers had inherited from the last defenders of paganism. He prided himself on walking in the footsteps of Plato, but the paths he followed had been well worn since the time of Fulgentius. (104)

Fulgentius is the first ancient we have seen who makes it a continual practice to quote from his predecessors: in his first book he quotes liberally from different Latin authors. He even composes a hymn to knowledge of the myths. Like the later mythographers, he is fond of posing alternative interpretations of the same myth: Saturn is the god of the heavens as well as the founder of a golden age in Italy, the nudity of Venus may signify either shame or the fact that the truth has nothing to hide or fear, and Mercury signifies different things under different names. Fulgentius constantly uses the etymological argument found in Renaissance criticism and works of controversy as well as in the later Italian mythographers. Finally he possesses a critical intelligence that goes beyond the scope of either Hyginus or Cornutus; for example, he writes a learned essay on the concept of *voluptaria* and both praises and damns the idea and its applications to Venus.[8] Similarly (as we've already noticed) Milton praises sexual desire and love in the unfallen Adam and Eve, but condemns their voluptuous behavior after the Fall, where they practice a sexuality tainted by lust.

Albricus Philosophus or Albericus of London, who was reputed to have been a twelfth century Englishman (one Alexander Neckam, 1157–1217), anticipates by several centuries the iconographical approach to the myths, as practiced by Georgius Pictor and Vincenzo Cartari. Like Cartari, everything he says about the pagan deities (in his *Allegoricae poeticae*) is based on what they are supposed to have looked like. For example, Mercury's staff represents both eloquence and the power of inducing sleep, while the wallet he carries marks him as the god of both business and thievery (Commelinus 315–16), an ancient identification of bargaining and stealing we have already observed (see chap. 4). Mercury's association with the hermaphrodite[9] is also hinted at by the caduceus, the snake-encircled staff that denotes ambiguous sexuality, as well as eloquence and the hypnotic powers of sleep. Milton's Comus, whose father is the effeminate transvestite Bacchus, deceives the Lady through his eloquence, and while he does not put her to sleep, he does immobilize her with his wand and reduce her to the condition of an asexual statue:

> *Spirit.* What, have you let the false enchanter scape?
> O ye mistook, ye should have snatcht his wand
> And bound him fast; without his rod revers't
> And backward mutters of dissevering power,
> We cannot free the Lady that sits heer
> In stony fetters fixt and motionless
>
> (*Comus* 814–19[10])

Fulgentius himself was honored by a fourteenth century commentary on *his* commentary, the *Fulgentius Metaforalis* of Joannes Ridevallus (fl. 1330). Besides commenting on Fulgentius's observations on classical myth, Ridevallus supplements Fulgentius with commentary from the Bible, the church fathers and earlier mythographers. And, in the spirit of Albericus, he provides a point by point description of various illustrations of the gods, which accompany his text in surviving manuscripts. Thus Ridevallus follows the model of iconographical exegesis found in Albericus, and provides yet another model for Pictor and Cartari. He discusses just four gods *in extenso* as particular virtues (Juno, Memory, Pluto, Benevolence). Unfortunately, his interpretations are devoid of both reason and logic. Juno, for example, is hung in golden fetters by Jupiter because gold is precious and so is memory (90)!

The persistence of the mythographic tradition as it developed from Fulgentius (and perhaps Albericus) is attested to by the existence of a series of mythographies loosely referred to as the *Mythographi Vaticani*, because they were edited in the nineteenth century from twelfth century manuscripts in the Vatican Library.[11] These three mythographies testify to the persistence of the mythographic tradition as it developed from Fulgentius both in the recital of their sources and in their symbolic interpretations of the myths. *Mythographus III* is particularly representative of the Fulgentius tradition in its concentration on physical and moral meanings, although it does provide a historical interpretation of Saturn. *Mythographus I* and *II* are both extremely brief in their accounts of the gods, and *Mythographus II* is strikingly similar in content to *Mythographus I*. The Siren account in M*ythographus II*, for example, is almost verbatim from *Mythographus I*, and the same quotation is found in both mythographies to support an almost identical interpretation of the myth of Pan (Bode 1.42, 108).

In contrast, *Mythographus III* presents very full accounts of the gods (Pluto occupies 24 pages of the Bode edition, and Apollo, 14) and arranges them in terms of their supposed chronology, beginning with Saturn. It is much more concise than either *Mythographus I* or *Mythographus II* (they are each easily ten times its length), but it is also more detailed, both in the accounts presented and in the citation of sources. Unfortunately, as Professors Elliott and Elder have shown, attempts to form generalizations about any one of the three "Vatican" mythographers are dangerous, since the editions of Mai and Bode have actually emended much of their texts from the pages of Fulgentius and other mythographers, and the existence of only one manuscript of *Mythographus I* and a handful for *Mythographus II* vitiate any possible case for widespread influence.

The mythographic tradition really comes into its own with Boccaccio. The *Genealogiae deorum gentilium libri*, written at the request of King Hugo IV of Cyprus, occupied Boccaccio for 25 years—from the time of his first meeting with Petrarch in 1350 to the end of his life.[12] This great compendium of myth and interpretation became the model for all of the great Renaissance mythographies of Italy: the *De deis gentium* of Lilio Gregorio Giraldi (1548), the *Imagini de i dei de gli antichi* of Cartari (1556) and the *Mythologiae* of Conti (1567).[13] An overview of these four great works (combined with some brief references to the less significant efforts of Alexander ab Alexandro [Alexander of Naples], Georgius Pictor and François Pomey) should serve to explain why Cartari's *Imagini* and Conti's *Mythologiae* came to be so popular and so widely used by the literary and artistic fraternities of the English and continental Renaissance.

BOCCACCIO

Boccaccio's *De genealogia* was an immensely popular work. There were at least 27 manuscripts, ten printed editions between 1472 and 1532, at least 12 printings of

Betussi's Italian version, and a number of Spanish and French versions.[14] Oddly enough, aside from Osgood's translation of the final two books, the work has never been translated into English. In the *De genealogia* Boccaccio continued the medieval tradition of allegorical interpretation that had been codified by Dante in his *Convivio* and *Epistola con Grande*, combining this with the medieval encyclopedic tradition, the exhaustive treatment of human knowledge typified by the *Summa theologica* of Thomas Aquinas and the *Etymologiae* of Isidore of Seville. "Boccaccio makes the first attempt on a large scale to assemble, arrange, incorporate, and explain the vast accumulation of legend, and reduce it, after the manner of his times, to convenient encyclopaedic form."[15] Boccaccio employs a fourfold method of interpretation of the myths that seems to combine the qualities of medieval and Renaissance allegorical interpretation: the literal-historical, the physical or "scientific," the moral or ethical, and the anagogical, the obscure shadowing forth of the Christian mysteries.

Boccaccio combines the allegorical and encyclopedic genres in his *De genealogia* for two basic purposes: to provide the reader with a compendium of classical myth and to justify the reading of pagan literature in a Christian society. He operates on the premise of earlier allegories that great truths are hidden beneath the cortex of classical myths, and that only the superior mind can penetrate that cortex. In his dedication to King Hugo of Cyprus, Boccaccio promises to "tear the hidden significations from their tough sheathing...," to "explain the meaning which wise men had hidden under this cover of absurd tales..." (Osgood 11, 6), the kind of occultism we have noted in the Egyptological tradition (chap. 6) and which Milton appears to condemn in *Paradise Lost* 1.480 ("Fanatic Egypt and her Priests,..."). Like the earlier mythographers, Boccaccio is uncritical of his sources (for example, he cites Homer and the later commentators on the Trojan war as equal authorities) and unhistorical in his approach to the study of mythology. "Like his mediaeval predecessors, Boccaccio is content to quote at second or third hand, without mention of his immediate source" (Coulter 327).

However, Boccaccio's most serious weaknesses are his genealogical approach to the myths (which necessitates reading perhaps five to ten chapters of his book to gather all the essential facts about any one god and involves the reader in constant, boring repetition) and his almost complete ignorance of Greek (he quotes many Greek sources in Latin translations, but he is not above making etymological arguments based on another writer's knowledge of Greek). He develops his list of gods from a genealogical tree that originates with the supposed god Demogorgon.[16] References to this pseudo-God are the only real evidence we have that Milton read Boccaccio, although there are scattered references to Demogorgon in Conti, Cartari and Giraldi as well. Milton speaks of ". . . the dreaded name / Of *Demogorgon*" in the second book of *Paradise Lost* (964–65), and invokes the whole mythological tradition in introducing the god to his college audience in the first *Prolusion*: "I find it stated by the most ancient authorities on mythology that Demogorgon, the ancestor of all the gods (whom I suppose to be identical with the Chaos of the ancients), was the father of Earth, among his many children" (*YP* 1.222–23), but not to be confused with Night (*YP* 1.226). Apparently, Boccaccio's method of reconciling contradictory accounts of myths is to cite them all without distinction. In short, Boccaccio provides the reader with a random account of miscellaneous gods and the different sacrifices attributed to them, but not in a form easily referenced by the Renaissance poet or artist. Although Boccaccio's treatise was certainly available to Milton, later mythographers were much more accessible. Moreover, references to the *De Genealogia* in the emblem books, dictionaries and classical commentaries are exceedingly rare.

Alexander of Naples

A work that slips between the medieval mythography of Boccaccio and the mythographies of his sixteenth century Italian successors is the *Genialium Dierum libri sex* (first ed., Rome 1522; ed. cited, Lyon, 1532) of Alexander ab Alexandro or Alexander of Naples (d. 1523). Alexander is constantly quoted by Cartari but virtually ignored by Conti. He combines several features that appear in the later mythographers, including a fascination with divine cognomens or surnames (Giraldi),[17] the description of sacrifices (Conti) and the divine temples and statuary associated with the pagan deities (Cartari). To these varied phenomena, he attaches meanings that are either extremely trivial or tantalizingly brief, or sometimes both. Readers seeking an interpretive essay on myth are pretty much left to their own devices. Alexander does speak of the superstitions and inept, false opinions of the Egyptians, but for the most part he assembles iconographical details to form an interpretation, as in the following sketch: "In Cypro Venus barbata virili specie, & habitu muliebri: apud Tussas in Aegypto cum cornibus bubulis effingebatur" (107b) (In Cyprus Venus was imaged in a man's beard and a woman's dress; among the Tussans in Egypt with an ox's horns). A description of the different guises she takes among the Arabs, Egyptians, Athenians, etc. follows, but nary a word of interpretation. That will be supplied by Cartari, as he plucks whole descriptions out of Alexander and appropriates them as his own.

Giraldi

Giraldi's *De Deis Gentivm varia & multiplex Historia* first appeared in Basel in 1548. The second and fourth editions (1560 and 1580) were also published at Basel, the third in London in 1565, and the fifth and final edition, in the *Opera Omnia*, was published in Leyden in 1696, some

44 years after Giraldi's death.[18] Interestingly, no editions of Giraldi's *Historia* were being printed during the period when interest in mythological manuals was at its height, while the mythographies of Conti and Cartari were constantly being reprinted and reedited. Unlike any of the other major Italian mythographies, Giraldi's *Historia* was never translated into any other language; perhaps this is an ironic tribute to its appeal to scholars (including Milton), who would be perfectly comfortable with the original Latin. Its appearance in the London 1565 edition certainly suggests that it was accessible to Milton.

In contrast to Boccaccio's free and often casual allegorical interpretation of pagan mythology, Giraldi seldom expresses an independent opinion about any of the gods. He tries to avoid a formal allegorical interpretation of each god along literal, historical, ethical and physical lines.[19] Although the *Historia* does represent an advance over earlier mythographies in Giraldi's attempt to present an objective history of the gods, with a minimum of allegorical interpretation, the author frustrates the practical-minded reader by surrounding this information with near-exhaustive citations from ancient authorities (he is less full on medieval authorities and practically ignores Boccaccio) and extremely detailed, sometimes fanciful etymological derivations of the names of the gods. Typical is his entry on the bearded, masculine Venus (*Venus barbata*), which is dense with scholarly citations and etymological evidence, but which never explores the notion that Venus might represent the bisexual nature of love, the equal participation of man and woman in the sex act:

> Barbata Venus et mascula teste Macrobio dicebatur.... idque Calvi et Levini auctoritatibus comprobat et Aristophanis, qui *aphroditun,* non *aphroditén* hanc deam appellat. sed plane et Aristoteles primo Elenchorum idem adfirmat, eodem auctore Levino, ubi de soloccismo agit; hoc idem et Servius grammaticus ostendit. Iulius quoque Firmicius eadem, ut puto, ratione biformem Venerem dixisse visus est—libro tertio. quin et alios deos pari modo

aliquando a scriptoribus enunciatos videmus, hoc est mares et feminas.[20]

[Venus was called bearded and masculine, according to the evidence of Macrobius,.... He verifies this by the sound opinions of Calvus and Levinus and Aristophanes, who call this goddess *Aphroditun* not *Aphroditén*. But surely Aristotle in the first book of the *Refutations of the Sophists* maintains the same thing—the source, the same Levinus—where he is discussing the solecism. And Servius the grammarian points out the very same thing as well. Moreover, Julius Firmicus, in his third book, using (as I see it) the same reasoning, seems to have called Venus double-formed. And in fact we can see that other gods were sometimes described in the same way by writers (i.e. as male and female).]

The jagged style of this passage is typical of the *Historia*, as is the mixture of ancient (Aristophanes, Aristotle, Firmicus) and medieval (Servius, Macrobius) authorities. Some of the editions do contain lengthy, detailed indexes, but these merely refer the reader back to the ponderous, relatively indigestible material of the text. Still, Giraldi did provide the Renaissance with the first scholarly history of the gods, and he was the first compiler of myths to see a connection between local rites of devotion in pagan times and the developing history of the pagan gods. However, his reluctance to provide multiple interpretations of pagan literature rendered his work less useful to the Renaissance artist or writer in search of a theme and an approach to his subject derived from pagan mythology. The *Historia* is a forbidding book, both in size and in organizational scheme; its main usefulness in the history of mythological interpretation was to act as a source for the more accessible manuals of Cartari and Conti, as well as the Ovidian commentaries, Renaissance dictionaries, and Latin editions of Alciato.

Pictor

The mythographical treatises of Georgius Pictor (1500–1569) pick up on the iconographical emphasis of Albericus and anticipate the method, if not the success, of Cartari's *Imagini*. His *Theologia Mythologica* (Freiburg, 1532), for example, contains a section on Venus (dealing with the same *Venus barbata* discussed in the previous quote from Giraldi) that follows the iconographical method of Albericus (acknowledged in his list of sources), but also provides an interpretive section that borrows from and acknowledges the encyclopedic work of Caelius Rhodiginus (see chap. 7):

> In ueterum monumentis statuam Veneris sic formatam legimus: superior corporis pars cingulo tenus maris barbati praeferebat effigiem, mulieris autem inferior. . . . quia Venerem omnis generationis ut authorem & praesidem venerati sunt veteres, teste Coelio lib. 16. (chap. 6, fol. 16b)

> (This is what the ancient accounts tell us about the shape of Venus's likeness: the upper part of the body down to the waist was made in the image of a bearded male, while the lower part was made in a woman's image. . . . . because the ancients worshiped Venus as the creator and ruler of all generation, according to the testimony of Coelius in his sixteenth book.)

Each section of the *Theologia mythologica* discusses the name of the deity, what it looks like, and what symbolic meanings can be generated from that likeness. Moving a step beyond this dependence on appearances, Pictor's *Apotheseos* (Basel, 1558) is perhaps the first illustrated mythography, unless one includes Hyginus's *Poeticon Astronomicon* under that rubric. In this dialogue between the teacher Theophrastus and the student Evander, the student questions the teacher about the physical appearance of the gods (based on statues and pictures that are themselves the result of "paper archaeology" [McGrath]); in his response, the teacher explains the symbolic implications of these divine images. Despite the new format, it is not surprising that the textual commentary on the pictures is cribbed from the earlier *Theologia mythologica*, which was itself derived from Albericus, Caelius, Palaephatus, Cornutus, Martianus, etc.[21]

POMEY

This catechetical mode was employed in still another mythography, François Pomey's *Pantheum Mythicum* (Lyon, 1659), itself heavily indebted to Boccaccio's *Genealogy*, Giraldi's *Historia* and Conti's *Mythologiae*, as Pomey himself freely acknowledges in his preface to the reader. Here the student is Paleophilus ("Love of Ancient Things") and the master teacher Mystagogus ("Master of Occult Knowledge"). It too concentrates on the physical attributes of the gods and the meanings that can be derived from them. The ambivalent character of Milton's Eve, first (prelapsarian) as loving and then (postlapsarian) as lustful is caught in Pomey's chapter on Venus (12). Although her name is attached to many shameful acts and perverted loves, she is still one of the greatest of all the goddesses (12.5.6).

CARTARI

Cartari's *Imagini*[22] saw at least 14 Italian editions from 1556 to 1674, four Latin editions, three French, one German, and an abridged English paraphrase falsely presented as an original work by Richard Linche (*The Fountaine of Ancient Fiction*, 1599). (Milton, of course, would have had no difficulty reading the Italian original). Substantive revisions were made in the 1571 editions,[23] which contain a preface by the author indicating his active hand in supervising the changes in the text. Of almost equal importance, this is the first systematically illustrated edition of an Italian mythographer;[24] the work contains 85 etchings by

Bolognino Zaltieri, which reappear in most sixteenth century editions, and are reissued with additional illustrations in most of the seventeenth century editions.[25] They are also found in the Padua 1616 and 1637 editions of Conti's *Mythologiae* (also by Zaltieri), which has caused some confusion for modern critics who have assumed that the outlandish gods presented in the illustrations actually bear some relation to Conti's text.[26]

These illustrations are, however, linked very closely with Cartari's text, for while Giraldi elects to be a historian of the gods, Cartari limits himself almost entirely to a moral interpretation in the pictorial tradition. Francesco Marcolini, in the preface to the first edition of 1556, notes that the book was meant to be useful to sculptors and artists as well as poets (A3–A3^v), and Cartari is indeed the first modern writer to attempt to explain the meanings of ancient works of art.[27]

The *Imagini* deals almost exclusively with the artifacts of the pagan gods; after a few generalizations in his opening chapters on religion as the principal distinction between man and beast, Cartari gets down to the serious business of summarizing the different ways ancient peoples depicted the gods, and of explaining the appearance of individual gods in paintings, statues and (occasionally) coins. The meanings conveyed by the artifacts are primarily moral, but Cartari's method does not encourage innovation or comprehensive coverage of even the moral allegory. Unlike his contemporary Conti, Cartari seldom pauses to reflect on the details of a myth or to assign a coherent set of meanings to the events of the narrative. Like the *Historia* of Giraldi, his work is thoroughly indexed (particularly in the later editions), and subdivisions of the chapters on individual gods are indicated in the margins. His coverage of source material is much less comprehensive than Giraldi's; in fact, Cartari is derivative of both Boccaccio and Giraldi but Giraldi is his major source for classical references. The *Imagini* was obviously meant to appeal to painters and sculptors, but it also proved valuable to writers working with the hybrid form of the masque, including Ben Jonson and Samuel Daniel. To some extent, the emphasis on the pictorial restricts the use of the *Imagini*, but it nonetheless proved more useful to the creative artist of the Renaissance than the minute historical observations of Giraldi.

Conti

Over 30 editions of Conti's *Mythologiae* are extant in the original Latin, and there are several editions of the French translation (first published in 1600 and followed by editions in 1604, 1607, 1611 and 1612) by Jean de Montylard (1530–1610?).[28] An error traceable to eighteenth century bibliographies created a ghost edition (Venice, 1551), which gave the impression that the *editio princeps* of the *Mythologiae* preceded that of Cartari's *Imagini* by five years. This created a second impression that Cartari was influenced by Conti, while in fact the reverse is true. Thus Milton scholars have focused on the *Mythologiae* and have almost totally neglected the *Imagini*. This is not the place to trace Conti's use of Cartari, but rather to remind ourselves that both Cartari and Conti contributed extensively to Milton's grasp of the mythological tradition. Conti was used as a schooltext in England; Cartari was not. Conti wrote in Latin, rendering his work accessible to all Renaissance humanists. But Milton's Italian was superb, so Cartari's Italian text would have been as readable to him as Conti's smooth Latin. Then again, Cartari was translated into both French and Latin as early as 1581.[29] But there are, as will be demonstrated, some features of the *Mythologiae* that are lacking in the *Imagini*.

Of the four mythographies, the *Mythologiae* is the one most obviously structured for the convenience of its readers. The introductory chapters outline Conti's philosophy of myth and his intention to supply physical, moral and historical interpretations of the myths; he also supplies the reader with a brief history of polytheism and of the sacrifices that the ancients offered to the pagan deities. The contents of books 2 through 9 can only be described as the christianization of myth: each book begins with a statement of its contents, usually explaining how the pagan gods anticipate and reaffirm the Christian faith, e.g. book 2, *De uno rerum omnium principio & autore Deo* (On the One God, the Originator and Creator of all Things); book 8, *Quàm sapienter Deorum multitudo antiquorum ad unum Deum referatur* (How to Make Sensible Connections Between the Many Ancient Gods and the One God); and book 9, *Quàm sapienter religionem, & sacerdotum honores, & inferorum locum introduxerint antiqui* (How Wise the Ancients Were to Introduce Us to Religion, Priestly Honors and the Underworld Kingdom). The tenth and final book is an epitome of the preceding nine books; the introduction sums up the contents of book 1, and all of the information about the principal deities discussed in books 2 through 9 is summarized in brief paragraphs followed by capsule statements of their symbolic meanings, as in the headings "Jove Physice," "Jove Ethice," etc. Most editions are equipped with a list of sources and at least one subject index.

Within the lengthy chapters of books 2 through 9, a very clear transition is made between the discussion of the essential information about the myth and the allegorical interpretations that the myth allows. Although Conti provides a threefold interpretation for almost all of the myths, he clearly emphasizes the moral or ethical meaning. At all times he adopts the persona of the moral philosopher weighing the potential value of each myth for the Renaissance Christian, separating the essential from the nonessential, and providing an implied rule of conduct for the "vir bonus." Thus his work is no mere anthology of myth and symbol; it is also a manual of behavior, squarely in the courtesy book tradition, and in some ways more immediately useful than *Il Libro del Cortegiano* (The Book of the Courtier) of Baldassare Castiglione (1478–1529).[30] For example, Conti places great emphasis on such subjects as the relationship of ruler and ruled, corruption in government, the duties of magistrates, the counselors that surround the king, antimilitarism and the keeping of state secrets.

Finally, Conti is the most lucid stylist of the four Italian mythographers (although comparisons break down with Cartari's vernacular text). His oratorical flourishes of statement, shifts from long to short sentences, constant interplay of statement and counterstatement, and decided preference for the periodic sentence all mark him as a disciple of Cicero. His Latin is clear, and his rhythmic and formal rhetoric confers a sense of dignity on his subject matter; making his work more accessible to the Renaissance artist whose own knowledge of Latin was something less than scholarly.

Natale Conti was both popular and influential during the English Renaissance; his *Mythologiae* appeared early enough (1567) to influence Spenser's *Shepheardes Calender* and late enough (1653) to form part of Milton's intellectual milieu as he prepared to compose the first books of *Paradise Lost*. Thomas W. Baldwin (1.421–22, 396) and J. W. Adamson (157–58) point out that Conti's *Mythologiae* was used as a textbook in an English school in the seventeenth century; copies of the work were to be found in the library of James I and the libraries of Spenser's alma mater, the Merchant Taylor's school, as well as Milton's Christ's college at Cambridge (Starnes and Talbert 25). John Florio (in his translation of Traiano Boacalini) makes specific reference to Conti and Apollo.[31] Henry Reynolds, who regards Conti as the greatest of the mythographers, makes frequent references to him in his *Mythomystes*,[32] as do John Jones in his translation of Ovid's *Invective Against Ibis* (Oxford, 1667) and Chapman in the glosses to his poetry.[33] Robert Burton cites Conti on the abstruse subject of love melancholy: "These above-named remedies have happily as much power as that bath of Aix, or Venus's enchanted girdle, in which saith Natalis Comes Love-toys and dalliance, pleasantness, sweetness, persuasion, subtilities, gentle speeches, and all witchcraft to enforce love, was contained" (Dell and Jordan-Smith 2.721). Both the encyclopedic Sir Thomas Browne and the popular Thomas Nashe refer to him as an authority on mythology and ancient customs: "And besides what you find in Natalis Comes, concerning Acharnania, the exiccation of meeres and fennes seems to have been no unknowne thing in Greece."[34] "*Natalis Comes* [Conti], if he were above ground, would be sworne upon it" (McKerrow 3.185). More significantly for our purposes, Carlo Diodati refers John Milton to Conti as the primary reference to a version of the Venus myth: ". . . I say that the birth of Venus from the sea is very well known, as amply indicated by Natalis Comes' *Mythology*,. . . ." (*YP* 2.771). Ben Jonson cites some passages directly from Conti in the notes to his masques,[35] and John Marston, no mean cribber of Conti himself, turns on his benefactor and reduces him to the status of a handy reference book:

> O darknes palpable! Egipts black night!
> My wit is stricken blind, hath lost his sight.
> My shins are broke, with groping for some sence
> To know to what his words haue reference.
> Certes (*sunt*) but (*nonvidentur*) that I know.
> Reach me some Poets Index that will show.
> *Imagines Deorum*, Booke of Epithites,[36]
> *Natalis Comes*, thou I know recites,
> And mak'st Anatomie of Poesie.
> ("Certain Satyres," II, p. 72)

Marston's explicit reference to Conti (and the Latin translation of Cartari by Antoine Du Verdier—the *Imagines Deorum*) in this passage was taken by Seznec and others as positive proof of Conti's and Cartari's influence on Renaissance literature. More recently, John Steadman[37] has maintained that it is very difficult to prove such a direct influence on Renaissance literature, and that specific use of the mythographers can be demonstrated only among such learned poets as Ben Jonson and George Chapman.

However, Steadman (in my view) does not take full account of the overwhelming evidence that Edmund Spenser consulted Conti at every stage in his composition of *The Faerie Queene*,[38] that John Marston himself uses the *Mythologiae* as his primary reference book,[39] that Conti makes otherwise inaccessible Greek texts available in his own fluent Latin verse (or where appropriate, prose) translations, that perhaps one third of the text of the *Mythologiae* is composed of Greek and Latin quotations, and that Conti himself is quoted extensively by rival sources of mythographical interpretation. In the Padua 1621 edition of Alciato's *Emblemata*, for example, Conti is used as a gloss on the emblems, and many editions of Renaissance dictionaries cite Conti as the major source for their definitions and explications of mythological figures. Moreover, George Sabinus, in creating his own mythological manual (Cambridge, 1584), takes Conti as his point of departure, as does François Pomey.[40]

Even though Steadman is skeptical about the possibility of ascertaining the mythographers' "influence" in specific contexts, he provides the most lucid summary of their importance to Renaissance literature. His remarks, however, apply more to Conti's *Mythologiae* and Cartari's *Imagini* than to other mythographical treatises:

> First, they constitute possible sources for classical allusions or quotations that Renaissance authors conceivably encountered in the classics themselves but which they might, with equal or greater probability, have encountered in contemporary reference works. Secondly, in selecting and combining classical allusions on particular themes, these reference books encroached on the poet's own domain. They usurped, to a degree, the eclectic and synthetic prerogatives of the poetic imagination. (In some instances, Renaissance poets have been praised for achieving a synthesis that they probably owed to mythographers or lexicographers). Thirdly, by moralizing and allegorizing classical motifs, these works further aided the poet or artist by suggesting the interpretation or application he might appropriately

give them; here again they provided the spadework for the creative imagination. Finally, these reference works helped to create or diffuse a common stock of ideas and symbols that the poet or painter might share with his audience. (*Nature into Myth* 55)

English Mythographers

A word, but no more than a word, needs to be said about the "English" mythographers. Most are plainly derivative of the Italian mythographers, and their only virtue is that they made the parings of their masters available to those who knew no language but English. For Milton, they would have been decidedly redundant.

Steven Batman

Some follow the model of Cartari rather than Conti, like Stephen Batman's (d. 1584) *Golden Booke of the Leaden Goddes* (London, 1577), which provides a rather lurid physical description of Jupiter, complete with three eyes and no ears. Each physical detail is mentioned and interpreted, including his full breasts (he nourishes us all) and his feet that tread on the Giants (overcoming Titan and the rest). His lightning bolt represents his power, his eagle the soul (f. 1). The representation of the upper and lower air as, respectively, Jupiter and Juno (f. 1–2), is taken directly from Conti (2.1.4). his extensive list of sources, it should be noted, does not include either Cartari or Conti. The brief sketches he provides of selected deities are no more extensive than the snippets provided by Albricus or the fables of Hyginus.

Samuel Daniel

Samuel Daniel's *The Vision Of the 12 Goddesses* (London, 1604; rpt. Evans) is not only derivative of the mythographers, but Daniel goes out of his way to disassociate himself and his work from them. For him, the "mythologers" have given the myths a multiplicity of meanings that serve only to confuse the reader, for they are needlessly abstruse: "And therefore owing no homage to their [the mythographers'] intricate obseruations. . . . to take no other knowledge of them, then fitted our present purpose" (A3). As befits the masque, Daniel's mythological references are primarily pictorial, as in the description of Diana: "*Diana*, in a greene Mantle imbrodered with siluer halfe Moones, and a croissant of pearle on her head: presents a Bow and a Quiuer" (A5). Daniel is also aware of the hieroglyphic tradition (a tradition, as we have seen, that is sometimes viewed as the source of the emblematic tradition), which he interprets as the *selection* and imaging of a single meaning of the myth from among many possibilities:

> And though these Images haue oftentimes diuers significations, yet it being not our purpose to represent them, with all those curious and superfluous obseruations, we tooke them only to serue as Hierogliphicqs for our present intention, according to some one property that fitted our occasion, without obseruing other their mysticall interpretations. . . . (A4)

Abraham Fraunce

Abraham Fraunce's *The Third part of the Countesse of Pembrokes Iuychurch* (London, 1592) lifts an interpretation of Tantalus directly from Conti: "Philosophers and learned men, whilst they wholly addict themselues to contemplation, neglecting their worldly and domesticall affaires, loose sometimes their goods, sometimes their children, or wife, or otherwise" (Fraunce fol. 30a; cf. Conti 6.18). And his interpretation of Venus maintains Conti's emphasis on lust and lasciviousness: ". . . Venus is faire, bewty enticeth to lust. She is naked, loue cannot be concealed. She is borne of the sea, louers are inconstant, like the troubled waues of the sea. . . . Swans and Doues drawe her chariot; Doues are wanton, and Swans are white and musicall, both being means to procure loue and lust" (Fraunce, fol. 45a; cf. Conti 4.13).

Francis Bacon

Francis Bacon's *De Sapientia Veterum* (Of the Wisdom of the Ancients) (London, 1609; *Works* Vol. 6) proclaims in its very title its ancestry from the manuals of Cartari, Giraldi and Conti, but his main source is clearly Conti.[41] In fact, whole passages of the work consist of very close paraphrases or direct quotations from the *Mythologiae*.[42] Consider, for example, the close verbal parallels between Conti's account of the Sphinx and Bacon's:

> Haec muliebri facie ac pectore fuisse proditur, pedes & caudam habuisse leonis, pennas autem volucris. At Clearchus caput & manus puellae, corpus canis, vocem hominis, caudam draconis, leonis vngues, alas auis, illam habuisse scripsit.
>
> Haec Sphinx singulis hominibus praeteriuntibus in Phyceo colle residens obscura sanè aenigmata proponebat, quae capiebat à Musis atque quicunque illa soluere nequiuisset, is vnguibus Sphingis laniabatur.... Significari hominis senescentis naturam per haec pronuncuiauit OEdipus, qui cùm baculo indiget vt susteniatur, aut cùm infans quatuor pedibus incedit, manibusque, vtitur pro pedibus, tunc maximè est inualidus. (Conti 9.18.1018–019)

> (The Sphinx had the breast and face of a woman, the feet and tail of a lion, and the wings of a bird. However, according to Clearchus, she had the head and hands of a girl, the body of a dog, the voice of a man, the tail of a dragon, and the wings of a bird.
>
> The Sphinx, having nothing to do as she lay on the Phycean hill, used to question each man that passed by with a puzzling riddle she had stolen from the Muses. If the man could not answer, she tore him to pieces with her claws.... Oedipus solved it by explaining the effects of age on man; who then needs to support himself with a staff; and as an infant, when he walks on all fours and uses his hands for feet, he is very weak indeed.)

Milton and the Mythographers 221

... facie et voce virginis; pennis volucris; unguibus gryphi: jugum autem montis in agro Thebano tenebat, et vias obsidebat; mos autem ei erat, viatores et insidiis invadere ac comprehendere, quibus in potestatem redactis, aenigmata quaedam obscura et perplexa proponebat, quae a Musis praebita et accepta putabantur. Ea si solvere et interpretari miseri captivi non possent, haesitantes et confusos in illis, magna saevitia dilaniabat.... Ille praesenti animo respondit, illud in Hominem competere, qui sub ipsum partum et infantiam quadrupes provolvitur, et vix repere tentat; nec ita multo post erectus et bipes incedit; in senectute autem baculo innititur et se sustenat, ut tanquam tripes videatur; extrema autem aetate decrepitus senex, labantibus nervis, quadrupes decumbit, et lecto affigitur. (Bacon, chap. 28, 677–78)

(She had the face and voice of a virgin, the wings of a bird, the claws of a griffin. She dwelt on the ridge of a mountain near Thebes and infested the roads, lying in ambush for travellers, whom she would suddenly attack and lay hold of; and when she had mastered them, she propounded to them certain dark and perplexed riddles, which she was thought to have obtained from the Muses. And if the wretched captives could not at once solve and interpret the same, ... she cruelly tore them to pieces.... Oedipus.... answered readily that it was man; who at his birth and during his infancy sprawls on all four, hardly attempting to creep; in a little while walks upright on two feet; in later years leans on a walking-stick and so goes as it were on three; and at last in extreme age and decreptitude, his sinews all failing, sinks into a quadruped again, and keeps his bed.) (755–56)

Although Bacon ultimately refers all of the pagan myths to a "physical" or "scientific" meaning, his approach is conventional in the extreme. We learn that "ut non paucis antiquorum poëtarum fabulis mysterium et allegoriam ... subesse ..." ("Praefatio," 626) (beneath no small number of the fables of the ancient poets there lay from the very beginning a mystery and an allegory) (696), and that "Habemus etiam et aliud sensus occulti et involuti signum non parvum, quod nonnullae ex fabulis tam absurdae narratione ipsa et insulsae inveniantur, ut parabolam etiam ex longinquo ostentent, et veluti clament" ("Praefatio," 626) (there is yet another sign, and one of no small value, that these fables contain a hidden and involved meaning; which is, that some of them are so absurd and stupid upon the face of the narrative taken by itself, that they may be said to give notice from afar and cry out that there is a parable below) (697). And in a passage reminiscent of the Christianizing allegories of the *Ovide Moralisé* and the church fathers, he even hints at a connection between pagan myth and Christian truth:

> quae ad Christianae fidei mysteria miro consensu innuant; ante omnnia navigatio illa Herculis in urceo ad liberandum Prometheum, imaginem Dei Verbi, in carne tanquam fragili vasculo ad redemptionem generis humani properantis, prae se ferre videtur. Verum nos omnem in hoc genere licentiam nobis ipsi interdicimus, ne forte igne extraneo ad altare Domini utamur. (chap. 26, 676)
>
> (It is true that there are not a few things beneath which have a wonderful correspondency with the mysteries of the Christian faith. The voyage of Hercules especially, sailing in a pitcher to set Prometheus free [also in Cartari and Conti], seems to present an image of God the Word hastening in the frail vessel of the flesh to redeem the human race. But I purposely refrain myself from all license of speculation in this kind, lest peradventure I bring strange fire to the altar of the Lord.) (753)

Bacon's sketch of the dangerously gift-giving Pandora[43] may recall God's dubious gift of Eve to Adam, and the libidinous nature of that gift: "et tamen recte positum, per Pandoram significari Voluptatem et Libidinem..." (chap. 26, 674) (Pandora has been generally and rightly understood to mean pleasure and sensual appetite...) (751). And, perhaps recalling Conti's account of the smoky Vulcan (2.6.159–60), he is contemptuous of the alchemists' vain efforts to turn base metals into gold,[44] "et magis insulse Chymici ludos et delicias poëtarum in corporum

transformationibus ad fornacis experimenta transtulerunt")
(Bacon, "Praefatio," 625) ". . . (and that the Alchemists more
absurdly still have discovered in the pleasant and sportive
fictions of the transformation of bodies, allusion to experiments of the furnace) (695). This is a labor that Milton (as
we have seen) transfers to the bowels of hell:. "This Desart
soil / Wants not her hidden lustre, Gemms and Gold; / Nor
want we skill or Art, from whence to raise / Magnificence;
and what can Heav'n shew more?" (Mammon, *PL* 2.270–
73). Bacon clothes modern science in the fabric of ancient
mythology, but he cannot fully resist the influence of centuries of mystical and occult interpretation.

Henry Reynolds

Henry Reynolds's *Mythomystes* (London, 1632) treats, as
its title indicates, the "mysteries" of classical mythology
and poetry. He does not discuss or allegorize the details
of individual myths.[45] Reynolds views modern writers as
catering to "the vnworthy vulgar" and being subject "to
the rape and spoile of euery illiterate reader" (155), and he
traces the occultism of ancient poets back to a now familiar source—the Egyptians:

> Let such then as are to learne whither to conceale their
> knowledges was the intent and studied purpose of the
> Auncient Poets all, and most of the aunctient Philosophers
> also; let such, I say, know that, when in the worlds youth
> & capabler estate, those old wise *AEgyptian* Priests be-
> ganne to search out the Misteries of Nature (which was
> at first the whole worlds only diuinity), they deuized, to
> the end to retaine among themselues what they had found,
> lest it should be abused and vilefied by being deliuered
> to the vulgar, certaine marks and characters of things,
> vnder which all the precepts of their wisdome were con-
> tained; which markes they called *Hieroglyphicks* or sacred
> grauings. (156)

Reynolds also repeats the oft-told (and erroneous) tale of
the transmission of knowledge from Egyptian to Greek to

Latin: "This learning of the *AEgyptians* (thus concealed by them, as I haue shewed) being transferred from them to the *Greekes*, was by them from hand to hand deliuered still in fabulous riddles among them, and thence downe to the *Latines*" (159). His remarks are hardly consistent with the narrator of *Paradise Lost*'s contemptuous dismissal of "Fanatic *Egypt* and her Priests" (*PL* 1.480), but they certainly represent of the occult tradition (including numerology and alchemy—cf. Reynolds 159, 170) that Milton inherited, and the widespread assumption that Hebrew learning preceded and surpassed that of all other nations.

Like Bacon, whose title Reynolds echoes (". . . the precious treasure of that wisdome of the Auncients," 177), he sees the myths as reflecting "the mysteries and hidden properties of Nature" (162). In fact, he seems to have adopted Bacon's interpretation of the wrestling contest between Pan and Cupid as an allegory of Love and Chaos, which ultimately descends from Conti:

> Dicunt illum fuisse cum Cupidine colluctatum, & ab eo victum, quia, vt diximus, amor & litigium principium fuisse rerum naturalium putata sunt. Amor enim procreandi materiam excitat, & in omnes formas ad generationem effingit, quae ita dicitur ab opifice superata dum cum illo colluctatur. (Conti 5.6.460)

> (They say that Pan wrestled with Cupid and was beaten by him, because, as we have already said, Love and Strife were supposed to be essential principles of Nature. In fact Love stimulates the substance for generation, and shapes it into all the different forms of creation, which is thus supposed to be overcome by its craftsman while it is struggling with him.)

> Quod vero attinet ad audaciam Panis, et pugnam per provocationem cum Cupidine; id eo spectat, quia materia non caret inclinatione et appetitu ad dissolutionem mundi et redivicationem in illud Chaos antiquum, nisi praevalida rerum concordia (per Amorem sive Cupidinem significata) malitia et impetus ejus cohiberetur et in ordinem compelleretur. (Bacon chap. 6, 639)

(With regard to the audacity of Pan in challenging Cupid to fight, it refers to this,—that matter is not without a certain inclination and appetite to dissolve the world and fall back into the ancient chaos; but that the overswaying concord of things (which is represented by Cupid or Love) restrains its will and effort in that direction and reduces it to order.) (712–13)

Whenas if they [scholars and writers] could but from that poore step learne the way to get a little higher vp the right scale of Nature, and really indeed accord and make a firme peace and agreement betweene all the discordant Elements, and (as the Fable of *Cupids* wrassle with *Pan* and ouercomming him teaches them the beginning of all Natures productions are loue and strife) indeauour to irritate, also, and force this *Pan*, or Simple Matter of things, to his fit procreatiue ability, by an industrious and wise strife and colluctation with him; then they might perhaps do somewhat in Philosophy not vnworth the talking of.... (Reynolds 173).

Thus Reynolds presents timeworn ideas in English garb without directly referencing his sources and without applying them to particular myths. He is a mythographer with few myths, a firm but somewhat shrill voice raised in favor of the past and against *any* kind of change.

Lord Herbert of Cherbury

Lord Herbert of Cherbury's (1583–1648) *De Religione Gentilium* first appeared in 1663 (Amsterdam) and was translated into English as *The Antient Religion of the Gentiles* (more correctly "Foreigners") by William Lewis in 1705 (London). Ostensibly a deistic treatise on the gods that attempts to demonstrate that all religions observe some essential truths in common, *The Ancient Religion of the Gentiles* is really a compilation of traditional materials with a slightly different slant. We are familiar by now with the ideas that "... almost all Religion and Superstition came from the East..." (13), that the common people are "ignorant and credulous" (14), that there are a huge number of pagan gods (184), that Chronos [Time] "like a Scyckle cuts down all things living" (188), that there is both a celestial (Urania) and a terrestrial Venus (215), and that Venus is the goddess of generation, pleasure and beauty. Herbert refers to other "mythologists," but not by name. He follows Conti in tracing the genesis of the pagan gods through Cicero's *On the Nature of the Gods*, and it is likely that he read Cicero as filtered through the *Mythologiae*.

Alexander Ross

A more pretentious but no less superficial mythography is Alexander Ross's *Mystagogus Poeticus* (London, 1647). His source list is limited to classical writers, but he is clearly dependent on Pictor, Cartari, Conti and other mythographers. For example, he divides each "god" section into a description followed by a second section entitled "The Interpreter" (which covers both the moral and the allegorical meanings of the god), a method borrowed directly from Pictor. Following both Pictor and Cartari, his method is also primarily pictorial. The chariot of Diana is borne by both black and white horses to symbolize the brightness and darkness of the moon. Like the Moon, she is androgynous, and her worshipers exchange their sexually defined clothing during her sacrifices (men dress as women, women as men), as Conti had previously observed (3.17.263). Ross's account of Cupid as being born from an egg that represents birth from Chaos echoes both Conti's citation from Aristophanes and Bacon's appropriation from one or both of those sources: "At Aristophanes in Auib. Noctem Zephyrium ouum peperisse scribit, è quo natus sit Cupido, qui cum Chao mistus omne Deorum genus ex illo excitauerit" (But Aristophanes, in *The Birds*, wrote that Night bore an egg from Zephyrus, from which Cupid was born. When mixed with Chaos Cupid became the catalyst for the birth of the entire lineage of the gods from that egg); (Conti 4.14.403) "... nisi quod a nonnullis ovum Noctis fuisse traditur. Ipse autem ex Chao et deos et res universas progenuit" (Bacon, chap. 17, 654–55) (... some say that he [Cupid] was an egg of Night. And himself out of Chaos begot all things, the gods included) (729); "... the informed and confused egge of the *Chaos* [which produced] all the creatures..." (Ross. 70). Ross also explores the paradox of Vulcan, the slowest of the gods, entrapping the swiftest: "*Mars*, who by *Homer* is described the swiftest of all the gods, was caught in a net by limping *Vulcan*, the slowest of them all" (265). This is Conti once again: (Quòd Mars omnium Deorum fortissimus & velocissimus arte Vulcani fuerit retibus implicitus, & debilis & claudicantis & tardi Dei) (2.7.165) (The disabled, lame, and sluggish god Vulcan used his great skill to tangle Mars, the bravest and swiftest of the gods, in a net trap). Ross's euhemeristic account of Endymion, who was said to have been loved by the Moon because she revealed her scientific secrets to him, was also anticipated by Conti (4.8.338).

Like Batman, Ross (in the second [1648] and third [1653] editions of *Mystagogus Poeticus*) acknowledges only some of his sources, eliminating those closest to his work: "Who would know more of these Genealogies, let him read *Pausanias, Bocatius, Hyginus, Apollodorus, Fulgentius, Austin, Eusebius, Lactantius, Homer, Hesiod*, and the other Poets" (London 1653 Preface unsigned). All of these sources (with the exception of Fulgentius) are discussed at length in both Conti and Cartari, and one suspects that Ross is dependent on their erudition rather than his own.

In short, Milton could find hardly anything in the English mythographers, that had not been first in Cartari, Conti or any of the other popular and ubiquitous Italian mythographers. And he had no reason to seek such derivative and incomplete versions of classical myth when more complete and more sophisticated versions were readily available. These English sources testify more to the durability and usefulness of the Italian mythographers, than to any native tradition of mythography. In fact, their appearance coincides with the decline of the tradition, for by the end of the seventeenth century mythology was already being dismissed as frivolous fantasy. Milton was the last great English poet to avail himself of this tradition, and several centuries would pass before another writer, James Joyce, would attempt to contain the encyclopedic range and complexity of his ideas within an equally complex mythological framework.

NINE

Milton, Vincenzo Cartari and Natale Conti

As we have seen, the mythographies of Vincenzo Cartari and Natale Conti incorporate almost all of the characteristics of other treatises on mythology (both earlier and later in the Renaissance) and at the same time provide their own distinctive approaches to the myths: pictorial or iconographic for Cartari, ethical for Conti. For example, while Conti does not eschew the theme of metamorphosis, so prevalent in Milton's *Paradise Lost*, there is a line beyond which he cannot and will not go: ". . . nullas hominum in arbores mutatorum, aut in corpora vel sensu vel ratione carentia, afferemus interpretationes nisi quae vtiliter afferri poterunt") (1.1.2) (We will not bother with interpretations about men changed into trees or bodies devoid of sense or of reason, unless they have some demonstrable worth). Thus Conti distances himself from the Ovidian tradition, while still taking full advantage of it. In

Conti as in Milton, metamorphosis is primarily a negative feature. Again, like Milton, Conti gives Hebrew theology precedence over the Egyptian: "... quòd ante Aegyptios, primi omnium mortalium Hebraei non solum religionem, sed etiam verum Dei cultum acceperunt: & non humanis consiliis, sed diuinis praeceptis ad veram religionem fuerunt instituti" (1.7.10) (... the Hebrews, not the Egyptians, were the first ones to discover both religion and the true worship of God. Their foundation in the true religion was fixed in divine teachings, not in human counsel). And Cartari as well: "Herodoto scriue che quelli di Egitto nominarono dodeci Dei solamente da principio, e paruero imitarli i Pitagorici, perche si legge che i Greci tolsero queste cose, e le altre scienze anchora dallo Egitto...." (intro. chap., 3) (Herodotus writes that from the very beginning the Egyptians named only twelve gods and in fact it seems that the Pythagoreans followed their example, for we read that the Greeks took these things as well as other branches of knowledge from Egypt).[1]

The Pagan Pantheon

Conti also joins the church fathers and others in ridiculing the Egyptian gods, but he also cites the two crucial passages that define this absurdity, viz. Anaxandrides of Rhodes the comic poet and Juvenal (previously cited in chap. 6; cf. chap. 6, ns. 16, 17):

> I couldn't have myself allied with you,
> Our ways and customs differing as they do.
> I sacrifice to Gods, to bulls you kneel,
> Your greatest god's our greatest treat, the eel;
> You don't eat pork; it's quite my favorite meat:
> You worship *your* dog, mine I always beat.

> Who knows not, O Bithyian Volsius, what monsters demented Egypt worships? One district adores the crocodile,
> .... but it is an impious outrage to crunch leeks and

onions with the teeth. What a holy race to have such divinities springing up in their gardens!²

Cartari limits himself to the observation that there were so many statues of the gods in Rome that they had a second population of stone (intro. chap., 13). The Son's tag line about the Greeks and Romans, "Thir gods ridiculous, and themselves past shame" (*PR* 4.342) is echoed in (among other places) Conti's account of Juno. As usual, Conti not only comments on the pagan gods, but he also provides the apposite passage from classical literature:

> Haec, cùm Dii caeteri territi ob metum Gigantum in AEgyptum aufugerent, ac alii aliam formam sumpsissent, in vaccam se conuertit, vt est apud Ouid.lib. 5 mutationum: .... (Ovid *Met* 225–31; cited in Conti 2.4.137)

> (When the Giants struck fear into the hearts of the gods, they fled into Egypt; and some even changed their shapes. Juno changed herself into a cow, as Ovid says in the fifth book of his *Metamorphoses*: How even there Typhoeus, son of Earth, pursued them, and the gods hid themselves in lying shapes: "Jove thus became a ram," said she, "the lord of flocks, whence Lybian Ammon even to this day is represented with curving horns; Apollo hid in a crow's shape, Bacchus in a goat; the sister of Phoebus, in a cat, Juno in a snow-white cow, Venus in an ibis bird.")

And in Milton:

>   After these appear'd
> A crew who under Names of old Renown,
> *Osiris, Isis, Orus* and thir Train
> With monstrous shapes and sorceries abus'd
> Fanatic *Egypt* and her Priests, to seek
> Thir wandring Gods disguis'd in brutish forms
> Rather then human.
>   (*PL* 1.476–82)

And the Greeks, according to Conti (and as we have already noted in Augustine)³ had innumerable gods: "Atque infinita est prope illorum Deorum multitudo, quos Graecia postea ceremoniis, altaribus, ac templis magnificentissimis auxit" (1.7.13) (The huge number of these gods that Greece later exalted with ceremonies, altars, and magnificent temples is almost infinite) Conti goes on to say that each and every one of the nations had its own special gods.

Following the polemical tradition established by the church fathers (themselves anticipated by the scoffing Lucian, another of Conti's sources), Conti continues to wax eloquent on the absurdities of these deities:

> Haec res fecit vt iidem Graeci, qui AEgyptiorum, aliarumque nationum acceptas ab iis superstitiones deriserant, in multò maiores errores sint postea collapsi. Nam & adulteros, & latrones, & ebriosos, ac facinorosos homines, qui multo erant brutis impuriores, pro Diis coluerunt, quare cùm de Diis loquerentur, adulteria, furta, parricidia, praelia, crudelitatemque illis iniunxerunt.... (1.7.15)

> (That is why the same Greeks, who had mocked the superstitions of the Egyptians and other nations which had adopted them, later collapsed into much greater errors. The Greeks gave divine worship to adulterers, thieves, drunkards, and men so wicked that they were even more degraded than animals. And when they spoke about the gods, they linked them with adultery, stealing, parricides, greed, and cruelty: transgressions which we expect from thieves and lawless men, and befitting gods like these.)

And, further, their human weaknesses:

> Non sunt igitur antiquorum Dij, cùm plures sint, cùm coelum contentionibus sit plenum, cùm multò sint mortalibus miseriores, cùm eos & dormire dixerint pöetae, & potationibus atque conuiuiis indulgere, & Veneris stimulis mirificè exagitari. Quis enim nesciat somnum & epulas esse ob corporis debilitatem...? (1.8.17)

> (Thus the "gods" of the ancients are not gods at all because they are numerous, because heaven is filled with quarrels, because they lead much more miserable lives than mortals, because the poets even said they sleep, indulge in drinking bouts and feasts, and are even amazingly aroused by the

goads of Venus. Is there anyone who does not know that meals and sleep are necessary because of the body's weaknesses?)

Cartari, because of his pictorial bias, concentrates on the number of representations of the gods, but feels no compunction to condemn polytheism or idolatry in any direct way. Conti also seems to be following Lactantius (or perhaps Cartari) when he insists that the existence of male and female goddesses indicates that the "gods" are really men:

> Si omnes Dii sint mares, aut foeminae, & ad procreandum apti, nihilque producant, multo magis sequetur absurdum: frustra enim potest is qui nunquam vim suam exercet. quare vbi sit sexus, ibi procreare necesse sit, atque ibidem Dei natura sempiterni esse non potest. (2. Intro. chap. 76)

> (... if all the gods are male and female and all are fertile, and they still don't have any children, the situation becomes even more absurd. There's no point in having power, if you never use your strength. If creatures have gender, they're supposed to produce children, and this situation is incompatible with the concept of an eternal god.)

CHRISTIAN MYTH

Conti also takes up the knotty theological problem of the "generation" of the Son by the Father:

> Erit igitur necessariò vnus Deus, qui neque genitus erit, neque generabit ex se alium, cuius substantia ab ipso dissideat. Nam veri piique theologi Deum generare Filium tradunt, sed eiusdem substantiae: & idem immortalis existens, cùm ex nullis principiis constet, nullum fortius est temporis principium. (76–77)

> (That's why there's only one god. This god was never born, and it is simply impossible that he would beget a child who differs in any way from himself. We learn from honest, God-fearing theologians that God did generate a son, just like himself; and that son also enjoys an immortal life, since he

has no part in the principles of creation and he had no "beginning" himself.)

In *Paradise Lost,* the Son is the image or manifestation of the Father's glory, which is an essential part of His substance: "... on his right / The radiant image of his Glory sat, / His onely Son..." (3.62–64). For Conti, the Christian god has no gender at all, while the pagan Jupiter partakes of both sexes:

> Quid enim esse potest idem mas ac foemina immortalis, nisi mundi anima, quae habeat in se haec omnia producendi facultatem? nam Deus omnino sexum non habet, vt diximus, cùm sexu omni sit magis perfectus. Neque spiritus quispiam ex his Deus est, neque vis ignis, sed omnibus his superior & omnibus imperans. (2.1.106)

> (But the same one can't be both male and female, and can't be deathless, unless it's the soul of the universe, that has the power within itself to bring everything else into being. For God has no gender at all, as we have said, since his perfection transcends gender. Nor is God any life-breath, nor is he fire power; God is greater than these forces, which are all at his command.)

ALCHEMICAL MYTH

As noted in chapter six (pp. 158–62), Milton's Mammon suggests that the rebellious devils can mitigate their pain by transforming the elements that make up their being, just as they can transform their environment by digging up the gold, the "precious bane" (*PL* 1.692) that lies beneath the baser elements of hell:

> ... This Desart soil
> Wants not her hidden lustre, Gemms and Gold;
> Nor want we skill or Art, from whence to raise
> Magnificence; and what can Heav'n shew more?
> Our torments also may in length of time
> Become our Elements, these piercing Fires
> As soft as now severe, our temper chang'd

Into their temper; which must needs remove
The sensible of pain ...

(*PL* 2.270-78)

This "skill or Art" is the province of the alchemist, whom Conti roundly condemns in his chapter on Vulcan (2.6), where he refers to the "empty" craft and "sooty trickery of chemists" [i.e., alchemists]:

> Nec me praeterit illorum qui torquendis metallis per ignem student, esse opiniones nonnullas, quas suis vasculis accommodare conantur. Neque enim credibile est metallorum formas posse per artem inter se conuerti,....
> *Ars fallax, inuisa bonis, dulcedine captos*
> *Iucunde vt perimis! dementibus improba siren.*
> *Naturam superare putas te posse per ignem?*
> *Stulta, quid insanis? te longis passibus illa*
> *Deserit, ac tandem nil perficis. illa colorum*
> *Te fallit, rerum te ludit mille figuris.*
> ....
> *Mendici fiunt: semper caligine barba*
> *Squallet, & immodico turpantur pallia fumo.*
> *Et noua quarentes semper mendacia iactant,*
> *Defecisse sibi vires....* (158-60)

(I'm aware that people who get all excited about reshaping metals with fire have their own opinions about this myth, and I also know how they've tried to adapt them to the experiments they perform with their beakers. But it is inconceivable that any craft could possibly change the shapes of metals,....

Treacherous skill, hateful to good men, how pleasantly you destroy men captivated by your charm! Wicked siren of maddened men! Do you think that you can conquer nature with fire? Oh fool, why do you rave? She leaves you behind by a long mark! And in the end you accomplish nothing. She, with appearance of colors, tricks you; she makes fun of you with a thousand shapes of things......
These wretches become poor men; their beards are filthy with soot; their cloaks are defiled from an excess of smoke; seeking out new things they are always telling lies; their strength has failed.)

Conti is outraged that mere men could presume to tamper with the principles of nature, a presumption that leaves them with the sooty image of Vulcan, but with no finished product to compensate for their labors.[4] Milton's Mammon presumes to tamper with the whole creation, thinking that he can emulate God and bring light out of darkness: "As he our darkness, cannot we his Light / Imitate when we please? . . ." (*PL* 2.269–70).

ATHENA

In *Paradise Lost*, Satan, listening to his own "devilish Counsel" (2.379), bears Sin, or the product of his imagination, from his head. In Conti's *Mythologiae*, Jupiter abducts and rapes Metis, or Good Counsel. Hearing the prophecy that she will bear him a daughter, and then a son who will depose him, Jupiter devours Metis. Now he has good counsel within himself, and after experiencing a violent headache, Hephaestus or Prometheus splits his skull open with an axe and Pallas Athena, goddess of wisdom, is born. Conti interprets it thus:

> hanc vxorem Iupiter deglutiuit, cuius caput grauidum factum est, quia vis ratiocinandi sedem praecipuam habet in capite. ex ea ratiocinatione nascitur Pallas armata, quo tempore pluit auro in Rhodiorum insula: per quae significatur imbibendum esse consilium bonorum & perpendendum, vt inde nascatur sapientia quam sequitur felicitas, & defensio tutissima rerum singularum, & tranquillitas, quam sapientia tuetur in rebus humanis, cùm sapientem nemo fallere, aut imparatum vnquam inuenire possit. (2.1.111–12)

> (Jupiter devoured his wife, and developed a pregnant head, because the faculty of reasoning has its special seat in the head. And the armed Pallas was born from reasoning power, when it rained gold on the island of Rhodes. This means that we must look at and give careful consideration to good men's judgment, so that it can become a source of wisdom, followed by good fortune and very sound protection for

everyone's property. It is also the source of a sense of security that wisdom cultivates in human life, for no one deceives the wise man, or ever finds him unprepared.)

Cartari rejects Martianus Capella's misogynist view that Wisdom was born without a mother because wisdom cannot issue from a woman. He interprets Wisdom or Minerva instead as the direct product of the divine mind:

> E fu anco finto che Minerua nascesse del capo di Gioue, come scriue Pausania che ne fu un simulacro nella rocca d'Athene, hauendogliele aperto Volcano con una tagliente scure di diamante, senza il seruitio della moglie, perche la uirtù intellettiua dell'anima sta nel ceruello, e discende ella, e tutta sua cognitione dal supremo intelletto, che è Gioue, conciosia che ogni sapienza venghi da Dio, e nasca dalla bocca dello Altissimo, non da queste cose basse e terrene, mostrate per Giunone. E cosi è meglio, e piu honesto esporre questa cosa, che come l'ha esposta Martiano à dispregio delle donne, il quale perche non fu forse troppo loro amico dice, fingersi Minerua essere nata senza madre, perche le donne non hanno consiglio, ne prudenza alcuna, o forse che disse cosi per andare dietro ad Aristotele, il quale scrisse nelle sue morali, che le donne non hanno punto buon consiglio. Cui non ardisco già di oppormi, ma dico bene che molte donne à tempi nostri si mostrano cosi prudenti & accorte, che lo fanno mentire. E se non che il valor loro le fa assai note al mondo, mettendo gli nomi, porrei anco infiniti essempi del senno, e della prudenza loro, mostrando quello, che altri forse non ha voluto vedere: & è che se bene Minerua nacque senza il seruitio della femina, nacque ella però femina, e uuole perciò il douere che si confacci piu alle donne, che à gli huomini. (Minerva 358, 360)

(They also imagined that Minerva was born from the head of Jupiter, as Pausanias writes (1.24.2). He says there was an image in the Athenian fortress that showed how Vulcan had already opened up Jupiter's head with a diamond cutting axe, without any help from Jupiter's wife. This means that the intellectual virtue of the soul is located in the brain, and that virtue and all of its knowledge descends from the supreme intellect, which is Jupiter. For all wisdom comes from

God, and is born from the mouth of the most high, and not from those base and earthly things, that Juno represented.

It is better and more honorable to explain her birth this way, than to follow the explanation of Martianus, which is disparaging to women. Martianus, who was apparently not very friendly to women, says that Minerva was imagined to have been born without a mother, because women possess neither counsel nor prudence.[5] Or perhaps he said that in imitation of Aristotle, who wrote in his moral works that women don't have even a speck of good counsel.[6] Naturally I don't dare to set myself against Aristotle, but I do say that many women in our own time have shown that they are prudent and shrewd enough to make a liar out of him. And even if the world takes little note of their value, if I put down their names I could provide almost infinite examples of women's prudence and good sense, perhaps showing others something that they didn't want to see. And even if Minerva was born without a woman's help, she was still born a woman, and this suggests that wisdom should be more suitable for women than for men.)

Milton perverts the myth. Wisdom is born because Jupiter has devoured Metis or good judgment, but Sin is born of Satan's head because he has conceived her in his imagination by conspiring against God, as his "fair" daughter reminds him:

> Hast thou forgot me then, and do I seem
> Now in thine eye so foul, once deemd so fair
> In Heav'n, when at th' Assembly, and in sight
> Of all the Seraphim with thee combin'd
> In bold conspiracy against Heav'ns King,
> All on a sudden miserable pain
> May surpris'd thee, dim thine eyes, and dizzy swumm
> In darkness, while thy head flames thick and fast
> Threw forth, till on the left side op'ning wide,
> Likest to thee in shape and count'nance bright,
> Then shining heav'nly fair, a Goddess arm'd
> Out of thy head I sprung...
>
> (PL 2.747–58)

Of course, in the pagan myth Jupiter does not go on to sleep with his own daughter and bear yet another monstrosity, Death, as Milton has it. In fact, Milton seems to combine the myths of Narcissus and Minerva in his account, for Satan is enamored of Sin because she reflects his own image: "Thy self in me thy perfect image viewing / Becam'st enamour'd, and such joy thou took'st / With me in secret, that my womb conceiv'd / A growing burden..." (PL 2.764–67).

Conti may also provide a clue as to why Milton used the myth of Athena (Pallas) springing from the head of Zeus, the origin of wisdom in humankind, to depict the birth of ugly Sin from the head of Satan. In other words, why did he give a negative twist to a basically positive myth? Where Milton's Sin is ugly and fearsome, Minerva repels her enemies with the fearsome, ugly image of the Gorgon on her shield: "Neque aduersus hanc insurgere quisquam audet, cùm faciem horrendam Gorgonis gestaret in pectore, quae viperas habebat pro capillis..." (4.5.310–11) (And no one dares to raise a rebellious hand against Minerva, because she sports the terrifying face of the Gorgon upon her breast, a monster who has snakes instead of hair....) For Conti, "Ex importunis igitur vitae peruturbationibus, & è coeno tenebrarum mentis & inscitiae nascitur sapientia..." (4.5.308) (wisdom is born from life's irritating problems, from the muddy shadows of the mind, and from ignorance.) He also focuses on the absurd aspects of her birth, the splitting "headache" of Jupiter, by citing that satiric atheist, Lucian: "acerrimus derisor humanae dementiae Lucianus in dialogis Deorum Iouem parturientem introducit, & Vulcanum cum acutissima & praeualida securi, vt sibi caput diuidat..." (4.5.300) (Lucian, who was a very great mocker of human stupidity, shows Jupiter giving birth in *The Dialogues of the Gods*, and Vulcan in attendance, using a very sharp, very powerful axe to split Jupiter's head....)

Prometheus, Pandora

If Milton wished to have the birth of Pallas mirror the birth of Sin, he could have completed the parallel by representing Prometheus as Satan. For Prometheus was supposed to have shaped both man and woman (at different intervals) from clay. (Or, in an alternative myth, woman is shaped from clay by Vulcan, Milton's Mulciber—see below). Just as Satan, "familiar grown," falls in love with Sin, the product of his own imagination, and suffers eternal torment for that evil choice, so, Conti informs us, "scripsit Duris Samius, quòd ita Prometheus torqueatur, quia Palladem amauerit" (4.6.329) (Duris of Samos wrote that Prometheus was tortured like that [the eagle continually devouring his liver] because he fell in love with Pallas.) And just as Satan introduces Eve and, through Eve, Adam to the knowledge of good and evil, so "Prometheum dictum fuisse ignem ad homines è coelo detulisse, quia rerum diuinarum & philosophiae cognitionem primus omnium mortalium hominibus ostenderit" (4.6.329) (Prometheus was supposed to have been the first person to bring fire from heaven to earth, because he was the first man to reveal the secrets of theology and philosophy to the rest of humankind.) Pallas also blinded Tiresias because he saw her naked, and because wisdom blinds us to everything else, just as sin blinds Satan to all other considerations (Conti 4.5.306). Satan corrupts Eve, but Eve is created by God through Adam. Similarly, Jupiter creates Pandora[7] who, like Eve, ". . . ensnar'd / Mankind with her fair looks, to be aveng'd / On him [Prometheus] who had stole *Joves* authentic fire" (*PL* 4.717–19). Or as Conti puts it:

> Id cùm resciuisset Iupiter, Vulcano imperauit vt foeminam è luto componeret, quae cùm astutissima esset & omnibus artibus à Dijs donata, vocata fuit Pandora. Neque ante illam extitisse foemineum sexum crediderunt, vt testatur Pausanias in Atticis. Hanc fabulantur missam fuisse à Ioue ad Prometheum cum omnibus malis in vasculo inclusis: quod munus cum spreuisset Prometheus, illa ad Epimetheum

contendit, qui dempto vasculi operculo omnia mala euolare sentiens, vix vltimam & in imo residentem spem occlusit, cum qua vas illud seruauit. Cum verò Prometheus Iouis munus reiecisset, quòd insidias formidaret, dicitur à Mercurio Iouis iussu ad Caucasum montem adductus,.... At Menander suauissimus poeta meritò torqueri Prometheum inquit, non quia ignem, sed quia multo grauis malum, quia foeminam scilicet omnium humanarum calimitatum autorem, & scelestum omnino animalis genus, inuenerit. (4.6.316, 318)

(When Jupiter found what Prometheus had done [his gift of fire to humankind], he ordered Vulcan to create woman from clay, and since she was so clever and blessed with so many accomplishments by the gods, they called her Pandora. The ancients believed that there was a female sex before Pandora, as Pausanias noted in his description of Attica. They fabled that Jupiter sent her to Prometheus with every kind of misfortune locked up in a little box. When Prometheus refused that gift, she rushed right over to Epimetheus. But once he pried open the lid of that little container and realized that all of the evils of the world were flying out of the box, he barely managed to get it shut. All that was left at the bottom was hope, and he kept that along with the box. After Prometheus spurned Jupiter's gift because he didn't trust the god, Jupiter (so the story goes) ordered Mercury to bring Prometheus to mount Cacausus.... But that very elegant poet Menander claims that Prometheus deserved to be tortured for a much more serious crime than revealing fire's secret: for he created woman, the cause of all our woe, the most criminal of all beings....)

In *The Doctrine and Discipline of Divorce*, as we have seen, Milton links Epimetheus's blunder to Adam's complicity in the Fall, for Adam failed to make proper use of his "gift": "... what a consummat and most adorned *Pandora* was bestow'd upon *Adam* to be the nurse and guide of his arbitrary happinesse and perseverance, I mean his native innocence and perfection, which might have kept him from being our true *Epimetheus*" (YP 2.293).

One might also relate The Judgment of Paris to Eve, Sin and "blest *Marie*, second *Eve*" (*PL* 5.387). Where Eve represents Venus or beauty, Sin can stand for Athena, wisdom or craft, and Mary the respectability and responsibility of Juno. And while Menander "... torqueri Prometheum inquit,... quia foeminam scilicet omnium humanarum calamitatum autorem, & scelestuum omnino animalis genus, inuenerit" (4.6.318) (... claims that Prometheus deserved to be tortured... [because] he created woman, the cause of all our woe, the most criminal of all beings, ...), a case can be made for Adam's culpability in insisting upon dividing himself from his new companion, Eve.

Death, Punishment and the Fall

In the third book of the *Mythologiae*, Conti deals with the mythical torments of the dead. While these might not seem to be immediately germane to Satan's condition in *Paradise Lost*, Conti emphasizes the *psychological* horrors of hell, and Milton picks this up in Satan's soliloquies. For example, the depth of Tartarus, the deepest hole in hell, reminds us of Satan's precipitous fall into ever deeper hellish chambers:

> Qui Tartarus quòd obscurissimus sit, indicauit his versibus Homerus libro Iliadis *th* ..... [8] (Conti 3.11.229; *Iliad* 8.13–16)

> (Homer, in the eighth book of his Iliad, described deep and gloomy Tartarus as follows [Zeus threatening any god who would dare to help the Trojans]: "Or I shall take and hurl him into murky Tartarus far, far away, where there is the deepest gulf beneath the earth, the gates whereof are of iron and the threshold of bronze, as far beneath Hades as heaven is above earth")

> Which way I flie is Hell; myself am Hell;
> And in the lowest deep a lower deep

Still threatning to devour me opens wide,
To which the Hell I suffer seems a Heav'n.

(*PL* 4.75–78)

More specifically, "the Sovran voice" decrees (*PL* 6.56) their eviction to the deep hole of Chaos: "Pursuing drive them out from God and bliss, / Into thir place of punishment, the Gulf / Of *Tartarus*, which ready opens wide / His fiery *Chaos* to receave thir fall" (*PL* 6.52–55).

Conti makes the connection with Chaos even more explicitly in a citation from Hesiod:

> Hesiodus in Theogonia videtur Tartarum ex illa confusa mole, quae Chaos vocabatur, genitum esse credidisse; vt ex his licet cognoscere:..... (Conti 3.11.228; Theog. 2.116-19)

> (Hesiod seems to think that Tartarus was created from the amorphous mass of chaos, as we can infer from these verses: "Verily at the first Chaos came to be, but next wide-bosomed Earth, the ever-sure foundation of all the deathless ones who hold the peaks of snowy Olympus, and dim Tartarus in the depth of the wide-pathed Earth...")

The depth of Tartarus, so explicitly referred to in the ancient sources (Conti cites both Plato and Homer to the effect that it is "an abyss"), is reiterated by Sin as she complains of her new home in hell:

> Into this gloom of *Tartarus* profound,
> To sit in hateful Office here confin'd,
> Inhabitant of Heav'n, and heav'nlie born,
> Here in perpetual agonie and pain,
> With terrors and with clamors compasst round
> Of mine own brood, that on my bowels feed.
>
> (*PL* 2.858–63)

Other images of Satan's "fall" appear in Conti's chapter on Phaethon (6.1).[8] Because of his arrogance and foolishness, Phaethon, son of the Sun, is struck down by his own father with a thunderbolt, just as God the Father dispatches Satan to bottomless perdition. Like Satan, this child of a god usurps his father's office (driving the chariot of the sun) and is known as "ambitious Phaethon" (Lucretius, *De Rerum Natura*, l. 400; cited in Conti 6.1.554). While Satan endures the heat of burning hell, Phaethon takes his name from the Greek *phaethw*, "I burn" (Conti 6.1.555). The attempt by the created, Satan, to usurp the authority of the creator, God, is dangerous, for "Alij maluerunt per hanc fabulam demonstrauisse antiquos rerum maximarum administrationem, ac summa imperia rerum publicarum iuuenibus aut adolescentibus aut imperitis non esse concedenda" (6.1.556) (Others claimed that the ancients used this story to warn us against permitting children, or adolescents, or untrained adults to have jurisdiction over matters of critical importance.) Conti's concluding statement on Phaethon reminds us of Satan's hierarchical arguments (first after God Himself) and devastating effect on human history: "Quod attinet ad mores, deprimere nonnullorum arrogantiam per haec voluerunt, qui nihil sibi non tribuunt, nihilque se nescire propter nobilitatem arbitrantur: quae arrogantia homines plerumque trahit in magnas calamitates" (6.1.557) (As for the moral interpretation of this myth, what the ancients were after here was to crush the insolence of people who thought a great deal too much of themselves just because they were members of the nobility. This kind of arrogance can really drag men into deep trouble.)

Three ambitious rebels who come to bad ends, whose conduct bears a remarkable resemblance to Satan's, and whose doom reprises Adam's, are Ixion, Sisyphus and Tantalus (Conti 6.16–18).[9] They are all aggressors against "God" (Jupiter or the Christian god), and receive punishments that are commensurate with their offenses, and which also reflect the grim reality of Satan's own punishments and pains. Thus Ixion, who dared to attempt to seduce Juno, Jupiter's own wife—as Satan attempts to seduce God's only woman, Eve—was bound to a wheel intertwined by serpents. Jupiter substituted a cloud for his wife Juno, from which Ixion begat those freaks of nature, the Centaurs:

> Hic igitur pro tanta Iouis in se liberalitate ac munificentia, Iunoni stuprum ferre conatus est. quod cùm illa Ioui

significasset, non facilè credidit Iupiter,..... sed rem palàm oculis intueri voluit. dicitur igitur nubem in Iunonis formam coegisse, quam Ixioni obiecit, cum qua congressus Centauros.... uit è coelo ad inferos ob suam loquacitatem deiectus. hic rotae ferreae fuit alligatus, circa quam angues complures conuoluebantur. (6.16.625)

(Ixion's way of thanking Jupiter for his kind and generous treatment was to try to rape his wife Juno. But when Juno told Jupiter what was going on, he found it difficult to believe her.... He wanted to see the seduction with his own eyes. So he's supposed to have made a cloud in Juno's shape, and given it to Ixion. Then Ixion had intercourse with that phantasm and fathered the centaurs.... Then he was cast out of heaven and tossed into the underworld because he couldn't keep his mouth shut. And he was tied to an iron wheel that had snakes coiling around it.)

And just as "Satan exalted sat, by merit rais'd / To that bad eminence..." (*PL* 2.5–6), ironically occupying (simultaneously) the most prestigious and the most painful part of hell, with an unsatisfied ("insatiate," l. 8) appetite to pursue revenge, so Ixion's pain is a measure of his ingratitude for Jupiter's great gifts:

quòd tanto grauius scilicet iure optimo supplicium esset Ixionis, quàm caeterorum omnium qui apud inferos torquentur; quanto maiora huc beneficia à Deo acceperat: quoniam id praeclarè scriptum est, quòd cui plus remittitur, is plus debet. (6.16.628)

(For the very severe and fully justified penalty that Ixion endured, a penalty that was much greater than what anyone else had to suffer in the underworld, was perfectly commensurate with all the great benefits this man had received from God. For it's clearly written that the man who receives much, owes much.)

From his fruitless union with a cloud, Ixion begets the Centaurs,[10] which Milton depicts as false wisdom in *Paradise Regained*:

> ... Who therefore seeks in these
> True wisdom, finds her not, or by delusion
> Far worse, her false resemblance only meets,
> An empty cloud.
>
> (4.318–21)

Conti manages to work Ixion's experience into a complex symbol encompassing both the arrogance of ambition and the ugly progeny of glory-seekers: "Illi enim qui pro virtute gloriam ex quibusuis rebus consectantur, aut qui pro vera sapientia falsam amplectuntur, multa indecora faciant oportet: quare monstro similes Cenaturi ex nube nascuntur" (6.16.627) (Anyone who prefers glorious to virtuous deeds under any circumstances, or embraces false instead of true wisdom, is certain to do some pretty nasty things. That's what the ancients meant by begetting abominable creatures like Centaurs out of clouds.) Like the Satan of the agonizingly self-revelatory soliloquies in *Paradise Lost*, Ixion's "cùm perpetua tamen ambitione gloriáque vexaretur" (6.16.627) (pride and ambition kept him in a constant state of emotional turmoil). Quoting Plutarch on "lovers of glory," Conti focuses on the evil births generated by such base motives: "For such men, consorting with glory, which we may call an image of virtue, produce nothing that is genuine and of true lineage, but much that is bastard and monstrous, being swept along one course and now along another in their attempts to satisfy desire and passion" (Plutarch, *Agis and Cleomenes* 1; Conti 6.16.627).

In *Tetrachordon*, Milton dramatizes the torturous fate of the husband yoked to an unsatisfactory wife by comparing him to Ixion and his monstrous brood of Centaurs:

> Nay such an unbounteous giver we should make him, as in the fables *Jupiter* was to *Ixion*, giving him a *cloud* instead of *Juno*, giving him a monstrous issue by her, the breed of *Centaures* a neglected and unlov'd race, the fruits of a delusive mariage, and lastly giving him her with a damnation to that wheele in hell, from a life thrown into the midst of temptations and disorders. (YP 2.597–98)

For Conti, Sisyphus, who was condemned to roll a huge stone up a hill in the underworld only to have it roll down again, represents the futility of human effort and the vanity of ambition. Approaching Satan in intelligence—Conti terms him "astutissimum omnium mortaliium" (6.17.629) (the sharpest person who ever lived)—Sisyphus made the fatal mistake of revealing the secrets of the gods, specifically Jupiter's seduction of Aegina. Just as Sisyphus is engaged in a pointless exercise that thwarts all of his ambitions, so Satan's mad search for revenge only underlines his failure to usurp the throne of God and insures his continued and constantly accelerating punishments:

> That with reiterated crimes he might
> Heap on himself damnation, while he sought
> Evil to others, and enrag'd might see
> How all his malice serv'd but to bring forth
> Infinite goodness, grace and mercy shewn
>
> (PL 1.214–18)

And just as Satan escaped from the underworld to plague humankind, only to return in an even more degraded state, so Sisyphus escapes from the underworld by a ruse, only to be dragged back forcibly by Mercury:

> nam moriturus iussit vxorem insepultum cadauer eiicere, quod cùm illa fecisset, petit à Plutone vt ad vxorem castigandam liceret accedere, à qua tantopere fuisset neglectus, quòd citò rediret. vbi Pluto illud concessisset, ad superos reuersus noluit ampliùs redire ad inferos; sed à Mercurio vi detractus illi supplicio addictus fuisse dicitur. (6.17.630)

> (Just before he died he ordered his wife to toss his body away without burying it. And once she had done that, he begged Pluto to let him return to the upper world and punish his wife for her egregious neglect; and he promised Pluto that he would come right back after he had done that. But when Pluto consented, he went back to the upper world without ever having any intention of returning to the lower world. But Mercury dragged him back by force, and he was supposed to have been punished in the manner described above.)

Tantalus, the third of these criminals, committed the ultimate abomination by feeding human flesh to the gods, and was therefore surrounded by food or drink that he could not touch or taste:

> qui tamen praesentes lautissimo regióque apparatu semper habet epulas, neque vllo pacto illas potest attingere, quamuis insatiabili fame excruciaretur. . . . perpetua siti vexari, & in aqua esse perpetuò, quae vsque ad mentum assurgit: sed quoties labris attingere conatur, illa statim refugit. . . .
> (6.18.634)

> (. . . he always had meals at his disposal that were sumptuously prepared and fit for a king; but he could touch none of them, even though he was almost mad with hunger . . . he was plagued by eternal thirst and condemned for all eternity to be in water up to his chin that flowed away instantly whenever he tried to bring any of it to his lips.)

Milton's Satan is similarly deprived. He eventually makes his way to Paradise, ". . . where the Fiend / Saw undelighted all delight . . ." (PL 4.285–86), where the mutual love of Adam and Eve only serves to remind him of his own loss and deprivation:

> Sight hateful, sight tormenting! thus these two
> Imparadis't in one anothers arms
> The happier *Eden*, shall enjoy thir fill
> Of bliss on bliss, while I to Hell am thrust,
> Where neither joy nor love, but fierce desire,
> Among our other torments not the least,
> Still unfulfill'd with pain of longing pines;
> (PL 4.505–11)

In a second version of the myth, Tantalus is threatened with an overhanging stone that fills his life with anxiety and foreboding: "Euripides in Oreste nullo in loco ob timorem posse Tantalum consistere scribit, cùm saxum illi perpetuò immineat: quam poenam illum pati inquit ob immoderatam linguae petulantiam & dicacitatem" (6.18.635). (Euripides (in his *Orestes*) said that Tantalus could never stand still in one place for fear of the eternally overhanging stone, a punishment that he had brought on himself by his own gross, petulant, and caustic language.) Satan experiences a similar anxiety, but from below rather than from above:

> Me miserable! which way shall I flie
> Infinite wrauth, and infinite despair?
> Which way I flie is Hell; my self am Hell;
> And in the lowest deep a lower deep
> Still threatning to devour me opens wide,
> To which the Hell I suffer seems a Heav'n.
>
> (*PL* 4.73–78)

Dreams

Both Cartari's and Conti's remarks on the symbolism of dreams can be useful to us in examining the nature of Eve's dream and how it defines her responsibility for her actions. Adam does not really make the connection between the dream and the temptation by Satan, although all the evidence is there, including Eve's identification of the dream-creature as "One shap'd and wing'd like one of those from Heav'n / By us oft seen..." (*PL* 5.55–56). Vergil (through Cartari) connects false dreams to the barren leaves of the elm tree, so there may well be a connection between Eve's dream and the fatal tree itself:

> Et il medesimo Virgilio ha finto anchora, che al mezzo della entrata dell'inferno sia un grande olmo, che sparga gli fronzuti rami, e che sotto le foglie di questi stiano attaccati i sogni uani e falsi. La quale cosa uuole dire, come l'espone Seruio, che alla stagione che cadono le foglie à gli alberi i sogni sono sempre uani. Et altri hanno detto, ch l'olmo arbore sterile, e che non fa frutto esprime da se la vanità de sogni. (Mercury 333)

> (Vergil also observes that a huge elm tree stood in the middle of the entrance to the underworld. The tree spreads its leafy branches, and the vain, false dreams are attached

to the underside of the leaves. As Servius explains, this means that during the season of falling leaves dreams are always false. Other commentators have remarked that the elm is a sterile tree, and its lack of fruit symbolizes the vanity of dreams.)

Adam reassures Eve that her dream is really a jumbling of their talk of the evening before,

> But with addition strange; yet be not sad.
> Evil into the mind of God or Man
> May come and go, so unapprov'd, and leave
> No spot or blame behind: Which gives me hope
> That what in sleep thou didst abhorr to dream,
> Waking thou never wilt consent to do.
>
> (*PL* 5.116–21)

But Conti's account of dreams might give Adam reason for concern:

> quamuis somnnia aliquando formae sint rerum optatarum, quae subministrantur ab ipsa phantasia. vt enim ait Artemidorus in lib. 1. de somniis. (Conti 3.14.239; Artemidorus 1.21[11]).

> (But sometimes dreams take the shape of a wish list. These wishes emerge from the vision itself, as Artemidorus notes in his first book *On Dreams*: "A dream is a movement or complex imagining of the mind, foretelling something good or bad about to happen.")

Thus according to Artemidorus, as filtered through Conti, dreams do foretell something that will in fact happen, and the dream vision itself gives birth to desires in the mind of the dreamer. While the fact that evil can pass without blame through the mind of the dreamer "gives [Adam] hope" (*PL* 5.119) that Eve would never act on the wishes provoked by her dream, Conti reminds us that hopes are about as dependable as dreams:

> Consimili ratione spes addiderunt sorores, quia saepius in rebus dubiis, vanosque habentibus exitus, collocantur, quare euanescunt tanquam somnia. (3.14.239)

(Employing a similar rationale, the ancients also claimed that the Hopes were Sleep's sisters, for one often encounters one's hopes under dubious conditions, or under conditions which yield inconclusive results. And so our hopes vanish, just like dreams.)

Those "inconclusive results" of Conti are also reflected in Cartari's description of dreams, which produce equal portions of falsehood and truth:

> Sopra di que Porfirio cosi discorre, come riferisce Macrobio, dicendo che l'anima ritiratasi quando l'huomo dorme in buona parte da gli ufficij del corpo se bene drizza gli occhi alla verità, non la pò vedere però mai drittamente per la scurezza dell'humana natura che l'adombra: ma se pure questa si assottiglia in modo che l'occhio dell'animo ci passi per dentro, vede sogni ueri per la porta del corno; ma se sta densa si, che l'animo non la possa penetrare con la uista, uengono per la porta dell'auorio i falsi sogni. (Mercury 333)

(Porphyrius also addresses this subject, as Macrobius reports, saying that during sleep the soul pretty much abandons the body's needs to concentrate more directly on the truth. Still, it can never quite pierce through the darkness of the human nature that clouds its view. But if the soul can render human nature so subtle that its eye can penetrate the truth, it will observe true dreams through the horned gate, but if human nature maintains its density, and it remains impenetrable to the soul's view, then false dreams come out of the ivory gate.)

This mingling of the true and the false, these crossed signals that emerge from our dreams, typify the ambiguous results of mythological explication: the myths are rich in meaning, but only for the wise and prudent person whose mind and heart are anchored in Christian truth.

Of the five underworld rivers mentioned by Milton, all five appear in Conti, although one (Phlegethon) only very briefly. Starnes and Talbert see Milton as absorbing this material from the dictionaries, particularly the etymology of the rivers. Conti, however, is often a primary source of the later editions of the dictionaries. He supplies not only the etymologies of four of the five rivers, but explanations for them as well.

Milton obviously locates the underworld rivers in Satan's hell:

> ... along the Banks
> Of four infernal Rivers that disgorge
> Into the burning Lake thir baleful streams;
> Abhorred *Styx* the flood of deadly hate,
> Sad *Acheron* of sorrow, black and deep;
> *Cocytus*, nam'd of lamentation loud
> Heard on the ruful stream; fierce *Phlegeton*
> Whose waves of torrent fire inflame with rage.
> Farr off from these a slow and silent stream,
> *Lethe* the River of Oblivion rouls
> Her watrie Labyrinth, whereof who drinks,
> Forthwith his former state and being forgets,
> Forgets both joy and grief, pleasure and pain.
> (*PL* 2.574–86)

According to Conti (speaking through Hesiod, his source), the Styx is such a terrible river that it lives apart from the rest of the gods; its terror also derives from its name:

> Hic fluuius, quoniam fluit sub terra, aquamque habet insuauissimam, creditus est ad inferos vsque descendere, & esse fluuius inferorum, qui ob insuauitatem suam dictus est Styx, quasi *stygeros*, quod odiosum significat apud Graecos. (Hesiod 776–79; Conti 3.2.194, 197)

("Terrible Styx, eldest daughter of back—flowing Ocean. She lives apart from the gods in her glorious house vaulted over with great rocks and propped up to heaven all round with silver pillars" ... Since the Styx flows underneath the ground, and its water is repulsive, it is supposed to descend into the underworld and to be an underworld river. It was called Styx after that repulsiveness, since the Greek word *stygeros* means "repulsive.")

Similarly, the sadness of the river Acheron resides in its etymology, but it also reminds us of the sadness experienced by the grim travelers to the underworld:

> Vbi verò quis vir bonus vel etiam malus omnem spem in Dei clementia & benignitate collocauerit post hanc praeteritae vitae ratiocinationem, tum moeror ille, qui Acheron dicebatur, per vallem profundam pectoris scilicet in lucem extollitur. (3.1.193)

> (When a good or even a bad man sets his hopes on the mercy and kindness of God after he has reviewed the events of his past life, a sadness (called the river Acheron) wells up in him, and cuts through the deep valley of his breast.)

Milton uses the word "lamentation" to describe Cocytus, and it is Conti's word as well:

> Dictus est autem Cocytus à querelis & lamentationibus, vt nomen ipsum significat, & veluti testatur Plato in tertio libro de rep. quia morituri plerique post commissorum poenitentiam lamentantur, quia illa contra Dei optimi omnium parentis leges commiserint. Alij maluerunt dictum esse, quia queruntur & grauiter ferunt, quia res charissimas sint relicturi: alij ob lamentationes coniunctorum dictum putant hunc fluuium, qui morituris est transeundus. (3.3.199)

> (Cocytus was named for weeping and lamenting; that's what his name means [Gr *kokuo* "to lament"], and that's what Plato said about it in the third book of his *Republic* [387C]. For most men on the brink of death usually cry after feeling sorry for what they have done, because they have disobeyed all the laws of God, all creation's perfect parent. Other commentators explain his name by observing that men complain and take it very poorly when they have to part with things that are very dear to them. Still others suppose that the river that must be crossed by those facing death takes its name from the tears of their relatives.)

Finally, in his description of the river Lethe, Milton mentions both the joys and sorrows that we forget when we drink its waters, an emphasis also found in Conti:

> Bibebatur autem duplici de causa aqua Lethaei fluminis, tvm vt obliuiscerentur animae illarum deliciarum quibus fruebantur in campis Elysijs, tum etiam vt fierent immemores earum molestiarum, quas antea in vita pertulissent:

quarum rerum si perdurasset memoria, nemo reperiretur qui vellet reuiuiscere, aut qui cùm primum posset, non vel sibi ipse manus inferret. (3.20.286)

(There were two reasons that the souls had to drink the water of the river Lethe: first to wipe out all memory of the delights they had enjoyed while they were living in the Elysian fields, and second to blot out all of the sorrows they had experienced in their previous lives. If these joys and sorrows had been maintained in memory, no one would ever want to come back to life, or, if he did, he would try to kill himself the first time he got the chance.)

Like Conti, Milton always discusses the Moon in terms of the Sun, the sister planet borrowing her light from her brother the Sun. He also uses the mirror image to describe it, as we can see from these apposite passages from both authors:

> less bright the Moon,
> But opposite in leveld West was set
> His mirror, with full face borrowing her Light
> From him, for other light she needed none
> In that aspect, and still that distance keeps
> Till night, then in the East her turn she shines,
> Revolv'd on Heav'ns great Axle, and her Reign
> With thousand lesser Lights dividual holds
>
> (PL 7.375–82)

Conti's explanation is much more technical and less poetic, but in substance the same:

Vbi fuerint oppositi isti planetae, ita, vt alterius centrum centro alterius ac centro terrae per rectam lineam opponatur, tunc Luna incidens in vmbram tota occultatur, ac deficit repentè illius lumen, cum nequeat tanquam speculum lumen ab eo accipere. At cum centra vtriusque planetae non opponuntur, tanto minus obscuratur, quanto magis centrum eius à linea recta distiterit alterius. . . . nam cum Sol per se sit lucidus, Luna nullum habet proprium lumen, sed tanquam speculum corpus diaphanes existens receptum à sole lumen ad terram transmittit. (3.17.258, 262)

(When those planets are set against one another in such a way that the center of the one is opposite the center of the other, and the center of the Earth is in a direct line, then the Moon lapses into the shadow, and is completely hidden; suddenly its light is lost, for it can no longer function as a mirror, receiving light by virtue of its position. When the centers of each planet are not set against one another, the more distant the center of the one is from the center of the other (measured in a direct line), the less it is hidden.... For while the Sun has its own brightness, the Moon has no light of its own; rather, just like a mirror, it is a transparent body which radiates light to the Earth that it receives from the Sun.)

It is interesting that, in Eve's dream, she hears Satan inviting her to come out and enjoy the shadowy half-lights of the Moon, where things are not what they seem: "... now reignes / Full Orb'd the Moon, and with more pleasing light / Shadowie sets off the face of things; in vain, / If none regard..." (*PL* 5.41–44). Cartari's Moon wears only black clothing because "non ha lume da se, ma da altrui lo riceue" (Diana 123) (the Moon has no light of its own, but receives it from someone else). The association of the moon with magic is sufficient reason for Eve to turn down the invitation: else she might join those in the lazar-house afflicted with "Moon-struck madness" (*PL* 11.486). Conti is very explicit about the relationship between the Moon and magic, perhaps the magic that Satan wishes to evoke in his invitation to Eve:

> Inde verò natam fuisse hanc opinionem scripserunt antiqui, quòd specula quaedam rotunda ita parabantur, vt in his Luna omnino appareret è coelo deducta. Atque Pythagorae ludicrum fuit quoddam Luna plena existente, vt quis in speculo quodam sanguine quaecunque collibuisset, scriberet: atque alteri praedicens à tergo illi assisteret, ea quae scripsisset Lunae ostentans: atque ille deinde intenta acie oculorum in Lunam, vniversa quae forent in speculo scripta perlegeret, tanquam in Luna scripta fuissent. Inde existimo artificium Cornelij Agrippae originem coepisse, qui in

occulta philosophia videtur rationem quandam attingere, vt qui maximè à nobis distant, possint quae volumus in Luna descripta perlegere. (3.17.257)

(According to ancient testimony this notion evolved from the practice of arranging some round mirrors to make the Moon look as if it were being pulled right down from the heavens. In fact Pythagoras had a little Moon game he liked to play: when the Moon was full, he would have someone use blood to write anything he wanted on a mirror. Then the writer would first reveal the contents of his message to someone else, and then stand behind Pythagoras and show the Moon what he had written. Then, while everyone had their eyes fixed on the Moon, Pythagoras would read off all the writing on the mirror, as if it had been written on the Moon. It is my opinion that this is the real source of Cornelius Agrippa's gambit, a kind of occult philosophical method, when people who are quite a distance from us can still read what we say is written on the Moon. The Moon was supposed to be heavily involved in sorcery, because the strength of planets placed in a certain fixed position is powerful, even awesome.)

According to Cartari, since the ancients couldn't understand the reasons for an eclipse, "dicevano, che la Luna era tirata in terra per forza d'incanti" (Diana 123) (they used to claim that the Moon was dragged down to Earth by the power of magic.) They also believed in enchantresses who used their evil charms "non solamente contra la Luna, ma contra il Sole anchora, e tutte le stelle, e contra tutti gli altri Dei cosi del Cielo, come dell'inferno..." (Diana 124) (not only against the Moon, but also against the Sun, all of the other planets, and both the heavenly and the underworld gods.)

Venus

Although accounts of Venus abound in mythological treatises of the ancient, medieval and Renaissance periods, the chapters that Cartari and Conti devote to the goddess of love and beauty form one of the most complete, both in terms of classical documentation and interpretive expertise. Their accounts would certainly have proved useful to Milton, for in describing Eve, Milton was caught in a time warp: although *Paradise Lost* is set in prelapsarian time, the narrator must still, in time-honored fashion, describe the first and most beautiful of women in terms of women yet unborn and goddesses yet unimagined, some of whom are not altogether what they should be—particularly that neo-prostitute and goddess of womanly shame (*vergogna*), Venus. Yet Milton had no real choice—Venus was the paradigm of female beauty for a Renaissance society steeped in the classics and convinced that all standards of beauty had to be derived from the tastes of ancient Greece and Rome. Thus the physical attributes, the deportment and the psychological bent of Eve all follow the model of Venus.

In our own time, when overpopulation is a continuing threat to both the quality of life in general and mere survival in particular, the praise of a woman for her fruitful womb seems decidedly out of place. Yet the "natural" Venus depicted in both Cartari and Conti, and filtered through Milton's *Paradise Lost*, represents the necessity of human love for human survival, as well as the importance of woman as childbearer. As Cartari states, "elle mostra quella virtù occulta, per la quale gli animali tutti sono tirati al desiderio di generare" (Venus 530) (she [Venus] shows that hidden virtue through which all the animals are drawn toward the desire to reproduce.) Conti also recognizes the need of the natural Venus, but he is so repelled by the act of physical love that he sees the myth of Venus (and Cupid) as a method of making "igitur apud imperitos homines horum nominum creditorum Deorum inuentio, vt minus turpe facinus coitus, & animalium coniunctio putaretur" (4.13.382) (intercourse or animal coupling into an act which might be considered a little less revolting and disgraceful for them). Quoting himself, Conti cites his own blushing embarrassment at the physical act of love: "ita expressimus illam amorem appellantes: '*Nil amor est aliud*

Veneris quàm parua voluptas, / Quae simul expleta est, inficit ora rubor'" (4.13.396) (And this is the way we once expressed the obscenity of the act of Venus: "Love is simply that small pleasure we get from Venus, and as soon as we're finished, our faces light up with a reddish glow.") We might recall Raphael's blush when asked by Adam how angels express their love for each other: "To whom the Angel with a smile that glow'd / Celestial rosie red, Loves proper hue, / Answer'd . . ." (*PL* 8.618–20).

Milton distinguishes, in book nine, between the chaste and the unchaste couplings of Adam and Eve. For Milton, Eve's nudity is at first the sign of innocence and true beauty, later a cause for shame. She, like Adam, is "with naked Honour clad / In naked Majestie" (4.289–90) before the Fall, but after the Fall, she is, like Adam, "naked left / To guiltie shame . . ." (9.1057–058). Before the Fall, the narrator tells us that Eve did not "the Rites / Mysterious of connubial Love refus[e] . . ." (4.742–43), and he defends the necessity of intercourse in terms of the natural Venus:

> Our Maker bids increase, who bids abstain
> But our Destroyer, foe to God and Man?
> Hail wedded Love, mysterious Law, true sourse
> Of human offspring, sole proprietie,
> In Paradise of all things common else.
>
> (4.748–52)

After the Fall, the naked beauty of Eve inflames Adam with lust that in turn causes the eye of Eve to "dart contagious Fire" (9.1036) until Adam seizes her hand and leads her "nothing loath" (1039) to their flower-strewn bed of lust. The experience is so enervating and exhausting that they become sated with sleep: ". . . they thir fill of Love and Love's disport / Took lately, of thir mutual guilt the Seal, / The solace of thir sin, till dewie sleep / Oppress'd them, wearied with thir amorous play" (9.1042–045).

The paraphrase of the verse in Genesis, "increase and multiply," is also found in Conti's chapter on Venus:

> Qui Coeli & Diei filiam tradiderunt, ij cum Theologis Christianis consenserunt, quoniam cùm Deus omnipotens coelum & lucem & sidera creasset, mox rebus omnibus imprimendi amoris ad procreandum vim addidit: quare creatis animalibus & herbis statim inquit, Crescite & multiplicamini. Haec eadem causa fuit cur fuerit praefecta nuptijs. (4.13.398)

> (Those who took the view that she was Heaven's and Day's daughter were in accord with the Christian theologians; for after the omnipotent god had created the sky, the sun, and the stars, he added the force that instills love and procreation on all of his creation. For once he had created all the plants and animals, God immediately said: "Increase and multiply" [Gen. 1.28]. And the same reasoning was used to put Venus in charge of marriage.)

But Conti feels that sexual intercourse "opes dilapidat, obest memoriae, vim oculorum labefactat, stomachum frigidiorem & imbecilliorem effecit" (4.13.393) (robs us of our possessions, disrupts our memory, weakens our eyesight, and makes the stomach colder and weaker...).

After the Fall, Eve is truly naked and exposed, bereft of all worldly *and* unworldly goods, including freedom from death, and subject to the continual prey of the world, the flesh, and the devil.

For Cartari, the nakedness of Venus means that she is eternally prepared for intercourse, eternally deprived of worldly goods because of her lascivious ways, and, as with Eve, eternally exposed to sin:

> Fu questa Dea fatta nuda per mostrare, come vogliono alcuni, quello à che sempre ella è apparecchiata, che sono i lasciui abbracciamenti, e perche questi godiamo meglio nudi che vestiti, ouero perche chi va dietro sempre à lasciui piaceri rimane spesso spogliato, e priuo di ogni bene, percioche perde le ricchezze, che sono dalle lasciue donne diuorate, debilita il corpo, e macchia l'anima di tale bruttura, che niente le resta più di bello. Oueramente si faceua Venere nuda per dare à conoscere, che i furti amorosi non ponno stare occulti, e se pure ui stanno qualche poco, si

scuoprono anco poi, e spesso auiene che si mostrino alhora che meno vi si pensa, e se ne dubita meno. (Venus 535)

(Some would have it that that goddess was made nude in order to show what she is always ready to perform, which are lecherous embraces—either because we always enjoy those better when we are nude than when we are dressed, or else because whoever constantly seeks after lecherous pleasures is often stripped and deprived of every good thing.[12] He loses his riches (which are devoured by lecherous women), weakens his body, and stains his soul with such brutishness that it is left without any beauty at all. Or perhaps Venus was made nude so that we could understand that secret love affairs can't be kept hidden, and even if they are for a little while, they are eventually discovered; and they often turn out to be less than they were supposed to be, and no less dubious.)

In the Judgment of Paris, the shepherd Paris chose Venus or pleasure over Juno (virtue) and Pallas Athena (wisdom). Conti explains: "traditum est in fabulis Venerem iudicatam à Paride fuisse pulchriorem Iunone ac Pallade, quia multo sunt plures qui corporis voluptates, quàm qui animi: qui vitia, quam qui virtutem; qui turpitudinem, quam qui gloriam sectantur" (4.13.402) (The myths tell us that Paris judged Venus to be more beautiful than either Juno or Pallas, because most men prefer fleshy to intellectual pleasure, vice to virtue, disgrace to glory.) When Adam first beholds Eve, he is so overcome by her beauty that, when he tells Raphael of his rapture, the angel sees fit to rebuke him for his bad judgment:

> ... be not diffident
> Of Wisdom, she deserts thee not, if thou
> Dismiss not her, when most thou needst her nigh,
> By attributing overmuch to things
> Less excellent, as thou thyself perceav'st.
> For what admir'st thou, what transports thee so,
> An outside? fair no doubt, and worthy well
> Thy cherishing, thy honouring, and thy love,
> Not thy subjection....
> (8.562–70)

Raphael continues, pointing out that Adam's attraction for Eve is of the passions, not of the mind, reminding us of Venus and the goddess whose existence excused physical delight in intercourse. The sense of touch, he says, is not all there is to love, and carnal love is the province of the beasts, not of men:

> In loving thou dost well, in passion not,
> Wherein true love consists not; love refines
> The thoughts, and heart enlarges, hath his seat
> In Reason, and is judicious, is the scale
> By which to heav'nly Love thou maist ascend,
> Not sunk in carnal pleasure, for which cause
> Among the Beasts no Mate for thee was found.
>   (8.588–94)

And just as Adam is overcome by his *love* for Eve's *beauty*, so Venus, the goddess of love and beauty, vanquished, according to both Conti and Cartari, all the deities of Heaven, even the all-powerful Zeus.

Both Conti and Cartari also award Venus the dubious distinction of being the goddess of prostitution. Conti cites the ever-censorious Lactantius, while Cartari implies a connection between the trade and Venus *Meretricia*, or the profit-making aspect of love:

> Venerem amorum Deam credidit Lactantius putatam, quia lena fuerit, quae prima meretriciam artem instituerit. (Conti 4.13.396–97)

> (Lactantius thought that Venus was supposed to be the goddess of love because she was the bawd who created the prostitute's profession.)

> Ma dico, che se ben Venere parue essere Nume principale delle meretrici, come ch'ella hauesse già trouata, e messa in uso l'arte loro, onde elle celebrauano solennemente la sua festa, pregandola, che desse loro gratia, bellezza, et leggiadria, si che da tutti fossero amate con loro utile, e guadagno. (Cartari, Venus 547–48)

> (But I do say that Venus certainly seemed to be the chief deity of the prostitutes, for she had discovered their skill

and put it to practical use. Thus the prostitutes were very serious about celebrating her feast, praying to her to give them grace, beauty, and elegance, so that everyone would love them in ways that would be both useful and profitable to them.)

In the eleventh book of *Paradise Lost*, when the archangel Michael gives Adam a vision of the future misery his sin has created, he sees

> A Beavie of fair Women, richly gay
> In Gems and wanton dress; to th'Harp they sung
> Soft amorous Dittics, and in dance came on:
> The Men though grave, ey'd them, and let thir eyes
> Rove without rein, till in the amorous Net
> Fast caught, they lik'd, and each his liking chose;
> (582–87)

The angel informs Adam that these appealing women are actually prostitutes, true daughters of Venus, a mockery of the pure love between men and women that existed before the Fall:

> For that fair femal Troop thou sawst, that seemd
> Of Goddesses, so blithe, so smooth, so gay,
> Yet empty of all good wherein consists
> Womans domestic honour and chief praise;
> Bred onely and completed to the taste
> Of lustful appetence, to sing, to dance,
> To dress, and troul the Tongue, and roul the Eye.
> To these that sober Race of Men, whose lives
> Religious titl'd them the Sons of God,
> Shall yield up all thir virtue, all thir fame
> Ignobly, to the trains and to the smiles
> Of these fair Atheists, and now swim in joy,
> (Erelong to swim at large) and laugh; for which
> The world erelong a world of tears must weep.
> (614–27)

Just as the savage, warlike men of history are primarily Adam's responsibility, so the brazen, shameless prostitutes are Eve's. This is Eve as Venus *meretricia*, or the commercial Venus, the one who uses her body as a commodity. Milton's Eve uses her charm to "sell" Adam on the idea of joining her in bliss or woe, and at this low point in her life, she has sunk to the subhuman level of the "bevy of fair women" who seduced the Israelite heros. It might not be too fanciful to speculate that the water imagery ("swim in joy," "swim at large," and then weep "a world of Tears") refers not only to the flood as the aftermath of sin, but also to Aphrodite, Venus rising from the foam of the sea.

Venus or Aphrodite is the child of sea foam and *Kronos or Saturn*, Devouring Time:[13]

> Venerem illam, quam vulgus mortalium, deliciarum, voluptatumque omnium, & blanditiarum, & elegantiae Deam esse putauit, natam esse fabulantur è Coeli genitalibus partibus à Saturno caesis, & in mare proiectis, sine matre, ex illa spuma scilicet, quae ex illarum iactu in summa aquae parte exorta est.... Tibullus lib. 1. Elegiarum hanc è spuma maris & sanguine Coeli. (Conti 4.13.381, 382)

> (Venus, whom the common people thought of as the goddess of every pleasure and delight, charm and grace, was fabled to have been born from the genitals of Heaven, which Saturn cut off and threw into the sea. She had no mother; instead she was conceived from the foam that was created when Saturn hurled the genitals into the sea.... Tibullus, in the first book of his *Elegies*, thought that she was born from the foam and blood of Heaven....)

"Devouring Time" is conflated with "Devouring Death" and invoked by Mother Sin in *Paradise Lost*:

> To whom [Death] th'incestuous Mother thus repli'd.
> Thou therefore on these Herbs, and Fruits, and Flours,
> Feed first, on each Beast next, and Fish, and Fowl,
> No homely morsels, and whatever thing
> The Sithe of Time mows down, devour unspar'd,
> Till I in Man residing through the Race,
> His thoughts, his looks, words, actions all infect,
> And season him thy last and sweetest prey.
>
> (10.602–09)

Eve's love is deadly, in the literal sense; Adam is her "dear," in the costly as well as the affectionate sense, and she loves him so much that ". . . Confirm'd then I resolve, / *Adam* shall share with me in bliss or woe: / So dear I love him, that with him all deaths / I could endure, without him live no life" (9.830–33).

According to one version of the myth of Venus and Adonis, Adonis was emasculated and killed by Mars, the jealous husband of Venus, in the shape of a boar. Venus mourns for the Adonis whose death she (unwittingly) caused:

> Fuerunt tamen qui dixerint non ipsum quidem Adonim in aprum irruisse, sed ab apro impetum factum fuisse in Adonini, & id Martis consilio contigisse. Nam cùm Mars Venerem, Venus Adonim amaret & sequeretur, ratus est Mars omnes Veneris amores posse in se conuerti, si Adonim de medio sustulisset. (Conti 5.16.531)

> (Some writers claimed that it was the boar and not Adonis that had initiated the attack, and that Mars had planned the assault. For since Mars loved Venus and followed her around, while she loved Adonis and followed him around, Mars felt that he could reverse the process just by killing Adonis.)

> Faceuasi oltre di ciò un simulacro di Venere simile à quello che nel monte Libano si uedeua, il qual haueua un manto intorno, che cominciando dal capo lo copriua tutto, e pareua stare tutto mesto, e sconsolato, e con mano pure auolta un nel manto sosteneua la cadente faccia, e come dice Macrobio credeua ognuno che lo vedeua che le lagrime gli cadessero da gli occhi, e quiui si mostraua Venere cosi addolorata per la morte di Adoni ucciso da un cinghiale. (Cartari, Venus 553)

> (Besides this, the ancients also made a statue of Venus that resembled the one visible on Mount Libanus, which was wrapped in a cloak that covered it from head to foot. It seemed to be overcome by sorrow and was very depressed; and one hand folded up inside the cloak propped up its

drooping head. And as Macrobius observes, everyone thought that they saw tears dropping from its eyes, for the image was showing Venus overcome with grief over the death of Adonis, who was killed by a boar.)

Eve goes one step further; she urges Adam to join her in a suicide pact, thus hastening the deaths of herself and the one she claims to love above all others:

> Let us seek Death, or he not found, supply
> With our own hands his Office on our selves;
> Why stand we longer shivering under feares,
> That shew no end but Death, and have the power,
> Of many ways to die the shortest choosing,
> Destruction with destruction to destroy.
> (10.1001–006)

One might recall the many images in Renaissance painting of Venus overcoming Mars, or Mars's admission of his weakness before Venus as described by Statius and recorded by Cartari:

> mettendo prima però quello, che Marte dice, mentre che tiene questa Dea in braccio,.... come scriue Statio, da che senza altro dirne si potrà comprendere molto bene, quale, e quanta sia la forza di Venere, onde non haurà da marauigliarsi più alcuno, quando uedrà talhora gli più saldi animi, e le più ferme menti essere vinte da lei, in modo che a gli amorosi piaceri si siano poscia date in preda. Queste dunque sono le parole di Marte tratte al uolgare, con le quali pongo fine alla imagine di Venere ..... (Cartari, Venus 555–56; Thebaid 3.295-99)

> (But first I want to mention what Mars says while he holds that goddess in his arms ... as Statius writes. From this speech alone, without an additional word, the reader will be able to understand very well just how great is Venus's power. Then he won't have to be amazed any more, when he sometimes sees how she defeats those with the steadiest spirits and the firmest minds, and then makes them slaves to amorous pleasures. So here are the words of Mars translated into the common tongue, and with these I conclude

the image of Venus: "O thou who art my repose from battle, my sacred joy and all the peace my heart doth know: thou who alone of gods and men canst face my arms unpunished, and check even in mid-slaughter my neighing steeds, and tear this sword from my right hand!")

In initiating a suicide pact, Eve attempts to embrace the power of both man (Adam) and woman (herself), *eros* combined with *thanatos*: "For contemplation hee and valour formd, / For softness shee and sweet attractive Grace, / Hee for God only, shee for God in him" (4.297–99). In his chapter on Venus, Cartari provides a number of mannish or dangerous Venuses: one in armor, another with a beard, a third holding the apple she won in the contest with Minerva (Pallas) and Juno (545–46, 550–51). The armed Venus mocks the warlike Pallas, reminding the goddess of how she defeated her in her naked "Edenic" state:

> ... della quale fa Ausonio un bello epigramma, e finge, che Pallade, uedendo Venere armata, come ella parimente andaua sempre, uoglia di nuouo uenire à contesa con lei etiandio sotto il giudicio di Pari, ma Venere la schernisse come temeraria, hauendo ardire di prouocarla hora che la uede armata, se da lei fu uinta già mentre che era nuda. Lo epigramma fatto uolgare è tale.... (Cartari 544–45; Ausonius, *Epigrams on Various Matters* 61)

Ausonius has a beautiful epigram about the image. He imagines that Pallas, seeing Venus in armor, the same way she always went herself, wants to start a new contest with her, under the judgment of Paris. But Venus scorned her as reckless for challenging her when she sees her armed, after Venus had already defeated her even when she was nude. This is how the epigram reads in the common tongue: "At Lacedaemon Pallas saw Venus armed. 'Now,' quoth she, 'let us contend, even with Paris for judge.' Venus replied, 'When I am armed, rash maid, dost thou despise me, seeing that when I conquered thee I was bare?'"

Conti speaks of three Venuses (4.13.399–400).[14] The first is the Heavenly Venus, who embraces the ethereal qualities of love, perhaps what Adam calls

> ... those graceful acts,
> Those thousand decencies that daily flow
> From all her words and actions mixt with Love
> And sweet compliance, which declare unfeign'd
> Union of Mind, or in us both one Soul
>
> (8.600–04)

The second is the Venus of the People, the earthly Venus who ensures procreation through the ubiquity of sexual desire. The last is Venus Apostraphia, Venus "turning away," who teaches men to say "no" to lascivious desires. This last Venus is not represented in Milton, as Eve herself becomes the desire she should dispel.

Thus the picture of Venus in Conti, Cartari and Boccaccio (their common source) is definitely *not* flattering, but it is most negative in Conti. All of these mythographers are uncomfortable with the mixture of ugly pleasure and physical beauty. But perhaps Cartari unconsciously (and most succinctly) drew the definitive parallel between Eve and Venus when he remarked that "Si che fu Venere nume commune a tutte qualità di donne" (Venus 548) (Venus was a deity common to every quality of women). Milton's Eve is not only a literary creation, but also a record of Milton's fascination with and terror of all that he found mysterious, compelling, beautiful, good and dangerous in women, a vision that drew its literary inspiration from Venus.

MERCURY

Of all the gods in the pagan pantheon, Mercury is perhaps the most versatile, and the one most apposite to the ambiguities in Satan's character. A thief, a businessman, a practitioner of the occult, guide of the souls of the dead, father of the hermaphrodite and master rhetorician: "Hunc finxerunt antiqui aurea cathena auribus hominum annexa, mortales quocunque collibuisset trahere solitum, sicuti de Hercule dicitur" (Conti 5.5.441) (The ancients thought that he dragged men around wherever he pleased by a golden chain fastened to their ears—and they said the same thing about Hercules as well.)[15] Since Satan is the ambassador of Death, he resembles Mercury who, according to Conti's quotation from Vergil, "calls pale ghosts from Orcus and sends others down to gloomy Tartarus, gives or takes away sleep and unseals eyes in death" (Conti 442; *Aen.* 4, 242–44). His caduceus, the shield framed by two snakes entwined in mutual amity, reminds one of Satan's own unfortunate resemblance to a snake. He is also, according to Homer, "a bringer of dreams," a particular talent he shares with Milton's Satan (Conti 5.5.446; Homer, *Hymn to Hermes*, 14), who appears "squat like a toad, close at the ear of Eve" (*PL* 4.800), and disturbs the Son's sleep with "ugly dreams" (4.408–09). He is also the bringer of Peace and War (Conti 5.5.447), the latter having been invented by Satan. Mercury, according to Cartari, also functions as the interpreter of the gods (Mercury 312), a function covered by both Raphael (the past) and Michael (the future) in *Paradise Lost*. He is the god of rhetoric, for the tongue is dedicated to him in his sacrifices (Conti 5.5.448).[16]

Despite (or perhaps because of) all of his training in rhetoric, Milton displays a healthy suspicion of the art in *Comus, Paradise Lost* and *Paradise Regained*. As Norman O. Brown has shown us, the ancients did not make a real distinction between the businessman and the thief, and the deceptive art of rhetoric was necessary to convince your customers to accept the worst of the bargain. Conti, for example, combines Mercury's rhetorical and thieving skills in his analysis of the god:

> nam cùm eloquentiae & orationis quanta vis esset vellent ostendere, dixerunt Mercurium esse nuntium Deorum & hominum, per orationem nimirum Deorum voluntas, & sententia diuinarum legum, & recta animorum nostrorum consilia, quae non nisi autore Deo proueniunt, explicantur. Inde creditus est etiam cathenae illi aureae annexos homines auribus quocunque libuisset attrahere. Hunc latronum & impostorum & fraudum Deum putarunt, non solùm quia si eloquentia cum malo & flagitioso sit ingenio,

plurimum obest caeteris hominibus, verùm etiam quia illorum quibus planetae Mercurij natura in ortu dominatur, ingenia sunt ad furta, & ad omne astutiae genus accommodata. (5.5.449)

(For when the ancients wanted to show us the incredible power of eloquence and rhetoric, they said that Mercury was the messenger of both men and gods. But rhetoric for them explained the will of the gods, the meaning of divine laws, and good moral counsel, all of which have God as their sole source. Thus even men's ears were fastened to Mercury's golden chain, so that he could drag them around wherever he pleased. They also claimed that Mercury was the god of robbers, impostors, and cheats, not only because an evil, shameful type of eloquence poses a real problem for the rest of men, but also because those whose horoscope is controlled by Mercury are disposed to be thieves and con artists.)

Thus Satan "sells" Eve on the apple, and his fellow devils on the plot to tempt Adam and Eve. Comus, in a kind of seductive persuasion paralleled by the Satan-Eve temptation tries, in vain, to "sell" the Lady on the loss of her chastity. Almost like stereotypes of the Renaissance seducer, Comus and Satan ply their sophistical trade against the Son, the Lady and Eve.

Cartari comes close to identifying Mercury (the trickster god) with the god of rhetoric, and with the Gallic Heracles as well, who led men about with chains that emanated from his lips (see n. 15, above):

& egli mandò con lui Mercurio con commissione di insegnare à quelli, ch'ei ne giudacaua degni, il modo di ben parlare, col quale essi potessero persuadere à gli altri quello che era necessario à fare per viuere vna vita dimestica, honesta, e ciuile. E per questo consecrarono gli antichi la lingua à Mercurio, & oltre à tutti gli altri sacrificij questo era à lui proprio e particolare di sacrificargli beendo certo poco vino le lingue delle vittime. (Mercury 328–29)

(Jupiter [assigned] Mercury... the responsibility of teaching the power of persuasive speaking to whatever men he thought were worthy of it, so that those men could eventually teach the others whatever they needed to lead an honest life, both in public and in private affairs. That was why the ancients dedicated the tongue to Mercury; in addition to all of the other sacrifices in his honor, the ritual of drinking a little wine while sacrificing the tongues of victims to Mercury was his own particular and fitting form of worship.)

The first of the smooth-tongued deceivers is Comus, who is accused by the Lady of being a "false traitor" who has "banisht" "truth and honesty" from his "tongue with lies" (691–93). She accuses him of being an "Impostor" and a "jugler" who "Would think to charm my judgement, as mine eyes / Obtruding false rules pranct in reasons garb" (762, 757–759). In *Paradise Lost* all the master rhetoricians are discovered among the fallen angels. Belial is almost a paradigm of hypocrisy, representing the sophists who "could make the worse appear / The better reason, to perplex and dash / Maturest Counsels . . . . ." Although "all was false and hollow," "yet he pleas'd the ear, / And with perswasive accent thus began" (*PL* 2.113–15, 112, 117–18). In fact, the narrator echoes the charges of the Lady against Comus: where Comus has "false rules pranckt in reasons garb," Belial uses "words cloath'd in reasons garb" (*PL* 2.226). Beëlzebub has a statesmanlike appearance, for "his look / Drew audience and attention still as Night," for ". . . deep on his Front engrav'n / Deliberation sat and public care; / And Princely counsel in his face yet shon, / Majestic though in ruin . . ." (*PL* 2.307–08, 302–05). In *Paradise Regained* Satan or "the subtle Fiend, / Though inly stung with anger and disdain, / Dissembl'd, and this Answer smooth return'd" (1.465–67). He practices a "gray dissimulation" (1.498) and in his urbane disguise greets the Son with "fair speech" (2.301). Even after the Son exposes his "weak arguing, and fallacious drift," Satan still manages to collect "his Serpent wiles" and renew his temptation with "soothing words" (3.4–6). Unlike Satan, the Son does what he says he will do, as even the devil has to admit:

"Thy actions to thy words accord" (3.9). He finds, to his chagrin, that "... the perswasive Rhetoric / That sleek't his tongue, and won so much on *Eve*, So little here, nay lost..." (*PR* 4.3-5). During that earlier triumph, Satan, in tempting Eve, summoned up all the eloquence "In *Athens* or free *Rome*," degrading himself to the point where he employed his rhetorically skilled tongue to lick "the ground whereon she trod." He deliberately developed a seductive speech that is as painstakingly structured as the most rigid classical oration: "So gloz'd the Tempter, and his Proem tun'd" (*PL* 9.671, 526, 549).

This seductively persuasive Satan and the erotically charged Eve meet in Cartari's silent woman, the one who lives through her husband's speech and (as in the hieroglyphic tradition) is symbolized by the mute tortoise beneath the foot of Venus (Venus 541).[17] Cartari's linkage of rhetoric with erotic desire fully captures the suggestibility of Eve and the eloquence of Satan. Cartari further observes that Mercury's statue was placed next to the statue of Venus because "che gli amorosi congiungimenti hanno bisogno di trattenimenti dolci e soaui, e di parole piaceuoli, perche queste fanno spesso nascere, e conseruano Amore fra le persone" (541) (amorous unions of necessity have sweet and mild delays [Milton's "sweet reluctant amorous delay" *PL* 4.311], and pleasant words, because they often cause love to be born among people, and to be preserved as well). Venus is also associated with *Pitho* or *Suadela*, the goddess of persuasion. Here one might envision Eve as the *rhetor* or speechmaker, convincing Adam to join her in death and corruption. The first eloquence, Cartari observes, was the rhetoric of lovers, for then "per piacere anch'essi a quelle trouarono mille belle cose, che prima non erano conosciute" (543) (these men would discover a thousand beautiful things to please women that they knew nothing about before.) For example, as a result of her interview with the devil, Eve "discovers" that she is a "goddess" and "empress" who is "resplendent" in her beauty, and both "fair" and unfair in any number of ways.[18] Venus, usurping Mercury's role, is also termed the Inventor or "Mechanic" because lovers are constantly inventing new ways to convince young women to accede to their desires (543).

As Cartari tells us,

> Fu anco creduto Mercurio il primo che mostrasse il modo di guadagnare, e perciò era Dio de mercatanti. Suida scriue che per questo metteuano una borsa in mano al suo simulacro. Fulgentio vuole che l'ali à piedi di Mercurio significhino il veloce, e quasi continuo mouimento di quelli che trafficano, li quali solleciti ne loro assari vanno quasi sempre hor qua, hor là. (Mercury 329)
>
> (Mercury was also supposed to be the first one to show men how to make a profit; thus he was the god of merchants. And that is why, as Suidas tells us, statues of Mercury showed him with a purse in his hand. Fulgentius explains Mercury's winged feet as symbols of speed, for those who are engaged in business are continually on the move, travelling swiftly from one place to another to conduct their affairs.)[19]

Satan is, of course, the original fallacious bargainer: he tempts Eve to give up eternal life for the taste of the forbidden fruit, but fails to convince Christ to exchange devil worship for food, learning, fame or power. He is also constantly on the move, from heaven to hell, from hell to earth and back again. Comus uses his considerable charm as a bargaining chip to assault the Lady's chastity, but is definitively repulsed. Certainly the devil's many evil missions take him to every corner of the kingdom, both high and low.

BACCHUS

In announcing the genesis of Comus from Bacchus and Ceres, the attendant Spirit provides an amalgam of details that receive careful analysis in both Cartari and Conti. Here is Milton's synthesis:

> *Bacchus*, that first from out the purple grape
> Crush't the sweet poyson of mis-used wine
> After the *Tuscan* mariners transform'd
> Coasting the *Tyrrhene* shore, as the winds listed
> On *Circe's* Iland fell (who knows not *Circe*
> The daughter of the Sun? whose charmed cup
> Whoever tasted lost his upright shape
> And downward fell into a groveling swine)
> This nymph that gaz'd upon his clustring locks
> With ivy berries wreath'd, and his blith youth
> Had by him ere he parted thence, a son
> Much like his father, but his mother more,
> Whom therfore she brought up, and *Comus* nam'd
> (*Comus* 46–58)

Milton makes a point of referring to the "sweet poyson of mis-used wine," for Bacchus is first associated with wine and almost always with its abuse. Cartari, who calls "ubbriachezza" (drunkenness) "il sacramento di Baccho" (the sacrament of Bacchus) (Bacchus 423), emphasizes its "grauissimi danni" (terrible consequences) (414):

> ei ne fu creduto il ritrouatore, mostrando à mortali già da principio come si haueuano da raccogliere l'vue dalle viti, e spremere il dolce succo tanto grato, & vtile anchora à chi temperatamente l'vsa, si come à gli disordinati beuitori apporta grauissimi danni. il che mostrarono gli antichi nelle imagini di Baccho. (414)

> (Bacchus was supposed to have invented wine and was the very first one to show men how to use it. He was the one who showed men, from the earliest times, how to harvest the grapes from the vines, and to squeeze that juice that is so delightful and useful to those who are temperate in its use, and holds such terrible consequences for the ones who drink to excess. And the ancients used the image of Bacchus to make this clear.)

Conti makes the point even more forcefully:

> cùm immoderatus illius vsus non parum obsit mortalibus, secretaque animi aperiat, & in insaniam propè impellat....

"Nam vbi vires corporis, mentemque vini imperium subegerit, multa effutire coguntur homines, vt scripsit in his etiam Theognis: . . ." (5.13.492–93; Theognis 157–58)

(For the excessive use of wine causes men considerable trouble; it unlocks the secrets of the mind, and also practically drives a person to madness. . . . For when the power of wine subdues the strength of the body and the mind, men are forced to babble about many things, as Theognis in fact wrote, in these words: "Wine maketh light the mind of wise and foolish alike, when they drink beyond their measure.")

Both Cartari and Conti make a point of the combined drunkenness and effeminacy of Bacchus, two negative qualities that Milton also associates with King Charles II:

Ma ritornando alla veste di Baccho, dicono ch'ella era di donna, perche il troppo bere debilita le forze, e fa l'huomo molle, & eneruato come femina. Onde Pausania scriue, che appresso de gli Elei nell'arca di Cipselo era intagliato Baccho con la barba, con veste lunga giù infino à terra, e che stando à giacere in certo antro circondato da viti, e da altri arbori frutti feri porgeua vna tazza con mano. (Cartari, Bacchus 425–26)

(But getting back to the clothing that Bacchus wore, it was supposed to be women's clothing, because excessive drinking weakens a man's virility, and makes him soft and weak like a woman. Thus Pausanias writes that the tomb of Cypselus, which is located in Elis, had an image of Bacchus carved on it. The image wore a beard, as well as a long gown that reached to the ground; it was reclining in a cave surrounded by vines and other fruit-bearing trees, and it was holding out a cup with one of its hands.)

Idem Deus pro bibentium ingenio alios facit audaciores, alios loquaces ac timidos tanquam foeminas: quare & mas & foemina creditus est. . . . Fingebatur hic Deus hinnulorum & caprarum pellibus indutus, quorum animalium alterum effoeminatam ebriosorum naturam significat, alterum insensum est vitibus. Idcirco etiam à mulieribus sacerdotibus plerunque [sic?] colebatur, quòd ebriosorum natura magis foeminis, quàm viris est similis. (Conti 5.13.506–07)

(Depending on a man's nature, this god can make him bolder, or as gabby and frightened as a woman, which is why the ancients thought that Bacchus was both male and female.... The ancients envisioned this god as wearing deerskins, which symbolize the drunkard's effeminate nature, and she-goat pelts, which stand for the goat's threat to the vines. That's why most of his ministers were women, because a drunken man is closer in nature to a woman than a true man.)

Referring doubtless to Charles II and perhaps to the poet's own plight under Restoration rule, Milton's narrator in *Paradise Lost* dismisses "... the barbarous dissonance / Of *Bacchus* and his revellers, the Race / Of that wild Rout that tore the *Thracian* Bard / In Rhodope..." (7.32–35). A second possible reference to the drunken Charles occurs in the first book, where we learn that "... when Night / Darkens the Streets, then wander forth the Sons / Of *Belial*, flown with insolence and wine" (500–02). In *The First Defense*, Milton refers to "... the younger Charles and his damned crew of emigrant courtiers...." (*YP* 4.534). As for effeminacy, Charles's hearkening to his wife's counsel shows how little competence he has "... to govern men, undervaluing and aspersing the great Counsel of his Kingdom, in comparison of one Woman" (*YP Eikonklastes* 3.421). Nor did that king respect women, "... when even in the theatre he kisses women wantonly, enfolds their waists and, to mention no more openly, plays with the breasts of maids and mothers" (*YP The First Defense* 4.408). Drunken and dissolute, with wild Bacchanalian companions, at once subservient to and lustful toward women, the king illustrates the legacy of Bacchus at its worst, a self-indulgent model of dishonor and incompetence.

FORTUNE, OCCASION, OPPORTUNITY

As we noticed in chapter five, there is no shortage of information about the images of Fortune and Occasion. Both Conti and Cartari deny the existence of Fortune, and

Milton clearly holds the same view. In fact, all three authors cite exactly the same passage from Juvenal to support their common denial of Fortune's divinity:

> ma cerchiamo quasi tutti sempre di hauerne; e perche non potiamo satiare il disordinato nostro desiderio, ci lamentiamo poi della Fortuna, la quale secondo la opinione di molti non è. onde Giuuenale cosi ne disse.... (Cartari, Fortune 458; Juvenal, Satire 10.365–66)

> We are always trying to acquire more things, and so we can never satisfy our perverted desire. This leads us to complain to Fortune, a being many people don't even believe in, as these words of Juvenal suggest: "Thou wouldst have no divinity, O Fortune, if we had but wisdom; it is we that make a goddess of thee, and place thee in the skies."

> Quare praeclarè scriptum est à Iuuenale stultè inter Deos collocatam fuisse Fortunam. Nam si prudentia potiùs, qùam temeritate quadam & caecitate mentis res humanae gubernarentur, oblitesceret penitus è mentibus hominum Fortunae nomen:.... Sed quòd inscitia mentibus hominum insidet, saepius illi admonendi sunt, quòd ... (Conti 4.9.341, 342).

> (That's why Juvenal was right on target when he wrote that it was foolish to make Fortune one of the gods. For if reason was our guide instead of blindness and stupidity, Fortune's name would drop right out of our minds.... But because we are so preoccupied by ignorance, we have to be reminded rather often that [Exact quote follows])

> But the name "fortune," as was said above, grew out of ignorance of causes; for when something occurs which is unplanned and unexpected, this is commonly called fortune.... Nor was the remark by Juvenal inappropriate: [exact quote follows].... For fortune surely is to be placed in heaven, but its name should be changed and it should be called "divine providence." (YP Art of Logic 8.229)

Where Milton renames "Fortune" as "Divine Providence," Conti takes a slightly different tack, seeing Fortune as a kind of scapegoat for the bad luck we do not wish to attribute to the divine: "Atque vt summatim dicam, nulla alia de causa excogitatum fuisse Fortunae nomen ab antiquis crediderim, nisi vt hominum lamentationes à summi Dei cogitatione ad inane nomen, & ad numen quod nusquam existeret, diuerterent" (4.9.344) (To put it in a word, it seems to me that the ancients invented Fortune's name for one simple reason: to divert men's complaining thoughts from the supreme god to a name that referred to a nonexistent deity.)

Conti, obviously borrowing from Cartari, refers to the oldest extant statue of Fortune, by one Bupalis, in which she is displayed with the cornucopia or horn of Amalthea (Horn of Plenty) in her hand:

> cominciando da quello, che mette Pausania, oue scriue, che tra le memorie de gli antichi non si troua statoa alcuna della Fortuna più antica di quella, che fece Bupalo architetto, e scultore eccellente à gli Smirnei, gente della Grecia, in forma di donna, che sul capo haueua un polo, e con l'una delle mani teneua il corno della copia. (Cartari, Fortune 459)

> (I'll begin with the one that Pausanias [4.30.6] provides. He writes that among the ancient memorials there is no record of any statue older than the one crafted by Bupalis, the superb architect and sculptor from the Greek city of Smyrna. He made her with a woman's shape, with a pole on her head, and with the Horn of Plenty in one hand.)

> Sapientissimè igitur Bupalus opinionem hominum secutus, vt est in Messeniacis Pausaniae, aedificandis templis, fingendisque simulacris ingeniosus ac solers, Fortunae signum apud Smyrnaeos omnium antiquorum primus effinxit: cuius capiti polum imposuit, cum altera manu vocatae Amaltheae cornu teneret. (Conti 4.9.342)

> (That's why Bupalis was very wise to conform to the common view of Fortune; Pausanias tells his story in his own description of Messenia. Bupalis was one of the great and

ingenious temple builders and statue makers of the ancient world, and the first man to sculpt a statue of Fortune in Smyrna. He placed the celestial pole upon her head, and the horn of Amalthea in her hand.)

As noted in chapter five, Satan has his own cornucopia, full of wealth and riches, which he carries in his hand, and which he rewards to whomever he favors:

> Get Riches first, get Wealth, and Treasure heap,
> Not difficult, if thou hearken to me,
> Riches are mine, Fortune is in my hand;
> They whom I favour thrive in wealth amain,
> While Virtue, Valour, Wisdom sit in want.
> (PR 2.427–31)

Cartari, in his image of Success or Macaria, seems to offer a rebuttal to Milton's Satan, maintaining that both virtue and wealth are needed for true human happiness:

> La imagine di costei, cio è della Felicità, che questo e il nome Latino, e Macaria il Greco, come ho detto, fu da gli antichi fatta, come si vede in alcune medaglie di Giulia Mammea, una donna sopra un bello seggio, che tiene nella destra il Caduceo, & ha nella destra un corno di douitia. Si può dire che quello significhi la virtù, questo le ricchezze, come che ne le virtù da se, ne le ricchezze per loro medesime possano fare qui l'huomo felice, che fu opinione di Aristotele. Imperoche quale felicità può essere di un virtuoso, che si troui in tanta pouertà che patisca disagio non solamente di molte cose che gli sarebbono commodè, ma di quelle anchora che gli sono necessarie? (Fortune 488–89)

> (The image of that goddess, whom the Romans called Success and the Greeks Macaria (as I have mentioned), was made, as we can tell from some of Julia Mammea's medals, in the following way. She is a woman seated on a beautiful throne holding the Caduceus in her right hand and the Horn of Plenty in her left. We can take the Caduceus to mean Virtue and the Horn of Plenty to represent wealth, for neither Virtue nor even riches can make men happy, as Aristotle opined. How can a virtuous man really be happy,

when he finds himself so poor that he suffers not only from the lack of conveniences, but of necessities as well? [Rackham, *Nicomachean Ethics* 1.7.15])

But Cartari moves even closer to Milton's opinion in his reference to Cebe's (fl. 5th c. B.C.) "Table," an imaginative rendering of the ups and downs of life,[20] where virtue alone is the key to success:

> Cebete nella sua tauola fa la Felicità vna donna che siede all'entrare di certa rocca in bel seggio, bene ornata, ma non però con molta arte, e coronata di bellissimi, e uaghi fiori. Alla quale ben pare che voglia andare ognuno, ma non vi arriuano però se non quelli che caminano con la scorta della virtù, lasciandosi alle spalle tutte l'altre cose; perche fu opinione di costui, come di molti altri anchora innanzi a lui, che la virtù sola potesse fare l'huomo felice. Il che dobbiamo dire noi anchora parlando christianamente, & intendendo non della Felicità, che qui brama alla cieca ognuno in questo mondo, perche non è, se ben pare, Felicità, ma di quella, che nelle celesti se di godono le anime beate, vera, immutabile, & eterna. Alla quale ha da sperare di guignere fermamente ognuno, che scorto da lucidissimi raggi della diuina bontà camini tutto il viaggio di questo mondo in compagnia della fede, calcando l'arido e sterile terreno co'piedi della carità. (Fortune 489-90)

> (Cebes, in his tableau, portrays Success as a woman placed at the entrance of a cave; she sits on a beautiful throne, really decked out (but with little art), and she is crowned with very beautiful, attractive flowers. It seems that everyone wants to get to her, but no one makes it except those who travel with virtue as their guide, leaving everything else behind them. For it was Cebes' opinion, as it had been the opinion of many earlier commentators, that virtue by itself was enough to make men happy. And speaking as Christians, we ought to say the same. But Success is not the proper symbol for that, even though each one of us blindly yearns for her in this world; she seems to be, but she isn't. Rather it is that true, unchangeable, and eternal bliss that the blessed souls enjoy from their celestial seats in the heavens. Each one of us keeps hoping to unite with Success,

guided by the gleaming rays of the Divine Goodness, as he walks the full length of his pilgrimage on earth, treading on the arid, sterile earth, with the feet of Charity.)

Cartari also employs the iconography of Fortune to dramatize the chaotic nature of world events: "mà le aggiunsero una rotonda palla sotto i piedi, e la fecero senza occhi, dandole poi un temone in mano, come che alla cieca, e senza prouidenza alcuna gouerni le cose del mondo") (476) (They also put a round ball underneath her feet, made her eyeless, and stuck a ship's rudder in her hand, for she rules over the things of this world as if she were blind and totally lacking in foresight). The Chorus in *Samson Agonistes* seems to be referring to this blind, seagoing guide when they commiserate with Samson for allowing Dalila to lead him astray: "What Pilot so expert but needs must wreck / Embarqu'd with such a Stears-mate at the Helm?" (1044–045).

As previously remarked in chapter five, Cartari connects Occasion with the Greek idea of *kairos* or the *appropriate time* to do something, without the sense of urgency that Satan uses to justify his rhetorical bullying of Eve. Since God controls all times and opportunities anyway, any undue haste in grasping the good times could be seen as a lack of faith. Indeed, our bad luck is usually the result of our inadequacies or a lack of provision for the future:

> come mostrarono pur'anche gli antichi nella imagine della Occasione; la quale fanno alcuni essere una medisima con la Fortuna: ma se non sono una medesima cosa queste due, ben sono tra loro molto simili, come dal ritratto di questa si potrà vedere, la quale fu fatta Dea da gli antichi, forse accioche dalla imagine sua riuerita, e spesso guardata imparasse ognuno di pigliare le cose in tempo, perche quelle con questo si mutano, e vanno via, lasciando poi chi non le seppe torre pieno di mestitia, e di pentimento. Fu adunque la imagine della Occasione cosi fatta. Staua una donna nuda con i piedi sopra una ruota, ouero su una rotonda palla, & haueua i lunghi capei tutti riuolti sopra la fronte, si che ne restaua la nucca scoperta, e come pelata, & à piedi

haueua l'ali, come si dipinge Mercurio, & era con lei una altra donna tutta addolorata, e mesta nello aspetto, e piena di pentimento.... Imperoche chi lascia passare la buona occasione, che si appresenta in qual si voglia cosa, altro non ha poi che pentirsi, e lagnarsi di se medesimo. Questa, che chiamarono i Latini Occasione, & opportunità, e riuerirono come Dea, fu da Greci detta tempo opportuno, e perciò da loro fatto Dio, non Dea, & era il suo nome Cero, che questa voce appresso de i Greci significa opportunità di tempo.... Fu dunque il Dio Cero de i Greci, il medesimo che era la Occasione de i Latini, del quale Posidippo fece uno epigramma descriuendo la sua imagine, onde Ausonio tolse forse l'argomento del suo quando dipinse la Occasione: perche sono in tutto simili, se non che Posidippo mette di più vn rasoio in mano al suo, & Ausonio alla sua de la Penitenza di più per compagna. Calistrato parimente nobile scultore fece il Dio Cero in forma di giouine nella sua più fiorita età, bello, e vago con i crini al uento sparsi, et in tutto il resto come lo descriue a punto Posidippo. Bisogna dunque stare con gli occhi aperti, e con le mani pronte per dare di piglio alle cose quando la Occasione ce le mostra, perch'ella tosto gira, e uolta la nucca pelata poi à chi non seppe cacciare le mani ne i lunghi crini, che ha sopra la fronte, e uia se ne camina con uelocissimi piedi. (Cartari, Fortune 478, 480)

(The ancients make this point again in their image of Occasion, whom some identify with Fortune. But even if these two are not the same, they are certainly very much alike, as we can see from Occasion's portrait. The ancients made her a goddess, perhaps so that each one of us could learn from her respected and frequently observed image to take things as they come, for things change with time and pass away, leaving those who don't know how to take advantage of them full of sadness and regret.

This is how the ancients made Occasion's image. A naked woman stood with her feet on a wheel or round ball, and her long hair was curled around her forehead, leaving the nape of her neck naked and exposed. Her feet had wings, in the same way that we picture Mercury. There was another woman with her [Penitence], who looked very sad, sorrowful, and full of regret. . . . For whoever allows a good opportunity to pass him by, when it offers him something that he wants, has no one to blame or complain about except himself.

This figure, whom the Latins called Occasion [feminine] and Opportunity [feminine], and worshiped as a goddess, was called Opportune Time [masculine] by the Greeks and therefore became their god, not their goddess. His name was Kairos, a word that for the Greeks means the opportunity time provides. . . .

Thus the Greek god Kairos was the same as the Latin god Occasion. Posidippus wrote an epigram describing Kairos, whose theme Ausonius probably borrowed when he pictured Occasion. They are the same in every respect, except that Posidippus places a razor in the hand of his image, and Ausonius gives Penitence to his image as a companion. The very noble sculptor Callistratus also made the god Kairos in the shape of a young man in the flower of his youth: handsome, attractive, his hair blowing in the wind, and every other detail in perfect accord with Posidippus's description of the god.[21]

Thus we must keep our eyes open and our hands ready to pick up things when Occasion shows them to us; for she twists herself around rapidly, turns her bare neck toward anyone who didn't think to send his hands in search of the long hair on her forehead, and skips away on her wonderfully swift feet.)

As Satan urges the Son: "If Kingdom move thee not, let move thee Zeal, / And Duty; Zeal and Duty are not slow; / But on Occasions forelock watchful wait" (*PR* 3.171–73). Or Comus to the Lady: "If you let slip time, like a neglected rose / It withers on the stalk with languish'd head" (743–44). Or Satan to his vengeful followers in *Paradise Lost*: "Let us not slip th' occasion. . . ." (1.178); or to himself as he prepares to tempt Eve: ". . . Then let me not pass / Occasion which now smiles, . . ." (9.479–80).

Also in chapter five, we saw that Satan in both *Paradise Lost* and *Paradise Regained*, Comus in *A Mask*, and Dalila in *Samson Agonistes*, all invoke a sense of urgency and haste along with the gift of Opportunity or "Occasion." The true Christian moves slowly and deliberately, and is not taken in by the hypocritical promises of malevolent deities or persons (e.g., Dalila) in their employ. Similarly, it is better to follow the fixed course of the godhead than the shifting, erratic path of blind Fortune.

ANTAEUS

The myth of Antaeus, the son of Mother Earth, and his struggle with Hercules, also receives extensive coverage in the emblem books. But Conti's summary of the myth provides all of the details Milton would have needed to create his parallel between the pagan battle and the Son's struggle with Satan in *Paradise Regained* (4.563-71):

> Antaeum Terrae filium obuium habuit, hominem admirandae proceritatis, quippe qui ad sexaginta & quatuor cubitorum longitudinem accederet, in omnes peregrinos inhumanum: quos secum luctari cogebat, & suffocabat. Hic cùm Herculem ad luctam prouocasset, ab eo penè extinctus ter prosternitur, at erat ea virtute vt quoties Terram matrem attingeret, toties fortior resurgeret, quod sentiens Hercules hunc comprehensum sublimem a terra tamdiu sustinuit, quamdiu spiraret, donec vi Herculea brachiisque denique strictus expirauerit. (7.1.691)

> (This Antaeus was famously tall, for he measured a full sixty-four cubits in height. And he acted like a savage toward people who were traveling through the area, for he used to challenge them to wrestling matches, and then strangle them. When he goaded Hercules into a similar match, the hero threw him on the ground three times in a row and he almost died. But the odd thing about his strength was that every time he touched his mother Earth, he sprang up stronger than he was before. Once Hercules figured that out, he grabbed him and lifted him high above the earth, where he continued to breathe until Hercules strangled him with his powerful arms. Then Earth's son finally expired.)

> To whom thus Jesus: also it is written,
> Tempt not the Lord thy God, he said and stood.
> But Satan smitten with amazement fell
> As when Earths Son *Antaeus* (to compare
> Small things with greatest) in *Irassa* strove
> With *Joves Alcides* [Hercules], and oft foil'd still rose,
> Receiving from his mother Earth new strength,
> Fresh from his fall, and fiercer grapple joyn'd,
> Throttl'd at length in th'Air, expir'd and fell;
> So after many a foil the Tempter proud,
> Renewing fresh assaults, amidst his pride
> Fell whence he stood to see his Victor fall.
>
> (*PR* 4.560–71)

Since Conti (in this instance) equates Hercules with the Sun (7.1.691) and Antaeus as the son of Earth, it would appear that Milton's "Son" of God, the heavenly principle, has triumphed over the son of Earth, the principle of Death or corruption. Satan's second fall literally brings him down to earth but no longer in a position to bounce back (or "spr[i]ng up stronger" as Conti puts it) to his former glory.

THE TWO-HANDED ENGINE

Lycidas (to take a final example) invites comparison with a number of parallel passages from both Cartari and Conti, but the passages relating to the Alpheus-Arethusa myth and the "two-handed engine" are particularly striking. As conventionally interpreted, the two-handed engine is seen as some kind of vague symbol of divine retribution for the sins of the clergy, who have not lived up to the moral example of Milton's dead friend, Edward King. The corrupt clergy may revel in the wool stolen from the shearer's feast, "But that two-handed engine at the dore / Stands ready to smite once and smite no more" (130–31). For Conti (quoting his own verses), greed, ambition, hatred or pure ignorance draws Lutherans away from God's holy church and into profound error. But if they don't see the light, vengeance is at hand: "*video splendentes aere cateruas, / Armorumque grauem sonitum, radiosque tremisco. / Ista mouente Deo loquimur, iam dira bipennis / Credite adest sterilis radicibus addita planta*" (4.6.327) (I see the troops in their shining bronze and tremble at the horrible sounds of gleaming arms. Even as we speak, God is managing these events; believe the awful two-edged sword is being applied to the roots of the sterile plant). Naturally, it will "smite no more," once it has cut away those sterile roots. The Protestant Milton might well have winced at a two-handed sword cutting through a swath of Lutherans, but he would not be hesitant to swing it himself at an episcopal establishment that, for him, denied true liberty.

ALPHEUS AND ARETHUSA

Finally, it might be convenient to discuss Milton's references to "Fountain *Arethuse*" (l. 85) and Alpehus ("Return *Alphéus*, the dred voice is past / That shrunk thy streams"—ll. 132–33) as a unit, since Conti treats them both in a single chapter of the *Mythologiae*. Here is the pertinent passage from Conti:

> Alij diuinam vim animorum nostrorum, virtutisque naturam per huiusmodi fabulam explicarunt, quippe quòd sicuti materia appetit formam, vt suum proprium bonum, quòd ipsa per se inutilis est & ociosa apparet, sic anima nostra virtutem tanquam formam suam expetit. Haec causa est cur Alpheus fingebatur sequi Arethusam, cùm *aiphos* sit macula, vt dictum est, siue imperfectio, & *arete* virtus à Graecis nominetur. (8.21.922)

(Other ancient writers used this type of myth to explain the immortal power of our spirits and the striving for excellence that we possess within our souls. Just as matter looks for a form to help it realize itself [for by itself and in itself matter has no value and seems to be uninvolved with anything] so our soul yearns for the excellence that is its own proper form. And that's why the ancients said that Alpheus followed Arethusa, for *alphos* means "stain" or "imperfection" [as we've already mentioned], and *arete* is what the Greeks call "virtue."}

As Hughes (119) observes, drawing from this same chapter in Conti, the stain of Alpheus and the virtue of Arethusa may signal the ultimate triumph of the good clergy (e.g., Edward King and his ilk) in England.

The aversion of the pure soul (Arethusa or Edward King) for any type of contact with the less than pure (Alpheus or the corrupt clergy) is also underscored by Conti's quotation from Vergil's tenth eclogue: "If, when thou glidest beneath Sicilian waves [recall Milton's reference to Alpheus as the Sicilian Muse in l. 133], thou wouldst not have briny Doris blend her stream with thine" (ll. 4–5; Conti 8.21.921).[22]

It should be clear by now that the parallels between Milton's writings and the mythographies of Cartari and Conti are legion; if they were his only bibliographical sources, they could easily have satisfied his needs for both information about and systematic, symbolical interpretation of pagan myth. As it stands, Conti and Cartari are really the great inheritors of a mythological tradition that began with the ancient Greek and Roman texts themselves and passed through many other forms before these helpful writers codified and synthesized its discordant elements. If not always the most insightful of commentators on the mythological tradition, they are certainly the most complete, and can serve as reliable guides to the quality and extent of information on classical mythology that was available to Milton.

Ten

Conclusions

This brief survey of Milton has revealed, if nothing else, the vastness and complexity of the mythological traditions available to Milton and the many options he had in applying them to his prose and poetry. Clearly, the continental tradition has been the most neglected by scholars, and the piecemeal attempts to relate his works to the emblem books require more serious application. Milton and the middle ages is another area of vast neglect, which has been barely touched on here. While Milton read the Greek and Latin classics as filtered through editions, translations and commentaries, it would be folly indeed to ignore the texts themselves as the primary sources of his ideas and information about mythology; that is a given in this discourse. At the same time, Milton himself was an annotator and commentator on classical mythology, an aspiring author of lexicons, a rigorous editor of Euripides, a master of Greek epic conventions.

Annotations to the classical texts of Homer, Vergil and Ovid are interesting but are more often philological than truly interpretive, except when they borrow readings or "allegories" from mythographers like Giraldi and Conti. The allegorized Ovid is somewhat more interesting; building on an already rich tradition of mythological commentary on the editions and translations of Ovid, the attempt to "christianize" myth enabled the commentator to move beyond simple philological analysis to the richer complexities and ambiguities of moral allegory. The allegory also became more systematized and less piecemeal, with every myth receiving approximately equal treatment.

The church fathers attempt to develop a theoretical approach to pagan mythology, if only to demolish it. Ironically, like the more positive orientation of the *Ovide Moralisé*, they place mythology in a Christian context and, in effect, anthologize large segments of the classical corpus. Their ambivalent attitude toward the pagan pantheon may well have encouraged Milton's own flexible attitude, now condemning, now endorsing pagan learning; now showing the gods as fiends, then modeling Adam, Eve, God the Father and the Son in the anthropomorphic terms of Homer and Hesiod.

Martianus Capella, Alan of Lille, and Bernard of Sylvester place myth in a purely literary context, particularly the myths of love, nature and creation. All three aspire to the epic strain and thus provide early generic models for the treatment of these themes in *Paradise Lost* and *Paradise Regained*. On a more empirical level, all three writers provided Milton with efficient guides for transferring human beings, gods and demons from the upper world to the lower world and back again, and spatial metaphors to bridge the gulf between material and spiritual forces.

In the *Trattato d'amore*, both the aesthetic and the philosophical aspects of mythology are united to form a new synthesis of philosophical ideas expressed through both myth and literature. The authors of these love treatises focus on the myths of Venus and Cupid, leading inevitably to a meditation on the nature of women and, in the Christian tradition, on Eve as an expression of the eternal feminine. Ficino's definition of love as the desire for enjoying beauty is certainly the working definition of Adam's relation to Eve, and the sophisticated bantering of Philo and Sophia is epitomized in Milton's description of amorous Eve's "sweet reluctant amorous delay" (*PL* 4.311). Ficino establishes the sanctity and worth of human love, and Bruno chronicles its extremes.

The Renaissance dictionaries provide a primarily factual analysis of the myths, succinct accounts of information gleaned from a variety of sources: the *Trattato d'amore*, the emblem books, the mythographers, editions of the classics, and even other dictionaries. The mythographies offer the most complete accounts of the myths and the most extended, systematic interpretations of their contents. Treatises like Conti's *Mythologiae* are veritable anthologies and interpretations of Greek and Latin literary texts, selected for the convenience of the busy Renaissance poet or artist. The convenient indexes in the texts of Giraldi, Conti and Cartari further encouraged their users to focus on the particular myth and interpretation they were looking for, say the uxorious Hercules, slave to the Lydian Queen Omphale.

The occult tradition filters through many, if not all, of the mythological works canvassed here. The emblem books are ambivalently pedagogical and mysterious—teaching plain truth through the veil of myth, simultaneously disguised and revealed in both verbal and pictorial symbols. The hieroglylphs form an obviously occult code, as do the blatantly sexual episodes glossed in the *Ovide Moralisé*. The mythographers—inconsistently to be sure—painstakingly explain the mythic allegories that only an intelligent audience can understand. The English mythographers follow falteringly (and sometimes belligerently) in their occult wake. One work proposes to decipher another, and in the process introduces new confusions, as Ridevallus explicates Fulgentius's explication of the myths. Works like Martianus Capella's *The Marriage of Mercury and Philology* are practically indecipherable, and complex analyses of *homo sapiens* in Alan of Lille prepare the way for Milton's own *homo erectus*, Adam.

As Patricia Vicari has remarked,

> The seventeenth century witnessed the decline and fall of classical mythology as a branch of knowledge, as a subject for poetry, and even as a rhetorical ornament. As the medieval world-view faded into a curiosity, so did the doctrine of hieroglyphs, that "sacramental view of nature" which upheld the mystical significance of the creatures made by God and the myths made by God's image, man. (214)

In this as in many other ways, Milton was the last great Renaissance humanist, the most creative and learned mythologist who ever wrote in English, the most brilliant synthesizer of pagan and Christian thought in any language.

Notes

Notes to Introduction

1. See Putnam, esp. 1.417–39; 2.3–87.
2. See Fletcher, *Intellectual Development*, and Parker esp. 1.3–182.
3. The earlier view is expressed in an anonymous work of the eighteenth century, *An Essay Upon Milton's Imitations of the Ancients*: "... vastly less invention and Judgment is required to make a good Original than a fine imitation" (6).
4. On the same theme see Anne Bowers Long, who uses the phrase "conjunctive allusion" (176) to describe Milton's simultaneous references to the Bible and the classics.
5. See esp. Starnes and Talbert's chapter on "Milton and the Dictionaries," in *Classical Myth and Legend in Renaissance Dictionaries* (cited hereafter as Starnes and Talbert) 226–339.
6. "Each Stair mysteriously was meant" (*Paradise Lost* 3.516). This and all other references to Milton's poetry are to the Shawcross edition.
7. Boswell's *Milton's Library* is the main study of Milton's accessibility to books.
8. See esp. *Nature Into Myth* and *The Lamb and the Elephant*.
9. See both *Milton's Eve* and *A Gust for Paradise*.
10. See Allen, *Mysteriously Meant*, ch. 10, "The Rationalization of Myth and the End of Allegory" 279–311.
11. Du Rocher's study of Milton and Ovid introduces Renaissance editions and allegories of Ovid only to dismiss them, treats the Homeric and Vergilian influences on Milton as appendages to Ovid, and cites Ovid in a modern edition. Since it is very rare

to find a "clean" text of Ovid in the seventeenth century (that is, one that corresponds exactly with a modern edition or that is bereft of commentary), Du Rocher's approach to Milton's interaction with Ovid is, in my view, virtually untenable.

12. For a useful corrective to this tendency, see my edition of essays on the subject of Milton's medievalism, *Milton and the Middle Ages*.

13. See references in Wolfe, *Complete Prose Works*, passim. All subsequent references to Milton's prose are to this edition and will be cited as *YP*.

14. One purpose of this chapter is to challenge Frye's reference to "Milton's apparent lack of interest in the emblem literature..." (18).

15. For an account of how the blind Milton might have worked his way through printed sources, see Grant McColley 48–49.

16. I am alluding to George Wesley Whiting's pioneering study, *Milton's Literary Milieu*.

17. On the former, see Patterson, Introduction 8.

18. Bouchard's evocation of the labyrinth as a controlling metaphor describing Milton's narrative art might also be enriched by a careful reading of Conti's chapters on Theseus and Daedalus (*Mythologiae* 7.9, 16).

19. "The Death of the Author," in *Image Music Text* 142–48.

20. *Feminist Milton*. Philip Gallagher makes a similar claim in *Milton, the Bible, and Misogyny*. See also Mary Nyquist, "The Genesis of Gendered Subjectivity in the Divorce Tracts and in Paradise Lost," in *Remembering Milton* 99–127.

Notes to Chapter One

1. Often he takes his cue from Conti as to the details surrounding a myth, but will attack him when Conti occasionally misdescribes or misspells a place name. He also cites the encylopedist Ludovicus Caelius Rhodiginus (see chapter 7) and the mythographer Fulgentius (see chapter 8). For a good general study of allegorical interpretations of Homer, see Lamberton's *Homer the Theologian*.

2. The mythological figure of *Occasio* and its relation to the similar figure of *Fortuna* will be discussed in several chapters of this study.

3. All translations from Greek, Latin, Italian and French not otherwise identified are my own.

4. The modern edition (with French translation) is by Félix

Buffière. Milton's signed copy is in the Special Collections library at the University of Illinois, Urbana-Champaign. I refer to the modern subdivisions in the text, but I have consulted both editions.

5. See Gallagher's essay on euhemerism.

6. On Renaissance ideas of the flood, see Allen's *Legend of Noah*.

7. See Boccaccio, *Genealogie Deorum Gentilium Libri* 1.2, 1.5.

8. McGrath employs this term in the title of his article on the illustrated editions of Vincenzo Cartari's *Imagini*.

9. This and all subsequent citations from Natale Conti's *Mythologiae* are to the Frankfurt 1581 edition. Although the first edition of the *Mythologiae* was printed in Venice (1567, second edition 1581), most editions are page-for-page reprints of Andreas Wechelus's Frankfurt edition and are therefore more likely to have been consulted by Milton than the Venice editions.

10. I cite the edition by Jones and Jones, and the translation by Schreiber and Maresca.

11. On Milton's distaste for women in power, see Le Comte, *Yet Once More*, especially chapter seven, "Women and Bishops" 123–41.

12. For a general study of Milton and the Muses, which depends heavily on the Renaissance dictionaries (discussed in my ch. 7), see Gregory's *Milton and the Muses*; see also Revard's "Milton's Muse and the Daughters of Memory."

13. Jane Chance traces the Latin appropriation of the Pythagorean Y, the choice of virtue or vice in human life, to Servius's commentary on Vergil: 'We know that Pythagoras the Samian divided human life like the letter Y: that is, the first part of life is undetermined being not yet given to either vices nor virtues; but the fork of the Y begins at adolescence, the time at which men pursue either vices, that is the left part, or virtues, the right part" (Servius On *Aen.* 6.136). Cited in Chance, *Medieval Mythography* 90. On Hercules at the Crossroads, see E. Tietze-Conrat, "Notes on 'Hercules at the Crossroads'" 305–09.

14. For the medieval Vergil and Vergil the magician, see Comparetti's *Virgil in the Middle Ages* and Spargo's *Virgil the Necromancer*.

15. In Smith's *Elizabethan Critical Essays* 1.136.

16. Although the *scholia* were not quite as detailed, classical writers other than Homer, Vergil, and Ovid also merited extensive commentary. See, for example, Johannus Passeratus's 1608 edition of Catullus, Tibullus and Propertius.

17. See note 5.

18. See Guy de Tervarent's study, "Eros and Anteros Or Reciprocal Love in Ancient and Renaissance Art."

19. Diane McColley invokes this tradition only to dismiss it: "Typically, the story is interpreted literally as male virtue undone by female concupiscence and figuratively as passion subjugating reason or the soul made thrall to the body's rebel powers" (*Milton's Eve* 9).

20. See Donald Swanson and John Mulryan, "The Son's Presumed Contempt for Learning in *Paradise Regained*: A Biblical and Patristic Resolution."

21. Cp. Zachary Bogan on Homer, above.

22. The point was made earlier by Albert C. Labriola in his essay, "The Titans and the Giants: *Paradise Lost* and the Tradition of the Renaissance Ovid."

23. For a more positive interpretation of Eve's sojourn at the stream, see Richard Corum, "Paradise Lost and Milton's Ideas of Women," in *Milton and the Idea of a Woman* 132–33.

24. Robert H. West, in his *Milton and the Angels*, shifts the focus and the responsibility to the fallen angels: "Milton seems to say in *Paradise Regained* and certainly to indicate in *Paradise Lost* that fallen angels in their own persons could and would embrace women with desire and even procreate with them" (169). James G. Turner, in *One Flesh*, his seminal study of seventeenth century ideas of the Fall, remarks on "the fatal coupling of male angels and female humans in Genesis 6.1–2" (20).

25. Commentators on Scripture, as Arnold Williams remarks in *The Common Expositor*, were even more careful: "They recognized a danger of large-scale reconciliation of Christianity and classical mythology" (210). See also John P. McCall, *The Poetics of Classical Myth*.

26. See note 36.

27. See Wind, ch. 3, "Father Time" 69–91.

28. While Martin Luther is not a classical author in the sense used here, his account of Moloch, as negotiated in the Henri Belle English translation (1652), has a verbal pattern similar to Milton's, while the horrible, repulsive cast of Moloch is emphasized with chilling detail. Bell places it under the category "Of Idolatrie" (chapter five) and the heading "The worshiping of the Idol *Moloch*, the Idol of the *Ammonites*":

> The holie Scripture often maketh mention of *Moloch*: and *Lyra* also, and the Commentaries of the Jews saie, It was an Idol made of Copper and Brasse, like a man that held his hands before him, wherein they put fierie glimmering

Coals. Now, when the Image was made very hot, then a father approached, and offered to the Idol, wherein the child was consumed and burned to death. In the mean time, they made a loud noise with Timbrels and Cymbals, and with blowing of horne, to th'end the parents should not heare the pitiful crying of the childe.

Other accounts of Moloch appear in the emblem books and Renaissance dictionaries (see chs. 5 and 7).

29. Harding, *Milton and the Renaissance Ovid* 13.
30. *Integumenta Ovidii, Poemetto Inedito Del Secolo XIII.*
31. De Boer, vol. 1, pp. 44–52.
32. "Fruit" throughout *Paradise Lost*; "apple" in *Areopagitica*.
33. Citations are designated by book, section, and page.
34. De Boer, *Ovide Moralisé en Prose*, 3.
35. Perhaps this is the source of Milton's remark in *The Doctrine and Discipline of Divorce* that divorce (the separating of the hermaphrodite) is, in a sense, an act of creation: "... when by his [God's] divorcing command the world first rose out of Chaos, nor can be renew'd again out of confusion but by the separation of unmeet consorts" (*YP* 2.273).
36. The term "hermaphrodite" embraced such a wide range of meanings during the Renaissance, including the possession of the presumed psychological traits as well as the reproductive organs of both sexes, that it is difficult to take Milton's denial of the phenomenon seriously. As Thomas Laqueur points out in *Making Sex: Body and Gender from the Greeks to Freud* (65), the medical literature of the period suggests that a woman might rise to the level of the "superior sex" and become a man, but very few writers thought it was possible for a man to become a woman. However, from Adam's perspective, Eve is "manlike" and yet "of different sex" the *summa* of everything that is beautiful in creation and at least in this sense superior to Adam himself (although the angel Raphael rebukes Adam for denigrating himself before Eve). Other traditions assume that Adam was sexless until the sexes were defined and delineated through the creation of Eve. See below (ch. 5) for the emblematic rendering of the hermaphrodite (Hermes plus Aphrodite, or Wisdom merging with Love). See also Caspar Bauhin's *De hermaphroditum natura* (Frankfurt 1614), and Helkiah Crooke's *Microcosmographia: A Description of the Body of Man* (Barbican 1615), an anthologized translation of various writers on the human body. The latter, unlike Augustine, distinguishes between the androgyne and the hermaphrodite: "In the sex, when they are of an vncertaine sex, so that you may doubt whether it be a male

or a female or both, as Hermophradites. Bi-sexed Hermophradites they call *Androgynas,.....*" (book 5, quest. 14, "Of Monsters and Hermophradites," p. 299). Thus the "manlike" but "different sex" description of Eve is closer to Bauhin's hermaphroditic than his androgynous model. I am grateful to Winfried Schleiner for these references.

37. Jean Hagstrum, in *Sex and Sensibility*, remarks on "how closely linked are innocent love and sinful lust" in Milton's paradise. In fact, after the fall, "Love has become lust" (39, 41). But Diane McColley (in *A Gust for Paradise*) claims that too much attention has been paid to the erotic in Eden. For McColley, Logos, not Eros, is the guiding principle of Adam and Eve.

38. See Mulryan, "The Heroic Tradition of Milton's *Samson Agonistes*" 217–29.

39. Cf. the narrator of *Paradise Lost*'s description of Eve as "More lovely than *Pandora*, whom the Gods / Endowd with all thir gifts, and O too like / In sad event, ..." (4.714–16). In *The Doctrine and Discipline of Divorce* (3.440–41) Milton laments the fact that Adam's natural gifts and basic innocence did not prevent him from becoming another Epimetheus, the unwitting husband of Pandora. Diane McColley (*Milton's Eve* 69) reads Milton's account of the myth as parody, and his version of the Eve story as "a rectified version of the story of Pandora." I think she exaggerates the ability of Milton (and his readers) to transcend the misogynistic tenor of both myths.

40. See De Boer, *Ovide Moralisé en Prose*, 6.

Notes to Chapter Two

1. A thorough but uncritical study of the church fathers and pagan lore is Gerald L. Ellspermann's *The Attitude of The Early Christian Writers Toward Pagan Literature And Learning*.

2. In *Select Letters of St. Jerome*, (# 22, "To Eustochium"), 127–29.

3. Milton refers directly to Jerome's dream in his *Areopagitica*, and rejects its vision in terms of a more positive one by Dionysius Alexandrinus (cited in Eusebius 7.7), which stresses the competence of the informed reader (presumably of scripture as well as pagan thought):

> And perhaps it was the same politick drift that the Divell whipt St. *Jerom* in a lenten dream, for reading *Cicero*; or else it was a fantasm bred by the feaver which had then seis'd him. For had an Angel bin his discipliner, unlesse it

were for dwelling too much upon Ciceronianisms, & had chastiz'd the reading, not the vanity, it had bin plainly partiall.... first to correct him only, and let so many more ancient Fathers wax old in those pleasant and florid studies without the lash of such a tutoring apparition.... But if it be agreed we shall be try'd by visions, there is a vision recorded by *Eusebius* far ancienter then this tale of *Jerom* .... [where Dionysius Alexandrinus enjoins us to] "Read any books what ever come to thy hands, for thou art sufficient both to judge aright, and to examine each matter" (*YP* 2.509–11).

4. In the *Areopagitica* Milton asserts that the pagans joined with the church in forbidding pagan learning to Christians: ".... Julian the Apostat, and suttlest enemy to our faith, made a decree forbidding Christians the study of heathen learning; for, said he, they wound us with our own weapons, and with our owne arts and sciences they overcome us" (*YP* 2.508).

5. St Augustine, *The City of God Against the Pagans.* See also Peter A. Fiore, *Milton and Augustine: Patterns of Augustan Thought in 'Paradise Lost,'* and John Paul Pritchard, *The Influence of the Fathers Upon Milton With Especial Reference to Augustine.*

6. Saint Justin Martyr, "The First Apology," ch. 5, p. 38; ch. 54, pp. 91–92.

7. See also a Renaissance translation of John Calvin: "... the infinite number of gods hath flowed out of the wit of man." In *The institution of Christian Religion, written in Latin by maisterr Iohn Calvin, and translated into Englysh according to the authors last edition.* London, 1561.

8. *Tertullian: Apological Works and Minucius Felix Octavius, Apology* 36.

9. See ch. 1, n. 36.

10. In *The Anti-Nicene Fathers,* 3.246, "On Prescription Against Heretics," chap. vii. For the Latin text ("Quid ergo Athenis et Hierosolymis?") see *Florilegium Patristicum tam veteris quam medii aevi auctores complectens,* "Librum de Praescriptione Haereticorum," 7.9 p. 13.

11. All references to *The Divine Institutes* are taken from the English translation by Sister Mary Francis McDonald.

12. See Rorty 4, 391.

13. See ch. 1, n. 13.

14. This jibe is found in Lucian and repeated in Giordano Bruno, *Lo Spaccio.* See chapter 4.

Notes to Chapter Three

1. My text is *The Marriage of Mercury and Philology*, trans. by William Harris Stahl and Richard Johnson, with E. L. Burge. For the Latin text see *De nuptiis Philologiae et Mercurii*, ed. Adolf Dick. Space does not permit discussion of Capella's many commentators. See Chance, *Medieval Mythography*, chs. 7, 11.

2. See Lucian, *Dialogues of the Gods*, "Hermes and Maia" 4.255.

3. See Mulryan, "The Heroic Tradition" 226–27. The Gallic Hercules will be discussed in greater detail in the chapter (5) on emblem books.

4. See Wind 106–08.

5. Brown emphasizes the trickery rather than the deceit of Mercury in the various sham agreements that he makes with other divinities.

6. *The Cosmographia of Bernardus Sylvestris*, trans. Winthrop Wetherbee 3. All subsequent references to the text of the *Cosmographia* are to this edition and will be cited in the text. The Latin text can be found in *Bernardus Silvestris: Cosmographia*, ed. Peter Dronke.

7. See Winthrop Wetherbee, *Platonism and Poetry in the Twelfth Century: The Literary Influence of the School of Chartres*, esp. the fourth chapter, "Form and Inspiration in the Poetry of Bernardus Sylvestris" 152–86.

8. See also my remarks on the Antwerp 1575 edition of Vergil in ch. 1, p. 23.

9. All subsequent references to the texts of *Anticlaudianus* and the *Plaint of Nature* are to the translations by James J. Sheridan. For the Latin text of the *Plaint of Nature*, see *The Anglo-Latin Satirical Poets and Epigrammatists of the Twelfth Century*, vol. 2, ed. Thomas Wright; for the *Anticlaudianus*, see *Anticlaudianus*, ed. R. Bossuat.

10. Cf. *Hermathena* 12 (1902–03), 439–40. Cited in the William H. Cornog translation of the *Anticlaudianus*, 42n.

11. For an excellent study of Alan and the school of Chartres, see Wetherbee, *Platonism and Poetry in the Twelfth Century*, esp. chapter 5, "Nature and Grace: The Allegories of Alain De Lille."

12. See C. S. Lewis, *English Literature in the Sixteenth Century, Excluding Drama* 124.

13. For a full list of manuscripts, see G. Raynaud De Lage, *Alain De Lille, Poète Du XII Siècle*, "Appendice: Manuscrits D'Alain De Lille" 175–86.

14. Cf. his "Milton and the *Roman de la Rose*: Adam and Eve

at the Fountain of Narcissus," in *Milton and the Middle Ages* 153–82.

15. Cf. Wetherbee, *Platonism and Poetry* 255–66.

16. For a provocative exploration of the tragic and heroic modes in *Paradise Lost*, see Barbara K. Lewalski, *Paradise Lost and the Rhetoric of Literary Forms*, esp. chs. 9 and 10.

17. To be explored in detail in the chapters on the emblem books (5) and the mythographers Vincenzo Cartari and Natale Conti (9).

18. The classic study is by Adolf Katzenellenbogen, *Allegories of the Virtues and Vices in Mediaeval Art From Early Christian Times to the Thirteenth Century.*

Notes to Chapter Four

1. Marsilio Ficino *Commentary on Plato's Symposium on Love*, trans. Sears Jayne. All references are to this edition. For the Latin text, see the *Theologia Platonica*.

2. *Leone Ebreo: The Philosophy of Love*, trans. F. Friedeberg-Seeley and Jean H. Barnes. All references are to this edition. For the Italian text, see the *Dialoghi d'amore*, ed. Santino Caramella.

3. *Giordano Bruno's "Heroic Frenzies,"* trans. Paul Eugene Memmo, Jr. All references are to this edition. For the Italian text, see *Degl'heroici fuori*.

4. *The Expulsion of the Triumphant Beast*, trans. Arthur D. Imerti. All references are to this edition. For the Italian text, see *Spaccio De La Bestia Trionfante*.

5. See McColley, *Milton's Eve*; and Shawcross, *With Mortal Voice: The Creation of "Paradise Lost."* Shawcross is the more explicit of the two: "The subject of man's disobedience has been used to exhibit the theme of God's love . . . (27). "*Paradise Lost* is about the losing of paradise, but the *theme* in the simplest terms is love" (31). For McColley, "The love that is wholly and ever-increasingly fulfilled because it is in right tune with God and all creation is the essence of Paradise" (64).

6. In assessing Milton's possible use of the *D'Amore*, I see no purpose in distinguishing between the various speeches and points of view of the different speakers of Ficino's dialogue, who in turn represent speakers from Plato's original dialogue, the *Symposium*. Professor Jayne provides a useful chart that indicates the parallel speakers and their topics (10).

7. See Jayne 4–7 on the lack of correspondence between the speech and chapter sections (which were not originally

published with the text) of the *De amore* and the actual units of meaning.

8. On the many faces of Venus in both the Middle Ages and the Renaissance, see my articles "The Three Images of Venus: Boccaccio's Theory of Love in *The Genealogy of the Gods* and His Aesthetic Vision of Love in *The Decameron*," and "Venus, Cupid and the Italian Mythographers."

9. See ch. 1, n. 36.

10. Cf. Bernard Sylvester (trans. ch. 3, p. 110).

11. See chap. 1, n. 5.

12. Chance (*Medieval Mythography* 347-48) refers to the tenth century poet "Theolodulus," who compares the symbolism of moral virtue in the Old Testament and in pagan myth, but from a Christian perspective, a perspective that is obviously not available to Ebreo.

13. For earlier sources of the Demogorgon, see ch. 8, n. 16.

14. See Mulryan, "The Three Images of Venus." Cartari, in his chapter on Venus, singles out Ebreo as the best commentator on the image of Venus rising from the sea (*Imagini* 530). This and all subsequent references to Cartari are taken from the Venice 1571 edition of the *Imagini*, edited by Vincentio Valgrisi. All translations are my own.

15. The common source of Ebreo and Milton may be Boccaccio's *Genealogiae*, 9:4, "De Cupidine 1 Martis filio, qui genuit Voluptatem" ("On the First Cupid, the son of Mars, who begot Desire"):

> Has aureas esse dicunt et plumbeas, et aureis amorem, plumbeis autem odium inferri, ut amantium ostendatur opinio.
> They said that these arrows were lead and gold, the gold to inspire love and the lead hatred, as the imagination of lovers demonstrates. (vol. 2, pp. 453-54)

16. Translators' brackets.

17. Cf. Crooke, *Microcosmographia*: "That Females are more wanton and petulant then Males, wee thinke hapneth because of the impotencie of their minds; for the imaginations of lustfull women are like the imaginations of bruite beastes which haue no repugnancie or contradiction of reason to restraine them" (book 5, question 2, "Of the Temperament of women, whether they are colder or hotter then men" p. 276). Before faulting Milton for sexism, or suggesting that he was particularly critical or contemptuous of women, we should ponder the fact that this passage appears in a Renaissance medical textbook! Diane

McColley (*Milton's Eve* 9) claims that Milton's version of the fall rejected the "dualism" of earlier verbal accounts, which interpreted the story "as male virtue undone by female concupiscence and figuratively as passion subjugating reason or the soul made thrall to the body's rebel powers."

18. For a provocative study of Bruno and the occult arts, see Frances A. Yates, *Giordano Bruno and the Hermetic Tradition*. More immediately pertinent to this study is John Charles Nelson's *Renaissance Theory of Love: The Context of Giordano Bruno's 'Eroici furori.'*

19. Cf. ch. 1, p. 46.

20. The interlocutors in these dialogues are Luigi Tansillo and Oboardo Cicada. Since their respective positions are not so clearly defined as those of Ebreo's Philo and Sophia, I have not identified the speakers in my citations from the *Heroic Frenzies*.

21. See Patricia Vicari, "The Triumph of Art, the Triumph of Death: Orpheus in Spenser and Milton."

22. See Lucian, *Dialogues of the Sea-Gods*, and *Dialogues of the Gods*, vol. 4.

23. See ch. 2, p. 58 ff., on Augustine's denunciation and mockery of the Egyptian gods.

24. This passage is discussed at length in Swanson and Mulryan, "The Son's Presumed Contempt for Learning in *Paradise Regained*: A Biblical and Patristic Resolution" 243–59.

25. See my article, "The Occult Tradition and English Renaissance Literature."

26. See Frederick Kiefer's seminal article, "The Conflation of Fortuna and Occasio in Renaissance Thought and Iconography."

Notes to Chapter Five

1. See also the entry for "Iconography" by Albert Labriola in *A Milton Encyclopedia*.

2. The phrase is found in McGrath and refers to artistic representations of the gods based on literary descriptions rather than true artifacts.

3. Shahla Anand's *Of Costliest Emblem*, the only book-length study of Milton and the emblems, is restricted to English emblem books.

4. 1588–1667. His *A Collection of Emblemes, Ancient and Moderne* (London 1635) includes both biblical and mythological emblems.

5. 1592–1644. His *Emblemes* (1635) went through many editions and were extremely popular. Unlike Wither's they are almost entirely biblical.

6. First printed in Augsburg in 1531, Alciato's (1492–1550) *Emblematum Liber* went through hundreds of editions in almost every European language. Many of these emblems of Quarles and Wither are simply translations from Alciato, whose emblems embrace both biblical and mythological themes.

7. See, e.g. Gayle Edward Wilson, below.

8. *Studies in Seventeenth Century Imagery*, vol. 2. See also the great thematic, worldwide index and epitome of emblems by Arthur Henkel and Albrecht Schöne *Emblemata Hanbuch: Zur Sinbildkunst des xvi und xvii Jahrunderts*. For a good general study, see Albert N. S. Thompson, *Literary Bypaths of the Renaissance* 29–67, or Rosemary Freeman, *English Emblem Books*. See also Peter M. Daly, ed., *The English Emblem and the Continental Tradition* and *Literature In The Light of the Emblem*. An *emblem* is meant to have a universal application and a clearly expressed meaning, while an *impresa* is supposed to be cryptic and obscure, with a meaning that is personal and particular to a person or a noble house, as in a coat of arms. In practice, however, the emblem sometimes affects obscurity and the *impresa* has significance beyond its immediate application. As David Mason Green observes, "by 1600 the terms *emblem* and *impresa* were virtually interchangeable everywhere" (27).

9. Cf. Edward Tayler, *Milton's Poetry: Its Development in Time* 167–68, 257. See also Frederick Kiefer, "The Conflation of Fortune and Occasio in Renaissance thought and iconography," and Mother M. Christopher Pecheux, "Milton and *Kairos*."

10. Emblem 122. For convenience all references to the Alciato emblems are taken from the facsimile edition edited by Peter M. Daly and Virginia M. Callahan: *Andreas Alciatus: 1 The Latin Emblems Indexes and Lists*. When I quote from their English translations of Alciato's epigrams, I silently omit the Latin equivalents they sometimes supply for individual words.

11. Emblem 54 ("A Tergo Calva Est" ["She is Bald from Behind"]).

12. *The Second Part of the Tritameron Of Love*, London, 1587. Greene misidentifies Fortune here both as one of the Furies (*Erineys*, who punish crimes to pacify the souls of the dead) and the Fates (the *Moerae* or *Parcae*, who determine the course of human life).

13. For this reference I am indebted to Professor Peter Medine of the University of Arizona.

14. This is the second edition. The first edition (in which the emblem is less clear) appeared in Bologna in 1555.

15. Eve is also a kind of grim reaper, for her sin makes a fatal harvest of Adam's welcoming bouquet of roses: "From his

slack hand the Garland wreath'd for *Eve* / Down drop'd, and all the faded Roses shed" (*Paradise Lost* 9.892-93); having lost her innocence and also destroyed Adam's flowers, Eve is "Defac'd, deflowrd, and now to Death devote" (901).

16. *Emblemata* (Antwerp 1585), #26. First edition 1565.

17. Amsterdam, 1610 [?]. First edition 1579. There are later editions in both Flemish and French.

18. Dalila is also compared (implicitly) to other evil female divinities: Circe and the Sirens ("Thy fair enchanted cup, and warbling charms") (934), and the curious Pandora ("Curiosity, inquisitive, importune / Of secrets, then with like infirmity / To publish them, both common female faults" (775-77).

19. In the prose, the meaning of fortune is usually restricted to the twists and turns of circumstance, particularly in *The History of Britain*. However, in speaking of Constantine, who was made emperor almost by accident (he was a common soldier who happened to have the same name as the reigning emperor), Milton speaks of ". . . the extent of his Fortune dilating his mind" and Constantine's practical ability to make the most of his situation [*Occasio*] (*YP* 3.150).

20. God the Father denies any influence on himself of either Fortune or Occasion, for, unlike the pagan Jupiter, he is not subject to Fate: ". . . Necessitie and Chance / Approach not mee, and what I will is Fate" (7.172-73).

21. Cf. *Faerie Queene* 2.11.45-46:

> He then remembred well, that had bene sayd,
> How th' Earth his mother was, and first him bore;
> She eke so often, as his life decayd,
> Did life with vsury to him restore,
> And raysd him vp much stronger then before,
> So soone as he vnto her wombe did fall;
> Therefore to ground he would him cast no more,
> Ne him commit to graue terrestriall,
> But beare him farre from hope of succour vsuall.
>
> Tho vp he caught him twixt his puissant hands,
> And hauing scruzd out of his carrion corse
> The lothfull life, now loosd from sinfull bands,
> Vpon his shoulders carried him perforse
> Aboue three furlongs, taking his full course,
> Vntill he came vnto a standing lake;
> Him thereinto he threw without remorse,
> Ne stird, till hope of life did him forsake;
> So end of that Carles dayes, and his owne paines did make.

22. See also *The Disgracers: The Fall of Icarus*, by Hendrik Goltzius, fig. 32 in Frye, *Milton and the Visual Arts*. Frye also reproduces many images of the fall of Satan beneath the feet of Michael: see esp. #s 17, 27, 28, 47.

23. See ch. 1, n. 13.

24. But Milton does not see moral choice entirely in terms of male virtue and enervating female weakness. In Sonnet Nine, for example, he praises the unidentified lady for choosing the path of virtue and shunning the easy road of pleasure: "Ladie, that in the prime of earliest youth / Wisely hast shun'd the broad way and the green" (1–2). And of course the "Lady" in *A Mask* ("Comus") is resolute against the libidinous choices offered by the vile enchanter.

25. On images of Omphale and the effeminate Hercules, see Raymond B. Waddington, "The Bisexual Portrait of Francis I: Fontainbleau, Castiglione, and the Tone of Courtly Mythology," in *Playing With Gender* 99–131. See Hagstrum, who notes that "Milton's conservative views animate *Samson Agonistes*, a work that includes an angry denunciation of dominating woman and an unrelenting dramatization of an enslaved sensual man" (33). But Ares and Hodge imagine a Milton at war with his own irreconcilable views: "His attitudes to women and sex entailed contradictions which he never fully resolved" (4).

26. See for example Achille Bocchi #88.

27. See Mulryan, "The Heroic Tradition" 226–27.

28. Cartari also distinguishes between "good" and "bad" women in his chapter on Fortune 484. This reference and all subsequent references to Vincenzo Cartari are taken from the Venice 1571 edition of the *Imagini* (ed. Vincentio Valgrisi), and will be cited by chapter title and page.

29. See ch. 1, n. 36.

30. Milton sometimes appears to revel in the ambiguity of his own sexuality. More than once he brings up his nickname as the Lady of Christ's college, and accusations that he played the woman (*Second Defense*) or appeared less than manly: "Perhaps my semblance might deceave the truth / That I to manhood am arriv'd so neer" (Sonnet 7.5–6). And the anonymous biographer claims that when Milton's amanuensis came later than usual in the morning to assist the blind Milton, "he would complain, saying *he wanted to be milked*" (Hughes 1044).

31. A recent critic takes a quite different view of the hermaphrodite's image. Gregory W. Bredbeck, in his "Milton's Ganymede: Negotiations of Homoerotic Tradition," refers approvingly "to a text Milton himself knew, Plato's *Symposium*, in which Aristophanes regards the creation of individuated gender and

sexuality as a godly punishment" (274), and suggests that for Milton and his age distinctions between male and female (the "patriarchical" splitting of the hermaphrodite) were the result of Adam's sin rather than the way things should be: "Read in its vernacular and historical contexts, *Paradise Regained* reveals gendered meaning in general to be a product of the Fall, a system distinctive of a separation from God.... Thus in *Paradise Regained* the language of patriarchy becomes the language of Satan and not of Milton" (273–74).

32. For a useful study of Maier, see H. M. E. De Jong, *Michael Maier's "Atalanta Fugiens": Sources of an Alchemical Book of Emblems.*

33. De Yong translation 255.

34. The same illustration appears in the Venice 1571 edition of Cartari (p. 304).

35. See ch. 1, n. 28. See also John Selden's *De diis syris* ("On the Syrian Gods"), 76–100.

36. Daly, *The English Emblem*, 2. In comparison, according to Daly, England produced just 50 emblem books, in over 100 editions.

Notes to Chapter Six

1. See Allen's excellent survey, "The Symbolic Wisdom of the Ancient Egyptians," *Mysteriously Meant* 107–33.

2. See S. K. Heninger, Jr. *Touches of Sweet Harmony* 155.

3. See my article, "The Occult Tradition and English Renaissance Literature."

4. Quoted in Allen, "Ben Jonson and the Hieroglyphs," 293.

5. Cf. Rudolf Wittkower, "Hieroglyphics in the Early Renaissance" 63, 91. See also Seznec, *Survival* 155–56: "Horapollo's [the reputed author of the first account of hieroglyphics] example inspired the humanists, above all, to look for some contemporary equivalent of the ancient cryptograms. This equivalent was provided by Alciati [Alciato] in his first collection, published in 1531."

6. The complete title reveals more fully the conflation of emblem, hieroglyphic, and a host of other terms to describe poetic and occult symbolism: *The Art Of making Devices: Treating of Hieroglyphicks, Symboles, Emblemes, AEnigma's, Sentences, Parables, Reverses Of Medalls, Armes, Blazons, Cimiers, Cyphres and Rebus.* Trans. Thomas Blount. As we will notice in chapter 7, Estienne (Stephanus) was a noted lexicographer.

7. *Emblems, By Fra. Quarles; With The Hieroglyphicks.* London, 1696. A3.

8. This emblem is added by the editor (Jacob Kerver?). Horapollo's Greek text is accompanied by a Latin translation. For an English translation, see George Boas, *The Hieroglyphics of Horapollo*.

9. *Theater of Fine Devices* (2nd ed. London, 1614). Combe's translation also stresses the historicity and occult nature of the hieroglyphs: ". . . it is not onely in our time that Emblemes are in account and singular regard, but it hath bene of ancient times and almost from the beginning of the world: for the Egyptians (which thinke themselues to be the first people of the world) before the vse of letters, wrote by figures & images, as well of men, beasts, fowles, and fishes, as of serpents, thereby expressing their intentions, as is written by most ancient authors . . . which haue laboured diligently and curiously to expound the saide hieroglyphicall figures. . . ." (A4). See also the first edition, London, 1593 [?].

10. In *Ben Jonson* 7.266–74. In his poem, "An Expostulacion with Inigo Jones," Jonson refers sarcastically to Jones's masques as "true / Court hieroglyphics" (ll. 42–43).

11. Cf. the description of Fortune and her cornucopia in Peacham, Du Choul, and Paradin (ch. 5, pp. 125–26).

12. See ch. 1, n. 36.

13. See also Conti's mocking poem on Vulcan/Mulciber in 2.6.159–60, to be taken up again in ch. 9.

14. As Hughes points out (229n.), the whole passage recalls the palace that Vulcan built for Apollo (cf. Ovid, *Met* 1.171–72, 4.762–64). Vulcan is both the god of fire and an alchemical god, and, as we shall have occasion to discuss in chapter nine, a symbol for alchemy's absurdities.

15. See ch. 2, p. 58. See also Giordano Bruno's remarks in ch. 4, p. 108.

16. Natale Conti, *Mythologiae* 1.7.12. I have taken the Conti material out of sequence because my emphasis is on the ancient sources Conti is citing here, not on his commentary.

17. *Protesilaos*, fr. 40. In *Fragments of Attic Comedy* 2.63.

18. Published separately, but also part of the former work.

19. See also Caussin, emblem 18, ll. 3–4: "First by the Tortesse at her feete is meant, / She must not gad, but learne at home to shrowd" (B7).

20. On the mythology of the tortoise, see my article, "The Tortoise and the Lady in Vincenzo Cartari's *Imagini* and John Webster's *The White Devil*."

21. One must qualify any endorsement of Milton's presentation of the separation scene by remarking that, in Genesis, Adam is *present* when Eve is tempted by the devil; Milton's creative

version of events is nothing less than a distortion of the biblical text. In *A Gust for Paradise*, Diane McColley rejects such conservative readings of female behavior by ancient writers and modern readers alike: "Whatever readers may think of Eve's departure from Adam, and however many partriarchical critics supposed it a feminine whim, Eve's reasons for it are not frivolous" (164). In contrast, Marilyn F. Farwell observes that "although we assume that Eve is a reasonable creature, many early images align her with the material world of passion, the senses, and the body" ("Eve, the Separation Scene, and the Renaissance Idea of Androgyny" 11).

22. Cf. ch. 9, p. 270.

23. See ch. 1, n. 32.

24. For the triumphant Satan, however, it is a trivial fruit: "... Him by fraud I have seduc'd / From his Creator, and the more to increase / Your wonder, with an Apple..." (*Paradise Lost* 10.485–87). See also Leonora L. Brodwin, "Milton and the Renaissance Circe."

25. As Iversen remarks, Kircher's mystical approach ensured that "... the texts themselves could not tell him anything he did not know in advance" (96).

26. Cf. Swanson and Mulryan, "The Son's Presumed Contempt," 250–59.

27. On Chaos, see ch. 1, p. 36.

Notes to Chapter Seven

1. For an overview, see Dillon, *Renaissance Reference Books*.

2. The first edition was published at Venice in 1516 and the last in 1566, in Frankfurt and Leipzig. See also my article, "The *Lectionum Antiquarum* of Ludovicus Caelius and the Italian Mythographers."

3. But William Kerrigan, commenting on Eve as naked hostess (*Paradise Lost* 5.443–50) in *The Sacred Complex*, suggests that "the libidinal power of Eve" is an *"excuse"* for not only Adam's passion, but the narrator's and the angel's as well (205).

4. See ch. 8, "Milton and the Dictionaries" 226–339. See also Starnes, *Renaissance Dictionaries English-Latin and Latin-English*.

5. Although Eliot does borrow some of his material from the Stephanus brothers, many of his entries are translated directly from Calepino (Starnes, *Renaissance Dictionaries* 53).

6. The other authors mentioned by Hoole (with the exception of Sandys, whom we have already discussed in chapter 1) will be discussed in chapter 9, "Milton and the Mythographers":

Mr. *Sandy's* Translation of this book [Ovid's *Metamorphoses*], in Folio, and Mr. *Rosse's English Mythologist*, will be very delightfull helps to your Scholars for the better understanding thereof; and if to these you adde *Sir Francis Bacon's little* book *de Sapientiâ veterum [On the Wisdom of the Ancients], Natales comes* [Natale Conti's *Mythologiae*], and *Verderius's Imagines Deorum* [The Latin translation of Vincenzo Cartari's *Imagini*], *Lexicon Geographicum, Poeticum, & Historicum* [Thomas Cooper's dictionary]; and the like fitting to be reserved for your Scholars use in the Schoole-librarie) it will invite them like so many bees to busie themselves sucking up matter and words to quicken their invention and expression. (Hoole 162–163; see also Starnes & Talbert 25–26.)

7. Starnes and Talbert 17. See also Fletcher, *The Intellectual Development of John Milton,* and D. L. Clark.

8. This is the third edition. The first edition was published in Milan in 1498. The person associated with the name "Suidas" flourished in the late tenth century, although the name may actually refer to the encyclopedia or "meadow." Thomas Eliot cites Suidas as one of his sources in the second edition of his dictionary (1538). Since all of the dictionaries, including Suidas's, are arranged alphabetically, I have not supplied page or signature references for these works.

9. According to Starnes, "During the whole period of the Renaissance scarcely an important dictionary was published which did not reflect directly or indirectly the influence of Calepine" (*Renaissance Dictionaries* 52).

10. Entered under "Saturnus."

11. See Edward Ewing Brandon, *Robert Estienne Et Le Dictionaire Français Aux XVI Siècle* 29. Brandon observes (26) that Estienne was apparently ignorant of the medieval lexicons that existed in manuscript form.

Notes to Chapter Eight

1. For Chance, "the moralization and allegorization of classical mythology, ... an explanation and rationalization of one or more myths, often in didactic form" (*Medieval Mythography* 1–2).

2. H. J. Rose (*Handbook*) agrees with Herodotus that Homer probably lived about 850 B.C. (33), but disagrees with the Greek historian's view that Homer was a contemporary of Hesiod; after reviewing the very scanty evidence available, Rose

very tentatively places Hesiod somewhere in the eighth century B.C. (65).

3. In *Auctores Mythographi Latini*, ed. Staveren (1742) 1–573. There were many compilations of the early mythographers extant around Milton's time. The four referred to here are: *Mythologici Latini*, ed. Commelinus (1599); *Opuscula Mythologica, Ethica Et Physica. Graece & Latine*, ed. Gale (1671); *Historiae Poeticae Scriptores Antiqui*, ed. Gale (1675); *Mythographi Latini*, ed. Muncker (1681). Titles of mythographies cited will be listed before the editors' names. For an overview of the classical mythographers, see the rather opinionated article by H. J. Rose ("Mythographers").

4. Frazer edition. Some very minor claimants to the title of mythographer are printed along with Apollodorus in Gale's edition (*Historiae Poeticae*). They are Cononis (*Narrationes*), Ptolemaeus (*Novae ad variam eruditionem historiae*), Parthenius (*Erotica*), and Antoninus Liberalis (*Metamorphoses*). Their Greek texts are accompanied by parallel Latin translations. Only Apollodorus is cited in Conti's *Mythologiae*.

5. See ch. 1, n. 5.

6. Cf. ch. 1, p. 32; ch. 6, p. 166.

7. There is an English translation in Gilbert Murray's *Four Stages of Greek Religion* 187–214.

8. Staveren 1: 612, 614; 2: 668–71; 3: 647–48.

9. Cf. ch. 1, n. 36.

10. If we are to believe Edward Le Comte (*Milton and Sex* 1–2) the phallic implications of the lady's immobilized position are elaborated upon in the reference to "... this marble venom'd seat / Smear'd with gumms of glutenous heat" (916–17), which Le Comte takes to mean sperm sticking to the *gluteous* (buttock). Venom is also the product of a snake (Mercury) or (in Le Comte's version) the phallus. Milton's immediate source is of course Spenser's Busyrane, whose charms must be reversed before Amoret can be made whole again (*Faerie Queene* 3.12).

11. Ed. Bode, 1834. See also the more recent edition of the first two Vatican mythographers by Kulcsàr, 1987.

12. Cf. the *Dizionario Biografico*; Chubb, 216.

13. Unless otherwise indicated, all subsequent references to the four great Italian mythographers will be to the Vincenzo Romano critical edition of the *De Genealogiae*, the English translation by Osgood (*Boccaccio on Poetry*) of the fourteenth and fifteenth books, the Basel 1560 edition of the *De Deis Gentium* (first published in 1548), the expanded Venice 1571 (ed. Vincentio Valgrisi) edition of the *Imagini*, and the expanded Frankfurt 1581 edition of the *Mythologiae*. For translations of

Giraldi, see note 20; translations from Conti are to the unpublished translation of the *Mythologiae* by John Mulryan and Steven Brown. Translations of Cartari are to my own unpublished translation of the *Imagini*. I have supplied Cartari's original Italian and Conti's original Latin, but English translations of their Latin and Italian translations from ancient Greek and Latin sources are taken from the Loeb series, but without the original Greek or Latin text.

14. Cf. A. Hortis, *Studi*, and Osgood, *Boccaccio on Poetry* xliv n. See also Wilkins, who builds on the work of Hortis; he gives detailed descriptions of editions and concludes that all editions of the *De Genealogia* are directly or indirectly derived from the Venice 1472 editions (437).

15. Osgood, *Boccaccio on Poetry* xii.

16. Cf. Harris Fletcher, "Milton's Demogorgon." Don Cameron Allen calls Demogorgon a "slip of the pen" that originated in a gloss of Statius by Lactantius Placidus (*Mysteriously Meant* 216). Seznec, in commenting on Boccaccio's "source," the lost author Theodontius, remarks that "Demogorgon is a grammatical error, become god" (*Survival* 222). See also Chance (*Medieval Mythography* 12).

17. Giraldi's etymological musings on the gods may owe something to an earlier work of uncertain date devoted to the subject, Julian Aurelius's *De Cognominibus Deorum Gentilium* (*On the Surnames of the Pagan Gods*) (Venice 1696).

18. See the *Biographie Universelle* and Gruppe.

19. Allen, *Mysteriously Meant* 221–25.

20. From the thirteenth *syntagma* of Giraldi's *Historia*. The text is taken from the unpublished translation of this section of the *Historia* by John Mulryan and Steven Brown, which is based on all known editions.

21. See the list of sources in the *Apotheseos* a4^v–a5.

22. Cf. Tiraboschi, *Storia Della Letteratura Italiana* 3.223–24; and Allen, *Mysteriously Meant* 228.

23. By Giordano Ziletti and Vincentio Valgrisi, both published at Venice.

24. The Venice 1566 reprint of the first edition contains a few illustrations, but not enough to be of any real value to its readers.

25. Cf. McGrath 213–26 and Mortimer 1.156–8. See also Allen, *Mysteriously Meant* 28.

26. Cf. Seznec's caustic analysis of the Italian mythographers in *The Survival of the Pagan Gods*, 236–56. He holds up Conti as well as Cartari to ridicule for "orientalizing" the supposed classical purity of the gods, but all of his references are to Cartari

rather than Conti, and he appears to be confusing the meaning of the illustrations for the Cartari text with what Conti actually says in the text of the *Mythologiae*. See also Seznec's own article, where he notices the misapplication of the Cartari illustrations to Conti's text: "Les manuels mythologiques italiens." The misapplication of the plates to Conti's text is also treated in McGrath and Mortimer.

27. For example, in the 1608 edition published at Padua, the title page boasts that the *Imagini* is an *"Opera utilissima historici, Poeti, Pittori, Scultori, & professori di belle lettere."* See also Allen, *Mysteriously Meant* 232.

28. See my article, "Translations and Adaptations of Vincenzo Cartari's *Imagini* and Natale Conti's *Mythologiae.*"

29. Both were published at Lyon and both were translated by the same man, Antoine du Verdier.

30. *The Courtier* was first published in 1533, and many times thereafter. The copy I examined at the Huntington library (Venice 1533, call # 30132) is bound with the Latin translation by Bartholomew Clerke (London 1585).

31. Cf. Yates, *Life of an Italian in Shakespeare's England* 303.

32. All subsequent references are to the Spingarn edition. I have also consulted Arnold's annotated edition.

33. Jones's references to Conti are often word for word. For Chapman, cf. the gloss on "The Shadow of Night," in Bartlett's edition of the poems 29.

34. "Letter #196," Dr. Browne to Mr. Dugdale, 11 Dec. 1658, Keynes 6:309.

35. See Gilbert 9 (Cf. Oceanus, Electra), and Mulryan, "Mythic Interpretations of Ideas in Jonson's *Pleasure Reconciled to Virtue*" passim.

36. Probably Jean Tixier's *Opus Epithetorum*, published at Basel in 1541 and in dozens of other editions through the seventeenth century.

37. *Nature Into Myth*, 46–51. While Steadman does attack the Starnes and Talbert claim that the mythographies were themselves made redundant by the Renaissance dictionaries, he does not grant them full generic integrity: "So far as the transmission of classical myth is concerned, a sharp dichotomy between lexicographical and mythographical works would not be a functional distinction. We might well bear in mind, therefore, that convenient, though equivocal, category (still preserved in library catalogues)—Dictionaries and Encyclopaedias" (52). See also his article, "Urania, Wisdom, and Scriptural Exegesis (*Paradise Lost*, VII, 1–12)."

38. Cf. Lotspeich, *Classical Mythology* passim.

39. While Steadman asserts that Marston's words "do not indicate that Marston himself really possessed these books or that he himself normally made a practice of consulting them" (49), Davenport, the editor of Marston's satires, asserts the opposite point, at least in relation to Natale Conti and his own study of Marston's poetry: "Practically all the mythology is taken direct from Natalis Comes' *Mythologia*. Marston paraphrases or translates whole passages from this popular text-book...." (29–30). Davenport's near-exhaustive notes plot the specifics of Marston's debt to Conti; the sheer weight of the evidence is irrefutable. Steadman cites Davenport on Marston's extensive use of Conti's *Mythologiae* (252 n. 4), but only to indicate that Joseph Hall, whom Marston is attacking, was not so clearly indebted to Conti.

40. His *Pantheum Mythicum* was first published in Lyon in 1559, and later translated into English in 1694 by "one J.A.A.B. [?]," and in 1698 by Andrew Tooke, who (in later editions) passed it off as his own work under the title *The Pantheon, Representing the Fabulous Histories of the Heathen Gods, and Most Illustrious Heroes* (London 1783). This translation was frequently reprinted for the next two centuries, and even found its way into American schools.

41. Some of my remarks here have been anticipated by Barbara Carman Garner in her fine study, "Francis Bacon, Natalis Comes [Conti] and the Mythological Tradition" passim.

42. To facilitate comparison I have provided the original Latin as well as the English translation.

43. See ch. 7, pp. 195–96.

44. See chap. six, pp. 158–62. I cite the Spingarn edition, but I have also consulted Arnold's edition.

45. For an extended discussion of Reynolds's symbolism, see Cinquemani.

Notes to Chapter Nine

1. This last phrase was a commonplace of medieval and Renaissance thought. Cf. *The Divine Institutes* of Lactantius: "... Pythagoras and afterwards Plato, inflamed with a love for seeking out the truth, had penetrated as far as the Egyptians and Magians and Persians in order to learn the practices and rites of these nations—for they suspected that wisdom was concerned with religion . . ." (4.2).

2. Milton quotes this exact passage in his *Art of Logic*. See the section on Fortune, below.

3. Cf. ch. 2, p. 57.

4. The alchemical symbolism in Conti's interpretation of Vulcan is discussed in John Mulryan and Steven Brown, "Natale Conti and the Alchemists."

5. Capella *De Nuptiis* 7.738.

6. *Politics* 1.13. "The counsel of a child is imperfect, of a woman invalid." Bekker edition, translation mine.

7. For the "gift-giving" Eve, see ch. 6, pp. 168–69; for Eve as Pandora, see ch. 7, 195–96, and ch. 8, 224.

8. Phaethon is not mentioned in the *Imagini*.

9. These mortal men are not discussed in the *Imagini*.

10. See my article, "The Heroic Tradition of *Samson Agonistes*," 230–31.

11. In *The Interpretation of Dreams* (the *Oneirocritica*), trans. Robert J. White.

12. Cf. Boccaccio *Genealogiae* 3.23.151.

13. In some versions of the myth, Jupiter emasculates his father Saturn (or *Kronos*), in others Saturn (or *Kronos*) emasculates his father Heaven (*Caelum*). In any case, Conti consistently refers to Saturn (*Kronos*) as devouring Time:

> cùm igitur rerum sit omnium vicissitudo, omniáque, quae quidem nata sunt, interire aliquando necesse sit, quia quae composita sunt, denique in sua principia soluuntur, quorum omnium mutationis architectus est tempus, dictus est Saturnus filios vorasse.... Pingebatur autem ab antiquis Saturnus senex pallidus, curuus, altera manu falcem gestans, & draconem caudam sibi mordentem: altera filium paruum ori apponebat, ac vorabat; caput galea tegebatur, & super illa erat amictus. Habebat iuxta se quatuor filios, è quibus Iupiter virilia amputabat, ac in mare proiiciebat, è quibus Venus oriebatur. (2.2.125, 129)

> (Since all things are subject to change, and everything that is born must inevitably die (for every created thing has its own unique composition and must return to its first principles, and time is the catalyst for change in every instance), Saturn is supposed to have devoured his sons.... The ancient image of Saturn showed a pale old man, bent, carrying a sickle and a serpent biting its tail in one hand, while he used his other hand to put his little son in his mouth, eating all the while. His head was covered by a helmet, which in turn was covered by a cloak. His four sons were next to him, and his son Jupiter was cutting off his father Saturn's genitals and throwing them into the sea, an act which caused the birth of Venus.)

14. Boccaccio has a different sequence. See my article, "The Three Images of Venus," 388–93.

15. Cp. with the Gallic Hercules discussed in ch. 5, pp. 135–38.

16. Cf. ch. 1, p. 32; ch. 6, p. 166; ch. 8, p. 201.

17. Cf. ch. 6, pp. 165–66.

18. While Eve is fair in appearance, she is, perhaps, unfair to Adam, when she goes "faring" to meet the devil, where she pays the ultimate "fare" of death for her passage to the forbidden tree.

19. Fulgentius *Mythologies* 1.18.

20. The *Pinax*, attributed to the Greek philosopher Cebes (fl. 5th century B.C.).

21. Posidippus was a Greek epigrammatist (ca. 312–280 B.C.). This epigram is from *The Greek Anthology* 16. "The Planudean Appendix," #275, "On a Statue of Time by Lysippus." For the sculptor Callistratrus see Pliny the elder *Natural History* 34.52.

22. This section on Alpheus and Arethusa first appeared in my article "Milton's *Lycidas* and the Italian Mythographers: Some Suggestive Parallels in their Treatment of Mythological Subjects," 39, 41.

BIBLIOGRAPHY

A. SOURCES BEFORE 1800

Alciato, Andreas. *Emblemata cum commentariis amplissimis....* Padua, 1621.

Alexander ab Alexandro [Alexander of Naples]. *Genialivm diervm libri sex varia ac recondita ervditione referti.* Paris, 1532.

Aneau, Barthelemy. *Picta Poesis: Vt Pictvra Poesis Erit.* Lyon, 1552.

Anon. *Rime De Gli Academici Occvlti Con Le Loro Imprese Et Discorsi.* Brescia, 1568.

Anon. *An Essay Upon Milton's Imitations of the Ancients.* London, 1791.

Appianus, Petrus. *Inscriptiones.* Ingolstadt, 1534.

Aurelius, Julian. *De Cognominibus Deorum Gentilium.* Venice, 1696.

Batman, Stephen. *The Golden Booke of the Leaden Goddes. Wherein Is Described the vayne imaginations of Heathen Pagans, and counterfaict Christians: wyth a description of their seueral Tables, what ech of their Pictures signified.* London, 1577.

Baudoin, Jean. *Recveil D'Emblemes Divers. Avec Des Discovrs Moravx, Philosophiqves, Et Politiqves, Tirez de diuers Autheurs, Anciens & Modernes.* Paris, 1646. 2 Vols.

Bauhin, Caspar. *De hermaphroditum natura.* Frankfurt, 1614.

Bocchi, Achille. *Bonon. Symbolicarvm.* Bologna, 1555.

———. *Bonon. Symbolicarvm Qvaestionvm, De vniuerso genere, quas ferio ludebat, LIBRI QVINQVE.* Bologna, 1574.

Bogan, Zachary. *Archaelologiae Libri Septem. . . . . . Francis Rous. With an Addition of their [the Athenians] Customes in Marriages, Burials, Feastings, Diviinations, etc. in the foure last Books. by Zachary Bogan, Schola of C. C. C. in Oxon.* Oxford 1658.

———. *Comparatio Homer: Cum Scriptoribus Sacris.* Oxford, 1658.

Boissard, Jean Jacques. *Iani Iacobi Boissardi Vesuntini Emblemata Cum Tetratichis Latinis.* [Metz, 1584]

Bolzani, Giovanni Pierio Valeriano. *Hieroglyphicorvm Collectanea, Ex Veteribvs, Et Neotericis Descripta, In Sex Libros, Ordine Alphabetico Digesta; ET NUNC PRIMUM IOANNIS PIERII VALERIANI, & anonymi cuiusdam sexaginta Hieroglyphicorum Libris aucta. In haec postrema editione recognita & expurgata. LVGDVNI, SVMPTIBVS PAVLI FRELLON, IN VIA MERCATORIA. M. DCXXVI.* Lyon, 1626.

Brune, Johan de. *Emblemata of Zinne-werck.* Amsterdam, 1624.

Caelius, Lodovicus Rhodiginus. *Ludovici Caelii Rhodigini Lectionvm Antiqvarvm Libri Triginta.* Cologne, 1620.

Calepino, Ambrogio. *Ambrosii Calepini Dictionarium In quo restituendo atque exornando haec praestitimus.* Venice, 1548.

———. *Ambrosii Calepini Bergomatis Lexicon Adavctvm Et Recognitvm Denvo.* The Hague, 1526.

———. *Ambrosii Calepini Dictionarivm Vndecim Lingvarvm.* Basel, 1598.

Calvin, John. *The Institution of Christian Religion, written in Latin by maisterr Iohn Calvin, and translated into Englysh according to the authors last edition.* [Translator Unknown] London, 1561.

Cameriarius, Joachim. *Commentarii Vtriusqve Linguae.* Basel, 1551.

Cartari, Vincenzo. *Le imagini con la spositione de i dei de gli anitichi, raccolte per vincenzo cartari.* Venice, 1556.

———. Venice, 1566.

———. *Le Imagini De I Dei De Gli Antichi. Nelle Quali Si Con-*

tengono gl'Idoli, Riti, ceremonie, & altre cose appartenenti all Religione de gli Antichi. . . . Venice: Vincentio Valgrisi, 1571.

———. *Le imagini de gli dei de gli antichi, del signor vincenzo cartari regiano*. . . . *Opera utilissima historici, Poeti, Pittori, Scultori, & professori di belle lettere*. Padua, 1608.

———. *Imagines Deorum, qui ab antiquis colebantur: in quibus simulacra, ritus, caerimoniae, magnaque ex parte veterum religio explicatur*. Transl. Antoine du Verdier. Lyon, 1581.

Castiglione, Baldassare. *Il Libro Del Cortegiano*. Venice, 1533.

———. *De Curiali siue Aulico*. Bartholomew Clerke, transl. London, 1585.

Caussin, Nicholas. *Symbolica Ægyptiorvm Sapientia. Polyhistor Symbolicvs*. Paris, 1634.

Cherbury, Lord Herbert. *De religione gentilivm*. Amsterdam, 1663.

———. *The Antient Religion of the Gentiles*. Transl. William Lewis. London, 1705.

Commelinus, Hieronymus, ed. *Mythologici Latini*. Heidelberg, 1599.

Conti, Natale. *Natalis Comitis Mythologiae, Sive Explicationum fabularum, Libri decem: In quibus omnia prope Naturalis & Moralis Philosophiae dogmata contenta fuisse demonstratur. Nuper ab ipso autore recogniti & locupletati. Eiusdem Libri Quatuor De Venatione. Cum Indice triplici; rerum memorabilium, urbium & locorum à variis heroibus denominatorum, ac plantarum & animalium singulis Diis dicatorum. Opus cuisuis facultatis studiosis perutile ac propé necessarium*. . . . Frankfurt, 1581.

Cooper, Thomas. *Bibliotheca Eliotae Eliotis Librarie. This Dictionarie Now Newly imprinted, Anno Domini. M.D.XLVIII, is augmented and inriched with aboue. xxxiij. thousande wordes and phrases, very nedefull for the knowlage of the latine tonge: besyde the descriuyng of the true significacions of wordes, whiche were greatly amisse by ouer muche folowyng of Calepine*. London, 1548.

———. *Thesavrvs Lingvae Romanae & Britannicae, tam accurate congestus, vt nihil penè in eo desyderari possit, quod vel Latinè complectatur amplissimus Stephani Thesaurus, vel Anglicè, toties aucta Eliotae Bibliotheca: opera & industria Thomae Cooperi Magdalenensis*. London, 1565.

Cope, Antonye. *THE HISTORIE OF TVVO THE MOSTE NOBLE CAPITAINES OF the worlde, Anniball and Scipio, of theyr dyuers battailes and uictories, excedyng profitable to reade, gathered and translated into Englishe, out of Titus Liuius, and other authourities, by Antonye Cope esquier.* London, 1544.

Corrozet, Giles. *Hecatomgraphie.* Paris, 1543.

Crooke, Helkiah. *Microcosmographia: A Description of the Body of Man.* Barbican, 1615.

Dinet, Pierre. *Cinq livres des Hieroglyphiqves, ov sont contenvs les plus rares secrets de la nature, & proprietez de toutes choses.* Paris, 1614.

Dolce, Lodovico. *L'Achille Et L'Enea De Messer Lodovico Dolce. Dove Egli Tessendo L'Historia Della Iliade D'Homero A'Qvella Dell'Eneide Di Vergilio. Ambedve L'Ha Divinamente Ridotte In Ottava Rima. Con Argomenti, Et Allegorie Per Ogni Canto: Et due Tauole: l'una delle Sentenze; l'altra de i Nomi, & delle cose piu notabili.* Venice, 1572.

Du Choul, Guillaume. *Discovrs de la Religion Des Anciens Romains.* Lyon, 1556.

Eliot, Thomas. *The Dictionary of syr Thomas Eliot knyght.* London, 1538.

Estienne, [Stephanus] Henri. *The Art Of making Devices: Treating of Hieroglyphicks, Symboles, Emblemes, AEnigma's, Sentences, Parables, Reverses Of Medalls, Armes, Blazons, Cimiers, Cyphres and Rebus.* Transl. Thomas Blount (London, 1646).

Fabrici, Principio. *Delle Allusione.* Rome, 1588.

Flammel, Nicholas. *His Exposition of the Hieroglyphicall Figures which he caused to bee painted vpon an Arch in St. Innocents Church-yard, in Paris. Together with the secret Booke of Artephivs, And The Epistle of Iohn Pontanus.* London, 1624.

Fraunce, Abraham. *The Third Part of The Countesse of Pembrokes Ivychurch: Entitled, Amintas Dale. Wherein are the most conceited tales of the Pagan Gods in English Hexameters: together with their auncient descriptions and Philosophical explications.* London, 1592.

Fulgentius Metaforalis. *Fulgentius Metaforalis, ein beitrag zur geschichte der antiken mythologie in mittelalter.* Leipzig: B. G. Teubner, 1926.

Gale, Thomas, ed. *Historiae Poeticae Scriptores Antiqui.* Paris, 1675.

———, ed. *Opuscula Mythologica, Ethica Et Physica. Graece & Latine.* Cambridge, 1671.

Giraldi, Lilio Gregorio. *De Deis Gentium.* Basel, 1560.

Goidtsenhoven, Laurens Van Haecht. *Mikrokosmos: Parvvus Mvndvs.* Amsterdam, 1610 [?].

Greene, Robert. *The Second Part of the Tritameron of Love.* London, 1587.

Heraclitus of Pontus. *Allegoriae in Homeri fabulas.* Basel, 1544.

Herbert, Lord of Cherbury. *De Religione Gentilivm, errorumque apud eos causis.* Amsterdam, 1663.

Homer. *Homeri Quae Extant Omnia Ilias, Odyssea, Batrachomyachia, Hymni, Poematia aliquot Cum Latina versione....* Basel, 1583.

———. *Commentarius Explicationibus primi libri Iliados Homeri.* ed. Ioachim Cameriarius. Strassburg, 1583.

———. *Comparatio Homer: Cum Scriptoribus Sacris.* ed. Zachary Bogan. Oxford: 1658.

———. *L'Vlisse Di M. Lodovico Dolce da Lui Trattato Dall'Odissea D'Omero Et Ridotto In Ottava Rima.* transl. Lodovico Dolce. Vinegia, 1573.

Hoole, Charles. *A New Discovery Of the old Art of Teaching Schoole, In four small Treatises.* London, 1660.

Horus Apollo. *Ori Apollinis Niliaci, De Sacris notis & sculpturis libri duo....* Paris, 1551.

Junius, Adrian. *Hadriani Ivnii Medici Emblemata. Eivsdem Aenigmatvm Libellvs.* Antwerp, 1585.

Kircher, Athaneseus. *Ad Alexandrvm V11. Pont. Max. Obelisci Aegyptiaci nuper inter Isaei Romani rudera Effossi Interpretatio Hieroglyphica Athanasii Kircheri E Soc. Iesv.* Rome, 1666.

Lactantius Placidus. *Fabularum Ovidii Abbreviatio.* Padua, 1474.

La Perrière, Guillaume de. *The Theater of Fine Devices.* trans. Thomas Combe. London, 1614.

Luther, Martin. *Dris Martini Luther. Colloquia Mensalia: Or, Dr. Martin Luther's Divine Discourses at his Table.... Translated out of the high Germaine into the English Tongue by Capt. Henrie Bell.* London: 1652.

Maier, Michael. *Atalanta Fvgiens, hoc est, Emblemata Nova De Secretis Naturae Chymica, Accommodata partim oculis & intellectui, figuris cupro incisis, adjectisque sententiis, Epigrammatis & notis, partim auribus & recreationi animi plus minus 50 Fugis Musicalibus trium Vocum, quarum duae ad unam simplicem melodiam distichis canendis peraptam, correspondeant, non absque singulari jucunditate videnda, legenda, meditanda, intelligenda, dijudicanda, canenda & audienda.* Oppenheim, 1618.

———. *Arcana Arcanissima Hoc Est Hieroglyphica Agyptio-Graeca, Vulgo necdum cognita, ad demonstrandam falsorum apud antiquos deorum, dearum, heroum, animantium & institutorum pro sacris receptorum, originem, ex uno Ægyptiorum artificio, quod aureum animi & Corporis medicamentum peregit, deductam, Vnde tot poëtarum allegoriae, scriptorum narrationes fabulosae & per totam Encyclopaediam errores sparsi clarissima veritatis luce manifestantur, suaeque tribui singula restituuntur, sex libris exposita.* [London, 1614.]

Mercier, Jean. *Emblemata.* Bourges, 1592.

Muncker, Thomas, ed. *Mythographi Latini. C. Jul. Hyginus. Fab. Planciades Fulgentius. Lactantius Placidus. Albricus Philosophus.* Amsterdam: 1681.

Ovid. *P. Ovidii Nasonis Metamorphoseos Libri Cum Commento.* Venice, 1493.

———. *Fabularum Ovidii Abbreviato.* Padua, 1474. [Lactantius Placidus?].

———. *Opera.* Lyon, 1518.

———. *Opera.* Basel, 1549.

———. *Le Metamorphose D'Ovide Figuree.* transl. Jean de Tournes. Lyon, 1583.

———. *Le Metamorphoses D'Ovide Traduites en Prose Francoise,* transl. N. Renoüard. Paris, 1651.

———. *Le Metamorforsi Di Ovidio Ridotte Da Gio Andrea Dell'Angvillara In Ottava Rima. Con le Annotationi Di M. Gioseppe Horologgi. & gli Argomenti & Postille Di M. Franceso Tvrchi.* Venice, 1584.

———. *Ovid's Invective Or Curse Against Ibis.* Transl. John Jones. London, 1658.

Paradin, Claude. *Deuises Heroiques.* Lyon, 1557.

Passeratus, Johannus. *Ioannis Passeratii Professoris Et Interpretis Regii Commentari In C. Val. Catullum, Albivm Tibullum Et. Sex. Aur. Propertium.* Paris, 1608.

Peacham, Henry. *Minerva Britannia Or A Garden of Heroical Devises.* London, 1612.

Perotti, Niccolò. *Cornucopiae.* Venice, 1490.

Pictor, Georgius. *Theologia mythologica.* Antwerp, 1532.

———. *Apotheseos Tam Exterarvm Gentivm Qvam Romanorvm Deorvm Libri Tres.* Basel, 1558.

Pomey, François. *Pantheum Mythicum; seu, Fabulosa deorum historia....* Lyon, 1659.

J. A. B. [?] transl. *The Pantheon, Representing the Fabulous Histories Of The Heathen Gods And Most Illustrious Heroes.* London, 1694.

———. Andrew Tooke, transl. *The Pantheon, Representing the Fabulous Histories Of The Heathen Gods, And Most Illustrious Heroes.* London, 1783.

Pontanus, Jacobus. *Symbolarum Libri XVII Qvibus P. Virgilii Maronis Bvcolica, Georgica, Aeneis, Probatissimis auctoribus Declaruntur, Comparuntur, Illustrantur.* Augsburg, 1599.

Purchas, Samuel. *Pvrchas his Pilgrimage. Or Relations Of The World And The Religions Observed In All Ages And Places discouered, from the Creation unto this Present.* London, 1614.

Quarles, Francis. *Hieroglyphikes of the life of Man* London, 1638.

———. *Trinitas Emblemes.* London, 1635.

———. *Emblems, By Fra. Quarles; With the Hieroglyphicks.* London, 1696.

Reusner, Nicholas. *Emblemata Nicolai Revsneri Ic. Partim Ethica, Et Physica: Partim verò Historica, & Hieroglyphica, sed ad virtutis, morumque doctrinam omnia ingeniosè traducta: & in quatuor libros digesta, cum Symbolis & inscriptionibus illustrium & clarorum virorum. Qvibus Agalmatvm, Sive Emblematum sacrorum Liber vnus superadditus.* Frankfurt, 1581.

Ripa, Cesare. *Della Piv Che Novissima Iconologia.* Padua, 1630.

Ross, Alexander. *Mystagogus Poeticus, Or The Muses Interpreter: Explaining The historicall Mysteries, and mysticall Histories of the ancient Greek and Latine Poets. Here Apollo's Temple is opened, the Muses Treasures discovered, and the*

Gardens of Parnassus disclosed, whence many flowers of usefull, delightfull, and rare Observations, never touched by any other Mythologist, are collected. London, 1647.

———. *Mystagogus Poeticus.* 2nd ed. London, 1648.

———. *Mystagogus Poeticus.* 3rd ed. London, 1653.

Sabinus, George. *FABVLARVM OVIDII INTERPRETATIO, ETHICA, PHYSICA, ET Historica, tradita in Academia Regiomontana a Georgio Sabino, & in vnum collecta & edita studio & industria T. T. Accessit etiam ex Natalis Comitis Mythologiis de fabularum vtilitate, varietate, partibus & scriptoribus, deque apologorum, fabularum, aenorumque differentia, tractatio.* Cambridge, 1584.

Selden, John. *De diis syris.* London, 1617.

Spencer, John. *De Legibus Hebraeorum Ritualibus Et Earum Rationibus, Libri Tres.* Cambridge, 1685.

———. *Dissertatio De Urim & Thummim. In Deuteron. C,33.v.8.* Cambridge, 1669.

Staveren, Augustino Van, ed. *Auctores Mythographi Latini.* Amsterdam, 1742.

Stephanus [Estienne], Charles. *Dictionarium Historicum, Geographicum, Poeticum.* London, 1686.

Stephanus [Estienne], Robert. *Thesavrvs Lingvae Latinae.* Basel, 1578.

"Suidas." *Svidae Historica, Caeteráque omnia quae ulla ex parte ad cognitionem rerum spectant, solis uerborum explicationibus (quae quidem in uulgatis Lexicis passim extant) praetermissis: Opus iucunda rerum uarietate & multiplici eruditione refertum.* Basel, 1564.

Thomas, Thomas. *Dictionarivm Linguae Latinae Et Anglicanae.* London, 1587.

———. *Thomae Thomasii Dictionarivm Svmma Fide Ac Diligentia Accvratissime Emendatvm, Magnaqve Insvper Rervm Scitv Dignarvm. Et Vocabulorum accessione, longè auctiùs locupletiusque redditum.* 5th ed. Cambridge, 1596.

———. *Thomae Thomasii Dictionarivm Svmma Fide Ac Diligentia Accvratissime Emendatvm, Magnaqve Insvper Rervm Scitv Dignarvm, Et Vocabvlorvm Accessione, Longe Avctivs locupletiusque redditum.* 11th ed. London, 1619.

Tiraboschi, Girolamo. *Storia Della Letteratura Italiana*. Modena, 1772–81. Vol. 3.

Tixier, Jean. *Opus Epithetorum*. Basel, 1541.

Tooke, Andrew. *The Pantheon: Representing the Fabulous Histories of the Heathen Gods, and Most Illustrious Heroes*. London, 1694.

Valeriano Bolzani, Giovanni Pierio. *Hieroglyphicorvm Collectanea, Ex Veteribvs, Ex Neotericis Descripta*. Lyon, 1626.

Van Veen, Octavio. *Amorvm Emblemata, Figvris Aeneis Incisa*. Antwerp, 1608.

Vergilius, Publius Maro. *Opera*. Nuremberg, 1492.

———. *Opera Virgiliana Cum Decem Commentis . . . . . Servio, Donato, Mancinello & Probo nuper addito: cum annotationibus Beroaldinis. . . . Augustino Datho. . . . Domitio Calderino. . . . Iodoco Badio Ascensio*. Lyon, 1529.

———. *P. Virgilii Maronis Opera. . . .* Paris 1532.

———. *P. Virgilii Maronis, Poetae Mantuani, Vniversum Poema: Cum Absolvta Servii Honorati Mauri, Grammatici, & Badii Ascensij Interpretatione*. Venice, 1562.

———. *P. Virgilius Maro, Et In Eum Commentationes, & Paralipomena Gerani Valentis Guelli, PP. Eivsdem Virglii Appendix, Cum Joseph Scaligeri Comentariis & Castigationibus*. Antwerp, 1575.

———. *Publii Virgilii Maronis Poemata. Henrici Stephani Scholijs Illustrata. Qvae Partim Dominata, Partim è Virorum Doctissimorvm Libris Excerpta Dedit*. Geneva, 1599.

———. *L'Opere . . . con ordine, che l'espositione volgare dichiara la latina, & la latina la volgare. . . .* ed. Giovanni Fabrini, Malatesta da Rimene, and Filippo Venuti. Venice, 1609.

———. Boys, John. *Aeneas His Descent into Hell . . . Together with an ample and learned comment upon the same, wherein all passages Critical, Mythological, Philosophical, and Historical, are fully and clearly explained*. London, 1661.

Wither, George. *A Collection of Emblemes, Ancient and Moderne*. London, 1635.

B. Modern Editions and Translations of Sources Before 1800

Alan of Lille. *De Planctu Naturae*. In *The Anglo-Latin Satirical Poets and Epigrammatists of the Twelfth Century*. Volume 2. Ed. Thomas Writer, the Rolls Series. London: Her Majesty's Stationery Office, 1872; rpt. Kraus 1964.

———. *The Anticlaudian of Alain de Lille*. Transl. William H. Cornog. Diss. University of Pennsylvania, 1935.

———. *The Plaint of Nature*. Transl. James J. Sheridan. Toronto: Pontiical Institute of Medieval Studies, 1980.

———. *Anticlaudianus*. ed. R. Bossuat. Paris: Libraire Philosophique J. Vrin, 1955.

———. *Anticlaudianus or The Good and Perfect Man*. Transl. James J. Sheridan. Toronto: Pontifical Institute of Medieval Studies, 1973.

Alciato, Andreas. *Andreas Alciatus 1 The Latin Emblems and Lists*, ed. Peter M. Daly and Virginia M. Callahan. Toronto: Toronto UP, 1985.

Anaxandrides of Rhodes. *Protesilaos*. In Edmonds, J. M., ed. and transl. *Fragments of Attic Comedy After Meineke, Bergk, and Kock*. Leiden: E. J. Brill, 1957–61, 2.63.

Apollodorus. *Apollodorus: The Library*. Trans. Sir James George Frazer, 2 vols. New York: G. P. Putnam's Sons, 1921.

Aristotle. *The Nicomachean Ethics*. Transl. H. Rackham. Cambridge, MA: Harvard UP, 1934.

———. *Aristoteles Philosophus*. ed. I. Bekker. Berlin, 1831–70.

Artemidorus, Daldianus. *The Interpretation of Dreams*. [the *Oneirocritica*]. Transl. Robert J. White. Park Ridge, New Jersey, Noyse Press, 1975.

Augustine, St. *The City of God Against the Pagans*. Transl. Eva Matthews Sanford and William McAllen Green. 7 vols. Cambridge, MA: Harvard UP, 1947–65.

Ausonius. *Ausonius*. Transl. Hugh G. Evelyn White. Cambridge, MA: Harvard UP, 1919. Vol. 2.

Bacon, Francis. *The Works of Francis Bacon*. ed. James Spedding, Robert Leslie Ellis, and Douglas Denon Heath. London, 1861. Vol. 6. "De Sapientia Veterum."

Bernard of Sylvester. *Bernardus Silvestris: 'Cosmographia'*. ed. Peter Dronke. Leiden: E. J. Brill, 1978.

———. *The Cosmographia of Bernardus Sylvestris*. Transl. Winthrop Wetherbee. NY: Columbia UP, 1973.

———. *The Commentary on the First Six Books of 'The Aeneid' of Vergil Commonly Attributed to Bernardus Silvestris*. ed. Julian Ward Jones and Elizabeth Frances Jones. Lincoln, Nebraska, UP, 1977.

———. *Commentary on the First Six Books of Vergil's 'Aeneid.'* Transl. Earl G. Schreiber and Thomas F. Maresca. Lincoln: Nebraska UP, 1979.

Boccaccio, Giovanni. *Genealogie Deorum Gentilium Libri*. ed. Vincenzo Romano. 2 vols. Bari: Giuseppe Laterza & sons, 1951.

———. *Boccaccio on Poetry: Being the Preface and the Fourteenth and Fifteenth Books of Boccaccio's 'Genealogia Deorum Gentilium.'* Trans. Charles G. Osgood. Princeton: Princeton UP, 1956.

Bode, Georg H., ed. *Scriptores Rerum Mythicarum Latini Tres Romae Nuper Reperti*. 2 Vols. Celle, 1834.

Bouchard, Donald F. *Milton: A Structural Reading*. Montreal: Queens UP, 1974.

Browne, Thomas. *The Works of Thomas Browne*, ed. Geoffrey Keynes. London: Faber & Faber, 1931. Vol. 6.

Bruno, Giordano. *Degl'heroici fuori*. Torino: Unione typografico-editrice torinese, 1928.

———. *Giordano Bruno's "The Heroic Frenzies"*, transl. Paul Eugene Memmo, Jr. Chapel Hill: North Carolina UP, 1966.

———. *Spaccio De La Bestia Trionfante*. Milan: G. Daelli, 1863.

———. *The Expulsion of the Triumphant Beast*. Transl. Arthur D. Imerti. New Brunswick, New Jersey: Rutgers UP, 1964.

Burton, Robert. *The Anatomy of Melancholy*, ed. Floyd Dell and Paul Jordan-Smith. New York: Tudor Books, 1927.

Chapman, George The Poems of George Chapman, ed. Phyllis Brooks Bartlett. New York: Russell & Russell, 1962.

Cicero, Marcus Tullius. *De officiis*. Transl. Walter Miller. Cambridge, MA: Harvard UP, 1913.

———. *De Natura Deorum, Academica*. Transl. H. Rackam. NY: G. P. Putnam's Sons, 1933.

Daniel, Samuel. *The Vision Of the 12 Goddesses, presented in a Maske the 8. of Ianuary, at Hampton Court: By the Queenes most excellent Maiestie, and her Ladies.* London, 1604. In *English Masques*, ed. Herbert Arthur Evans. Freeport, NY: Books for Libraries, 1897, rpt. 1971.

Ebreo, Leone. *Diagloghi d'amore.* Ed. Santino Caramella. Bari: G. Laterza & sons, 1929.

———. *The Philosophy of Love.* Transl. F. Friedeberg-Seeley and Jean H. Barnes. London: Socino Press, 1937.

Felix, Marcus Municius. *Tertullian: Apologetical Works and Minucius Felix Octavius.* Transl. R. Arbesmann, J. Daly, and E. A. Quain. New York: Fathers of the Church, 1950.

Ficino, Marsilio. *Theologia Platonica: de immortalitate animorum.* Paris, 1559. Rpt. Olms, Hildesheim, Germany, 1975.

———. *Commentary on Plato's Symposium on Love.* Transl. Sears Reynolds Jayne. Dallas: Spring Publications, 1985.

Golding, Arthur. *Shakespeare's Ovid: Being Arthur Golding's Translation of the 'Metamorphoses',* [London 1567] ed. W. H. D. Rouse. NY: W. W. Norton, 1961.

The Greek Anthology. Trans. W. R. Paton. NY: Putnam, 1916–1918. Vol. 5.

Heraclitus of Pontus. *Heraclité Allégories D'Homére.* Ed. and transl. Félix Buffière. Paris: Société D'Édition Les Belles Lettres, 1962.

Hermes Trismegistus. *Hermetica: The Ancient Greek and Latin Writings Which Contain Religious or Philosophical Teachings Ascribed to Hermes Trismegistus.* Transl. and ed. Walter Scott. Oxford: Clarendon, 1924. Vol. 1.

Hesiod. *Hesiod: The Homeric Hymns and Homerica.* Trans. Hugh G. Evelyn White. Cambridge, MA: Harvard UP, 1914.

Homer. *The Iliad.* Transl. A. T. Murray. Cambridge, MA: Harvard UP, 1924–25. Vol. 1.

Horus Apollo. *The Hieroglyphics of Horapollo.* Trans. George Boas. Bollingen Series 23. NY: Partenon, 1950.

Jerome, St. *Selected Letters of St. Jerome.* transl. F. A. Wright. NY: G. P. Putnam, 1933.

John of Garland. *Integumenta Ovidii, Poemetto Inedito Del Secolo XIII,* ed. Fausto Ghisalberti. Milan: Giuseppe Principato, 1933.

Jonson, Ben. *Ben Jonson*, ed. C. H. Herford and Percy Simpson. Oxford: Oxford UP, 1963, vols. 7, 11.

———. *The Complete Poetry of Ben Jonson*, ed. William B. Hunter, Jr. NY: NYUP, 1963.

Justin Martyr, St. *St. Justin Martyr*. Transl. Thomas B. Falls. New York: Christian Heritage, Inc., 1948.

Juvenal. *Juvenal and Persius*. Transl. G. G. Ramsay. Cambridge, MA: Harvard UP, 1940.

Lactantius. *The Divine Institutes*. Transl. Sister Mary Francis McDonald. Washington, DC: Catholic University of America Press, 1964.

Lucian. *Lucian*. Transl A. M. Harmon, et al. NY: G. P. Putnam's Sons, 1931–67. 8 vols.

Martianus Capella. *De nuptiis Philologiae et Mercurii*. Ed. Adolf Dick. Leipzig: Teubner, 1925.

———. *The Marriage of Mercury and Philology*. transl. by William Harris Stahl, and Richard Johnson, with E. L. Burge. In *Martianus Capella and the Seven Liberal Arts*. NY: Columbia UP, 1977. Volume 2.

Marston, John. *The Poems of John Marston*, ed. Arnold Davenport. Liverpool: Liverpool UP, 1961.

Milton, John. *John Milton: Complete Poems and Major Prose*. ed. Merritt Y. Hughes. Indianapolis: Bobbs-Merrill, 1957.

———. *The Complete Poetry of John Milton*. ed. John T. Shawcross. Rev. ed. NY: Doubleday, 1971.

Mythographi Vaticani I et II. Ed. Peter Kulcsàr. CCSL, no. 91c (Turnhout: Brepolis, 1987).

———. Wolfe, Don M. ed. Complete Prose Works of John Milton. 8 vols. New Haven: Yale UP, 1956–.

———. John Milton: Complete Poems and Major Prose. ed. Merrit Y. Hughes. Indiana: Bobbs-Merrill, 1957.

Nashe, Thomas. The Works of Thomas Nashe. ed. Ronald B. McKerrow. New York: Barnes & Noble, 1966. Vol. 3.

Ovid. *Integumenta Ovidii, Poemetto Inedito Del Secolo XIII*. ed. Fausto Ghisalberti (Milan: Giuseppe Principato, 1933).

———. *Metamorphoses*. Transl. Frank Justus Miller. Cambridge, MA: Harvard UP, 1984. Vol. 1.

———. *'Ovide Moralisé': Poème du commencement du quatorzième siècle. De Boer, C., et al., eds. 5 vols. Amsterdam: Johannes Müller, 1915–38.

———. *Ovide Moralisé En Prose (Texte Du Quinzième Siècle)*. Ed. C. De Boer. Amsterdam: North Holland, 1954.

Plato. *The Republic*. Transl. Paul Shorey. NY: G. P. Putnam's Sons, 1930. Vol. 1.

Pliny the Elder. *Natural History*. Transl. H. Rackham. 11 vols. Cambridge, MA: Harvard UP, 1962.

Plutarch. *Plutarch's Lives*, Transl. Bernadotte Perrin. Cambridge, MA: Harvard UP, 1921. Vol. 10.

Porphyry. *Porphyry: The Cave of the Nymphs in the Odyssey*. Rev. text with transl. by John M. Duffy, Philip M. Sheridan, Leendert G. Westernink, and Jeffrey A. White. Intro. by Michael Psellus. Arethusa Monographs. Buffalo, NY: SUNY Buffalo, 1969.

Reynolds, Henry. *Mythomystes*. in J. E. Spingarn, ed. *Critical Essays of the Seventeenth Century*. Oxford: Oxford UP, 1908, rpt. 1957. Vol. 1, pp. 141–79.

———. *Henry Reynolds' 'Mythomystes': An Edition of the Text with an Introductory Essay*. Claude Graveley Arnold. 2 vols. Diss. University of Michigan, 1964.

Sallustius. *On the Gods and the World*. In Gilbert Murray, *Four Stages of Greek Religion*, pp. 187–214. NY: Columbia UP, 1912.

Sandys, George. *Ovid's 'Metamorphosis' Englished, Mythologized, and Represented in Figures*. [Oxford, 1632]. ed. Karl K. Hulley and Stanley T. Vandersall. Lincoln: Nebraska UP, 1970.

Seneca. *Seneca*. Transl. Frank Justus Miller. Cambridge, MA: Harvard UP, 1953. Vol. 1.

Spenser, Edmund. *The Faerie Queene*. Ed. A. C. Hamilton. New York: Longman, 1977.

Stanyhurst, Richard. *The First Foure Bookes of Virgil his Aeneis translated into English Heroical Verse*. Leiden, 1582. [The Preface] In *Elizabethan Critical Essays*, ed. Gregory Smith. 2 vols. Oxford: Oxford UP, 1904.

Statius. *Thebaid*. Transl. J. H. Mozley. Cambridge, MA: Harvard UP, 1955. Vol. 1.

Tertullian. *Florilegium Patristicum tam veteris quam medii aevi auctores complectens*. Ed. B. Geyer and J. Zellinger. Bonn: Peter Hanstein, 1930.

———. *Tertullian: Apologetical Works and Minucius Felix Octavius*. Transl. R. Arbesmann, J. Daly, and E. A. Quain. New York: Fathers of the Church, 1950.

———. *The Anti-Nicene Fathers*. Vol. 3. Ed. and transl. Alexander Roberts and James Donaldson. Grand Rapids, Mi.: Wm. B. Eerdmans, 1973.

[Vatican Mythographers], ed. Bode, Georg H. *Scriptores Rerum Mythicarum Latini Tres Romae Nuper Reperti*, 2 vols. Celle, 1834. 2 Vols.

Vergil. *Virgil*. Transl. H. Ruston Fairclough. 2 vols. Cambridge, MA: Harvard UP, 1967.

Webbe, William. *A Discourse of English Poetrie*. London, 1586. In *Elizabethan Critical Essays*, ed. Gregory Smith. 2 vols. Oxford: Oxford UP, 1904. 1.206–302.

Xenophon. *Memorabilia and Oeconomicus*. Trans. E. C. Marchant. Cambridge, MA: Harvard UP, 1953.

C. MODERN SOURCES

Adamson, J. W. *Pioneers of Modern Education*. Cambridge: Cambridge UP, 1905.

Aers, David, and Bob Hodge. "Rational Burning": Milton on Sex and Marriage." *Milton Studies*, ed. James Simmonds. Pittsburgh: Pittsburgh UP, Vol. 13, 1979, 3–34.

"Alain." *The Gods*. Transl. Richard Pevera. NY: New Directions, 1934, rpt. 1973.

Allen, Don Cameron. *The Legend of Noah: Renaissance Rationalism in Art, Science, and Letters*. Urbana: Illinois UP, 1963.

———. *Mysteriously Meant: The Rediscovery of Pagan Symbolism and Allegorical Interpretation in the Renaissance*. Baltimore: Johns Hopkins UP, 1970.

———. "Ben Jonson and the Hieroglyphs." *Philological Quarterly* 18 (1939), 290–300.

Anand, Shahla. *Of Costliest Emblem: 'Paradise Lost' and the Emblem Tradition*. Washington DC: University Press of America, 1980.

Bakhtin, M. M. *The Dialogic Imagination: Four Essays by M. M. Bakhtin*, ed. Michael Holquist (trans. Carl Emerson and Michael Holquist). Austin: Texas UP, 1981.

Baldwin, Thomas. W. *William Shaksper's Small Latine & Lesse Greeke*. Urbana, Illinois: Illinois UP, 1944. Vol. 1.

Barthes, Roland. *Image Music Text*. Transl. Stephen Heath. NY: Hill and Wang, 1977.

Belsey, Catherine. *John Milton: Language, Gender, Power*. Oxford: Basil Blackwell, 1988.

Biographie Universelle Ancienne et Moderne. Paris, 1813. Vol. 16.

Blessington, Francis C. *Paradise Lost and the Classical Epic*. London: Routledge & Kegan Paul, 1979.

Bloom, Harold. *A Map of Misreading*. NY: Oxford UP, 1975.

Boswell, J. *Milton's Library: A Catalogue of the Remains of John Milton's Library and Ancillary Readings*. NY: Garland, 1975.

Bouchard, Donald F. *Milton: A Structural Reading*. Montreal: McGill-Queen's UP, 1974.

Brandon, Edward Ewing. *Robert Estienne Et Le Dictionaire Français Aux XVI Siècle*. Baltimore: J. H. Furst, 1904.

Bredbeck, Gregory W. "Milton's Ganymede: Negotiations of Homoerotic Tradition." *PMLA* 106 (March 1991): 262–76.

Brodwin, Leonora L. "Milton and the Renaissance Circe." *Milton Studies*, Vol. 6, ed. James Simmonds. Pittsburgh: Pittsburgh UP, 1974: 21–83.

Brown, Norman O. *Hermes the Thief: The Evolution of a Myth*. Madison: Wisconsin UP, 1947.

Bush, Douglas. *Mythology and the Renaissance Tradition in English Poetry*. rev, ed., NY: W. W. Norton and Company, 1963.

Chance, Jane. *Medieval Mythography: From Roman North Africa to the School of Chartres A.D. 422–177*. Gainesville: Florida UP, 1004.

Chubb, Thomas Caldecot. *The Life of Giovanni Boccaccio*. Port Washington, NY: Kennikat Press, 1969.

Cinquemani, A. M. "Henry Reynolds' *Mythomystes* and the Continuity of Ancient Modes of Allegoresis in Seventeenth-Century England." *PMLA* 85 (1970): 1041–049.

Clark, D. L. *John Milton at St. Paul's School: A Study of Ancient Rhetoric in English Renaissance Education*. NY: Archon Books, 1964.

Collett, Jonathan. "Milton's Use of Classical Mythology in *Paradise Lost*." *PMLA* 85 (1970): 88–96.

Comparetti, Domineco. *Virgil in the Middle Ages*, transl. E. F. M. Benecker (NY: Macmillan, 1908).

Corum, Richard. "'Paradise Lost' and Milton's Ideas of Women," In *Milton and the Idea of Woman*. Ed. Julia Walker. Urbana: Illinois UP, 1988, 120–47.

Coulter, C. C. "The Genealogy of the Gods." *Vassar Mediaeval Studies*, ed. Christabel Forsyth Fiske. NY: Yale UP, 1923. 314–41.

Daly, Peter M., ed. *The English Emblem Book and the Continental Tradition*. NY: AMS, 1988.

Daly, Peter M., ed. *Literature in the Light of the Emblem*. Toronto: Toronto UP, 1979.

De Jong, H. M. E. *Michael Maier's "Atalanta Fugiens": Sources of an Alchemical Book of Emblems*. Leiden: E. J. Brill, 1969.

De Lage, G. Raynaud. *Alain De Lille, Poète Du XII Siècle*. Montreal: Institutes D'études médiévales, 1951.

Dillon, John B. "Renaissance Reference Books as Sources for Classical Myth and Geography: A Brief Survey, with an Illustration from Milton," in the *Acta Conventus Neo-Latini Bononiensis* (August–September 1979), ed. R. J. Schoeck (Binghamton, NY: MRTS, 1985), 437–50.

DuRocher, Richard J. *Milton and Ovid*. Ithaca: Cornell UP, 1985.

Elliott, Kathleen O., and J. P. Elder, "A Critical Edition of the Vatican Mythographers," *Transactions of the American Philological Association*, 78 (1947), 189–207.

Ellsperman, Gerald L. *The Attitude of the Early Christian Writers Toward Pagan Literature and Learning*. Washington, DC: Catholic University of America Press, 1949.

Farwell, Marilyn P. "Eve, the Separation Scene and the Renaissance Idea of Androgony." *Milton Studies*, ed. James D. Simmonds. Pittsburgh: Pittsburgh UP, 1982 (14.3-20).

Fiore, Peter A. *Milton and Augustine: Patterns of Augustan Thought in 'Paradise Lost'*. University Park, PA: Penn State UP, 1981.

Fletcher, Harris. "Milton's Demogorgon—*Prolusion I* and *Paradise Lost*, II, 960–65," *Journal of English and Germanic Philology*, 57 (October 1958): 684–89.

———. *The Intellectual Development of John Milton*. 2 vols. Urbana: Illinois UP, 1965.

Freeman, Rosemary. *English Emblem Books*. London: Chatto & Windus, 1948.

Frye, Roland M. *Milton and the Visual Arts: Iconographic Tradition in the Epic Poems*. Princeton: Princeton UP, 1978.

Gallagher, Philp. J. *Milton, the Bible, and Misogyny*. Columbia: Missouri UP, 1990.

———. "Milton and Euhemerism: *Paradise Lost* X.578–84," *Milton Quarterly* 12 (1978): 16–23.

Gilbert, Allan H. *The Symbolic Persons in the Masques of Ben Jonson*. Durham: Duke UP, 1948.

Green, David Mason. *Medieval Backgrounds of the Elizabethan Emblem Book*. Diss. Berkeley 1958.

Gregory, E. R. *Milton and the Muses*. Tuscaloosa: Alabama UP, 1989.

Gruppe, Otto. *Geschichte der Klassichen Mythologie und Wahrend der Neuzeit*. Leipzig: B. G. Teubner, 1921.

Hagstrum, Jean H. *Sex and Sensibility: Ideal and Erotic Love from Milton to Mozart*. Chicago: Chicago UP, 1980.

Harding, Davis P. *Milton and the Renaissance Ovid*. Urbana: Illinois UP, 1946.

Hartwell, Kathleen Ellen. *Lactantius and Milton*. Cambridge, Mass.: Harvard UP, 1929.

Heninger, S. K. Jr. *Touches of Sweet Harmony: Pythagorean Cosmology and Renaissance Poetics*. San Marino: The Huntington Library, 1974.

Henkl, Arthur, and Albrecht Schöne, *Emblemata Hanbuch: Zur Sinbildkunst des xvi und xvii Jahrunderts*. Stuttgart: J. B. Metzlersche, 1976.

Hortis, A. *Studi delle opere Latine del Boccaccio*. Trieste, 1879.

Iversen, Erik. *The Myth of Egypt and Its Hieroglyphics in European Tradition*. Copenhagen: Gad, 1961.

Katzenellenbogen, Adolf. *Allegories of the Virtues and Vices in Mediaeval Art From Early Christian Times to the Thirteenth Century*. London: Warburg Institute, 1939.

Kerrigan, William. *The Sacred Complex: On the Psychogenesis of "Paradise Lost."* Cambridge: Harvard UP, 1983.

Kiefer, Frederick. "The Conflation of Fortuna and Occasio in

Renaissance Thought and Iconography." *The Journal of Medieval and Renaissance Studies* 9 (1979), 1–27.

Kolenda, Konstantin. *Rorty's Humanistic Pragmatism: Philosophy Democratized.* Tampa: South Florida UP, 1990.

Labriola, Albert C. "Iconography." In *A Milton Encylopedia.* ed. G. K. Hunter et al. Vol. 4. Lewisburg, PA: Bucknell UP, 1970.

———. "The Titans and the Giants: *Paradise Lost* and the Tradition of the Renaissance Ovid," *Milton Quarterly* 12 (1978): 9–16.

Lacan, Jacques. *Écrits: A Selection.* Transl. Alan Sheridan. NY: W. W. Norton, 1977.

Lamberton, Robert. *Homer the Theologian: Neoplatonist Allegorical Reading and the Growth of the Epic Tradition.* Berkeley: California UP, 1986.

Laqueur, Thomas. *Making Sex: Body and Gender from the Greeks to Freud.* Cambridge, MA: Harvard UP, 1990.

Le Comte, Edward. *Milton and Sex.* NY: Columbia UP, 1978.

———. *Yet Once More: Verbal and Psychological Pattern in Milton.* NY: Liberal Arts Press, 1953.

Lewalski, Barbara K. *Paradise Lost and the Rhetoric of Literary Forms.* Princeton: Princeton UP, 1985.

Lewis, C. S. *English Literature in the Sixteenth Century, Excluding Drama.* Oxford: Clarendon, 1953.

Long, Anne Bowers. *The Relations Between Classical and Biblical Allusions in Milton's Later Poems.* Diss. U. of Illinois 1967.

Lotspeich, Henry Gibbons. *Classical Mythology in the Poetry of Ednumd Spenser.* Princeton: Princeton UP, 1932. Rpt. NY: Octagon, 1965.

McCall, John P. *The Poetics of Classical Myth.* University Park: Penn State UP, 1979.

McColley, Diane. *Milton's Eve.* Urbana: Illinois UP, 1983.

———. *A Gust for Paradise: Milton's Eden and the Visual Arts.* Urbana: Illinois UP, 1993.

McColley, Grant. *Milton's Technique of Source Adaptation.* NY: Haskell House, 1966 [?].

McGrath, R. L. "The 'old' and 'new' illustrations for Cartari's

Imagini dei dei degli antichi: a study of 'paper archaeology' in the Italian Renaissance." *Gazette des beaux arts* , 59 (1962): 213–26.

Martindale, Charles. *Milton and the Transformation of Ancient Epic*. Totwa, New Jersey: Barnes and Noble, 1986.

Martindale, Charles, ed. *Ovid Renewed: Ovidian Influences on Literature and Art from the Middle Ages to the Twentieth Century*. Cambridge: Cambridge UP, 1988.

Mommsen, Theodor E. "Petrarch and the Story of the Choice of Hercules." *Journal of the Warburg and Courtauld Institutes*. 15 (1952), 178–92.

Mortimer, Ruth, comp. *Catalogue of Books and Manuscripts II: Italian 16th Century Books* [Harvard College Library Department of Printing and Graphic Arts]. Cambridge: Belknap Press, 1974.

Mulryan, John. "The Heroic Tradition of Milton's *Samson Agonistes*." *Milton Studies*, Vol. 18, ed. James D. Simmonds (Pittsburgh: Pittsburgh UP, 1983): 217–34.

———. "The *Lectionum Antiquarum* of Ludovicus Caelius and the Italian Mythographers." ACTA, Neolatin Congress, Wolfenbüttel Germany. Binghamton, NY: MRTS, 1988, pp. 99–105.

Mulryan, John, ed. *Milton and the Middle Ages*. Lewisburg: Bucknell UP, 1982.

———. "Milton's *Lycidas* and the Italian Mythographers: Some Suggestive Parallels in their Treatment of Mythological Subjects." *Milton Quarterly*. 15 #2 (May 1981), 37–44.

———. "Mythic Interpretations of Ideas in Jonson's *Pleasure Reconciled to Virtue*." *The Ben Jonson Journal* 1 (1994), 63–76.

Mulryan, John, and Steven Brown. "Natale Conti and the Alchemists: The Wedding of Myth and Science in the Renaissance." *Cauda Pavonis* (Fall 1990), 9.2: 1–3.

Mulryan, John. "The Occult Tradition and English Renaissance Literature." *Bucknell Review* 20.3 (Winter 1972): 53–72.

———. "The Three Images of Venus: Boccaccio's Theory of Love in *The Genealogy of the Gods* and His Aesthetic Vision of Love in *The Decameron*," *Romance Notes* 19 (1979), 388–94.

———. "The Tortoise and the Lady in Vincenzo Cartari's *Imagini* and John Webster's *The White Devil,"* *Notes and Queries*, 38 n.s. (March 1991), 78–79.

———. "Translations and Adaptations of Vincenzo Cartari's *Imagini* and Natale Conti's *Mythologiae*: The Mythographic Tradition in the Renaissance." *Canadian Review of Comparative Literature*, 8.2 (Spring 1981), 272–83.

———. "Venus, Cupid, and the Italian Mythographers," *Humanistica Lovaniensia* 22 (1974): 31–41.

Nelson, John Charles. *Renaissance Theory of Love: The Context of Giordano Bruno's 'Eroici furori'*. New York: Columbia UP, 1958.

Nyquist, Mary. "The Genesis of Gendered Subjectivity in the Divorce Tracts and in *Paradise Lost*." In *Remembering Milton: Essays on the Texts and Traditions*. Ed. Mary Nyquist and Margaret W. Ferguson. NY: Methuen, 1987, pp. 99–127.

Osgood, C. V. *The Classical Mythology of Milton's English Poems*. New York: Henry Holt, 1900.

Panofsky, Erwin. *Studies in Iconology: Humanistic Themes in the Art of the Renaissance*. NY: Harper & Row, 1939.

Parker, W. R. *Milton: A Biography*. Oxford: Oxford UP, 1968. 2 Vols.

Patterson, Annabel., ed. *John Milton*. NY: Longman, 1992.

Pecheux, Mother M. Christopher. "Milton and *Kairos*." *Milton Studies*, ed. James D. Simmonds. Vol. 12. Pittsburgh: Pittsburgh UP, 1978: 197–212.

Porter, William M. *Reading the Classics and 'Paradise Lost.'* Lincoln: Nebraska UP, 1993.

Praz, Mario. *Studies in Seventeenth-Century Imagery*. 2 vols. London: Warburg Institute, 1947.

Pritchard, John Paul. *The Influence of the Fathers Upon Milton With Especial Reference to Augustine*. Diss. Cornell University, 1955.

Putnam, Geo. H. *Books and Their Makers in the Middle Ages*. 1897 rpt. NY: Hilary House, 1962. 2 Vol.

Rapaport, Herman. *Milton and the Postmodern*. Lincoln: Nebraska UP, 1983.

Revard, Stella P. "Milton's Muse and the Daughters of Memory." *English Literary Renaissance* 9.3 (Autumn 1979): 432–41.

Rorty, Richard. *Philosophy and the Mirror of Nature*. Princeton: Princeton UP, 1979.

Rose, H. J. *A Handbook of Greek Literature*. New York: E. P. Dutton, 1960.

———. "Mythographers." In *The Oxford Classical Dictionary*, ed. N. G. L. Hammond & H. H. Scullard. Oxford: Clarendon, 1970.

Seznec, Jean. *The Survival of the Pagan Gods: The Mythological Tradition and Its Place in Renaissance Humanism and Art*. Transl. Barbara F. Sessions. NY: Harper & Row, 1953.

———. "Les manuels mythologiques italiens et leur diffusion en Angleterre à la fin de la Renaissance." *Melanges d'histoire et d'archeologie*, 50 (1933): 276–92.

Shawcross, John. *With Mortal Voice: The Creation of 'Paradise Lost'*. Lexington: Kentucky UP, 1982.

Spargo, John W. *Virgil the Necromancer: Studies in Virgilian Legends* (Cambridge: Harvard UP, 1934).

Starnes, DeWitt T. *Renaissance Dictionaries English-Latin and Latin-English*. Austin, Texas: Texas UP, 1954.

Starnes, DeWitt T. and Ernest William Talbert. *Classical Myth and Legend in Renaissance Dictionaries: A Study of Renaissance Dictionaries in Their Relation to the Classical Learning of Contemporary English Writers*. Chapel Hill: North Carolina UP, 1955.

Steadman, John M. *The Lamb and the Elephant: Ideal Imitation and the Context of Renaissance Allegory*. San Marino, Calif.: The Huntington Library, 1974.

———. *Nature Into Myth: Medieval and Renaissance Moral Symbols*. Pittsburgh: Duquesne UP, 1979.

———. "Urania, Wisdom, and Scriptural Exegesis (*Paradise Lost*, VII, 1–12)," *Neophilologus*, 47 (January 1963), 61–73.

Swanson, Donald, and John Mulryan. "The Son's Presumed Contempt for Learning in *Paradise Regained*: A Biblical and Patristic Resolution." in *Milton Studies*, Vol. 27, ed. James D. Simmonds (Pittsburgh, 1991): 243–62.

———. "Milton's *On the Morning of Christ's Nativity*: The Virgilian and Biblical Matrices." *Milton Quarterly*. 23.2 (May 1989), 59–66.

Tayler, Edward. *Milton's Poetry: Its Development in Time*. Pittsburgh: Duquesne UP, 1979.

Tervarent, Guy de. "Eros and Anteros or Reciprocal Love in Ancient and Renaissance Art." *Journal of the Warburg and Courtauld Institutes* 28 (1965): 205–08.

Thompson, Albert N. S. *Literary Bypaths of the Renaissance*. New Haven: Yale UP, 1947.

Tietze-Conrat, E. "Notes on 'Hercules at the Crossroads.'" *Journal of the Warburg and Courtauld Institutes* 13 (1950): 305–09.

Tillyard, E. M. W. "Milton and the Classics." In *Transactions of the Royal Society of Literature*, ed. Joseph Bard. London: Oxford UP, 1923. 26: 59–72.

Turner, James G. *One Flesh*. Oxford: Oxford UP, 1987.

Vicari, Patricia. "The Triumph of Art, The Triumph of Death: Orpheus in Spenser and Milton." In *Orpheus: the Metamorphosis of a Myth*. ed. John Warden. Toronto: Toronto UP, 1982, 207–30.

Waddington, Raymond B. "The Bisexual Portrait of Francis I: Fontainbleau, Castiglione, and the Tone of Courtly Mythology." In *Playing With Gender: A Renaissance Pursuit*. Ed. J. R. Brink, Maryanne C. Horowitz, and Allison P. Couder. Urbana: Illinois UP, 1991. 99–131.

West, Robert H. *Milton and the Angels*. Athens: Georgia UP, 1955.

Wetherbee, Winthrop. *Platonism and Poetry in the Twelfth Century: The Literary Influence of the School of Chartres*. Princeton: Princeton UP, 1972.

Whiting, George Wesley. *Milton's Intellectual Milieu*. Chapel Hill: North Carolina UP, 1939.

Wilkins, E. H. "The Genealogy of the Editions of the *Genealogia Deorum*." *Modern Philology*, 17 (1919): 425–38.

Williams, Arnold. *The Common Expositor: An Account of the Commentaries on Genesis, 1527–1633*. Chapel Hill: North Carolina UP, 1948.

Wilson, Gayle Edward. "Emblems in *Paradise Regained*." *Milton Quarterly*, 6.4 (1972): 77–81.

Wind, Edgar. *Pagan Mysteries in the Renaissance*. 2nd ed, Harmondsworth: Penguin, 1967.

Wittkower Rudolf. "Hieroglyphics in the Early Renaissance." In *Developments in the Early Renaissance.* ed. Bernard S. Levy. Albany: SUNY Press, 1972, 63–91.

Wittreich, Joseph. *Feminist Milton.* Ithaca: Cornell UP, 1987.

Yates, Frances A. *Giordano Bruno and the Hermetic Tradition.* Chicago: Chicago UP, 1964.

———. *Life of an Italian in Shakespeare's England.* Cambridge: Cambridge UP, 1934.

INDEX

Abundance, 154
Acheron, 252
Actaeon, 107, 198
Adam: as androgyne, 101, 103; and Christ, 97; as dreamer, 250, 262; and Eve, 39, 41, 51, 58, 69, 82, 93, 99, 105–06, 130, 139, 142, 164, 173–74, 193; and the Fall, 67, 76, 81, 242; and God, 84, 91; and love, 48, 89, 95–96, 100, 248; and Mercury; and Raphael, 190; and Samson, 52, 86, 134; and sexuality, 5, 62, 79, 144, 153, 155; and time, 42; as thinker, 102; and the Tree of Life, 142; as victim, 264–65; as weak, 87, 94, 132, 143, 149, 175, 181, 258
Aegina, 247
Aesculapius, 64, 69
Agrippa, Cornelius, 256
Alan of Lille, 80–88
Albericus ("Philosophicus," "Of London"), 202–03, 210, 218
Alchemy, 69, 156–60, 222–23, 234–36
Alciato, Andrea 7, 44, 114–16, 122, 127, 129, 134, 147, 151, 163, 171, 189, 217
Alexander ab Alexandro. *See* Alexander of Naples
Alexander of Naples, 204, 207
Allegory, 6, 44, 53, 98, 104, 173, 191, 197, 223
Alpheus, 284–86
Anaxandrides of Rhodes, 160, 230
Androgyne the, 101, 103, 157, 185, 190, 226, 304n30. *See also* Hermaphrodite, the
Andromeda, 198
Aneau, Barthelemy, 140, 141
Angels: demonic, 40; evil, 170; fallen, 65, 157; good, 85, 88, 108; sexed, 294n24; Raphael, 68, 73, 84–87, 94, 107, 175, 190, 258–60, 268; Michael, 67–68, 73, 79, 88, 107, 262, 268. *See also* Demons, Devil, the, and Devils, the
Antaeus, 126, 176, 184–86, 194, 196, 283–84
Antichrist, 50
Anubis, 200
Aphrodite, 143, 173, 178, 180, 182, 185, 263. *See also* Venus
Apollo, 40, 64, 69–70, 84, 166, 204
Appianus, Petrus, 153
Apollodorus, 197–198, 227
Aquinas, St. Thomas, 205
Arethusa, 284–85
Aristophanes, 41, 209, 226
Aristotle, 102, 162, 209, 238, 278
Arnolph of Orleans, 45
Artemidorus, 250
Atropos, 178
Atalanta, 143, 166
Athena, 13, 39, 49, 65, 69, 136–39, 185, 191, 236–39. *See also* Pallas (Athena), Minerva, *Phronesis*, Wisdom
Atlas, 59
Auctores, 74
Ausonius, 183, 266, 282

339

Bacchae, 45
Bacchus, 65, 73, 163, 166, 272–75
Bacon, Francis, 199, 220–23, 226
Batman, Steven, 218
Baudoin, Jean, 134–35, 154
Bernard of Sylvester, 74–80
Bersuire, Pierre, 45, 50
Bible: the Old Testament, 10, 98; and pagan texts, 41, 55, 57, 62, 99, 203; as the Word, 159; Corinthians, 138; Genesis, 88, 98, 100, 104, 258–59; Matthew, 132
Boccaccio, Giovanni, 50, 96–99, 204–06, 208, 211–12, 227
Bocchi, Achilles, 118, 120, 140
Boissard, Jacques, 116
Boreas, 140
Botticelli, 69
Browne, Sir Thomas, 216
Brune, Johan de, 144, 147, 149
Bruno, Giordano, 7, 68, 104–13
Burton, Robert, 96
Bupalis, 277

Cabala, the, 110, 157
Caelius, Lodovicus, 8, 173–76, 189, 210
Caelum, 46. See also Caelus
Caelus, 42. See also Caelum
Caenis, 83
Calepino, Ambrogio, 179, 181–85, 189
Callistratus, 282
Camerarius, Joachim, 177–80
Capella, Martianus, 68–74, 84, 86, 237, 238
Cartari, Vincenzo, 115–16, 136, 163, 182, 202–04, 207–18, 226–27, 229–86
Castiglione, Baldessar, 96, 214
Caussin, Nicholas, 153
Cebes, 278–79
Centaurs, 244–45
Ceres, 185
Chance, 75. See also Fate(s), Fortune, Kairos, Occasio(n), Opportunity
Chaos, 74–77, 85, 90, 104, 169–70, 224–27, 243
Chapman, George, 215–16
Chartres, School of, 81
Chione, 40
Christ, 80, 97, 116, 121. See also Jesus, Savior, the Son
Choul, Guillaume de, 115

Church Fathers, the: and allegory, 222; and Milton, 54–66; and mythography, 203; and paganism, 7, 40, 99, 121, 201–03, 230, 232; Augustine, 55–59, 68, 160, 227, 231; Clement of Alexandria, 169; Justin Martyr, 56, 64–65; Lactantius, 40–41, 60–65, 227, 233, 261; Jerome, 55–56, 296–97n3; Lactantius, 227; Marcus Minucius Felix Octavius, 55–56, 64; Tertullian, 57, 60, 189
Cicero, Marcus Tullius 55, 159, 183–85,189–90, 226
Circe, 45, 167
Cocytus, 253
Combe, Thomas, 153
Comus, 269–70, 282
Conti, Natale: and Alciato, 149; and Alexander of Naples, 207–08; and Francis Bacon, 220, 224; and the cabala, 110; and Cartari, 211–18; and the dictionaries, 178, 180, 186, 188; and Egyptology, 160, 163, 171; and Fortune, 125; and love, 182; and Milton, 229–86; and the mythographic tradition, 204; and Henry Reynolds, 224; and Alexander Ross, 226–27; and Vulcan, 222
Cooper, Thomas, 179, 192–95
Cope, Sir Antonye, 118, 136
Cornutus, 198, 202
Corrozet, Giles, 122, 129, 138–40, 153
Cronos, 182, 225. See also Time
Cupid: appearance of, 99, 184; and Boccaccio, 300n15; cast out of heaven, 127, 149; and Chaos, 226–27; defeated by Pan, 138–39; and love, 100, 105, 175, 178, 224–25; and pain, 106; and Venus, 144, 182
Cybel, 42
Cynocephali, 58

Dagon, 121, 138
Daniel, Samuel, 213, 218
Dalila, 121–22, 132–33, 181, 187, 193
Dante, 69, 205
Death, 39–41, 77–78, 132, 144–49, 240, 242–49, 284
Demogorgon, 98, 206, 310n16
Demons, 56, 65, 190, 170. See also Angels, Devil, the and Devils,

Index 341

Desire, 112
Devil, the, 49, 87, 95, 103, 106, 116, 122, 142, 165. *See also* Satan
Devils, the, 41, 58, 157–58. *See also* Angels, Demons the,
Deyanira, 52–53
Diana, 182, 184, 219, 226
Dictionaries, Renaissance, 115, 149, 165, 172–96, 206, 217
Dinet, Pierre, 155–56
Diodati, Carlo, 216
Discord, 49
Dreams, 54, 249–56, 296–97n3
Du Choul, Guillaume, 122
Du Rocher, Richard, 2, 291–92n11
Duty, 165
Du Verdier, Antoine, 216

Earth, 127, 255–56, 283
Ebreo, Leone, 7, 96–104, 132
Echo, 51
Eden, 92, 248. *See also* Garden, the
Eliot, Sir Thomas, 179, 191–92, 194, 196
Elysian Fields, the, 254
Endymion, 227
Epimetheus, 194, 241
Estienne (family), 1. *See also* Stephanus, Charles and Stephanus, Robert
Euhemerism, 45, 47, 55, 98–99, 184, 194
Euripides, 248
Eurydice, 193
Eusebius, 184, 227
Eve: and Adam, 39, 41, 51, 58, 69, 82, 93, 99, 105–06, 132, 139, 142, 164, 173–74, 193; and the Fall, 134, 142, 155, 174; and love, 39, 48, 89, 95–96, 248, 264; and Pandora, 49, 52, 101, 194, 222; and sexuality, 5, 13, 37, 39, 41, 43, 48, 58, 69, 99, 102–05, 143, 153, 175, 211, 258–59, 265, 266, 300–01n17, 307n3; and her sons, 40; and Venus, 132

Fabricio, Principio, 144, 148
Fall, the, 52, 80, 98, 106, 174, 202, 258
Fame, 118, 163
Fate(s), 111, 147, 152, 165. *See also* Chance, Fortune, *Kairos*, Occasion, Opportunity

Felicity, 122
Ficino, Marsilio, 7, 43, 89–96, 130, 147, 163
Firmicus, Julius Maternus, 200–01, 209
Flamel, Nicholas, 156
Florio, John, 215
Fortune: as blind, 75; in Caelius (Ludovicus Rhodiginus), 176; as Chaos, 88; bearing the cornucopia, 86, 154, 165; as emblem, 115–26; as good and evil, 182–83; names of, 191; as Occasio[n], 149, 275–82, as Ruler, 110–12, Sources of, 186; and Time, 178. *See also* Chance, Fate(s), *Kairos*, Occasio(n), Opportunity
Fraud, 88
Frye, Ronald Mushat, 114, 292n14
Fraunce, Abraham, 219
Fulgentius, Fabricus Planciades, 201, 227

Galileo, 162
Ganymede, 178
Garden, the, 88. *See also* Eden
Genius, 170
Gesner, Conrad, 182, 184–85, 194
Giants, the, 43, 218
Giraldi, Lilio Gregorio: the *Historia*, 149, 178, 180, 204, 207–12; the *Syntagma de Musis*, 187
Goidtsenhoven, Laurens Van Haecht, 122, 126, 130, 133, 135–37, 143
Good Counsel. *See* Metis
Gorgon, the, 156, 239
Greene, Robert, 116, 118

Hades, 242
Harapha, 134
Harmony, 73
Heaven, 152, 170
Hebrews, the, 151, 156, 161–62, 169–71, 224, 230
Helios, 43. *See also* Sun, the
Hell, 107, 158, 249
Hephaestus, 236. *See also* Mulciber, Vulcan
Heracles. *See* Hercules
Hercules: and Antaeus 283; and the apple, 166; in Caelius (Ludovicus Rhodiginus), 176; Choice of, 63, 130, 293n13, 304n24; and Deyanira, 53; and emblems, 129–37; Gallic, 10,

69, 134, 187, 193, 269; and Omphale, 177, 189, 195; parentage of, 86, 127, 191; and Prometheus, 222; and the Sun, 284; and Samson, 52, 132, 187; and his twelve labors, 182, 185, 191; and the Trachiniae, 68
Hermaphrodite, the. *See also* Androgyne, the
Hermaphroditus, 51, 141–42, 177, 185, 194
Hermathena, the 68, 176, 182, 190, 192
Hermes (Trismegistus), 59, 69, 157, 159, 169, 180. *See also* Mercury
Herodotus, 230
Hesiod, 184, 193, 197, 243, 252
Heywood, Thomas, 150
Hieroglyphics, 44, 150–71, 180, 219, 223, 306n9
Hippomenes, 166
Homer: and Boccaccio, 205; and Christianity, 65; and Natale Conti, 243; and the *scholia*, 14–22; 65; as a source, 190; on Vulcan, 227; the *Hymns*, 268; the *Iliad*, 107, 188–89
Hoole, Charles, 179
Hopes, the, 251
Horace, 116
Horapollo, 180, 152–53
Hyginus, 197–198, 202, 218, 227

Icarus, 129, 147, 176, 182, 184, 192
Iconography, 109, 210, 171, 229
Idolatry, 109
Isidore of Seville, 205
Isis, 59, 61, 200
Ixion, 244–45

Jesus, 111. *See also* Christ, Savior the, Son the
Jocus, 83
John of Garland, 45
Jones, John, 44, 215
Jonson, Ben, 154, 213, 216
Josephus, 187
Jove. *See* Jupiter, Zeus
Joyce, James, 228
Junius, Adrian, 122
Juno, 51, 189, 218, 231, 242, 245, 260
Jupiter: Allegorized, 107–09, 214; appearance of, 218; and Athena, 13, 236–39; and Chaos, 129, 170; and Creation, 99; and Cupid, 126, 184; and Fortune, 111–12; and the Giants, 42–43; as God, 84, 244; and Juno, 245; and Mercury, 70–71; and Prometheus, 240–41; and Vulcan, 188–89. *See also* Zeus
Juvenal, 121, 160, 165, 230, 275–76

Kairos, 116, 119, 121, 183, 191, 282. *See also* Chance, Fate(s), Fortune, Occasio[n], Opportunity
King Charles II, 163, 193, 274–75
King Edward, 286
King Henry VIII, 118, 137
King James I, 215
Kircher, Athanasius, 90, 163, 167–71

Lethe, 253–54
Linche, Richard, 211
Logos, the, 9–10
Lord Herbert of Cherbury, 225–26
Lewis, William, 225
Lucian, 69, 107, 134, 160, 189, 232, 239
Lust, 155
Luther, Martin, 147, 294–95n28
Lutherans, 284
Lycus, 132

Macaria (Success), 278
Macrobius, 209, 251, 265
Maier, Michael, 143, 145, 156–57, 159
Mammon, 157–58, 223, 234, 236
Manoa, 121
Manutius, Aldus, 1
Marcolini, Francesco, 212
Mars, 88, 152, 173, 227
Marston, John, 216–17, 312n39
Mary (Mother of Jesus), 242
Medea, 167
Medusa, 156, 163
Menander, 241
Mercier, Jean, 126, 128
Mercury: and Aphrodite, 143; and Martianus Capella, 68–74; and Cicero, 184; and eloquence, 88, 107, 164, 198–202; and the fallen angels, 40; and Fortune, 125; and Hercules, 134; and learning, 99, 135; as merchant, 199; and the mythographers, 267–72; and Occasio[n], 122; as planet, 177; and Prometheus, 241; and Sisyphus, 247; and sleep, 202. *See also* Hermes (Trismegistus)

Index   343

Metanoeia (Regret, Penitence), 116, 122
Metis (Good Counsel), 236, 238
Meun, Jean de, 81
Michael. *See* Angels
Micyllus, Jacobus, 45
Midas, 45
Milton, John: *An Apology for Smectymnuus*, 183; *Arcades*, 97, 147, 152; *Areopagitica*, 161, 167; *Art of Logic*, 276; *At A Solemn Musick*, 97; *Comus*, 86, 119, 122, 139, 163–64, 202, 268, 270, 282; *Doctrine & Discipline of Divorce*, 194, 241; *Eikonoklastes*, 275; *1st Defence of the English People*, 275; *The History of Britain*, 183; *Il Penseroso*, 59, 68, 159, 191, 193; *Life of Ramus*, 177; *Lycidas*, 65, 152, 193, 284; *Nativity Ode*, 166; *Paradise Lost*, 70–106, 234–43, passim; *Paradise Regained*, 12, 37, 58–65, 70, 76–78, 87–88, 109–11, 124–26, 130, 135, 162, 165, 169, 199–200, 231, 246, 268, 270–71, 282–83; *Prolusions*, 83; *Samson Agonistes*, 63, 112, 121–22, 125, 130, 134, 193, 200, 280, 282; *Tetrachordon*, 51, 246
Minerva, 190, 237–39. *See also* Athena, Pallas (Athena), *Phronesis*, Wisdom
Mnenosyme, 176
Modesty, 155
Moloch, 42–43, 144, 147, 176, 180, 194
Montlyard, Jean de, 213
Moon, the, 152, 164, 226–27, 254–56
Moses, 43, 59, 65, 71, 76, 98–99, 102, 104, 151, 159
Mulciber, 187, 190, 240. *See also* Hephaestus, Vulcan
Muse, the, 84–86
Muses, the, 176–77, 182, 185, 187, 190–92, 220–21
Mythographers: ancient, 197–218; English, 218–28; medieval, 104, 201–04; Renaissance, 115, 149, 310n26, 311n37
Myyrha, 39

Narcissus, 38, 48, 51, 216, 239
Nature, 76–77, 81, 88, 166, 224
Necessity, 144
Neckham, Alexander. *See* Albericus ("Philosophicus," "Of London")
Nessus, 52

Obelisk, 167
Oedipus, 220–21
Occasio(n), 86, 111, 115–26, 165, 176–78, 182–83, 186, 191, 195, 278–81. *See also* Chance, Fate(s), Fortune, Opportunity, *Kairos*
Occultism, 8, 11, 104, 110, 150–73, 180, 205, 221–24, 256
Omphale, 134, 177, 182, 185, 189–91, 195
Opportunity, 111, 115–26, 282. *See also* Chance, Fate(s), Fortune, *Kairos*, Occasio(n)
Orpheus, 45, 65, 107, 169–70, 192–93
Osiris, 159, 161, 200
Ovid: and commentaries, 105, 175, 291n11; and mythology, 2, 99, 104; *Invective Against Ibis*, 215; *Metamorphoses* 62, 83, 179, 182, 184
Ovide Moralisé, 45–50, 99, 222
Ovide Moralisé en Prose, 49–53

Palephatus, 198
Pallas (Athena), 240, 260. *See also* Athena, Minerva, *Phronesis*, Wisdom
Pan, 68, 99, 140, 166, 224–25
Pandora, 193–94, 222, 240–42, 296n39
Paradin, Claude, 125
Paradise, 76, 96, 105–06, 248
Paris, 49, 51, 242, 260
Pasiphae, 198
Paul, St., 176
Pausanias, 227, 237, 241, 274
Peacham, Henry, 122
Pegasus, 163
Penitence, 281. *See also Metanoeia*
Perotti, Nicolai, 189
Perriere, Guillaume De, 153
Perseus, 163
Phaethon, 37–38, 43–44, 47, 50, 127, 147, 176, 184, 243–44
Philo, 96–104
Philology, 68–74, 84, 88
Phlegethon, 251
Phornutus, 198. *See* Cornutus
Phronesis, 71. *See also* Athena, Pallas (Athena), Minerva, Wisdom

Pictor, Georgius, 202–04, 210–11, 226
Placidus, Lactantius [Luctatius], 44–45
Plato, 41, 64–67, 77, 92–105, 132, 154, 201, 243, 253
Platonism, 156
Pliny, 185
Plutarch, 68, 247
Pluto, 203
Poems on Obscure Scholarly Subjects, 154
Pomey, François, 204, 211
Posidippus, 282
Priscian, 83
Prometheus, 59, 240–42
Prudence, 110
Purchase, Samuel, 161
Pythagoras, 63, 97, 256

Quarles, Francis, 114, 151

Regius, Raphael, 45
Reusner, Nicholas, 141, 146
Regret. *See Metanoeia*
Reynolds, Henry, 215, 223–25
Rhodiginus, Ludovicus Caelius. *See* Caelius, Ludovicus Rhodiginus
Ridevallus, Joannes, 203
Ripa, Cesare, 154–55
Romance of the Rose, 81
Ross, Alexander, 226–27

Sabinus, George, 217
Salmacis, 51, 141–44, 185, 187, 194
Samson, 63, 86, 121–22, 132–34, 165, 181, 187, 193
Sallustius, 199
Sandys, George, 6, 36–44
Satan: as Antaeus, 126–27; and Athena, 165; and Chaos, 85; and the Choice of Hercules, 130; and the cornucopia, 277; and Death, 147, 268; and dreams, 79; and Eve, 142; and Fortune, 125; and Heaven, 150; and Hell, 242, 243; and independence, 94; and Ixion, 245; and learning, 10, 60; and madness, 95; and the Moon, 255; and Occasion, 111, 115, 121; and Phaethon, 37, 43, 47, 50, 127, 240; and Sin, 236, 238, 239; and Sisyphus, 247; and sophistry, 76, 87, 164–65, 269, 271; and Tantalus, 249, and woman, 133
Saturn, 42, 50, 77–78, 88, 170, 178, 201
Savior, the, 68, 87. *See also* Christ, Jesus, and Son, the
Scylla, 45
Seneca, 134, 173–74
Servius, 190, 209
Sexuality, 12–13, 139–43
Seznec, Jean, 201, 216
Shakespeare, 12
Shame: Honorable, 155; Womanly, 257
Shawcross, John, 89, 299n5
Sidney, Sir Philip, 105
Silenus, 73
Sin, 39, 41, 78, 136–38, 185, 238–43, 263
Sirens, the, 147
Sisyphus, 244, 247
Sleep, 251
Socrates, 61, 65
Solomon, 134
Son, the, 10, 58, 60–65, 77, 87, 109–110, 125–26, 129, 130–35, 138, 165, 200, 233, 270–71. *See also* Christ, Jesus, and Savior, the
Sophia, Ficino, 96–104; Bruno, 107–08
Sophists, 76
Spencer, John, 161–62
Spenser, Edmund, 126, 140, 215, 217
Sphinx, the, 220
Stanyhurst, Richard, 44
Starnes, Dewitt T., 177–78, 251
Statius, 265
Steadman, John, 3, 216–18
Stephanus, Charles, 179, 185–91
Stephanus, Robert, 179, 194
Stoics, the, 61
Styx, the river, 252
Success. *See Macaria*
Suidas, 178, 180–81, 308n8
Sun, the, 129, 152, 164, 254–55. *See also Helios*

Talbert, Ernest William, 79–80, 251
Tantalus, 219, 244, 248
Tartarus, 242–43, 268
Taurus, 198
Tetragrammaton, the, 150

Thomas, Thomas, 179, 195–96
Time, 41–42, 77–78, 118, 225, 263. *See also* Cronos
Tiresias, 82, 218, 240
Trismegistus, Hermes. *See* Hermes (Trismegistus)
Tritons, 154
Two-Handed Engine, the, 284
Typhon, 161, 200

Ulpian, 195
Urania, 44, 71–74, 85, 88, 191, 226. *See also* Muses, the

Valeriano, Pierio, 153, 163–67, 171
Van Veen, Octavio, 121–23
Varro, 57, 68
Vatican Mythographers, the, 203–04
Venus: physical appearance, 105, 207–09, 210; celestial, 45, 92, 99–100, 177, 226, 266; and death, 86; and Eve, 88, 167; and euhemerism, 108; and love, 46, 175, 178; and the mythographers, 256–67; names of, 173, 190; and sexuality, 48, 81, 73, 132, 166, 261–262; sources of, 7, 89, 152, 184–85, 195; warlike, 165–66, 265; womanly, 267
Vergil, 2, 69, 190, 286
Vicari, Patricia, 290
Virtue, 112, 125, 130
Voluptas, 132
Vulcan, 64, 137–38, 159, 173, 187–88, 222, 227, 235–37, 240–41, 306n14. *See also* Hephaestus, Mulciber

Whitney, Geoffrey, 116
Wisdom, 70, 111, 125. *See also* Athena, Minerva, Pallas (Athena), *Phronesis*
Wither, George, 114

Yole, 52

Zaltieri, Bolognino, 212
Zeal, 165
Zeno, 61
Zeus, 39, 69, 107, 137. *See also* Jupiter